D0182126

Writing, Teaching, Learning

Writing, Teaching, Learning

A Sourcebook

4th edition of
Rhetoric and Composition

Edited by
Richard L. Graves

BOYNTON/COOK PUBLISHERS
HEINEMANN
PORTSMOUTH, NH

Boynton/Cook Publishers, Inc.
A subsidiary of Reed Elsevier Inc.
361 Hanover Street
Portsmouth, NH 03801–3912
http://www.boyntoncook.com

Offices and agents throughout the world

© 1999 Boynton/Cook Publishers, Inc.

All rights reserved. No part of this book may be reproduced in any form or by any electronic or mechanical means, including information storage and retrieval systems, without permission in writing from the publisher, except by a reviewer, who may quote brief passages in a review.

The author and publisher wish to thank those who have generously given permission to reprint borrowed material:

"The Winds of Change: Thomas Kuhn and the Revolution in the Teaching of Writing," by Maxine Hairston was originally published in *College Composition and Communication*, 33 (February 1982). Copyright © 1982 by the National Council of Teachers of English. Reprinted with permission.

"Pedagogy of the Distressed," by Jane Tompkins was originally published in *College English*, 52 (October 1990). Copyright © 1990 by the National Council of Teachers of English. Reprinted with permission.

"What Do We Know About the Writing of Elementary School Children?," by Julie M. Jensen was originally published in *Language Arts*, 70 (January 1994). Copyright © 1994 by the National Council of Teachers of English. Reprinted with permission.

"On Stories and Scholarship," by Richard J. Murphy, Jr. was originally published in *College Composition and Communication*, 40 (December 1989). Copyright © 1989 by the National Council of Teachers of English. Reprinted with permission.

"Laura's Legacy," by Carol S. Avery was originally published in *Language Arts*, 65 (February 1988). Copyright © 1988 by the National Council of Teachers of English. Reprinted with permission.

"Writing for Life: Language Arts in the Middle," by Linda Rief was originally published in *Language Arts*, 71 (February 1994). Copyright © 1994 by the National Council of Teachers of English. Reprinted with permission.

"Scott's Gift," by Peggy A. Swoger was originally published in *English Journal*, 78 (March 1989). Copyright © 1989 by the National Council of Teachers of English. Reprinted with permission.

"'Whispers of Coming and Going': Lessons from Fannie," by Anne DiPardo reprinted from *Writing Center Journal* 12 (Spring 1992): 124-144. Used with permission.

"Crossing Lines," by Carole Deletiner was originally published in *College English*, 54 (November 1992). Copyright © 1992 by the National Council of Teachers of English. Reprinted with permission.
(continued on p. 354)

Library of Congress Cataloging-in-Publication Data
Writing, teaching, learning : a sourcebook / edited by Richard L. Graves.— 4th ed.
    p.   cm.
    Rev. ed. of: Rhetoric and composition. 3rd ed. 1990.
    Includes bibliographical references.
    ISBN 0-86709-488-5 (alk. paper)
    1. English language—Rhetoric—Study and teaching. 2. English language—
Composition and exercises. 3. Report writing—Study and teaching. 4. English
language—Rhetoric. I. Graves, Richard L. (Richard Layton), 1931– .
II. Rhetoric and composition.
PE1404.R48   1999
808'.042'07—dc21   99-21953
                                                          CIP

Editor: Lisa Luedeke
Production: Elizabeth Valway
Cover design: Joni Doherty Design
Manufacturing: Louise Richardson

Printed in the United States of America on acid-free paper
Docutech RRD 2007

for Bob Boynton

Contents

Preface

The teacher of writing is the luckiest person on Earth. Never mind the stacks of papers to grade. Never mind the mindless bureaucracy that always seems to work at cross-purposes. Never mind the minimal salary. All this will pass. Eventually we will come to see that our best work is not in grading papers but in the quality of our responses to our students. Our classes will go on despite the bureaucrats, who themselves are not teachers anyway. No, we will never receive a good salary, but with luck and grace we will learn to live on what we make, which in the long run is more valuable than having wealth. And what remains? Our students. Our classes. Our blessed work, the growth of the human mind and spirit. And lest we forget, our being involved in an emerging academic discipline that is at the heart of a renaissance in education and that continues to see more clearly ways of contributing to the well-being of the human race.

Even though some thorny problems remain—the status of adjunct faculty members, for example—there are many good reasons for optimism. One such reason was revealed to me during the recent work of editing this fourth edition of *Rhetoric and Composition,* now retitled *Writing, Teaching, Learning.* When this edition was in the early planning stages, we envisioned a comprehensive collection that would highlight the forty-year period from the "birth" of the discipline in the early 1960s to the year 2000. Representing the very best of what had been published about the teaching of writing during that period, it would serve as a foundation for the continuing growth of the discipline on into the twenty-first century. It was a good idea, but it was not to be.

In the process of surveying literally hundreds of essays published since 1990 (the date of the publication of the third edition), I was astonished to find an abundance of excellent material. Not only is there a large amount of current material, but so much of it treats issues heretofore unexplored. I realized then that a decision had to be made. Would the fourth edition be a comprehensive survey covering the period of time we originally planned? Or would it truly be a new edition, focusing on new ideas and fresh directions in the discipline? I became convinced that the latter path was the best way to go, and the editors at Heinemann agreed. What we need as we enter this new century is a celebration of all that is fresh and useful at the present time, not a rehashing of older material that has become a part of the mainstream.

Of the total thirty-two essays in the fourth edition, only seven appeared in the earlier editions; twenty-five are new. At the outset, no preconceived guidelines were established for the selection process. This was intentional. I wanted to see, as objectively as possible, everything that was out there and to identify those essays that stood on their own merits as excellent. This first search yielded some fifty essays, and at that point criteria began to emerge, somewhat unconsciously, for the final selection process:

- Is it useful for the teacher of writing, for the experienced as well as the young teacher just beginning to learn the trade?

- Is it readable and well-written? Does it have a voice, a persona? Does the reader perceive a real person behind the printed page?

- Is the length appropriate for the subject? Or is it wordy, unnecessarily obscure or convoluted, strewn with references, footnotes, citations, and other impediments that seem more designed to impress editors than inform readers?

- Is it universal? Does it have broad application even though it speaks of a certain grade level or class or local situation?

- Is it fresh? Does it point toward a new and higher level of understanding? Does it emphasize both teacher and student becoming better people as well as better writers?

In this process, unfortunately, some superb essays were cut, essays with quality, imagination, and insight. But those that emerged, in my opinion, are the *best of the best*. I hope you will agree.

Also early in the planning stages, it was assumed that the format of the fourth edition would follow the earlier format. The abundance of excellent new material, however, influenced some changes in format. It should be noted too that an evolving format, as well as specific criteria, influences the selection of material. A superb article that does not fit the format, obviously, cannot be included.

The most obvious change in format concerns the section on style. In all the earlier editions, at least one section was devoted to style, but the fourth edition does not include such a section. It is interesting to note that between 1990 and 2000 very little has appeared in the journals on the subject of style. If such a section were to be included, it would have drawn most of its material from the 1960s and 1970s. This current lack of emphasis on style, in my opinion, is a healthy sign. Style in our discipline is similar to the study of anatomy in the health professions. Style, like anatomy, is a foundational subject. It is expected that professionals know the foundations of their field: their practice is based on it. The professional journals, however, do not revisit such basic material over and over. What we are now seeing in our journals is *advancement* of the discipline, new and fresh insights that assume a general knowledge of the field. The fourth edition reflects this current emphasis.

Even though the section on style has been deleted, the fourth edition includes more sections than earlier editions. The overall length, however, is about the same. The final section of the third edition, "New Perspectives, New Horizons," now appears as Part Four, "Perspectives 2000." Part Five, "Attunement Through Shared Experience," and Part Six, "Spiritual Sites of Composing," are new. Both have their roots in the writings of Paulo Friere, though this is not always explicit. Indeed the 1990s might be viewed as the decade when American education began to reflect the same ideas that inspired Friere. "Attunement Through Shared Experience" speaks for a greatly expanded role of the teacher, one that reaches beyond the walls of the classroom as well as the artificial limits of the discipline. Going beyond the walls of the classroom, it should be noted, implies something revolutionary about what should go on inside the classroom.

Whereas Part Five explores the social dimensions of our work, Part Six, "Spiritual Sites of Composing," reaches toward an understanding of the inner life—depth in writing, depth in ourselves. Ann Berthoff reminds us that Friere saw the "prophetic church" as the driving moral energy for his work, which in many ways corresponds to what we see as the spiritual basis of our work. What has been bubbling under the surface of the discipline for years began to emerge in the 1990s—writing as a healing force; creativity, writing, and the arts; meditation; silence; intuition; feminine ways of knowing; images, archetypes, and symbols; mystical experience; transcendence; the whole range of human emotions. All this and more can be characterized as *spiritual*. Embracing the spiritual dimension, many believe, brings wholeness to our teaching. Without it, our work is incomplete and fragmented, having the form but no life. Those who have pioneered in this area might be compared to the early explorers of the cave of Lascaux whose flickering lights first illumined those primitive drawings of our ancestors. All that is included in Part Six is superb, and yet it represents just the first step in exploring a vast, uncharted area of learning. It is deeply gratifying for me to devote a full section to this dimension of our work.

Needless to say, *Rhetoric and Composition* would never have been possible without the support and encouragement of Bob Boynton, founder and former editor, friend of the profession, champion of literacy and educational reform. This fourth edition would not have been possible without the support of the current editor, Lisa Luedeke, whose energy, insight, good humor, and common sense I have come to admire. The staff at Heinemann, Lynne Mehley, Elizabeth Valway, and so many others have been helpful throughout the project.

Like teachers everywhere, I have learned so much from my students. There have been so many I could not name them all, so I name one as representative—Amy McCall, whose lesson "Rivers" continues to inspire me. During the planning stages of each edition, we have conducted a survey of writing teachers, asking them which articles have been most helpful in their work. I want to express my thanks to all of them, including those who responded anonymously, from the first edition to the present: Hugh Agee, Bob Bain, Lynn Bloom, Laura Brady, Lil Brannon, Tom Brennan, P. A. Carroll, Don Cunningham, Frank D'Angelo, Jim Davis, Anne Ruggles Gere, Dorothy

Grimes, I. Hashimoto, Paul Kameen, Terry Ley, Richard Lloyd-Jones, Carolyn Matalene, Marian Mohr, Lyn Zalusky Mueller, Keith Miller, Janice Neuleib, Elizabeth Cowan Neeld, Gretchen Niva, Twila Yates Papay, Gordon Pardl, David Roberts, Mike Rose, Dennis Rygiel, Bob Shafer, John Simmons, Fred Standley, Patricia Stock, Ann Trousdale, Lynn Troyka, Betty Jane Wagner, Tom Waldrep, Barbara Walvoord, Sam Watson, Ed White, Harvey Wiener, Lisa Williams, and Bill Wolff.

Susan Becker of Peoria, Illinois, and Isabelle Thompson of Auburn, Alabama, have been superb proofreaders, offering insights, suggestions, and continuing support, more than I could ever repay. Tom Nash has continued to stay in touch, though he is miles away, in Oregon. Susan Villaume has provided keen insights about the acquisition of literacy. I continue to be amazed at Sherry Swain's intuition about teaching and learning and thankful for her support and encouragement of my work. Over the years Jim Gray and members of the National Writing Project have taught me so much about writing and the writing classroom. Regina Foehr, friend and colleague, has made so many positive suggestions and numerous valuable contributions. Martha Goff Stoner's insights have always been sound as well as inspirational.

Finally, through it all over many years, my wife, Lois, has been supportive, quietly proud, always giving more than I deserve. Without her vision and faith, none of this would be possible.

R. L. G.

Part One

Introduction

Except he come to composition, a man remains un-put-together, more than usually troubled by the feuds within, and therefore a little more addicted to those without.

—Robert D. Hellman

Welcome to the world of writing. Though demanding, sometimes even frustrating, writing nevertheless remains one of the most deeply satisfying experiences in which humankind engages. Whether we come to writing as a student or as a teacher, we all find that writing itself is a great teacher. Some of us find that it can also be a friend who comforts in difficult times, or a companion who accompanies us through the routine events of daily life. Ideally we come to writing early, as children, and let it continue to feed and inform us throughout a lifetime. The invitation to write is always there, both beckoning and challenging us to ever higher levels of growth.

The first essay in this section is a classic—Maxine Hairston's "The Winds of Change: Thomas Kuhn and the Revolution in the Teaching of Writing," which was originally published in 1982. Hairston borrows the term *paradigm shift* from Thomas Kuhn to describe a wholly new way of seeing our work as writers and teachers of writing. She cites several assumptions from the "old paradigm" and goes on to describe ideas and activities that view writing as a process. For the past few years, *writing as process* and *new paradigm* have been generally viewed as synonymous.

Those readers who would like to see how the new paradigm has developed since 1982 should turn to the very last essay in this text, Susan A. Schiller's "Writing: A Natural Site for Spirituality." Taken together, these two essays provide a brief recent history of the teaching of writing and point the way toward a, yes, a breathtaking future.

Has the teaching of writing changed in recent years? Jane Tompkins' thoughtful and provocative response in "Pedagogy of the Distressed" suggests that it has changed profoundly. Tompkins describes a moment of transformation—"walking down the empty hall to class"—that initiated her journey into another teaching life. The old self, characterized by fear, desperately sought approval and contemptuous academic pride, is swept away. In its place is the quest for freedom, spontaneity, and authenticity. This is not a method, Tompkins

1

suggests, but something much deeper. Tompkins refers explicitly to Paulo Freire's work, but in some ways she goes beyond Freire, especially in her understanding of the dynamics of the American classroom experience. Those familiar with Freire's work will observe that his ideas are consistent with much of the thinking about the teaching of writing over the past decade.

In Julie M. Jensen's "What Do We Know About the Writing of Elementary School Children?" we hear the voices of several well-known and highly respected writing teachers. These brief quotations should be read slowly and thoughtfully, for brief though they may be, they contain ideas of great merit and wisdom. What is true of the way children learn to write is also true of the way adults continue to learn and grow and write. Listen to James Moffett, for example: "The writer has a reason to write, an intended audience, and control of subject matter and form . . . composing is staged across various phases of rumination, investigation, consultation with others, drafting, feedback, revision, and perfecting" (30). Moffett's final three words are almost prophetic in invoking the magic of language: "Literacy is sorcery" (30).

The Winds of Change

Thomas Kuhn and the Revolution in the Teaching of Writing

Maxine Hairston

In 1963, the University of Chicago Press published a book titled *The Structure of Scientific Revolutions,* written by Thomas Kuhn, a University of California professor of the history of science. In the book Kuhn hypothesizes about the process by which major changes come about in scientific fields, and conjectures that they probably do not evolve gradually from patient and orderly inquiry by established investigators in the field. Rather, he suggests, revolutions in science come about as the result of breakdowns in intellectual systems, breakdowns that occur when old methods won't solve new problems. He calls the change in theory that underlies this kind of revolution a *paradigm shift.* I believe we are currently at the point of such a paradigm shift in the teaching of writing, and that it has been brought about by a variety of developments that have taken place in the last 25 years.

Briefly, Kuhn's thesis in *The Structure of Scientific Revolutions* is this:

When a scientific field is going through a stable period, most of the practitioners in the discipline hold a common body of beliefs and assumptions; they agree on the problems that need to be solved, the rules that govern research, and on the standards by which performance is to be measured. They share a conceptual model that Kuhn calls a paradigm, and that paradigm governs activity in their profession. Students who enter the discipline prepare for membership in its intellectual community by studying that paradigm.

But paradigms are not necessarily immutable. When several people working in a field begin to encounter anomalies or phenomena that cannot be explained by the established model, the paradigm begins to show signs of instability. For a while, those who subscribe to the paradigm try to ignore the contradictions and inconsistencies that they find, or they make improvised, *ad hoc* changes to cope with immediate crises. Eventually, however, when enough anomalies accumulate to make a substantial number of scientists in the field question whether the traditional paradigm can solve many of the serious problems that face them, a few innovative thinkers will devise a new model. And if

College Composition and Communication, 33 (February 1982), pp. 76–88. Copyright © 1982 by the National Council of Teachers of English. Reprinted with permission.

enough scientists become convinced that the new paradigm works better than the old one, they will accept it as the new norm.

This replacement of one conceptual model by another one is Kuhn's *paradigm shift*. He cites as classic examples the astronomers' substitution of the Copernican model of the solar system for the Ptolemaic model and the development of Newtonian physics. Such shifts are usually disorderly and often controversial, and the period in which they occur is apt to be marked by insecurity and conflict within the discipline.

Kuhn believes that because these shifts are so disruptive, they will occur only when the number of unsolved problems in a discipline reaches crisis proportions and some major figures in the field begin to focus on those unsolved problems. But even with mounting evidence that their conceptual model doesn't work, supporters of the traditional paradigm resist change because they have an intellectual and sometimes an emotional investment in the accepted view. They particularly resist abandoning the conventional textbooks that set forth the precepts of their discipline in clear and unqualified terms. Those texts, as Richard Young points out in his essay, "Paradigms and Problems: Needed Research in Rhetorical Theory," are usually so similar that one way to discover the traditional paradigm of a field is to examine its textbooks.[1]

Finally, however, most of the resistance to the new paradigm will dissipate when its advocates can demonstrate that it will solve problems that the traditional paradigm could not solve. Most of the new generation of scholars working in the field will adopt the new model, and the older practitioners will gradually come around to it. Those who cling to the old paradigm lose their influence in the field because the leaders in the profession simply ignore their work. When that happens, the paradigm shift is complete, and the theory that was revolutionary becomes conventional.

This summary of Kuhn's book is sketchy and too simple, but I think it accurately reflects the key points in his theory. When he developed the theory, he considered only the so-called hard sciences, particularly chemistry, astronomy, and physics. He did not claim or even suggest that his model for scientific revolution could or should apply to social sciences or the humanities, where research is not done in laboratories and usually does not involve measurements or formulas. Nevertheless, I believe that composition theorists and writing teachers can learn from Thomas Kuhn if they see his theory of scientific revolutions as an analogy that can illuminate developments that are taking place in our profession. Those developments, the most prominent of which is the move to a process-centered theory of teaching writing, indicate that our profession is probably in the first stages of a paradigm shift.

The Current-Traditional Paradigm and Its Proponents

In order to understand the nature of that shift, we need to look at the principal features of the paradigm that has been the basis of composition teaching for several decades. In "Paradigms and Patterns" Richard Young describes it this way:

> The overt features . . . are obvious enough: the emphasis on the composed product rather than the composing process; the analysis of discourse into description, narration, exposition, and argument; the strong concern with usage . . . and with style; the preoccupation with the informal essay and research paper; and so on.[2]

Young adds that underlying the traditional paradigm is what he calls the "vitalist" attitude toward composing: that is, the assumption that no one can really teach anyone else how to write because writing is a mysterious creative activity that cannot be categorized or analyzed.

In an article in the Winter, 1980, *Freshman English News* James Berlin and Robert Inkster ascribe other features to the conventional paradigm. Basing their conclusions on an analysis of repeated patterns in four well-known and commercially successful rhetoric texts, they add that the traditional paradigm stresses expository writing to the virtual exclusion of all other forms, that it posits an unchanging reality which is independent of the writer and which all writers are expected to describe in the same way regardless of the rhetorical situation, that it neglects invention almost entirely, and that it makes style the most important element in writing.[3]

I would make three other points about the traditional paradigm. First, its adherents believe that competent writers know what they are going to say before they begin to write; thus their most important task when they are preparing to write is finding a form into which to organize their content. They also believe that the composing process is linear, that it proceeds systematically from prewriting to writing to rewriting. Finally, they believe that teaching editing is teaching writing.

It is important to note that the traditional paradigm did not grow out of research or experimentation. It derives partly from the classical rhetorical model that organizes the production of discourse into invention, arrangement, and style, but mostly it seems to be based on some idealized and orderly vision of what literature scholars, whose professional focus is on the written product, seem to imagine is an efficient method of writing. It is a prescriptive and orderly view of the creative act, a view that defines the successful writer as one who can systematically produce a 500-word theme of five paragraphs, each with a topic sentence. Its proponents hold it *a priori;* they have not tested it against the composing processes of actual writers.

At this point some of my readers may want to protest that I am belaboring a dead issue—that the admonition to "teach process, not product" is now conventional wisdom. I disagree. Although those in the vanguard of the profession have by and large adopted the process model for teaching composition and are now attentively watching the research on the composing process in order to extract some pedagogical principles from it, the overwhelming majority of college writing teachers in the United States are not professional writing teachers. They do not do research or publish on rhetoric or composition, and they do not know the scholarship in the field; they do not read the professional journals and they do not attend professional meetings such as the annual Conference on College Composition and Communication; they do not participate in faculty development workshops for writing teachers. They are trained as literary critics first and as teachers of literature second, yet out of necessity most of them are doing half or more of their teaching in composition. And they teach it by the traditional paradigm, just as they did when they were untrained teaching assistants ten or twenty or forty years ago. Often they use a newer edition of the same book they used as teaching assistants.

Out of necessity, apathy, and what I see as a benighted and patronizing view of the essential nature of composition courses, English department administrators encourage this unprofessional approach to the teaching of writing. In the first place, they may believe that they have so many writing classes to staff that they could not possibly hire well-qualified professionals to teach them; only a comparatively few such specialists exist. Second, most departmental chairpersons don't believe that an English instructor needs special qualifications to teach writing. As one of my colleagues says, our department wouldn't think of letting her teach Chaucer courses because she is not qualified; yet the chairman is delighted for her to teach advanced composition, for which she is far more unqualified. The assumption is that anyone with a Ph.D. in English is in expert writing teacher.

I think, however, that the people who do most to promote a static and unexamined approach to teaching writing are those who define writing courses as service courses and skills courses; that group probably includes most administrators and teachers of writing. Such a view, which denies that writing requires intellectual activity and ignores the importance of writing as a basic method of learning, takes away any incentive for the writing teacher to grow professionally. People who teach skills and provide services are traditionally less respected and rewarded than those who teach theory, and hiring hordes of adjuncts and temporary instructors and assigning them to composition courses reinforces this value system. Consequently there is no external pressure to find a better way to teach writing.

In spite of this often discouraging situation, many teachers who cling to the traditional paradigm work very hard at teaching writing. They devote far more time than they can professionally afford to working with their students, but because they haven't read Elbow or Bruffee they have no way of knowing that their students might benefit far more from small group meetings with each other than from the exhausting one-to-one conferences that the teachers hold. They both complain and brag about how much time they spend meticulously marking each paper, but because they haven't read Diederich or Irmscher they don't know that an hour spent meticulously marking every error in a paper is probably doing more harm than good. They are exhausting themselves trying to teach writing from an outmoded model, and they come to despise the job more and more because many of their students improve so little despite their time and effort.

But the writing teacher's frustration and disenchantment may be less important than the fact that if they teach from the traditional paradigm, they are frequently emphasizing techniques that the research has largely discredited. As Kuhn points out, the paradigm that a group of professionals accepts will govern the kinds of problems they decide to work on, and that very paradigm keeps them from recognizing important problems that cannot be discussed in the terminology of their model. Thus teachers who concentrate their efforts on teaching style, organization, and correctness are not likely to recognize that their students need work in invention. And if they stress that proofreading and editing are the chief skills one uses to revise a paper, they won't realize that their students have no concept of what it means to make substantive revisions in a paper. The traditional paradigm hides these problems.

Textbooks complicate the problem further. As Kuhn repeatedly points out, the standard texts in any discipline constitute a major block to a paradigm shift because they represent accepted authority. Many, though certainly not all, of the standard textbooks in rhetoric and composition for the past two decades have been product-centered books that focus on style, usage, and argumentation; Sheridan Baker's *The Practical Stylist* and Brooks and Warren's *Modern Rhetoric* are typical examples. When Donald Stewart made an analysis of rhetoric texts three years ago, he found that only seven out of the thirty-four he examined showed any awareness of current research in rhetoric. The others were, as he put it, "strictly current-traditional in their discussions of invention, arrangement, and style."[4] And textbooks change slowly. Publishers want to keep what sells, and they tend to direct the appeals of their books to what they believe the average composition teacher wants, not to what those in the vanguard of the profession would like to have.

Signs of Change

Nevertheless, changes are under way, and I see in the current state of our profession enough evidence of insecurity and instability to suggest that the traditional prescriptive and product-centered paradigm that underlies writing instruction is beginning to crumble. I think that the forces contributing to its demise are both theoretical and concrete and come from both inside and outside of the profession. Changes in theory probably started, in the middle 1950s, from intellectual inquiry and speculation about language and language learning that was going on in several fields, notably linguistics, anthropology, and clinical and cognitive psychology. To identify and trace all these complex developments would go far beyond the scope of this article and beyond my current state of enlightenment. I can only touch on some of them here.

Probably one of the most important developments to affect writing theory was the publication of Noam Chomsky's *Syntactic Structures* in 1957. His theory of transformational grammar, with its insistent look at the rules by which language is generated, caused a new focus on the process by which language comes into being.* The publication of Francis Christensen's essays on the generative rhetoric of the sentence and the paragraph in the early 1960s also stimulated new interest in the processes by which writers produce texts. Certainly the tagmemicists also provoked a fresh look at the act of writing when they urged writers to generate ideas by thinking about subjects from a dynamic, three-faceted perspective. And when the humanistic psychologist Carl Rogers began to criticize behaviorist psychology just as Chomsky had criticized behaviorist theories of language, he probably hastened the shift away from the product-response evaluation of writing.

A major event that encouraged the shift of attention to the process of writing was the famous Anglo-American Seminar on the Teaching of English, held at Dartmouth College in the summer of 1966. In the final report of this gathering of eminent educators from Britain and the United States, the participants deemphasized the formal teaching of grammar and usage in the classroom and emphasized having children engage directly in the writing process in a nonprescriptive atmosphere.

So the intellectual climate conducive to this change has been developing for more than two decades. Of course, if these shifts in theory and attitudes were the only forces that were putting pressure on the traditional approach to teaching writing, revolution in the profession would probably be long in coming. But other concrete and external forces have also been putting pressure on writing teachers. These teachers are plagued by embarrassing stories about college graduates who can't pass teacher competency tests, and by angry complaints about employees who can't write reports. And the professors agree. Their students come to them writing badly and they leave writing badly. Handbooks won't solve their problems, and having them revise papers does no good.

Worse, just at this time when they are most disheartened about teaching writing, large numbers of English professors are beginning to realize that most of them are going to be teaching a lot of writing to a lot of students from now on. The prospect is grim, so grim that the English departments at Harvard and the University of Michigan have given up and turned the bulk of their composition teaching over to specialists outside the departments. But most professors can't do that, and instead they feel insecure and angry because they know they are teaching badly. In Kuhn's terminology, their methods have become anomalous; the system that they have always depended on no longer seems to work.

But why should the paradigm begin to break down just now? After all, as Richard Young points out, thousands of people have learned to write by the trial-and-error method of producing a text and having it criticized. Why shouldn't that slow, but often effective, method continue to work most of the time? Once more, I think, Kuhn has the answer. He says, "One need look no further than Copernicus and the calendar to discover that external conditions may help to transform a mere anomaly into a source of acute crisis."[5] I believe that the external conditions which have hastened the crisis in the teaching

---

*I am indebted to my colleague Stephen Witte for bringing this development to my attention.

of writing are open admissions policies, the return to school of veterans and other groups of older students who are less docile and rule-bound than traditional freshmen, the national decline in conventional verbal skills, and the ever larger number of high school graduates going on to college as our society demands more and more credentials for economic citizenship. Any instructional system would come close to collapse under such a strain, and our system for teaching writing has been particularly vulnerable because it has been staffed largely by untrained teachers who have had little scholarly interest in this kind of teaching.

Following the pattern that Kuhn describes in his book, our first response to crisis has been to improvise *ad hoc* measures to try to patch the cracks and keep the system running. Among the first responses were the writing labs that sprang up about ten years ago to give first aid to students who seemed unable to function within the traditional paradigm. Those labs are still with us, but they're still giving only first aid and treating symptoms. They have not solved the problem. Another *ad hoc* remedy took the form of individualized instruction, but it has faded from the scene along with computer-assisted instruction. The first was too costly and too isolated, the second one proved too limited and impersonal. And the experiments with expressive writing also turned out to be *ad hoc* measures, although for a while they seemed to have enough strength to foreshadow a paradigm shift. Sentence combining, I predict, will prove to be another *ad hoc* measure that serves as only a temporary palliative for serious writing problems.

All these remedies have proved temporarily or partially useful; none, however, has answered the crucial question: What is the basic flaw in the traditional paradigm for teaching writing? Why doesn't it work?

The Transition Period

Someone who cares has to ask that question before the revolution can start because, as Kuhn points out, "novelty ordinarily emerges only for the man who, knowing *with precision* what he should expect, is able to recognize that something has gone wrong."[6] In the teaching of composition, the essential person who asked that question may not have been a man, but a woman, Mina Shaughnessy. In her book *Errors and Expectations,* Shaughnessy describes the educational experience that made her, a professor at a prestigious university, stop to ask, "What went wrong?"

> In the spring of 1970, the City University of New York adopted an admissions policy that guaranteed to every city resident with a high school diploma a place in one of its eighteen tuition-free colleges, thereby opening its doors not only to a larger population of students than it had ever had before . . . but to a wider range of students than any college had probably ever admitted or thought of admitting to its campus. . . . One of the first tasks these students faced when they arrived at college was to write a placement essay. . . . Judged by the

results of these tests, the young men and women who were to be known as open admissions students fell into one of three groups: 1. Those who met the traditional requirements for college work, who appeared from their tests . . . to be able to begin at the traditional starting points; 2. those who had survived their secondary schooling . . . and whose writing reflected a flat competence; 3. [those] who had been left so far behind the others in their formal education that they appeared to have little chance of catching up, students whose difficulties with the written language seemed of a different order from those of other groups, as if they had come, you might say, from a different country.

. . . The third group contained true outsiders, . . . strangers in academia, unacquainted with the rules and rituals of college life, unprepared for the sorts of tasks their teachers were about to assign them. . . .

Not surprisingly, the essays these students wrote during their first weeks of class stunned the teachers who read them. Nothing, it seemed, short of a miracle was going to turn such students into writers. . . . To make matters worse, there were no studies nor guides, nor even suitable textbooks to turn to. Here were teachers trained to analyze the belletristic achievements of the ages marooned in basic writing classrooms with adult student writers who appeared by college standards to be illiterate.[7]

Relying on their previous experience with selectively admitted students at the City University, Shaughnessy and her colleagues thought they knew what to expect from "college writers." The shock of facing a kind of writing that fit no familiar category, that met no traditional standards, forced Shaughnessy, at least, to recognize an anomaly. If these students had come through schools in which writing had been taught with standard textbooks and standard methods, then one had to conclude that the method and the textbooks did not work, at least not for a substantial and important group of students. The question was, "Why?"

To find the answer, Shaughnessy analyzed the placement essays of 4,000 students and over a period of five years worked at trying to get at the roots of their problems and devise a way to overcome them. Eventually she became persuaded

. . . that basic writers write the way they do, not because they are slow or nonverbal, indifferent to or incapable of academic excellence, but because they are beginners and must, like all beginners, learn by making mistakes. . . . And the keys to their development as writers often lie in the very features of their writing that English teachers have been trained to brush aside with a marginal code letter or a scribbled injunction to "Proofread!" Such strategies ram at the doors of their incompetence while the keys that would open them lie in view. . . . The work [of teaching these students to write] must be informed by an understanding not only of what is missing or awry, but of *why this is so.*[8] (italics added)

Shaughnessy's insight is utterly simple and vitally important: we cannot teach students to write by looking only at what they have written. We must also understand *how* that product came into being, and *why* it assumed the form that it did. We have to try to understand what goes on during the internal act of writing and we have to intervene during the act of writing if we want to affect its outcome. We have to do the hard thing, examine the intangible process, rather than the easy thing, evaluate the tangible product.

Although Shaugnessy was not the first investigator to try to move behind students' written products and find out how those products came into being—Janet Emig and Charles Stallard had both done limited studies at about the same time as Shaughnessy, and James Britton and his colleagues in Great Britain were working on a very ambitious study of the development of writing abilities—she was the first to undertake a large-scale research project whose goal was to teach the new students of the seventies to write. Her example, her book, and her repeated calls for new research in composition have undoubtedly been important stimuli in spurring the profession's search for a new paradigm.

Others in the profession have also given impetus to the search. In 1968 a journalist and professor named Donald Murray published a book called *A Writer Teaches Writing,* in which he suggests that if we want to teach students to write, we have to initiate them into the process that writers go through, not give them a set of rules. He insists that writers find their real topics only through the act of writing. In fact, Murray may have originated the admonition, "Teach Writing as a Process not Product" in a 1972 article by that title.[9] A resurgence of interest in classical rhetoric in the seventies also sparked interest in a new approach to the teaching of writing. The books by rhetoricians Richard Weaver and Edward P. J. Corbett provided the theoretical foundations for the view that writing cannot be separated from its context, that audience and intention should affect every stage of the creative process. When this premise became widely accepted at major universities—for example, the University of Iowa and the University of Texas—it inevitably put strains on the old product-centered paradigm.

Another major influence on the teaching of writing across the nation has come from California's Bay Area Writing Project, initiated in 1975. A cardinal principle of that project has been the revolutionary thesis that all writing teachers should write in order to understand the writing process firsthand. When teachers began to do so, the traditional textbook model for writing inevitably came into question. And as spin-offs of the Bay Area Writing Project have proliferated across the country, largely funded by grant money donated by agencies and foundations alarmed about the writing crisis, a growing number of teachers are changing to process-centered writing instruction.

The Emerging Paradigm

But the most promising indication that we are poised for a paradigm shift is that for the first time in the history of teaching writing we have specialists who are doing controlled and directed research on writers' composing processes. Sondra Perl of Herbert Lehman College of the City University of New York and Linda Flower and John Hayes of Carnegie-Mellon University are tape-recording students' oral reports of the thoughts that come to them as they write and of the choices they make. They call their investigative strategy "protocol analysis," and they supplement it with interviews and questionnaires to put together composite pictures of the processes followed by working writers. Sharon Pianko of Rutgers University has done a study in which she matched groups of traditional and remedial writers, men and women writers, and 18-year-old and adult writers and compared their composing habits. Nancy Sommers of New York University has done a study comparing the revising practices of college freshmen and experienced professional writers, and Lester Faigley and Stephen Witte of the University of Texas now have a federal grant to do a more comprehensive study on revising. (An article based on this study appeared in the December, 1981, issue of *CCC.*) Lee Odell of Rensselaer Polytechnic Institute and Dixie Goswami are currently involved in a federally funded study of the practices of writers in business.

From these and other studies we are beginning to find out something about how people's minds work as they write, to chart the rhythm of their writing, to find out what constraints they are aware of as they write, and to see what physical behaviors are involved in writing and how they vary among different groups of writers. So far only a small amount of data has been collected, and the inferences we can draw from the studies are necessarily tentative. As Linda Flower puts it, because we are trying to chart and analyze an activity that goes on largely out of sight, the process is rather like trying to trace the path of a dolphin by catching glimpses of it when it leaps out of the water. We are seeing only a tiny part of the whole process, but from it we can infer much about what is going on beneath the surface.[10]

What are we finding out? One point that is becoming clear is that writing is an act of discovery for both skilled and unskilled writers; most writers have only a partial notion of what they want to say when they begin to write, and their ideas develop in the process of writing. They develop their topics intuitively, not methodically. Another truth is that usually the writing process is not linear, moving smoothly in one direction from start to finish. It is messy, recursive, convoluted, and uneven. Writers write, plan, revise, anticipate, and review throughout the writing process, moving back and forth among the different operations involved in writing without any apparent plan. No practicing writer will be surprised at these findings: nevertheless, they seriously contradict the traditional paradigm that has dominated writing textbooks for years.

But for me the most interesting data emerging from these studies are those that show us profound differences between the writing behaviors of skilled and unskilled writers and the behaviors of student and professional writers. Those differences involve the amount of time spent on writing, the amount of time preparing to write, the number of drafts written, the concern for audience, the number of changes made and the stages at which they are made, the frequency and length of pauses during writing, the way in which those pauses are used, the amount of time spent rereading and reformulating, and the kind and number of constraints that the writers are aware of as they work. This kind of information enables us to construct a tentative profile of the writing behaviors of effective writers; I have sketched such a profile in another paper, not yet published.

From all this activity in the field, the new paradigm for teaching writing is emerging. Its principal features are these:

1. It focuses on the writing process; instructors intervene in students' writing during the process.
2. It teaches strategies for invention and discovery; instructors help students to generate content and discover purpose.
3. It is rhetorically based; audience, purpose, and occasion figure prominently in the assignment of writing tasks.
4. Instructors evaluate the written product by how well it fulfills the writer's intention and meets the audience's needs.
5. It views writing as a recursive rather than linear process; prewriting, writing, and revision are activities that overlap and intertwine.
6. It is holistic, viewing writing as an activity that involves the intuitive and nonrational as well as the rational faculties.
7. It emphasizes that writing is a way of learning and developing as well as a communication skill.
8. It includes a variety of writing modes, expressive as well as expository.
9. It is informed by other disciplines, especially cognitive psychology and linguistics.
10. It views writing as a disciplined creative activity that can be analyzed and described; its practitioners believe that writing can be taught.
11. It is based on linguistic research and research into the composing process.
12. It stresses the principle that writing teachers should be people who write.

Portents for the Future

I believe that important events of the recent past are going to speed the revolution and help to establish this new paradigm in the nation's classrooms.

First, the University of Iowa's Writing institute, which received a $680,000 grant from the National Endowment for the Humanities to train freshman composition directors, has this year completed its work and sent out forty administrators for writing programs who will almost certainly base those programs on the new model. They are bound to have a profound influence on their institutions.

Second, graduate programs in rhetoric are rapidly increasing across the country. The last count in the Spring, 1980, *Freshman English News* showed that fifty-three institutions have added graduate rhetoric courses since 1974,

and that was not a complete list. Enrollment in these programs is climbing because students realize that English departments now offer more jobs in rhetoric
and composition than in any other specialization. Most of these programs are
going to produce young professionals who have been taught by scholars who
know recent research and are committed to the new paradigm: Richard Young,
Ross Winterowd, Joseph Comprone, James Kinneavy, Andrea Lunsford, Elizabeth Cowan, Linda Flower, to name just a few. When these new graduates go
into English departments where the traditional paradigm prevails, they are certain to start working for change.

Third, in many schools, even graduate assistants who are in traditional literary programs rather than rhetoric programs are getting their in-service training from the rhetoric and composition specialists in their departments. They are
being trained in process-centered approaches to the teaching of composition,
and when they enter the profession and begin teaching lower-division writing
courses along with their literary specialties, they are most likely to follow the
new paradigm. And, more and more, the methods courses for high-school teachers are also being taught by the rhetoric specialists; that change will have a profound effect on secondary school teaching.

Fourth, we now have process-based texts on the teaching of writing.
Shaughnessy's *Errors and Expectations* is well-known and widely used. It has
been joined by Irmscher's *Teaching Expository Writing* and Neman's *Teaching
Students to Write*. The authors of both these latter books incorporate research
findings and recent developments in the profession into their philosophies of
and methodologies for teaching writing.

Fifth, college composition textbooks are changing. Along with their traditional books, most publishers are now publishing at least one process-oriented,
rhetorically based writing text. Several are now on the market and more are
forthcoming, most of them written by scholars and teachers who are leaders
in the profession. Moreover, many major publishing houses now retain well-
known composition specialists to advise them on manuscripts. The publishers
sense change in the wind and realize that the new crop of well-informed and
committed writing program directors who will be taking over are going to insist on up-to-date textbooks. The change will even reach into some high schools
because one large company has hired one of the country's leading rhetoricians
to supervise and edit their high school composition series. Many others will
probably follow their example.

But no revolution brings the millennium nor a guarantee of salvation, and
we must remember that the new paradigm is sketchy and leaves many problems
about the teaching or writing unresolved. As Kuhn points out, new paradigms
are apt to be crude, and they seldom possess all the capabilities of their predecessors. So it is important for us to preserve the best parts of earlier methods
for teaching writing: the concern for style and the preservation of high standards for the written product. I believe we also need to continue giving students
models of excellence to imitate.

Kuhn contends that "the transition between competing paradigms cannot be made a step at a time, forced by logic. . . . Like the gestalt switch, it must occur all at once (though not necessarily in an instant) or not at all." [11] He says, however, that, "if its supporters are competent, they will improve it [the paradigm], explore its possibilities, and show what it would be like to belong to the community guided by it." [12] I see this last opportunity as the challenge to today's community of composition and rhetoric scholars: to refine the new paradigm for teaching composition so that it provides a rewarding, productive, and feasible way of teaching writing for the nonspecialists who do most of the composition teaching in our colleges and universities.

Notes

1. Richard Young, "Paradigms and Problems: Needed Research in Rhetorical Invention," *Research in Composing,* ed. Charles Cooper and Lee Odell (Urbana, IL: National Council of Teachers of English, 1978), p. 31.

2. Young, p. 31.

3. James A. Berlin and Robert P. Inkster, "Current-Traditional Rhetoric: Paradigm and Practice," *Freshman English News,* 8 (Winter, 1980), 1–4, 13–14.

4. Donald Stewart, "Composition Textbooks and the Assault on Tradition," *College Composition and Communication,* 29 (May, 1978), 174.

5. Thomas Kuhn, *The Structure of Scientific Revolutions,* Second Edition (Chicago; University of Chicago Press, 1970), p. x.

6. Kuhn, p. 65.

7. Mina Shaughnessy, *Errors and Expectations* (New York and London: Oxford University Press, 1977), pp. 1–3.

8. Shaughnessy, p. 5.

9. Donald Murray, "Teach Writing as a Process not Product," *The Leaflet,* November 1972, pp. 11–14 (The New England Association of Teachers of English).

10. Linda Flower and John Hayes, "Identifying the Organization of the Writing Processes," *Cognitive Processes in Writing,* ed. Lee W. Gregg and Erwin R. Steinberg (Hillsdale, NJ: Lawrence Erlbaum Associates, 1980), pp. 9–10.

11. Kuhn, p. 150.

12. Kuhn, p. 159.

Pedagogy of the Distressed

Jane Tompkins

Fear is what prevents the flowering of the mind.

—J. Krishnamurti,
On Education

I

As professors of English we are always one way or another talking about what we think is wrong with the world and to a lesser extent about what we'd like to see changed. Whether we seek gender equality, or economic justice, or simply believe in the power and beauty of great literature, we preach some gospel or other. We do this indirectly, but always. What I have to say is very simple and comes directly off this point: our practice in the classroom doesn't often come very close to instantiating the values we preach.

I was led to think about the distance between what we do as teachers and what we say we believe in by Paulo Freire's *Pedagogy of the Oppressed,* whose great theme is that you cannot have a revolution unless education becomes a practice of freedom. That is, to the extent that the teaching situation reflects the power relations currently in force, which are assumed to be oppressive and authoritarian, to that extent will the students themselves, when they come to power, reproduce that situation in another form. He argues that if political revolution is to succeed, pedagogy must first enact that very unalienated condition which the revolution presumably exists to usher in. Now the situation that currently pertains in the classroom, according to Freire, can best be understood through the analogy of banking. "In the banking concept of education," he writes, "knowledge is a gift bestowed by those who consider themselves knowledgeable upon those whom they consider to know nothing. . . . Education thus becomes an act of depositing, in which the students are the depositories and the teacher is the depositor. Instead of communicating, the teacher issues communiques and makes deposits which the students patiently receive, memorize, and repeat" (58).

College English, 52 (October 1990), pp. 653–60. Copyright © 1990 by the National Council of Teachers of English. Reprinted with permission.

16

I don't think that this is the model we have to contend with in the United States today, at least not in higher education, at least not for the most part. We have class discussion, we have oral reports, we have student participation of various kinds — students often choose their own paper topics, suggest additional readings, propose issues for discussion. As far as most of us are concerned, the banking model is obsolete. But what we do have is something no less coercive, no less destructive of creativity and self-motivated learning, and that is something I'll call the performance model.

I became aware of this phenomenon some four or five years ago when I was teaching a combined graduate-undergraduate course at Columbia University. Why the realization came to me then I cannot explain. I remember walking down the empty hall to class (always a little bit late) and thinking to myself, "I have to remember to find out what they want, what they need, and not worry about whether what I've prepared is good enough or ever gets said at all." Whereas, for my entire teaching life, I had always thought that what I was doing was helping my students to understand the material we were studying — Melville or deconstruction or whatever — I had finally realized that what I was actually concerned with and focused on most of the time were three things: a) to show the students how smart I was, b) to show them how knowledgeable I was, and c) to show them how well-prepared I was for class. I had been putting on a performance whose true goal was not to help the students learn but to perform before them in such a way that they would have a good opinion of me. I think that this essentially, and more than anything else, is what we teach our students: how to perform within an institutional academic setting in such a way that they will be thought highly of by their colleagues and instructors.

What is behind this model? How did it come to be that our main goal as academicians turned out to be performance? I think the answer to the question is fairly complicated, but here is one way to go. Each person comes into a professional situation dragging along behind her a long bag full of desires, fears, expectations, needs, resentments — the list goes on. But the main component is fear. Fear is the driving force behind the performance model. Fear of being shown up for what you are: a fraud, stupid, ignorant, a clod, a dolt, a sap, a weakling, someone who can't cut the mustard. In graduate school, especially, fear is prevalent. Thinking about these things, I became aware recently that my own fear of being shown up for what I really am must transmit itself to my students, and insofar as I was afraid to be exposed, they too would be afraid.

Such fear is no doubt fostered by the way our institution is organized, but it is rooted in childhood. Many, perhaps most, people who go into academic life are people who as children were good performers at home and in school. That meant that as children they/we successfully imitated the behavior of adults before we were in fact ready to do so. Having covered over our true childish selves, we have ever since been afraid of being revealed as the unruly beings we actually are. Fear of exposure, of being found out, does not have its basis in any real inadequacies either of knowledge or intelligence on our part, but rather in the performance model itself which, in separating our behavior from what we really felt, created a kind of false self. (This notion of the false self comes from Alice Miller's *The Drama of the Gifted Child*). We became so good at imitating the behavior of our elders, such expert practitioners at imitating whatever style, stance, or attitude seemed most likely to succeed in the adult world from which we so desperately sought approval that we came to be split into two parts: the real backstage self who didn't know anything and the performing self who got others to believe in its expertise and accomplishments. This pattern of seeking approval has extended itself into our practice as teachers. Still seeking approval from our peers and from our students, we exemplify a model of performance which our students succeed in emulating, thus passing the model down to future generations. Ironically, as teachers we are still performing for the teachers who taught us.

There is one other kind of fear that I want to mention here, institutional in its origin, and that is the fear of pedagogy itself as a focus of our attention. We have been indoctrinated from the very start, at least I was, to look down on pedagogy as a subject matter and to deride colleges of education. I was taught to see them as a sort of natural repository for the unsmart, the people who scored in the 50th percentile on their tests and couldn't make it into the higher realms to which I had so fortunately been admitted.

I remember quite vividly my introduction to this point of view. It was in an anteroom at Swarthmore College while waiting to be interviewed by a committee representing the Woodrow Wilson Foundation. While I sat there in a state of abject terror, I overheard a conversation between two young men also hoping to convince the committee's greybeards to find them worthy of a fellowship. One of them said to the other—I no longer remember his exact words— that thinking about teaching was the lowest of the low and that anyone who occupied himself with it was hopelessly beyond the pale and just didn't belong in higher education. I'll never forget my surprise and dismay at hearing this opinion which had never occurred to me before, for I had previously thought (coming from a family of teachers) that teaching was an important part of what any college professor would do. As things turned out, I subsequently embraced the view I overheard and held it as my own for some thirty years; or rather, this view embraced me, for my antipedagogical indoctrination went on pretty steadily throughout graduate school.

Now obviously, despite all this, I must have given some thought over the years to what went on in my classroom. One cannot be a total somnambulist and still survive, though I think a lot of people, myself included, have come pretty close. But I paid attention only when forced to because things weren't going well, and even then I felt I was doing something vaguely illegitimate. I used to wonder by what mysterious process others managed their classes, since no one I knew had been trained to do it and no one ever talked, really talked, about what they did. Oh, there were plenty of success stories and the predictable remarks about a discussion that had been like pulling teeth but never anything about how it really felt to be up there day after day.

In this respect teaching was exactly like sex for me—something you weren't supposed to talk about or focus on in any way but that you were supposed to be able to do properly when the time came. And the analogy doesn't end there. Teaching, like sex, is something you do alone, although you're always with another person/other people when you do it; it's hard to talk about to the other while you're doing it, especially if you've been taught not to think about it from an early age. And people rarely talk about what the experience is really like for them, partly because, in whatever subculture it is I belong to, there's no vocabulary for articulating the experience and no institutionalized format for doing so.

But there is one thing people do sometimes talk about in relation to teaching, and they do this now more frequently than in the past. They talk about using teaching as a vehicle for social change. We tell ourselves that we need to teach our students to think critically so that they can detect the manipulations of advertising, analyze the fallacious rhetoric of politicians, expose the ideology of popular TV shows, resist the stereotypes of class, race, and gender; or, depending on where you're coming from, hold the line against secular humanism and stop canon-busting before it goes too far.

But I have come to think more and more that what really matters as far as our own beliefs and projects for change are concerned is not so much what we talk about in class as what we do. I have come to think that teaching and learning are not a preparation for anything but are the thing itself. There is a catch-22 in the assumption that what you say in class or what you write for publication is the real vehicle for change. For if you speak and write only so that other people will hear and read and repeat your ideas to other people who will repeat them, maybe, to other people, but not so that they will do something, then what good are your words?

I've come to realize that the classroom is a microcosm of the world; it is the chance we have to practice whatever ideals we may cherish. The kind of classroom situation one creates is the acid test of what it is one really stands for. And I wonder, in the case of college professors, if performing their competence in front of other people is all that that amounts to in the end.

II

I've now made an awkward lunge in the direction of creating a different world in the classes I teach. It wasn't virtue or principle that led me to this but brute necessity caused by lack of planning. A year ago last fall, because I knew I wouldn't have time to prepare my classes in the usual way, I borrowed a new teaching method from a colleague and discovered, almost by accident, a way to make teaching more enjoyable and less anxiety-producing.

More enjoyment and less anxiety do not sound like very high-minded goals. In fact, they are self-centered. My upbringing taught me never to declare to anything I did was self-centered, especially not if it had to do with an activity like teaching, which is supposed to be altruistic. But I had discovered that under the guise of serving students, I was being self-centered anyway, always worrying about what people thought of me. So I tried something else for a change.

What the method boils down to is this: the students are responsible for presenting the material to the class for most of the semester. I make up the syllabus in advance, explain it in detail at the beginning of the course, and try to give most of my major ideas away. (This is hard; holding on to one's ideas in case one should need them to fill some gap later on is bred in the bone after twenty-odd years in the classroom). The students sign up for two topics that interest them, and they work with whoever else has signed up for their topic; anywhere from two to four people will be in charge on any given day. On the first round of reports the groups meet with me outside of class to discuss their ideas and strategies of presentation. I give plenty of feedback in written form, but no grades.

I find that my classes are better. The students have more to say in every class, more students take part in the discussions, students talk more to each other and less to me, and the intensity and quality of their engagement with the course materials is higher than usual. Because I don't have the burden of responsibility for how things are going to go every time, I can contribute when I feel I really have something to say. I concentrate better on what is being said, on who is talking, and on how the class is going—how things feel in the class.

The upshot is I do less work and enjoy class more. But I feel guilty about this. Partly because somewhere along the way I got the idea that only back-breaking work should produce good results. I struggle not to feel guilty at teaching in a way that is pleasurable to me and free from fear because part of what I now try to do as a teacher conveys a sense of the way I think life ought to be. This means, among other things, offering a course that is not a rat race, either for me or for the students. I no longer believe that piling on the work is a good in itself or that it proves seriousness and dedication. The point is not to make people suffer. The trial-by-fire model that graduate school sets is a bad one for the classroom. Education is not a preparation for war; the university is not a boot camp.

Still, there is the question of whether, in shifting the burden of performance onto the students, I'm not making them do work I'm too lazy to do myself, sending them off on a journey with inadequate supplies, telling them to go fishing without a rod or bait, demanding that they play the Kreutzer Sonata before they can do a scale. It's true that in some cases the students don't deal with the material as well as I could, but that is exactly why they need to do it. It's not important for me to polish my skills, but they do need to develop theirs and to find a voice.

When the same person is doing the presenting all the time, inevitably one line of approach to the materials is going to dominate. But when it's not the teacher who is always calling the shots, the interests of the individual students have a chance to emerge. You find out what they want to focus on, think is important, believe in. Several points of view get to be enunciated from the position of designated speaker: students get practice in presenting material in a way that is interesting and intelligible to other people; the variety keeps the class entertained and passes responsibility around so that even the quietest students have to contribute and end up feeling better about themselves.

Almost every class I've conducted in this way has had its own intellectual center of gravity. A cluster of issues, or sometimes a single problem, keeps on coming up; the students develop a vocabulary and a common set of references for discussing it. This gives the class a sense of identity, a coherence as much social as intellectual.

But I want not so much to make a pitch for this method, which, after all, is not that new, as to relay what I have learned from these experiences.

Last spring I taught a course on a subject I had been wanting to explore but knew little about: the subject was emotion. The course was offered under the rubric Feminist Theory in the Humanities, one of three core courses in a women's studies graduate certificate program newly launched at my university. I'd gotten the idea for this course from a brilliant lecture Alison Jaggar had given entitled "Love and Knowledge." Jaggar argued that since reason, in Western epistemology, had traditionally been stipulated as the faculty by which we know what we know, and since women, in Western culture, are required to be the bearers of emotion, women were automatically delegitimized as sources of knowledge, their epistemic authority cut off from the start.

Using this idea as my inspiration, I decided we would look at the way emotion had been dealt with in the West—in philosophy, psychology, anthropology, literature and literary criticism, and religious studies (this was an interdisciplinary course both in subject matter and in enrollment). We ended by looking at examples of feminist writing that integrated emotion and ideation both in substance and in form.

This was the most amazing course I've ever taught, or rather the most amazing course I've never taught, because each class was taught by the students. Since I had no expertise in any of the areas we were dealing with except the literary, there was no way I could be responsible for presenting the material every time. So, having put together a syllabus by hook or by crook, I distributed responsibility for class presentations in the way I've just outlined. I encouraged the students to be creative in their modes of presentation, and, since this was a course in emotion, encouraged people to be free in expressing their feelings and to talk about their own experiences whenever they seemed relevant. One of the points of the course was, in practice, to break down the barrier between public discourse and private feeling, between knowledge and experience.

You see, I wanted to be iconoclastic. I wanted to change the way it was legitimate to behave inside academic institutions. I wanted to make it OK to get shrill now and then, to wave your hands around, to cry in class, to do things in relation to the subject at hand other than just talking in an expository or adversarial way about it. I wanted never to lose sight of the fleshly, desiring selves who were engaged in discussing hegemony or ideology or whatever it happened to be; I wanted to get the ideas that were "out there," the knowledge that was piled up impersonally on shelves, into relation with the people who were producing and consuming it. I wanted to get "out there" and "in here" together. To forge a connection between whatever we were talking about in class and what went on in the lives of the individual members. This was a graduate course, and the main point, for me, was for the students, as a result of the course, to feel some deeper connection between what they were working on professionally and who they were, the real concerns of their lives.

This may sound utopian. Or it may sound childlike. But I did and do believe that unless there is some such connection, the work is an empty labor which will end by killing the organism that engages in it.

The course was in some respects a nightmare. There were days when people went at each other so destructively that students cried after class or got migraine headaches (I started getting migraines after every class before long). There were huge misunderstandings, factions, discussions at cross-purposes, floundering, a sense of incoherence, everything that one might have feared. There were days when I decided I had literally opened Pandora's box and that we would all have been better off conducting business as usual. One day I myself was on the verge of tears as I spoke.

But this was also the most exciting class I've ever been in. I never knew what was going to happen. Apart from a series of stunning self-revelations, wonderful readings added to the reading list by the students, and reports whose trajectory came as a total surprise, we were led, as a class, by various reporting groups into role-playing, picture drawing, and even on one occasion into participating in a religious ceremony.

I learned from this class that every student in every class one "teaches" is a live volcano, or, as James Taylor puts it in his song, "a churnin' urn o' burnin' funk." There is no one thing that follows from this discovery, but for me it has meant that I can never teach in the old way again. By which I mean that I can never fool myself into believing that what I have to say is ultimately more important to the students than what they think and feel. I know now that each student is a walking field of energy teeming with agendas. Knowing this I can conduct my classes so as to tap into that energy field and elicit some of the agendas.

Which brings me, in conclusion, to my current rules of thumb reminders of what I've learned that keep me pointed in the right direction.

- Trust the students. Years of habit get in the way, years of taking all the responsibility for the class on yourself. You have to believe that the students will come through and not be constantly stepping into the breach. The point is for the students to become engaged, take responsibility, feel their own power and ability, not for you, one more time, to prove you've got the right stuff.

- Talk to the class about the class. For mnemonic purposes, we might call this the "good sex directive." Do this at the beginning of the course to get yourself and the students used to it. Make it no big deal, just a normal part of day-to-day business, and keep it up, so that anything that's making you or other people unhappy can be addressed before it gets too big or too late to deal with.

- Less is more. It's better to underassign than to overassign. Resist the temptation to pile on work. Work is not a virtue in and of itself. Quality of attention is what you're aiming at, not burnout.

- Offer what you have. Don't waste time worrying that your thoughts aren't good enough. A structure for people to use in organizing their thoughts, to oppose, to get their teeth into is what is needed. Not *War and Peace*.

- Don't be afraid to try new things. This is a hard one for me. I'm always afraid a new idea will flop. So it flops. At least it provides variety and keeps things moving. I call this the Shirley MacLaine Principle: if you want to get the fruit from the tree, you have to go out on a limb.

- Let go. Don't hang on to what's just happened, good or bad. In some situations you probably can't tell which is which anyway, so let things happen and go on from there. Don't cling to the course, to the students, to your own ideas. There's more where they all came from. (A corollary to this rule is: you can't do it all. The whole point of this approach is that the teacher doesn't do everything.)

Gay Hendricks writes in *The Centered Teacher*:

It is easy, if we view teaching as a one-way street, to fall into the trap of doing more than 50% of the work in the classroom. If we see teachers as having the answers and the students as having the questions we invite an imbalance in the relationship which can only cause a drain on teachers' energy. It is important to have a relationship with students which generates energy for *all* concerned rather than drains it. (27)

Teaching is a service occupation, but it can only work if you discover, at a certain point, how to make teaching serve you. Staying alive in the classroom and avoiding burnout means finding out what you need from teaching at any particular time. I went from teaching as performance to teaching as a maternal or coaching activity because I wanted to remove myself from center stage and get out of the students' way, to pay more attention to them and less to myself. On an ideological plane, then, you might say I made the move in order to democratize the classroom. But on a practical plane I did it because I was tired. Sometimes, I used to think of my teaching self as the character played by Jane

Fonda in a movie about a couple who had entered a dance marathon to earn money during the Depression; it was called *They Shoot Horses, Don't They?* In moving from the performance to the coaching model, I was seeking rest.

I'm not suggesting that other teachers should adopt this particular method. There are a million ways to teach. (Nor do I think the method is suitable only for graduate students or students in elite institutions: Freire worked with illiterate peasants.) What I'm suggesting are two things. First, what we do in the classroom is our politics. No matter what we may say about Third World this or feminist that, our actions and our interactions with our students week in, week out prove what we are for and what we are against in the long run. There is no substitute for practice. Second, the politics of the classroom begins with the teacher's treatment of and regard for him- or herself. A kinder, more sensitive attitude toward one's own needs as a human being, in place of a desperate striving to meet professional and institutional standards of arguable merit, can bring greater sensitivity to the needs of students and a more sympathetic understanding of their positions, both as workers in the academy and as people in the wider world.

Works Cited

Freire, Paulo. *Pedagogy of the Oppressed.* Trans. Myra Bergman Ramos. New York: Continuum, 1970.

Hendricks, Gay. *The Centered Teacher.* Englewood Cliffs, NJ: Prentice, 1981.

Jaggar, Alison M. "Love and Knowledge: Emotion in Feminist Epistemology." *Gender/Body/Knowledge: Feminist Reconstructions of Being and Knowing.* Eds. Alison M. Jaggar and Susan R. Bordo. New Brunswick: Rutgers UP, 1989.

Miller, Alice. *The Drama of the Gifted Child.* New York: Basic, 1983.

What Do We Know About the Writing of Elementary School Children?

Julie M. Jensen

Comments from various teachers and researchers across the United States remind us of what we have learned about children's writing in the 30 years since the publication of "The Braddock Report."

Celebrating anniversaries seems instinctive to our profession. In 1992, a banner year, we acknowledged the 50th anniversary of the awarding of the Caldecott Medal to Robert McCloskey's *Make Way for Ducklings* (1941) and the 30th anniversary of the appearance of a book widely credited as launching the environmental movement, Rachel Carson's *Silent Spring* (1962). It was no coincidence that children's books about Mozart were in evidence last year, the 200th anniversary of his birth. And when have we seen more books about Christopher Columbus than in 1992, the 500th anniversary of the explorer's arrival in the new world? If we so eagerly use language to pay tribute to milestones in life and in print, the obvious question is, What's in store for the current year? Certainly one possibility springs to mind.

Thirty years ago, a new book signaled the start of an era in the teaching of writing. Referred to as "the charter of modern Composition" (North 1987, p. 17), it has been credited with leading the profession "to new breadth and depth of interest in the teaching of writing" (Hillocks 1986, p. xvii). The book came in response to concerns of NCTE's Executive Committee about the nature of public pronouncements on how writing should be taught and its appointment of a "Committee on the State of Knowledge in Composition." The charge to the Committee was "to review what is known and what is not known about the teaching and learning of composition and the conditions under which it is taught, for the purpose of preparing for publication a special scientifically based

I am grateful to Arthur Applebee, Nancie Atwell, Glenda Bissex, Colette Daiute, Anne Haas Dyson, Peter Elbow, Susan Florio-Ruane, Robert Gundlach, George Hillocks, Jr., Martha King, Richard Lloyd-Jones, Ken Macrorie, James Moffett, Thomas Newkirk, W. Charles Read, and William Teale for their contributions to this manuscript.

Language Arts, 70 (April 1993), pp. 290–94. Copyright © 1993 by the National Council of Teachers of English. Reprinted with permission.

report on what is known in this area" (p. 1). The result, informally called "The Braddock Report," is formally known as *Research in Written Composition* by Richard Braddock, Richard Lloyd-Jones, and Lowell Schoer, published in 1963 by NCTE.

The 30th anniversary of an acknowledged milestone in the teaching of writing is, like other anniversaries, an opportune time to take stock. Braddock, Lloyd-Jones, and Schoer gave us a baseline, a starting point, an introduction for a new story about the teaching of writing. They did it most concisely in this short and frequently quoted passage:

> Today's research in composition, taken as a whole, may be compared to chemical research as it emerged from the period of alchemy: some terms are being defined usefully, a number of procedures are being refined, but the field as a whole is laced with dreams, prejudices, and makeshift operations. (p. 5)

If writing research was alchemy 30 years ago, what is it now? What can be said in 1993, after 30 years of explosive interest in and intense research on the writing of elementary school children?

In pursuit of an answer, I turned to experts, specifically to 24 scholars cited most frequently in "Writing," a chapter written by Anne Dyson and Sarah Freedman (1991) for the *Handbook of Research on Teaching the English Language Arts.* I invited each to compose a brief written response to this question: "What is the single most important thing that we as a profession know now that we didn't know 30 years ago about the teaching and learning of writing in the elementary school?" I am indebted to 16 of them for returning usable questionnaires.

After multiple readings, I sorted the responses into four overlapping categories and composed for each category a possible generalization about the current state of knowledge about writing. Thus, according to my sample of experts, we now know that (1) writing during the early years is a natural "gateway to literacy"; (2) all children can be writers; (3) understanding writing and writers means understanding complex and interrelated influences—cognitive, social, cultural, psychological, linguistic, and technological; and (4) we write so that both we and others can know what we think, who we are. Following are the responses, clustered by category, alphabetized by author. I close with a list of publications for "Further Reading," a single title by each respondent taken from the "Writing" chapter of the *Handbook* cited above.

Writing During the Early Years Is a Natural "Gateway to Literacy"

> . . . [V]ery young children can learn to write before they can read. They can write anything they can say, whereas they can read only a fraction of the words they can say. And so writing is easier, quicker, and, in a sense, more "natural" than reading—certainly more easily and naturally learned. Thus

writing naturally *precedes* reading. Writing is the gateway to literacy, not reading. Writing is the realm where children can attain literacy first and best feel on top of it—feel ownership and control over the written word.

We need to follow up this insight in the teaching of older children: to make sure that writing is not always used to serve reading and follow reading; but that just as often writing can come first, and reading can serve writing.

Peter Elbow
University of Massachusetts

. . . From my perspective, the most important insight is that, given appropriate time and nurturing, even very young children may produce extended writing of high quality without first having had to undergo a program of servitude in the supposed 'building blocks' of writing: correct spelling, sentence structure, and so forth. The research has shown that children can transfer much of what they have learned about language to writing. This is not, of course, to say that there is nothing more to learn about written discourse than what appears in daily talk. We do know, however, that children can begin using what they do know far earlier and more effectively than we thought.

George Hillocks, Jr.
University of Chicago

Certainly the most surprising, exciting, and stimulating "thing" we know is that children **can, will,** and **do** write very early if they are in an environment where writing is done and their efforts are received as containing a real message. Knowledge of children's early "invented" spellings and "concept of message" has brought fundamental changes in the way teachers, parents and publishers see writing and its relationship to literacy and to language learning generally. This knowledge, plus that concerning children's early concept of story, elements, and structure of story as well as other critical features of text, changed expectations of teachers and led to a virtual explosion of writing in the early years which surely impacts on later writing because children learn its **value**—and that **they can do it.**

Martha L. King
The Ohio State University, emerita

I would say that the single most important thing we have learned is the systematic way children learn about written language from a very early age. Fifteen years ago writing was generally viewed as a relatively late-developing competence, built on a foundation of fluent reading. Researchers like Graves, Sowers, Bissex, Calkins, Harste, and Dyson have essentially rewritten this developmental map. We now expect primary children to write and share writing, where 15 years ago this would have been a novelty.

Thomas Newkirk
University of New Hampshire

All Children Can Be Writers

Thirty years ago, I was the artist of my fifth-grade class. We also boasted a singer, a scientist, a pitcher, a gymnast, a funny boy, a pretty girl, a bookworm, and a writer. Back then a writer's voice was a rare gift from the stingy fairy godmother of language arts.

Today, all of the children in the elementary school I direct are writers. We know that every child can write—given enough time and appropriate tools, given a teacher who has learned how to observe kids and how to help, given demonstrations of what writers do and encouragement to break new ground, given opportunities to learn from successes and from failures, too.

Thirty years later we know that writing is the most democratic of all the arts. Every child, regardless of ability or background, can have a voice as a writer.

Nancie Atwell
The Center for Teaching and Learning
Edgecomb, Maine

We've expanded our view of what constitutes writing so that many more children are seen and see themselves as writers: not only the young poets and storytellers, but the inventive spellers who are working to understand and use our writing system, the children who write about dinosaurs and kittens, those who write letters to friends or strangers, writers of lists, and of narratives of their own lives. Why is such inclusiveness important? Because education aims at inclusion—at inviting children into a literate society.

Glenda L. Bissex
Northeastern University

Understanding Writing and Writers Means Understanding Complex and Interrelated Influences— Cognitive, Social, Cultural, Psychological, Linguistic, and Technological

. . . What we have now is a better understanding of language learning processes and the ways they are embedded in the social and cultural contexts of the classroom, which in turn helps us better understand the consequences of what we choose to do as teachers.

Arthur N. Applebee
State University of New York at Albany

The major contribution to understanding writing in the past 30 years has been the realization that writing, like reading, is a complex process, influenced by many factors. After many years of focusing on the text in English and English Education, teachers and researchers shifted in the 1970s to focus on the processes of creating and comprehending texts. This shift has brought to light psychological, cultural, and social influences on the writing and reading processes. While understanding these diverse influences has been a major advance in the field, we still have partial understandings of writing and reading because these influences have not been integrated. In my current work, I am exploring details of teacher/student and peer interactions around literacy among diverse groups of students: and by considering this research in relation to research by others, I am working to develop a theory that integrates social, cultural, psychological, and linguistic explanations of literacy. I think that gaining an interdisciplinary view of the myriad influences on writing will increase our ability to help children who have serious difficulties with literacy.

Colette Daiute
Harvard Graduate School of Education

. . . [W]hat we know more about now than we did 30 years ago is the complexity of the relationship between oral and written language. I have a methods book from the Dewey period when people sure knew about "authentic" writing tasks and about the importance of talking about ideas before writing. But I don't think we knew so much about (a) the developmental history of children's figuring out in what way writing is "talk written down", (b) the sociolinguistic details of how writing is not "talk written down"; (c) the sociopolitical issues involved in the academic valuing of writing that is most removed from at least some people's "talk written down"; (d) the ethnographic vision of writing "practices" that are talked about and shape talk in varied ways.

Anne Haas Dyson
University of California, Berkeley

For me, the single most important thing we now know about the teaching and learning of writing in elementary school that we did not know in 1960 is that these processes are inherently social. We now know a considerable amount about the social organization of schools and classrooms and about how that social order constrains instruction. In addition, we know that students experience different kinds of literacy events in school and nonschool contexts. The forms and functions of literacy in school children's lives transcend classroom reading and writing instruction. Educational policy and practice are challenged to confront both the different home and community experiences children have around literacy and the nature (and limitations) of classrooms as places to learn and practice literacy. Knowledge gained especially by ethnographic research in both school and community settings has greatly informed the discourse about policy, teaching practice, curriculum, and assessment in recent decades— especially in the areas of elementary reading and writing instruction.

Susan Florio-Ruane
Michigan State University

Over the past few decades we have become more conscious of the linguistic and cultural complexities of how children learn to write. I am not sure that we have learned "one most important thing" that we didn't know 30 years ago. I do think that we have become more interested in children as writers and in ourselves as teachers of writing. I suspect that the most dramatic change in how we think about the learning and teaching of writing in the current age will turn out to have to do with changes in the nature of writing itself, as computer technology increasingly provides the basic tools for written expression and communications.

Robert Gundlach
Northwestern University

We have learned that writing has to be learned in school very much the same way that it is practiced out of school. This means that the writer has a reason to write, an intended audience, and control of subject matter and form. It also means that composing is staged across various phases of rumination, investigation, consultation with others, drafting, feedback, revision, and perfecting. And finally, this new pedagogical realism means that writing is not learned in isolation but in the same mixture with other activities that obtains in writing outside of school, as part of a way of life that includes it, entails it, and calls for it. For children of elementary years, this way of life means that writing is a form of play from invented spelling to story dramas, that literacy is sorcery.

James Moffett
Mariposa, California

Many educators, I believe, would now agree with some version of the following:

Close study of children's writing reveals interesting and sometimes profound and original attempts to overcome fundamental difficulties of knowledge, language, and audience. These cognitive, linguistic, and social difficulties inhere in the process of writing.

This view denies that one can comprehend children's writing development in relation to adult standards of correctness in spelling, punctuation, usage, diction, paragraph structure, coherence, organization, and so forth. It implies that development crucial to writing begins even before elementary school, and that it is interesting at every level. This thesis presents a formidable challenge which many teachers, teacher-educators, and researchers have taken up.

W. Charles Read
University of Wisconsin-Madison

We now see writing as a goal-directed activity and the writer as an active constructor of written language. The result of this view of writing/writer is that we understand much better what goes on in children's heads — with respect to both composing and spelling —while they're planning their writing, while they're writing, and while they're revising their writing.

William H. Teale
University of Texas at San Antonio

We Write So That Both We and Others Can Know What We Think, Who We Are

More of us believe that writing emerges from the desire to say something important to us. It may be important partly because we don't yet know what we want to say, but we ought to feel that the writing itself is worth the effort. We have said something worth saying, and we have made ourselves closer to another person.

Richard Lloyd-Jones
University of Iowa, emeritus

We know that all people are language-using animals with powers of telling stories of their lives.

Ken Macrorie
Santa Fe, New Mexico

My one-item questionnaire is hardly the first effort in three decades to monitor emerging signs that research in the teaching of composition has evolved from "the period of alchemy" (Braddock et al. 1963, p. 5). George Hillocks, Jr., for example, in *Research on Written Composition: New Directions for Teaching* (1986) amassed for his bibliography 6,000 titles covering just 20 years, 1963–1982. After detailed analysis of that research, Hillocks commented, "Perhaps all of the research on composing in the past two decades raises more questions than it answers. But it has answered some, and in raising others, it promises to answer more" (p. 61).

Lloyd-Jones, in his introduction to Hillocks' book, took note of the changes in research on composition over the two decades following the volume he co-authored. The studies cited by Hillocks were prepared more carefully, were more varied, often involved "reductions of the number of instances examined and greater emphasis on close and complicated examination of those instances" (p. xiii), and demonstrated an awareness of a theoretical or philosophical base. Concluding, Lloyd-Jones wrote, "I find these reviews rouse in me a sense of great optimism" (p. xiv). Hillocks, in fact, credits recommendations made in the 1963 report for shaping the course of subsequent research.

Dozens of researchers whose voices are not heard above (e.g., Janet Emig, Donald Graves, Kellogg Hunt, Mina Shaughnessy) are nonetheless represented by their achievements. All have helped to move us beyond alchemy. All have enabled their fellow researchers to ask more enlightened questions. All have brought into clearer focus our role as writing teachers, enabling us to make better informed decisions as we guide young writers. Still, as was true 30 years ago, concerns remain about public pronouncements on the teaching of writing, and the need continues to take stock of what we know and need to know.

"What Do We Know About the Writing of Elementary School Children?" On the 30th anniversary of the publication of an acknowledged milestone, we care more, we do more, we know more. But, clearly, our understanding is far from complete. Of one thing we can be sure: students and teachers and researchers, standing on a more secure foundation, are constructing new milestones in composition, ones whose anniversaries may well be celebrated in these pages in 2023.

References

Braddock, R., Lloyd-Jones, R., & Schoer, L. (1963). *Research in written composition.* Urbana, IL: National Council of Teachers of English.

Carson, R. (1962). *Silent spring.* Boston: Houghton Mifflin.

Dyson, A. H., & Freedman, S. W. (1991). Writing. In J. Flood, J. M. Jensen, D. Lapp, & J. R. Squire (Eds.), *Handbook of research on teaching the English language arts* (pp. 754–774). New York: Macmillan.

Hillocks, Jr., G. (1986). *Research in written composition: New directions for teaching.* Urbana, IL: National Conference on Research in English and ERIC Clearinghouse on Reading and Communication Skills.

McCloskey, R. (1941). *Make way for ducklings.* New York: Viking.

North, S. (1987). *The making of knowledge in composition: Portrait of an emerging field.* Portsmouth, NH: Boynton/Cook-Heinemann.

Part Two

Stories from the Writing Classroom

Their story, yours, mine—it's what we all carry with us on this
trip we take, and we owe it to each other to respect our stories and
learn from them.

> —William Carlos Williams
> as told to Robert Coles

The stories in our lives are a remarkable source for growth and understanding.
In the teaching of writing, stories are especially important, first because writing itself is personal, and second because the general pull of our culture is toward abstraction rather than story. Teachers tend to overlook the value of story as a rich storehouse for learning, turning instead to methodology, professional jargon, the adoption of a teacher persona, and other impersonal means that sometimes stand between teacher and student and inhibit the learning process. Included in this section are stories from writing teachers at all grade levels, for stories somehow transcend age and other superficial kinds of difference. The college teacher can learn much from the elementary teacher, and vice versa. There is something personal and compelling in all these stories, something that invites us to learn and grow.

Although the stories in this section have theory embedded in them, it is the story itself which seems most compelling. A story has several advantages over a theoretical statement. For example, the story provides a richer context than a description of theory. It provides a "feel" or "flavor," something of the human dimension purposefully omitted in the abstraction. The story occurs at a deeper, more primal level, and it has the power to speak directly to another— at its own level and on its own terms. Stories may be described as "raw" data, but an even better description would be "pure" or "uncontaminated" data. In the story, we see the original events, before someone else has drawn conclusions or made assumptions, a process which itself is open to bias and error. There is, of course, a place for theory, but story has its place too. This section is an eloquent reminder of the power of story and its ability to communicate in ways which theory doesn't understand.

In the opening essay, "On Stories and Scholarship," Richard Murphy not only provides a rationale for using story but weaves marvelous examples of stories from his own experience throughout the account. "The irony of my argument," he laments, "is that I am making it at all. I should just use this space to tell a story . . ." (41). His argument is compelling and deserves close reading.

The legacy which Carol Avery describes is about Laura, a child in her first-grade classroom, but it is also about herself, the teacher, and about every other child in the class. Ultimately, it touches the life of the reader, thus spreading over many miles and through time.

A day in October in New Hampshire. The setting is Linda Rief's classroom, and yet it could be anywhere, any class. The story that unfolds in "Writing for Life: Language Arts in the Middle" has subtle universal qualities from which all teachers can draw understanding. Both Carol Avery and Linda Rief exemplify the paradox: the more personal the story, the richer its possibility for universal application, the greater its truths resonate within our own lives.

In "Scott's Gift," Peggy A. Swoger describes a growth and transformation experience that occurred over the span of a school year. "Tell me your story," she asked Scott, a special-education student diagnosed with attention deficit disorder. At first his growth was slow and tentative, but his small steps in learning accumulated and the results were amazing. This story, like that of Helen Keller and her teacher, Annie Sullivan, is a testimony to what a teacher's loving patience can accomplish in the life of a student.

In "'Whispers of Coming and Going': Lessons from Fannie" Anne DiPardo writes of the experience of Fannie, a young Navajo woman, and Morgan, her tutor in the writing center, also a member of a minority race. In her quest for literacy in English, as well as her quest to be bicultural, Fannie reveals something of the rich fabric of the Navajo culture. Especially prominent is the Navajo genius for the wisdom of silence and the concomitant reluctance to articulate the insights that arise therein. "What Morgan [the tutor] most needed," writes DiPardo, "was advice to *listen more*—for the clues students like Fannie would provide, for those moments when she might best shed her teacherly persona and become once again a learner" (68). Good advice for writing teachers everywhere!

"Pain is the thing that we all know so much about and are so reluctant to reveal and share with one another" (78), writes Carole Deletiner, an "outsider" and adjunct lecturer at Hunter College. But sometimes you write about the pain. Sometimes you write, hoping to exorcise the pain. Her essay "Crossing Lines" describes how the author crosses subtle bureaucratic boundaries and steps out of the traditional role of teacher to touch the lives of her students. Carol Deletiner's story challenges writing teachers to look for those often invisible lines that restrict our effectiveness and to cross them when it's in the best interest of our students.

On Stories and Scholarship

Richard J. Murphy, Jr.

In *The Making of Knowledge in Composition* (Boynton/Cook, 1987), Stephen North claims that we need to give credit again to a kind of knowledge that has in recent years been deprecated. According to North, this knowledge—what he calls "lore"—has a profound influence on all of us involved in composition studies. It is practitioner knowledge, the knowledge of teachers. Teachers need to defend it, and themselves, North says, "to argue for the value of what they know, and how they come to know it" (55).

This is the task I want to work toward here. These are notes toward a reevaluation of teacher knowledge and of what I think is the most important form in which that knowledge is represented—stories.

Making Autobiography

Barbara Hardy says that human beings cannot keep from telling stories. Sleeping and waking we tell ourselves and each other the stories of our days: "We mingle truths and falsehoods, not always quite knowing where one blends into the other. As we sleep we dream dreams from which we wake to remember, half-remember and almost remember, in forms that may be dislocated, dilapidated or deviant but are recognizably narrative . . . [Stories are the] autobiography we are all engaged in making and remaking, as long as we live, which we never complete, though we all know how it is going to end" (*Tellers and Listeners,* Athlone, 1975, 4).

During a graduation party across the street last spring, I stood in my neighbor's kitchen drying dishes and talking with her about her son David's writing. She had recently read something he had written for one of his high-school teachers. She had found it almost unintelligible, full of what she called "gunk." When she asked him why he didn't just come out and say what he meant, David told her that his teachers don't want that. They want it all gunked up, he said. They want it indirect, hidden. "*Do* they?" she asked me suddenly, looking at me intently as if I knew. "Do they want *that?*" I said no as quickly as I could, and

College Composition and Communication, 40 (December 1989), pp. 466–72. Copyright © 1989 by the National Council of Teachers of English. Reprinted with permission.

she went on: "Well, I didn't think so. I thought they wanted kids to make sense, but David was *sure*. No doubt in his mind at all. Bullshit. The kids know it's bullshit, and they think the teachers want it anyway."

I was drying the dishes and setting them on the kitchen table. She was putting them away. Thinking about David and David's teacher reminded me of Rhonda and me.

A student in one of my introductory composition courses, Rhonda had done some writing one day in class, open-ended writing, free, a memory trace. In it she suddenly happened on a moment from her childhood. She was rocking her little sister (the sister she never liked) in the front-porch rocker at their home in Buchanan, Virginia. Both girls were giggling gaily when the chair— and Rhonda's little sister—tipped off the porch into the yard. Everyone rushed out of the house and tried to comfort the fallen child. Even Rhonda looked concerned for her sister, asking if she was hurt, saying she was sorry it happened, patting her on the head. Soon it was clear that no real harm had been done. The chair was returned to the porch, and the girls were cautioned against rocking too close to the rail-less edge. But no one knew—not her sister, not her parents— what really happened: that she deliberately flipped her sister into the yard because she disliked her so.

When Rhonda called me over in class to ask me what she should do next, I suggested that she write more, that she go back through the incident, enlarge it, texture it, sharpen its meanings. I crouched down in the aisle next to her plastic and steel desk, balanced myself with my right hand on the edge of the desktop, and urged her to write more. What was it like to have a little sister you never liked? Why didn't you like her? What was it like to have her sitting in that chair and you rocking and hearing her squeals of delight? What was it like to be giggling so hard and then to hear yourself giggle, to be intent on rocking your sister and then to have the thought steal up on you that you could hurt her? What was it like to notice how the chair was edging slowly, almost imperceptibly, toward the side of the porch, and then to keep on rocking and laughing as it moved? I urged her to write more because already, in reading that first rush of memory, I could feel in it not only Rhonda's story but yours and mine as well, not the story of just one moment but of her whole childhood, perhaps of her whole life.

When I heard my neighbor describe her son's guess about what his teachers wanted, I began to imagine what Rhonda must have thought. I pictured her getting back to her dorm room in Stuart Hall and trying to tell her roommate about what had happened during English. About how her teacher liked what she wrote and told her to go on writing. About how she didn't really understand what he wanted her to do. "He told me to write more," she's likely to have said, "but I don't know . . . I wrote all there was to it already. I don't know what more there is to say. I guess I could put some other gunk in, but I don't know if it'll be what he wants."

This story of Rhonda and David, of high school and Freshman English, of kitchens and classrooms, has little in the way of data. It is based on no tape-recorded conversation, no protocols, and—because I did not keep copies of Rhonda's writing—no scripts. It has no systematic analysis, no findings, no conclusion even. To ask if it is valid or reliable is to ask an impertinent question. It is just a story of a teacher trying to think about his work, remembering some, making some up, trying to sort out the puzzle of his experience. It is very hard—even for him—to tell where memory ends and imagination begins.

In Book I of *The Prelude,* Wordsworth tells of a harrowing experience made up of both memory and imagination. Once, as a young boy, he stole a boat and rowed stealthily out onto a moonlit lake. It was an act, he says, "of troubled pleasure." The night was clear and silent, the lake beautiful, but the traces of the boy's movements were everywhere— in the voices of the mountain echoes that followed his oars, in the line of moonwashed pools that stretched out behind the boat as he rowed. He felt a wonderful exhilaration in his skill, in the speed and power with which he rowed through the stillness, but all the while he trembled with fear. Then he noticed something. Behind the small ridge under which the boy had found the boat, there was a huge cliff hidden from his sight when he was close to shore. As he rowed onto the lake, however, this cliff gradually came more and more into view. It seemed to rise up as he rowed. Wordsworth says that it seemed alive. We know the cliff was solid and inanimate, and the boy knew it too, but the more he rowed away from the edge of the lake the larger it loomed. The faster he rowed the more insistently it rose. All his guilt and fear amassed themselves in that mountain and strode after him, until finally he shrank, turned the boat, and crept back to where he had found it moored.

Memory and imagination are inseparable in this story; fact and fiction merge. The story is *about* their merging. Did the mountain live that night? Did the boy steal that boat? We cannot answer these questions; we probably do not ask them. The story invites us to enter lyrically into this moment of troubled pleasure and to reexperience the animation of a vast guilt. For days after that night, Wordsworth says, he was cut off from his ordinary world:

> No familiar shapes
> Remained, no pleasant images of trees,
> Of sea or sky, no colours of green fields;
> But huge and mighty forms, that do not live
> Like living men, moved slowly through the mind
> By day, and were a trouble to my dreams. (I.395–400)

The forms that move by day through our minds as teachers may not be huge and mighty, and they may not always be the trouble of our dreams, but they have a profound impact on our teaching. They are the stories by which, as teachers, we come to understand ourselves.

Teacher Knowledge

"Teacher knowledge" is a term developed recently by educational researchers to identify the subtle understanding that grows out of teacher practice. Our knowledge enables us to respond to the complex, specific, and dynamic demands of particular teaching situations. It combines knowledge of content, pedagogical skill, and what Lee Shulman calls the "wisdom of practice" ("Knowledge and Teaching," *Harvard Educational Review* 57 [February 1987]: 11). As such, teacher knowledge is not abstract or generalized, but embedded in actual school experience. According to Walter Doyle, "[W]hat teachers know about chunks of content, instructional actions, or management strategies is tied to specific events that they have experienced in classrooms" ("Curriculum in Teacher Education," Meeting of the American Educational Research Association, April 1988). Teacher knowledge is represented, then, in one of its most important forms in the stories we tell ourselves and perhaps our fellow teachers and students of moments of our teaching and learning, moments in which we were thrilled or troubled or surprised by the most complicated joy.

During the first class meeting one semester in Freshman English, I talked too much. I do not remember why. Usually I ask students the first day to interview and introduce each other to the rest of us, but that day I did something else, so it took me far longer than usual to learn their names. It was several weeks before I felt I had a fairly sure grasp of who was who, and even then some students eluded me.

The class met in the basement of Curie, the science building, a huge black lab table at the front of the room with two sinks and a couple of gas jets. The ceiling was a maze of pipes and heating ducts. She was the quietest student. She never spoke in class. The first three class days devoted to group reading of drafts, she was absent. She sat in the second row, in the fifth desk. Even when she was present she seemed absent. Our eyes never connected. When I looked over to her, she was always looking down, writing some note or other, picking paper scraps out of her notebook spiral.

She gave me her first and third essays to read and mark. I cannot remember what they were about. The second essay she brought to my office for a conference. The fourth essay she did not submit. The rest of her record is blank. On the twelfth of October, I received a form memo from the dean, addressed to me and all her other teachers, informing us that she had withdrawn from the university. Almost our entire relationship, then, is bound up for me in that one conference in my office during which we talked about her second essay. I do not have a copy of her paper, but I remember it.

It was a letter to her grandfather who lived in northern California, a letter of thanks for the summer she had just spent with him. She was trying to explain why the visit was so important to her. Having grown up in the East, she had never seen the West Coast, never seen the grey, fog-bound Pacific. All summer she and her grandfather had lived together in his small house near the water. They had wandered along the beach, watched the weather and the shore birds, talked, permitted each other to sit alone in silence. She wanted him to know how much it had meant to her, that summer, and the feeling was practically beyond words.

She told me that she couldn't read the paper to her classmates. When she tried to read it aloud to me in my office, she was unable to make it all the way through. Coming to college had been hard for her, she said by way of explanation, far harder than she had thought it would be. But she wanted to send the letter to her grandfather; she had something to tell him that she wanted him to know. When she stopped reading, I read the rest aloud myself.

One day she was down on the beach alone. At the edge of the ocean, on a shelf of still wet sand she came upon a dying seal. She didn't know what to do. The seal's glistening body heaved, but otherwise it did not move. Its eyes were open. She knelt down next to it and waited. All day she waited there, watching. Once, when she reached her hand out and rested it on the fur of the seal's neck, she could feel its labored breathing in her fingers. She quickly pulled her hand away. Later she found that she could caress its side without feeling that she was making its work harder, so for a while she did that. Eventually the seal's eyes closed, and before the tide came back in its panting also stopped. She still sat there for a time. When she finally rose to dig a grave for the seal, her legs were sore and locked tight, so she stumbled in her awkward work. When she was done with the burial, she smoothed the sand with her hands and left the water to do the rest.

The reason she was writing this to her grandfather was that she had not told him about it at the time. She had made up some story about her day—she didn't know why, couldn't say even now, something about how she felt, well, *responsible* for that death—and now she wanted him to know the truth.

By the end of the fourth week of the semester, she had stopped coming to class. By the end of the fifth, she was gone.

Such a story reminds me that I am sometimes helpless as a teacher, that sometimes all I can do is sit by and watch. But I want to resist turning the story into a parable. If I try to say what its "point" is, I have to generalize the experience—her, me, the seal, the paper, and that mythic seashore where she knelt. If it can be analyzed into domains, if it can be reduced to findings or implications for research, I want to insist that it was not made to have any. It is a story, one fragment of my knowledge as a teacher.

Literary Scholarship

As we reconsider teacher knowledge, we need to distinguish such stories from case study. However much a case depends on rich description and narration, its meaning is propositional, a statement of abstract generalization. As

Lee Shulman puts it in "Those Who Understand: Knowledge Growth in Teaching" (*Educational Researcher* [February 1986]: 4–14), "To call something a case is to make a theoretical claim—to argue that it is a 'case of something,' or to argue that it is an instance of a larger class" (11). The meaning of the stories we tell ourselves about our lives and work, on the other hand, is aesthetic. We recreate the past, selecting its particulars and making them vivid, in order to reexperience them imaginatively. The meaning of a case depends on its systematic construction—on the internal validity with which it is drawn from the data, reduced, analyzed, and interpreted. The meaning of the stories I think we should tell and value lies in their forceful representation of the experience of teaching and learning, in their believability, in their memorability. Case study aspires to science. Stories of teaching and learning aspire to poetry.

Jerome Bruner makes a parallel distinction between two different ways or modes of knowing. In "Narrative and Paradigmatic Modes of Thought" (*Learning and Teaching the Ways of Knowing*, Ed. Elliot Eisner, National Society for the Study of Education, 1985, 97–115), Bruner claims that the two modes differ radically. Both are important ways of making sense of the world, and they complement one another. But they are irreducible, and the differences between them are so profound that the paradigmatic cannot be said to be the "refinement" or "abstraction" of the narrative. "Moreover," Bruner concludes, "there is no direct way in which a statement derived from one mode can contradict or even corroborate a statement derived from the other" (97–98).

The distinction Bruner makes here is a familiar one. James Britton contrasts poetic and transactional writing in *Language and Learning* (U of Miami P, 1970), arguing that "one 'has meaning' in a way the other does not—and *vice versa*. If we ask 'What does it mean?' of a piece of transactional writing, we shall not expect the same sort of answer as we expect when we ask it of a poem or a novel" (178). James Moffett puts it differently in *Teaching the Universe of Discourse* (Houghton, 1968), but he too claims that the narrative and the paradigmatic are irreducible. According to Moffett, "The essence of story is once-upon-a-time. Once. Unique and unrepeatable events—not 'recurring' events, as in science" (121).

We need to remember this distinction as we develop the argument for stories in the literature of composition studies. We need to keep in mind the peculiar power of narrative to shape and articulate what we know as teachers. Stephen North calls for a new understanding of teacher lore "such that other kinds of knowledge can *usefully* interact with it" (371), but in the interest of "useful interaction" we ought not to try to make stories into something else. The meanings and methods of the stories we tell ourselves are unlike those of any systematic mode of inquiry. Their value to us depends on this difference. A renewed appreciation of them, then, will require acceptance of their nonscientific, essentially literary character.

Story

The irony of my argument is that I am making it at all. I should just use this space to tell a story, but I have been afraid to. I have included some fragments—moments of memory, spots of time—but the argument has abashed me with its claim: that the stories we tell will be deeply valuable to us, that in telling them we will define ourselves and what we know, that in hearing them we will remember who we are and what teaching and learning have come to mean to us. Still, this characterization of stories does not describe their purpose so much as their effect. The *purpose* is the same as has always moved tellers and listeners—the pleasure of the story.

My youngest son, Stephen, is in the fifth grade. He had to do a report this year on Marco Polo, a written report and an oral presentation in front of the class. The report was due on Friday, so on Monday he rode his bike down to the public library, looked up two encyclopedia articles on Marco Polo, made photocopies of them, and brought them home. Tuesday and Wednesday he spent at the computer, typing what he titled the "1rst Draft" of his report.

We had some grief over this draft: he wanted to use the copies of the articles he had brought home (he kept calling them his "data"; "I can't write it without my data," he kept saying); but I wanted him to write it out at least once without looking at the articles, just the way he had told it to us in the car on the way home from Kmart. And by the way, I told him, when you get all done with this, remind me to read you a poem about Kubla Khan, the emperor with whom Marco lived and worked. He waved this away with an OK and went on with his complaint.

"You're making me do it *your* way," he said.

"Yes," I said. "Now get to work. I'm trying to type. You type, too."

By the time his mom called from the National Reading Conference in Tucson where she was spending the week, he was reconciled to his work. He had almost a page, he told her happily, pointing at the screen as he talked into the phone. "This is my first draft," he told her. "I'm free-minding it."

Thursday night I showed him how to do the spellcheck and how to double-space (his freckled face beamed when suddenly he had two pages, not one). Then we saved his file under a new name so he wouldn't lose the earlier draft.

"You mean I get to keep them both?" he asked, amazed.

When we printed out the final version, he was so excited by it that he kept thinking of people he wanted to give copies to—his teacher, of course, and one for himself and one for me and one for his sister and one for his brother in California.

At breakfast Friday morning, as he was reading it aloud to us over his cereal, he noticed a glitch. "That's not right," he said. "'*On* Marco and his father go back to Venice'? *That's* not right. It should be '*Then* Marco and his father go back.'"

Downstairs to the computer, load up the file, make the change, save it under a new name, draft three, no time to make extra copies now, but Stephen wants his teacher to see all three versions so he grabs them all for her and races for the school bus that's already honking at the corner.

The report was a success, he told me Friday afternoon. He was nervous in front of the class, and his teacher asked him to give his presentation twice, but she said it was *excellent,* an evaluation Stephen underlined in the air with his voice.

Then I read the poem to him.

> In Xanadu did Kubla Khan
> A stately pleasure dome decree:
> Where Alph, the sacred river, ran
> Through caverns measureless to man
>   Down to a sunless sea. (1–5)

I planned to give him all sorts of explanation, but at the last moment I decided just to read. No glosses on "athwart," "cedarn," "momently," or "Mount Abora." Just the poem, trying to revive within us its symphony and song. When I got to the end, Stephen said—his highest compliment—*"Cool."*

I think he meant it. As we went up the stairs from the basement to get some more stove wood, he said, "You know the part I like best? That part about the dome of sun and the caves of ice. *Yeah,*" he said. "That was *cool.*"

Laura's Legacy

Carol S. Avery

May 8, 1987
We celebrate Mother's Day in our first grade classroom this Friday afternoon.
The children perform a play for their mothers entitled "The Big Race," the
story of the tortoise and the hare. Laura is the "turtle" who wins the race.

A few minutes later Laura reads aloud the book she has authored about her
mother. The group laughs as she reads about learning to count with her cousins
when she was three years old. Laura writes: "I was learning six. Then my Mom
came in and asked what we were doing. I said, 'I'm learning sex!'" Laura's
mother was delighted. The reading continues with a hilarious account of a family squabble between Mom and Dad over a broken plate. Laura concludes the
anecdote, "So then I just went in and watched TV." Laura looks at me and
smiles as she pauses, waiting for her audience to quieten before she goes on. I
wink at her; I know she is thinking, "Wait till they hear the next part. It's the
funniest of all." She reads about a llama spitting in Mom's eye on a visit to the
zoo. Laura's way with words has brought delight to everyone. I remember a
week earlier when Laura and I sat to type her draft and she said, "This is the
best part. I put it last so that everyone will feel happy at the end."

May 9, 1987
Saturday night, around 11:45 P.M., a light bulb ignites fabric in a closet outside
Laura's bedroom. Laura wakes. She cannot get through the flames and by the
time firefighters reach her it is too late. Laura dies. No one else is injured.

May 11, 1987
The children and I gather on our Sharing Rug in the classroom on Monday
morning. I have no plans. We start to talk. There are endless interruptions until Michael says, "Mrs. Avery, can we shut the door so people stop bothering
us?" So Michael shuts the door. "Are you going to read us the newspapers?"
they ask. "Is that what you'd like?" "Yes," comes the unanimous response. The
children huddle close; a dozen knees nuzzle against me. I read aloud the four-
paragraph story on the front page of the *Sunday News* that accompanies a picture of our Laura sprawled on the lawn of her home with firefighters working

Language Arts, 65 (February 1988), pp. 110–11. Copyright © 1988 by the National Council of
Teachers of English Reprinted with permission.

over her. I read the longer story in Monday morning's paper that carries Laura's school picture. We cry. We talk and cry some more. And then we read Laura's books—writings which Laura determined were her best throughout the year and which were "published" to become part of our classroom library. These books are stories of Laura and her family, stories with titles such as *My Dad Had a Birthday* and *When My Grandmother Came to My House*. Laura's voice comes through loud and clear with its sense of humor and enthusiasm. We laugh and enjoy her words. "Laura was a good writer," they say. "She always makes us laugh when we read her stories." Then Dustin says, "You know, it feels like Laura is right here with us, right now. We just can't see her."

A short time later we begin our writing workshop. Every child chooses to write about Laura this day. Some write about the fire, some write memories of Laura as a friend. I write with them. After forty-five minutes it is time to go to art and there are cries of disappointment at having to stop. We will come back to the writing. There will be plenty of time. The last five weeks of school will be filled with memories of Laura as we work through our loss together. The children will decide to leave her desk in its place in the room because, "It's not in our way and anyway, this is still Laura's room even if she's not really here anymore." Laura's mother and little brother will come in to see us. On the last day they will bring us garden roses that Laura would have brought. Laura will always be a part of us and none of us will ever be the same.

In the days immediately following Laura's death and in the weeks since then certain thoughts have been rattling around in my head: I'm so glad that I teach the way I do. I'm so glad I really knew Laura. I know that I can never again teach in a way that is not focused on children. I can never again put a textbook or a "program" between me and the children. I'm glad I knew Laura so well. I'm glad all of us knew her so well. I'm glad the classroom context allowed her to read real books, to write about real events and experiences in her life, to share herself with us and to become part of us and we of her. I'm grateful for a classroom community that nurtured us all throughout the year and especially when Laura was gone. Laura left a legacy. Part of that legacy is the six little published books and the five-inch-thick stack of paper that is her writing from our daily writing workshops. When we read her words, we hear again her voice and her laughter.

Writing for Life

Language Arts in the Middle

Linda Rief

Early October in New Hampshire. On the drive to school each morning, I roll down the windows and drink in the air. It is green-pear crisp.

On this particular day in one eighth-grade class, Matt signs up for a conference. He reads aloud the piece he's written. It's a poem about death, about a suicide, about a father. His words are quick, and clean, and simple—right to the point.

> The leaves move left and right.
> The wind blows with all its might.
> I'm riding in a car It didn't feel
> Very far because I slept.
> I wake up and get out of my bed
> With an absurd feeling of dread.
> The words my mom said,
> are etched in my head,
> Your father is dead, shot through the head.
> The leaves don't move left or right.
> The wind doesn't blow with all its might.
> Birds no longer take to flight.
> All is silent.
> All is dead.

"What a sad, terrible thing," I say. "The poem is so depressing that I'm surprised you use rhyme. Rhyming poems are usually light and funny." This one's not funny, his shrug tells me.

I ask Matt where he got the idea for the poem. "Because it's true," he says.

"Oh, Matt, I'm so sorry." I'm stuck for words. I buy time. I ask Matt if he'd mind reading the piece to Carol, a University of New Hampshire doctoral student frequently in my classroom. Matt goes over to the carpet and reads his poem to her. I watch Carol listening intently as he reads and then answers her questions.

Matt's father was older and suffered a serious back problem. Several years ago, the entire family—except his dad, who excused himself by saying he wasn't

Language Arts, 71 (February 1994), pp. 92–94. Copyright © 1994 by the National Council of Teachers of English. Reprinted with permission.

feeling good—visited relatives for Thanksgiving dinner. The next morning, Matt noticed that his dad wasn't at breakfast. He asked when his dad would be home. He only heard his mother say, "He won't . . . he's dead."

While Carol is listening to Matt, I make my rounds of the students who have signed up for conferences. Debbie reads me an excerpt about a teenage boy, a runaway, who is deciding whether to stay in the cold alley filled with garbage and overflowing trash cans or to return to the family he's run away from. In real life, Debbie's 17-year-old brother ran away. No one has heard from him in 4 months. In her story, the boy decides to go home.

I welcome Sherri back to school after an extended absence. Her 7-year-old sister, Kaitlyn, had been hit and killed by a pickup truck just 2 weeks before, when she darted across a busy street. "I would have been back earlier," Sherri tells me, "but we got my sister's ashes yesterday."

"I'm so sorry," I say. But I wonder. How do you hold the ashes of your 7-year-old sister? Your 7-year-old daughter? Next to the teddy bear on the bed? Do you keep the nightlight on so she won't be afraid of the dark? Do you just throw away her toothbrush? How does her giggle fit in the box? How do you hold the ashes of your 7-year-old sister? I move on to the next table.

Ted, an awkward, bumbling kid who takes Ritalin to control his hyperactivity, has written his name on the board for a conference. His writing is long, and I'm not sure I'll have time to listen to the whole piece. But when he starts reading, after telling me, "I jus' wanna know if you like it," I tell him to keep reading. The writing is fresh, vivid, filled with humorous detail. It's about a boy named Trevor who wakes up to a day where everyone likes him and has gone out of his or her way to be kind to him: the school bus driver who's making pancakes and sausage for him on a portable grill at the bus stop . . . the math teacher who gives him an engraved leather chair to sit in for his great attitude and effort during fractions . . . the dance dedicated to him for being such a well-liked, all-around great kid. When he gets to the part about a blonde, blue-eyed Swedish "babe" saving a seat for him on the bus, Ted stops, leans in, looks me straight in the eye, and says, "Can I be honest with you about what would happen to a 14-year-old boy if this was true about the Swedish babe?"

"Of course," I say, all too quickly.

Ted reads, "Trevor got a hard-on the size of Florida as he sat down next to her." How can I say, "Nice detail. I can really see it"?

In the middle of our conference the fire drill wails. Once outside, Bevin, Laurie, and Kelly discover a new piece of jewelry. They remove their earrings and plunge the stems of autumn's best through their pierced ears. At the all-clear, we return to the classroom. Everyone starts writing again. Ted continues with Trevor. Mart thinks about what he might add to his dad's suicide poem. Debbie returns to writing her runaway piece.

I look up, and an entire table of girls has leaves dangling from their ears—maple red, oak orange, and the hickory's summer-squash yellow. Despite their topics, perhaps *because* of their topics, these kids bring the air of October into the classroom. It is green-pear crisp.

Carol looks at me and laughs. "I'm going back to first grade, where all they write about are hearts and rainbows. Life's too tough here. . . . I thought this was the All-American town, where every kid had his own mother and father, a dog, a cat, a brother, a sister. . . . How do you do it?"

How do *I* do? I think. How do *they* do it? Maybe this *is* the All-American town.

In *Gates of Excellence,* Katherine Paterson (1981) says:

> Why are we so determined to teach our children to read? So that they can read road signs? Of course. Make out a job application? Of course. Figure out the destination of the bus so that they can get to work? Of course. But don't we want far more for them than the ability to decode? Don't we want for them the life and growth and refreshment that only the full richness of our language can give? . . . [We should be reading] good or even great [books] because they make the right connections. They pull together for us a world that is falling apart. They are the words that integrate us, judge us, comfort and heal us. They are the words that . . . bring order out of chaos. (pp. 17–18)

I share Paterson's passion for reading and extend that passion to writing. Our students must be allowed their voices through writing because it helps them think and feel and play with language as they make order out of their chaotic lives: their school lives, their personal lives, and the chaos of the world around them.

Ted, Matt, Debbie, and Sherrie are only four of the reasons why we should be, in the words of Don Murray, "seeking diversity" in our classrooms, "not proficient mediocrity." Every child is unique and deserves to be valued for that uniqueness. We show our students we value them as individuals when we value their voices. And we hear their voices when we invite them to show us what they know and how they know that through their writing and reading.

Through giving kids choices as they read and write, we also teach them to take responsibility for their own learning. Rexford Brown, in *Schools of Thought* (1991), says that taking responsibility for their own learning " . . . is the only way to get them deeply engaged and committed to their education. It is a natural way to teach responsibility and reinforce the values that undergird all natural learning: courage, honesty, persistence, and respect" (p. 249).

At the end of the year I ask students to include in their portfolios a one-page synthesis of what they've discovered about themselves as learners by assembling and reflecting on the contents of the portfolio. Katie's one-pager shows she is deeply engaged and committed to her own learning:

> When you are a 14-year-old, it is often difficult to explain who you are and what your likes and dislikes are, because this is a time, at least for me, when

I want to experience many different things. When I was younger, my heart was set on being a ballerina. My whole life revolved around dance for 7 years. When I entered middle school, I found the need to expand my interests and set aside my toeshoes for field hockey cleats and track shoes. It was about this same time that I began to experience the power of the written word, both in the books I began to read, and the things I began to write. I was especially inspired by the books of Maya Angelou and Bette Greene, and it was through their words that my interest in women's rights and human rights really began. My writing has become a way for me to think and discover who I am.

I am a sensitive person who cares about the quality of life for others and the environment. I love the coast of Maine, where I spend my summers each year. . . . The feeling of the sand between my toes and the quiet solitude of the ocean make me happy and peaceful. I am an optimist because I try to look at all possibilities, but I am a pessimist, too, because my perceptions of the world around me often don't meet my expectations.

Right now, I'm trying to consider my Bazooka Bubblegum fortune which said, "Your success is only limited by your desire," and I'm trying to try on as many shoes as I can to try to find the one that best fits me in life.

We will hear the unique, honest, courageous voices of our students when they are allowed to show us what they think and know and feel when they are reading and writing *for life,* as Katie is. It is the kind of learning that matters. It is the only way to keep the air in our classrooms green-pear crisp.

References

Brown, R. (1991). *Schools of thought.* San Francisco, CA: Jossey-Bass.

Paterson, K. (1981). *Gates of excellence.* New York: E. P. Dutton.

Scott's Gift

Peggy A. Swoger

The urge to communicate must be as basic a need for humans as hunger and sex. I remember once a small, friendly girl approaching me on the sidewalk, smiling and gesturing to me. The child was mute, and I could see in the urgency of expression how desperately she wanted me to understand. Finally she tugged me down to her level and touched my necklace. "Oh, you like my necklace," I said. She smiled with delight at having communicated her thoughts and returned, contented, to her play.

Scott must have felt the same joy when he wrote on his self-evaluation after several weeks of writing workshop, "I feel good when I write." Scott was one of several learning-disabled students in my basic English class. Generally, I taught advanced and regular ninth-grade students, but this year I wanted to see how effective writing workshop would be for the basic writers. I set up the same class structure for my three gifted classes and basic class, hoping it would work equally well for all ability levels; for, if so, I could demonstrate that tracking of students is not necessary.

From the first day I had outside visitors to these classes, especially to Scott's first-period class. Nancie Atwell (1987) says in her book *In the Middle,* "Close your door and try it; open your door and share it." Well, my door never closed, and the students and I never tired of sharing our joy of writing.

Scott's Writing

That first day all fourteen of the students wrote on their own topics, but two of them needed extra prompting from me. When I said, "Now write three topics of your own on your topics list," Scott hunched over his clean paper and looked up helplessly at me. He is a tall, broad-shouldered boy, sixteen years old and going out for football. It is also his first year out of special-education classes, and he feels the pressure of "making it." His special-education teacher said that last year Scott became so depressed and withdrawn that they considered special counseling for him. He rarely tried to communicate; in fact, Scott's problems had always been complicated by his language and speech difficulties. He seemed not to be able to generate sentences, even orally.

English Journal, 78 (March 1989), pp. 61–65. Copyright © 1989 by the National Council of Teachers of English. Reprinted with permission.

Figure 1. Hambone

When I first got Hambone, I was only 6 years old. I was so exicted when I got him. He was a Dalamiun dog.

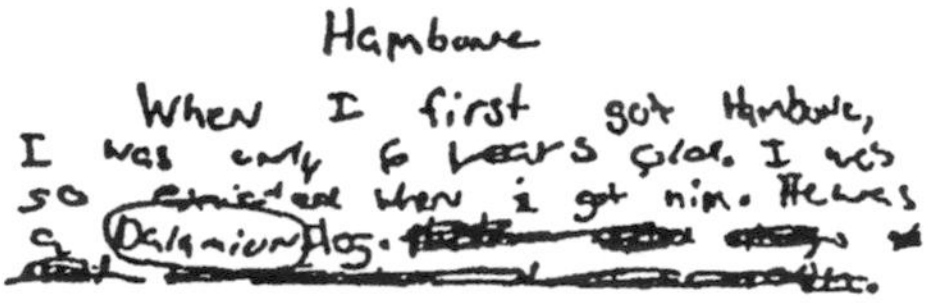

Figure 2. Hambone

When I first got Hambone, I was only 6 years old. I was so exicted when I got him. He was a Dalamiun dog with spots un him. He weuld always slept in the dinning room. Then he got old and sick. One day we took him to the vect. We came home. Got him some medican at the vect. Then he jus went off. We couldn't find him anywhere, and we looked everywhere. The neibhurs looked everywhere but they didn't find him. This went on for one week.

Some kids found him and came to us. They found him neer this fence. He was lying dead with flys flying around him. He looked pretty gross. We lifted him up to the fence. I was pretty scared.

So then we got a shvle and dig a good hole for him very deep. Then we buiried him. It was a little sad. We knew he would die sometime. So we buirded him in that hole and we covered it up, Tom and me. We were pretty sad.

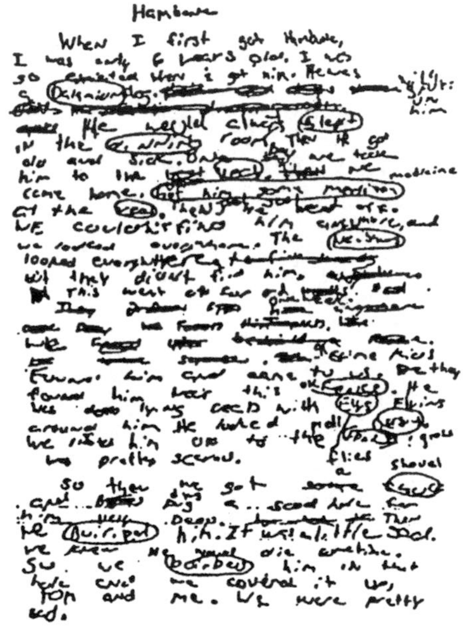

Scott's mother told me about his efforts to cultivate friends. He invited a boy from his special-education class to go home with him after school. Scott offered his friend everything he could think of in the kitchen: "You want Coke? You want potato chips?" But after that, neither boy could think of anything to say. They sat around the living room in embarrassed silence, thinking of nothing to do. Will Scott ever be able to talk with people, the mother wanted to know; will Scott's progress this year continue? I could not answer her questions because this was my first time around the track, my first experience with the learning disabled.

Perhaps that was a blessing because I just accepted whatever they could do and praised it. If they did not perform, I waited, but I revisited each desk every day. "Tell me about your story," I would say while looking with interest into their eyes at the person somewhere within. Scott was shy, but his soft brown eyes said that he liked my visits to his desk. He stumbled over each word and started over repeatedly. After three days he had written three sentences (Figure 1).

After three weeks he had finished this story (Figure 2), which he punched into the computer one painful letter at a time. The importance of this first story was not that, with help, he corrected most of the spelling and put periods in the right places. Instead, Scott, visualizing and reliving this experience of his earlier years, had touched a deep pool of emotions. Probably this had been his first realization of death and his first painful awareness of love. His special-education teachers were surprised and delighted at his expression of emotion, something they had never seen from him before.

With his first story published on the bulletin board, Scott was cooking. "What's your next story?" I asked. "Snow skiing," he announced, while already hunched over his paper and writing. As he read the first draft to me, he thoughtfully went back to his sentence: "I was real afraid of the mountain." He said, "I was real afraid of the *steep* mountain." Scott had entered the world of revision.

These two stories and a first draft of a visit to his grandmother's at the beach comprised his first nine weeks' work. Both Kellogg Hunt's T-Unit analysis and Fry's readability level suggest that Scott's first published story equaled that of an average first grader. Carol Avery, a first-grade teacher visiting my classes, had made that comment about several of the papers on our bulletin board. "This is about what my first graders can do by the end of the year," she said. Carol observed Scott at work in the computer room. He was capitalizing every word, and she, a wonderful observer of children's learning, asked him why. "She told me to capitalize all the important words," he said as he gestured toward the aide in the computer room who had been helping him with the title of his story. "Every word was important to Scott," Carol commented.

It is interesting to me that although Scott seldom used language, he had language. It's like those millions of seeds and deep roots lying dormant until the rains come. Scott's desert began to bloom. I first noticed changes in his choice of words. He wrote "obnoxious," his first three-syllable word, when describing his two new puppies. No doubt he had picked up some of his mother's vocabulary in relation to those dogs.

One day, later in the year, he came to my desk and asked if there were two meanings of the word "hospital." He wrote: "The friend's sister had a lot of people over to celebrate Mardi Gras. I met a lot of them and they were very hospitable." Scott seemed to be noticing words. He needed words; he was a writer.

He also needed details. "Scott notices everything," his mother told me. His writing began to show this attention to detail. He wrote: "It was the first time I ate crawfish. You suck the inside of the head and eat the tail. It was very spicy." These details were certain to entertain his classmates.

By March, his syntactic structures and vocabulary indicated a growth of nearly three years. The only activity that will produce syntactic growth, critics of sentence combining said, was intellectual development. My teacher instincts told me that Scott's growth was intellectual; the more complex his thinking, the more complex grammatical structures he required to carry his message.

Scott's Reading

But what was happening with Scott's reading was even more phenomenal. Even Scott commented that his reading had improved. Each week he had time for two periods of sustained, silent reading in English class, and he had five periods a week in reading class. Scott read slowly, agonizing over the fact that he

Figure 3. Retriever

My puppies by Scott

One morning i got up for school but, when my mom said, "Come down stairs i have suprise for you." I came down stairs and we went down in bhment. I looked and there were two pupies ouside i was so suriprise. They had brown colored hair. They were very obnoxious they would get on you and tire your cloths. One was a femal and another is male. When i got hom from school i played with them for an hour or two. I got on the flour and they would get on me. I play fesh with them. They were very cute. I played with everday when i got home. from school. My brother bought them in Aura so I don't know where he got them. My mom let them in time to time.

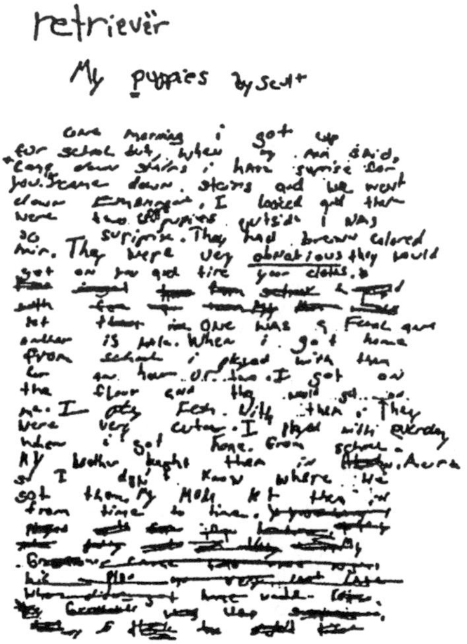

couldn't pass a simple five-question computer quiz on the books he finished. About a week before Christmas holidays, Scott finished *The Outsiders.* He loved it but, again, could not pass the multiple-choice quiz. He asked if he could write to me about the book. For the first time, with events organized for him already, he wrote with abandon. "Cutting loose," someone has called it. In two class periods Scott wrote three pages of readable prose. He enjoyed himself immensely.

His classmates suggested that he should read *Where the Red Fern Grows* because they wanted Scott to name his two new puppies Dan and Ann after those in this book. Scott selected three books to take home for the holidays. His mother exclaimed to me later, when she and I cried over his reading scores, "He was really reading all those books he carried up to his room!" In just eight months Scott's reading growth, measured by the Stanford Reading Diagnostic Test (Brown Level), moved from 2.8 to 7.3—over four years' growth!

As unbelievable as these scores were, they were not the best in the class. Scott's reading growth was fourth from the bottom of the class, and his syntactic growth was about the same as that of his peers. The length of Scott's pieces doubled in words, but many of his classmates tripled their output. The top student, with an IQ of 100, moved from approximately the fifth to the ninth stanine in reading and from 9.8 to 11.0 in syntactic maturity. His first story was 98 words and his final one 716. On an average, the class members increased their essay length by 100 words. But none of them had as much to overcome as Scott.

Scott's disability had been diagnosed as attention deficit disorder (ADD) with hyperactivity and speech difficulties. Paired with an IQ of 74, these are terrible hurdles. Scott could not have struggled harder if he had been wrestling Grendel's mother.

Scott's Growth: Some Lessons for Teachers

The question is, Why? What was happening here that had not happened before for these students? It is as though something clicked and suddenly written language made sense. The students made giant leaps, first in writing and then in reading, greater than I had ever seen before in my fifteen years of teaching. My instinct told me that the workshop approach worked because the students had the time and the freedom to work out of their own mental constructs. There were no assignments, no tests, no homework, nothing that the students had to see *My Way*.

Scott was telling his own story in his own way from what he knew. His mind was learning to "go around," to cope with the learning disability. Special-education teachers tell me there is no cure for a disability; the kid just learns to live with it.

Scott's efforts and successes surely must inspire us all. I would like to say to him the words of Beethoven: You, Scott, like all mankind, were "born with a divine spark; you deserve to be free." The fact that language was your liberator makes me realize as never before the importance of my job, of being called English teacher. You have unknowingly been both the writer and the teacher, showing us a way into your world, into your intellectual world. Your lesson is a rich tapestry, written as much by the patient silences between us as by your written and spoken words.

I know that you are ready to step out. Your mother told me, in a worried way, that for some time now you have been going to your room to stand in front of your mirror and talk to the person you see there. She seemed to think you do this out of loneliness, that your reflection is a kind of imaginary friend. She thought you might be "cracking up." But I think you are practicing as children do when they learn a new skill. You are using your language, listening to your voice, observing the movements of your lips as you form words. You are working on your speech, a speech that has always embarrassed you, to make it sound normal. You are practicing to enter that wonderful social whirl of the high-school hallway with the strutting jocks and the pretty girls; you are practicing to say "yes" the next time a girl asks you to a lead-out.

Some lessons seem obvious to me from Scott's experience. First, our students, even most of the handicapped, are little learning machines when, as Frank Smith says, they are learning what *they* need to know. Writing seems to be a catalyst, an ignition system to start up these learning machines. Scott and his classmates wrote every day in both English language class and reading class. Having school time to write and read in a community of learners is essential.

Next, we must, as language teachers, take advantage of the social purpose of language itself. Who taught language to the grunting cave dweller? We know that out of that basic drive to communicate, human beings have created language, our greatest invention. It happened naturally, out of daily needs and daily give-and-take. Language growth happens in a social context, and that is the only way it happens. If literacy is our goal, students need to be working and interacting purposefully in pairs and small groups.

Finally, perhaps no other children in our schools have had learning dissected into such small pieces as much as the learning disabled. We feed them like feeding crumbs to birds. Their natural learning has been stymied by contrived assignments, worksheets, and writing formulas. We must understand that the mind works naturally with whole pieces of discourse.

Let us sit at the feet of the learners and let them guide us into their worlds; let us trust and celebrate their potential by focusing on what they can do. Like Scott, these children have gifts to give us if we can learn to receive.

Work Cited

Atwell, Nancie. 1987. *In the Middle: Writing, Reading, and Learning with Adolescents.* Portsmouth, NH: Boynton/Cook Publishers.

"Whispers of Coming and Going"

Lessons from Fannie

Anne DiPardo

As a man with cut hair, he did not identify the rhythm of three
strands, the whispers of coming and going, of twisting and tying
and blending, of catching and of letting go, of braiding.
> —Michael Dorris,
> *A Yellow Raft in Blue Water*

We all negotiate among multiple identities, moving between public and private
selves, living in a present shadowed by the past, encountering periods in which
time and circumstance converge to realign or even restructure our images of
who we are. As increasing numbers of non-Anglo students pass through the
doors of our writing centers, such knowledge of our own shape-shifting can
help us begin—if *only* begin—to understand the social and linguistic challenges which inform their struggles with writing. When moved to talk about the
complexities of their new situation, they so often describe a more radically
chameleonic process, of living in noncontiguous worlds, of navigating between
competing identities, competing loyalties. "It's like I have two cultures in me,"
one such student remarked to me recently, "but I can't choose." Choice becomes a moot point as boundaries blur, as formerly distinct selves become or-
ganically enmeshed, indistinguishable threads in a dynamic whole.

Often placed on the front lines of efforts to provide respectful, insightful
attention to these students' diverse struggles with academic discourse, writing
tutors likewise occupy multiple roles, remaining learners even while emerging
as teachers, perennially searching for a suitable social stance—a stance existing somewhere along a continuum of detached toughness and warm empathy,
and, which like all things ideal, can only be approximated, never definitively
located. Even the strictly linguistic dimension of their task is rendered problematic by the continuing paucity of research on the writing of nonmainstream
students—a knowledge gap which likewise complicates our own efforts to
provide effective tutor training and support. Over a decade has passed since

The Writing Center Journal, 12 (Spring 1992), pp. 125–44. Copyright © 1992 by the National
Writing Centers Association. Reprinted with permission.

Mina Shaughnessy eloquently advised basic writing teachers to become students of their students, to consider what Glynda Hull and Mike Rose have more
recently called the "logic and history" of literacy events that seem at first glance
inscrutable and strange. In this age of burgeoning diversity, we're still trying to
meet that challenge, still struggling to encourage our tutors to appreciate its rich
contours, to discover its hidden rigors, to wrestle with its endless vicissitudes.

This story is drawn from a semester-long study of a basic writing tutorial
program at a west-coast university—a study which attempted to locate these
tutor-led small groups within the larger contexts of a writing program and campus struggling to meet the instructional needs of non-Anglo students. It is about
one tutor and one student, both ethnic minorities at this overwhelmingly white,
middle-class campus, both caught up in elusive dreams and uncertain beginnings. I tell their story not because it is either unusual or typical, but because it
seems so richly revealing of the larger themes I noted again and again during
my months of data collection—as unresolved tensions tugged continually at a
fabric of institutional good intentions, and as tutors and students struggled,
with ostensible goodwill and inexorable frustration, to make vital connection. I
tell this story because I believe it has implications for all of us trying to be worthy students of our students, to make sense of our own responses to diversity, and
to offer effective support to beginning educators entrusted to our mentorship.

"It, Like, Ruins Your Mind":
Fannie's Educational History

Fannie was Navajo, and her dream was to one day teach in the reservation
boarding schools she'd once so despised, to offer some of the intellectual, emotional, and linguistic support so sorely lacking in her own educational history.
As a kindergartner, she had been sent to a school so far from her home that she
could only visit family on weekends. Navajo was the only language spoken in
her house, but at school all the teachers were Anglo, and only English was allowed. Fannie recalled that students had been punished for speaking their native language—adding with a wry smile that they'd spoken Navajo anyway,
when the teachers weren't around. The elementary school curriculum had emphasized domestic skills—cooking, sewing, and, especially, personal hygiene.
"Boarding school taught me to be a housemaid," Fannie observed in one of her
essays, "I was hardly taught how to read and write." All her literacy instruction had been in English, and she'd never become literate in Navajo. Raised in a
culture that valued peer collaboration, Fannie had long ago grasped that Anglo
classrooms were places where teachers assume center stage, where students are
expected to perform individually: "No," her grade-school teachers had said
when Fannie turned to classmates for help, "I want to hear *only* from *you*."

Estranged from her family and deeply unhappy, during fifth grade Fannie
had stayed for a time with an aunt and attended a nearby public school. The ex-

perience there was much better, she recalled, but there soon followed a series of personal and educational disruptions as she moved among various relatives' homes and repeatedly switched schools. By the time she began high school, Fannie was wondering if the many friends and family members who'd dropped out had perhaps made the wiser choice. By her sophomore year, her grades had sunken "from A's and B's to D's and F's," and she was "hanging out with the wrong crowd." By midyear, the school wrote her parents a letter indicating that she had stopped coming to class. When her family drove up to get her, it was generally assumed that Fannie's educational career was over.

Against all odds, Fannie finished high school after all. At her maternal grandmother's insistence, arrangements were made for Fannie to live with an aunt who had moved to a faraway west-coast town where the educational system was said to be much stronger. Her aunt's community was almost entirely Anglo, however, and Fannie was initially self-conscious about her English: "I had an accent really bad," she recalled, "I just couldn't communicate." But gradually, although homesick and sorely underprepared, she found that she was holding her own. Eventually, lured by the efforts of affirmative action recruiters, she took the unexpected step of enrolling in the nearby university. "I never thought I would ever graduate from high school," Fannie wrote in one of her essays, adding proudly that "I'm now on my second semester in college as a freshman." Her grandmother had died before witnessing either event, but Fannie spoke often of how pleased she would have been.[1]

Fannie was one of a handful of Native Americans on the campus, and the only Navajo. As a second-semester first-year student, she was still struggling to find her way both academically and socially, still working to overcome the scars of her troubled educational history. As she explained after listening to an audiotape of a tutorial session, chief among these was a lingering reluctance to speak up in English, particularly in group settings:

Fannie: When, when, I'm talking . . . I'm shy. Because I always think I always say something not right, with my English, you know. (Pauses, then speaks very softly.) It's hard, though. Like with my friends, I do that too. Because I'll be quiet—they'll say, "Fannie, you're quiet." Or if I meet someone, I, I don't do it, let them do it, I let that person do the talking.

A.D.: Do you wish you were more talkative?

Fannie: I wish! Well I am, when I go home. But when I come here, you know, I always think, English is my second language and I don't know that much, you know.

A.D.: So back home you're not a shy person?

Fannie: (laughing uproariously) No! (continues laughing)

I had a chance to glimpse Fannie's more audacious side later that semester, when she served as a campus tour guide to a group of students visiting from a distant Navajo high school. She was uncharacteristically feisty and vocal that

week, a change strikingly evident on the tutorial audiotapes. Indeed, when I
played back one of that week's sessions in a final interview, Fannie didn't recognize her own voice: "Who's that talking?" she asked at first. But even as she
recalled her temporary elation, she described as well her gradual sense of loss:

> Sometimes I just feel so happy when someone's here, you know, I feel happy?
> I just get that way. And then (pauses, begins to speak very softly), and then it
> just wears off. And then they're leaving—I think, oh, they're leaving, you know.

While Fannie described their week together as "a great experience," she
was disturbed to find that even among themselves, the Navajo students were
speaking English: "That bothered me a lot," she admitted, surmising that
"they're like embarrassed . . . to speak Navajo, because back home, speaking
Navajo fluently all the time, that's like lower class." "If you don't know the
language," Fannie wrote in one of her essays, "then you don't know who you
are. . . . It's your identity . . . the language is very important." In striking contrast to these students who refused to learn the tribal language, Fannie's grandparents had never learned to speak English: "They were really into their culture, and tradition, and all of that," she explained, "but now we're not that way
anymore, hardly, and it's like we're losing it, you know." Fannie hoped to attend
a program at Navajo Community College where she could learn to read and write
her native language, knowledge she could then pass on to her own students.

Fannie pointed to the high dropout rate among young Navajos as the primary reason for her people's poverty, and spoke often of the need to encourage
students to finish high school and go on to college. And yet, worried as she was
about the growing loss of native language and tradition, Fannie also expressed
concerns about the Anglicizing effects of schooling. Education is essential, she
explained, but young Navajos must also understand its dangers:

> I mean like, sometimes if you get really educated, we don't really want that.
> Because then, it like ruins your mind, and you use it, to like betray your
> people, too. . . . That's what's happening a lot now.

By her own example, Fannie hoped to one day show her students that it is possible to be both bilingual and bicultural, that one can benefit from exposure to
mainstream ways without surrendering one's own identity:

> If you know the white culture over here, and then you know your own culture,
> you can make a good living with that . . . when I go home, you know, I know
> Navajo, and I know English too. They say you can get a good job with that.

Back home, Fannie's extended family was watching her progress with
warm pride, happily anticipating the day when she would return to the reservation to teach. When Fannie went back for a visit over spring break, she
was surprised to find that they'd already built her a house: "They sure give me
a lot of attention, that's for sure," she remarked with a smile. Many hadn't seen
Fannie for some time, and they were struck by the change:

Everybody still, kind of picture me, still, um, the girl from the past. The one who quit school— and they didn't think of me going to college at all. And they were surprised, they were really surprised. And they were like proud of me too . . . 'cause none of their family is going to college.

One delighted aunt, however, was the mother of a son who was also attending a west-coast college:

She says, "I'm so happy! I can't wait to tell him, that you're going to college too! You stick in there, Fannie, now don't goof!" I'm like, "I'll try not to!"

"I Always Write Bad Essays": Fannie's Struggles with Writing

On the first day of class, Fannie's basic writing teacher handed out a question-naire that probed students' perceptions of their strengths and weaknesses as writers. In response to the question, "What do you think is good about your writing?" Fannie wrote, "I still don't know what is good about my writing"; in response to "What do you think is bad about your writing?" she responded, "Everything."

Fannie acknowledged that her early literacy education had been neither re-spectful of her heritage nor sensitive to the kinds of challenges she would face in the educational mainstream. She explained in an interview that her first in-struction in essay writing had come at the eleventh hour, during her senior year of high school: "I never got the technique, I guess, of writing good essays," she explained, "I always write bad essays." While she named her "sentence struc-ture, grammar, and punctuation" as significant weaknesses, she also added that "I have a lot to say, but I can't put it on paper . . . it's like I can't find the vocabu-lary." Fannie described this enduring block in an in-class essay she wrote dur-ing the first week of class:

From my experience in writing essays were not the greatest. There were times my mind would be blank on thinking what I should write about.

In high school, I learned how to write an essay during my senior year. I learned a lot from my teacher but there was still something missing about my essays. I knew I was still having problems with my essay organization.

Now, I'm attending a university and having the same problems in writ-ing essays. The university put me in basic writing, which is for students who did not pass the placement test. Of course, I did not pass it. Taking basic writ-ing has helped me a lot on writing essays. There were times I had problems on what to write about.

There was one essay I had problems in writing because I could not ex-press my feelings on a paper. My topic was on Mixed Emotions. I knew how I felt in my mind but I could not find the words for expressing my emotions.

Writing essays from my mind on to the paper is difficult for me. From this experience, I need to learn to write what I think on to a paper and expand my essays.

"Yes," her instructor wrote at the bottom of the page, "even within this essay—which is good—you need to provide specific detail, not just general statements." But what did Fannie's teacher find "good" about this essay—or was this opening praise only intended to soften the criticism that followed? Fannie had noted in an interview that she panicked when asked to produce something within 45 minutes: "I just write anything," she'd observed, "but your mind goes blank, too." Still, while this assignment may not have been the most appropriate way to assess the ability of a student like Fannie, both she and her instructor felt it reflected her essential weakness—that is, an inability to develop her ideas in adequate detail.

At the end of the semester, her basic writing teacher confided that Fannie had just barely passed the course, and would no doubt face a considerable struggle in first-year composition. Although Fannie also worried about the next semester's challenge, she felt that her basic writing course had provided valuable opportunities. "I improved a lot," she said in a final interview, "I think I did—I know I did. 'Cause now I can know what I'm trying to say, and in an afternoon, get down to that topic." One of her later essays, entitled "Home," bears witness to Fannie's assertion:

The day is starting out a good day. The air smells fresh as if it just rained. The sky is full with clouds, forming to rain. From the triangle mountain, the land has such a great view. Below I see hills overlapping and I see six houses few feet from each other. One of them I live in. I can also see other houses miles apart.

It is so peaceful and beautiful. I can hear birds perching and dogs barking echos from long distance. I can not tell from which direction. Towards north I see eight horses grazing and towards east I hear sheep crying for their young ones. There are so many things going on at the same time.

It is beginning to get dark and breezy. It is about to rain. Small drops of rain are falling. It feels good, relieving the heat. The rain is increasing and thundering at the same time. Now I am soaked, I have the chills. The clouds is moving on and clearing the sky. It is close to late afternoon. The sun is shining and drying me off. The view of the land is more beautiful and looks greener. Like a refreshment.

Across from the mountain I am sitting is a mountain but then a plateau that stretches with no ending. From the side looks like a mountain but it is a long plateau. There are stores and more houses on top of the plateau.

My clothes are now dry and it is getting late. I hear my sister and my brother calling me that dinner is ready. It was beautiful day. I miss home.

"Good description," her instructor wrote on this essay, "I can really 'see' this scene." But meanwhile, she remained concerned about Fannie's lack of sophistication: "Try to use longer, more complex sentences," she added, "avoid short, choppy ones." Overwhelmed by the demands of composing and lacking strategies for working on this perceived weakness, Fannie took little away from such feedback aside from the impression that her writing remained inadequate.

Although Fannie was making important strides, she needed lots of patient, insightful support if she were to overcome her lack of experience with writing and formidable block. Only beginning to feel a bit more confident in writing about personal experience, she anticipated a struggle with the expository assignments that awaited her:

> She's having us write from our experience. It'll be different if it's like in English 101, you know how the teacher tells you to write like this and that, and I find that one very hard, cause I see my other friends' papers and it's hard. I don't know if I can handle that class.

Fannie was trying to forge a sense of connection to class assignments—she wrote, for instance, about her Native American heritage, her dream of becoming a teacher, and about how her cultural background had shaped her concern for the environment. But meanwhile, as her instructor assessed Fannie's progress in an end-of-term evaluation, the focus returned to lingering weaknesses: "needs to expand ideas w/ examples/description/explanation," the comments read, not specifying how or why or to whom. Somehow, Fannie had to fill in the gaps in her teacher's advice—and for the more individualized support she so sorely needed, she looked to the tutorials.

"Are You Learnin' Anything from Me?": The Tutorials

Morgan, Fannie's African American tutor, would soon be student teaching in a local high school, and she approached her work with basic writers as a trial run, a valuable opportunity to practice the various instructional strategies she'd heard about in workshops and seminars. Having grown up in the predominantly Anglo, middle-class community that surrounded the campus, Morgan met the criticisms of more politically involved ethnic students with dogged insistence: "I'm first and foremost a member of the *human* race," she often said, going on to describe her firm determination to work with students of all ethnicities, to help them see that success in the mainstream need not be regarded as cultural betrayal. During the term that I followed her—her second semester of tutoring and the first time she'd worked with non-Anglo students—this enthusiasm would be sorely tested, this ambition tempered by encounters with unforeseen obstacles.

Morgan's work with Fannie was a case in point. Although she had initially welcomed the challenge of drawing Fannie out, of helping this shy young woman overcome her apparent lack of self-confidence, by semester's end Morgan's initial compassion had been nearly overwhelmed by a sense of frustration. In an end-of-term interview, she confessed that one impression remained uppermost: "I just remember her sitting there," Morgan recalled, "and talking to her, and it's like, 'well I don't know, I don't know' . . . Fannie just has so many doubts, and she's such a hesitant person, she's so withdrawn, and mellow, and quiet. . . . A lot of times, she'd just say, 'well I don't know what I'm supposed to write. . . . Well I don't like this, I don't like my writing.'"

Although Fannie seldom had much to say, her words were often rich in untapped meaning. Early in the term, for instance, when Morgan asked why she was in college, Fannie searched unsuccessfully for words that would convey her strong but somewhat conflicted feelings:

Fannie: Well . . . (long pause) . . . it's hard . . .

Morgan: You wanna teach like, preschool? Well, as a person who wants to teach, what do you want outta your students?

Fannie: To get around in America you have to have education . . . (unclear).

Morgan: And what about if a student chose not to be educated—would that be ok?

Fannie: If that's what he wants . . .

At this point Morgan gave up and turned to the next student, missing the vital subtext—how Fannie's goal of becoming a teacher was enmeshed in her strong sense of connection to her people, how her belief that one needs an education "to get around" in the mainstream was tempered by insight into why some choose a different path. To understand Fannie's stance towards schooling, Morgan needed to grasp that she felt both this commitment *and* this ambivalence; but as was so often the case, Fannie's meager hints went unheeded.

A few weeks into the semester, Morgan labored one morning to move Fannie past her apparent block on a descriptive essay. Fannie said only that she was going to try to describe her grandmother, and Morgan began by asking a series of questions—about her grandmother's voice, her presence, her laugh, whatever came to Fannie's mind. Her questions greeted by long silences, Morgan admitted her gathering frustration: "Are you learnin' anything from me?" she asked. Morgan's voice sounded cordial and even a bit playful, but she was clearly concerned that Fannie didn't seem to be meeting her halfway. In the weeks that followed, Morgan would repeatedly adjust her approach, continually searching for a way to break through, "to spark something," as she often put it.

The first change—to a tougher, more demanding stance—was clearly signalled as the group brainstormed ideas for their next essays. Instead of waiting for Fannie to jump into the discussion, Morgan called upon her: "Ok, your turn in the hot seat," she announced. When Fannie noted that her essay would be about her home in Arizona, Morgan demanded to know "why it would be of possible interest to us." The ensuing exchange shed little light on the subject:

Fannie: Because it's my home!

Morgan: That's not good enough . . . that's telling me nothing.

Fannie: I was raised there.

Morgan: What's so special about it?

Fannie: (exasperated sigh) I don't know what's so special about it . . .

Morgan: So why do you want to write about it, then?

Morgan's final question still unanswered, she eventually gave up and moved to another student. Again, a wealth of valuable information remained tacit; Morgan wouldn't learn for several weeks that Fannie had grown up on a reservation, and she'd understood nothing at all about her profound bond with this other world.

Two months into the semester, Morgan had an opportunity to attend the Conference on College Composition and Communication (CCCC), and it was there that some of her early training crystallized into a more definite plan of action, her early doubts subsumed by a new sense of authoritative expertise. Morgan thought a great deal about her work with Fannie as she attended numerous sessions on peer tutoring and a half-day workshop on collaborative learning. She returned to campus infused with a clear sense of direction: the solution, Morgan had concluded, was to assume an even more low-profile approach, speaking only to ask open-ended questions or to paraphrase Fannie's statements, steadfastly avoiding the temptation to fill silences with her own ideas and asides. As she anticipated her next encounter with Fannie, she couldn't wait to try out this more emphatic version of what had been called—in conference sessions and her earlier training—a "collaborative" or "non-directive" stance.

Still struggling to produce an already past-due essay on "values," Fannie arrived at their first post-CCCC tutorial hour with only preliminary ideas, and nothing in writing. Remembering the advice of Conference participants, Morgan began by trying to nudge her towards a focus, repeatedly denying that she knew more than Fannie about how to approach the piece:

Morgan: What would you say your basic theme is? And sometimes if you keep that in mind, then you can always, you know, keep that as a focus for what you're writing. And the reason I say that is 'cause when you say, "well living happily wasn't. . . ."

Fannie: (pause) . . . Well, America was a beautiful country, well, but it isn't beautiful anymore.

Morgan: Um hm. Not as beautiful.

Fannie: So I should just say, America was a beautiful country?

Morgan: Yeah. But I dunno—what do you think your overall theme is, that you're saying?

Fannie: (long pause). . . . I'm really, I'm just talking about America.

Morgan: America? So America as . . . ?

Fannie: (pause) . . . Um . . . (pause)

Morgan: Land of free, uh, land of natural resources? As, um, a place where there's a conflict, I mean, there, if you can narrow that, "America." What is it specifically, and think about what you've written, in the rest. Know what I mean?

Fannie: (pause) . . . The riches of America, or the country? I don't know . . .

Morgan: I think you do. I'm not saying there's any right answer, but I, I'm— for me, the reason I'm saying this, is I see this emerging as, you know, (pause) where you're really having a hard time with dealing with the exploitation that you see, of America, you know, you think that. And you're using two groups to really illustrate, specifically, how two different attitudes toward, um the richness and beauty of America, two different um, ways people have to approach this land. Does that, does this make any sense? Or am I just putting words in your mouth? I don't want to do that. I mean that's what I see emerge in your paper. But I could be way off base.

Fannie: I think I know what you're trying to say. And I can kind of relate it at times to what I'm trying to say.

Morgan: You know, I mean, this is like the theme I'm picking up . . . (pause) I think you know, you've got some real, you know, environmental issues here. I think you're a closet environmentalist here. Which are real true, know what I mean. (pause) And when you talk about pollution, and waste, and, um, those types of things. So I mean, if you're looking at a theme of your paper, what could you pick out, of something of your underlying theme.

Fannie: (pause) . . . The resources, I guess?

Morgan: Well I mean, I don't want you to say, I want you to say, don't say "I guess," is that what you're talkin' about?

Fannie: Yeah.

Morgan: "Yeah?" I mean, it's your paper.

Fannie: I know, I want to talk about the land. . . .

Morgan: Ok. So you want to talk about the land, and the beauty of the land. . . .

Fannie: Um hm.

Morgan: . . . and then, um, and then also your topic for your, um, to spark your paper . . . what values, and morals, right? That's where you based off to write about America, and the land, you know. Maybe you can write some of these things down, as we're talking, as focussing things, you know. So you want to talk about the land, and then it's like, what do you want to say about the land?

What *did* Fannie "want to say about the land"? Whatever it was, one begins to wonder if it was perhaps lost in her tutor's inadvertent appropriation of these meanings—this despite Morgan's ostensible effort to simply elicit and reflect Fannie's thoughts. While Fannie may well have been struggling to articulate meanings which eluded clear expression in English, as Morgan worked to move her towards greater specificity, it became apparent that she was assuming the paper would express commonplace environmental concerns:

Fannie: I'll say, the country was, um, (pause), more like, I can't say perfect, I mean was, the tree was green, you know, I mean, um, it was clean. (long pause) I can't find the words for it.

Morgan: In a natural state? Um, un-, polluted, um, untouched, um, let me think, tryin' to get a . . .

Fannie: I mean everybody, I mean the Indians too, they didn't wear that (pointing to Morgan's clothes), they only wore buffalo clothing, you know for their clothing, they didn't wear like . . these, you know, cotton, and all that, they were so . . .

Morgan: Naturalistic.

Fannie: Yeah. "Naturalistic," I don't know if I'm gonna use that word . . . I wanna say, I wanna give a picture of the way the land was, before, you know what I'm, what I'm tryin' to say?

The Navajos' connection to the land is legendary—a spiritual nexus, many would maintain, that goes far beyond mainstream notions of what it means to be concerned about the environment. However, later in this session, Morgan observed that Fannie was writing about concerns that worry lots of people—citing recent publicity about the greenhouse effect, the hole in the ozone layer, and the growing interest in recycling. She then brought the session to a close by paraphrasing what she saw as the meat of the discussion and asking, "Is that something that you were tryin' to say, too?" Fannie replied, "Probably. I mean, I can't find the words for it, but you're finding the words for me." Morgan's rejoinder had been, "I'm just sparkin', I'm just sparkin' what you already have there, what you're sayin'. I mean I'm tryin' to tell you what I hear you sayin'."

Morgan laughed as, in an end-of-term interview, she listened again to Fannie's final comment: "I didn't *want* to find the words for her," she mused; "I wanted to show her how she could find 'em for herself." Still, she admitted, the directive impulse had been hard to resist: "I wanted to just give her ideas," Morgan observed, adding that although Fannie had some good things to say, "I wanted her to be able to articulate her ideas on a little higher level." Although it was obvious to Morgan that the ideas in Fannie's paper were of "deep-seated emotional concern," she also saw her as stuck in arid generalities: "'I don't know, it's just such a beautiful country,'" Morgan echoed as she reviewed the audiotape. While Morgan emphasized that she "didn't wanna write the paper for her," she allowed that "it's difficult—it's really hard to want to take the bull by the horns and say, 'don't you see it this way?'" On the one hand, Morgan noted that she'd often asked Fannie what she was getting out of a session, "'cause sometimes I'll think I'm getting through and I'm explaining something really good, and then they won't catch it"; on the other hand, Morgan emphasized again and again that she didn't want to "give away" her own thoughts.

Although Morgan often did an almost heroic job of waiting out Fannie's lingering silences and deflecting appeals to her authority, she never really surrendered control; somehow, the message always came across that Morgan knew more than Fannie about the ideas at hand, and that if she would, she could simply turn over prepackaged understandings. While her frustration was certainly understandable, I often had the sense that Morgan was insufficiently curious about Fannie's thoughts—insufficiently curious about how Fannie's understandings might have differed from her own, about how they had been shaped by Fannie's background and cultural orientation, or about what she stood to learn from them.

When asked about Fannie's block, a weary Morgan wrote it off to her cultural background:

> You know, I would have to say it's cultural; I'd have to say it's her you know,
> Native American background and growing up on a reservation . . . maybe . . .
> she's more sensitive to male-female roles, and the female role being quiet.

On a number of occasions Morgan had speculated that Navajo women are taught to be subservient, a perception that contrasted rather strikingly with Fannie's assertion that she wasn't at all shy or quiet back home.[2] Hoping to challenge Morgan's accustomed view of Fannie as bashful and retiring, in a final interview I played back one of their sessions from the week that a group of Navajo students were visiting the campus. Fannie was uncharacteristically vocal and even aggressive that morning, talking in a loud voice, repeatedly seizing and holding the floor:

Fannie: You know what my essay's on? Different environments. Um, I'm talking, I'm not gonna talk about my relationship between my brothers, it's so boring, so I'm just gonna talk about both being raised, like my youngest brother being raised on the reservation, and the other being raised over here, and they both have very different, um, um, (Morgan starts to say something, bur Fannie cuts her off and continues) characteristics or somethin' like that. You know, like their personalities, you know.

Morgan: Um. That's good. (Morgan starts to say something more, but Fannie keeps going.)

Fannie: It's funny, I'm cutting, I was totally mean to my brother here. (Morgan laughs.) Because, I called, I said that he's a wimp, you know, and my brother, my little brother's being raised on the reservation, is like, is like taught to be a man, he's brave and all that.

Luis (a student in the group): That's being a man?!

Fannie: And . . .

Luis: That's not being a man, I don't find.

Fannie: (her voice raised) I'm sorry—but that's how I wrote, Ok?! That's your opinion, I mean, and it's . . .

Luis: I think a man is sensitive, caring, and lov—

Fannie: (cutting him off) No, no . . .

Luis: . . . and able to express his feelings. I don't think that if you can go kill someone, that makes you a man.

Fannie: I mean . . .

Luis: That's just my opinion (gets up and walks away for a moment).

Fannie: (watching Luis wander off) Dickhead.

Morgan listened with a widening smile to the rest of this session, obviously pleased with Fannie's sometimes combative manner and unflagging insistence that attention be directed back to her. "Ha! Fannie's *so* much more forceful," Morgan exclaimed. "And just more in control of what she wants, and what she needs." When asked what she thought might have accounted for this temporary change, Morgan sidestepped the influence of the visiting students:

> I would love to think that I made her feel safe that way. And that I really um, showed her that she had, you know, by my interactions with her, that she really had every right to be strong-willed and forceful and have her opinions and you know, say what she felt that she needed to say, and that she didn't have to be quiet, you know. People always tell me that I influence people that way. You know? (laughs). "You've been hangin' around with Morgan too much!"

Hungry for feedback that she'd influenced Fannie in a positive way, Morgan grasped this possible evidence with obvious pleasure. Fannie was not a student who offered many positive signals, and it was perhaps essential to Morgan's professional self-esteem that she find them wherever she could. In this credit-taking there was, however, a larger irony: if only she'd been encouraged to push a little farther in her own thinking, perhaps she would have found herself assisting more often in such moments of blossoming.

Conclusion: Students As Teachers, Teachers As Students

When Morgan returned from the CCCC with a vision of "collaboration" that cast it as a set of techniques rather than a new way to think about teaching and learning, the insights of panelists and workshop leaders devolved into a fossilized creed, a shield against more fundamental concerns. Morgan had somehow missed the importance of continually adjusting her approach in the light of the understandings students make available, of allowing their feedback to shape her reflections upon her own role. At semester's end, she still didn't know that Fannie was a nonnative speaker of English; she didn't know the dimensions of Fannie's inexperience with academic writing, nor did she know the reasons behind Fannie's formidable block.

Even as Morgan labored to promote "collaborative" moments—making an ostensible effort to "talk less," to "sit back more," to enact an instructional mode that would seem more culturally appropriate—Fannie remembered a lifetime of classroom misadventure, and hung back, reluctant. Morgan needed to know something about this history, but she also needed to understand that much else was fluid and alive, that a revised sense of self was emerging from the dynamic interaction of Fannie's past and present. Emboldened by a few treasured days in the company of fellow Navajos, Fannie had momentarily stepped into a new stance, one that departed markedly from her accustomed behavior on reservation and campus alike; but if her confidence recalled an earlier self, her playful combativeness was, as Fannie observed in listening to the tape, a new and still-strange manifestation of something also oddly familiar, something left over from long ago.

Rather than frequent urgings to "talk less," perhaps what Morgan most needed was advice to *listen more*—for the clues students like Fannie would provide, for those moments when she might best shed her teacherly persona and become once again a learner. More than specific instructional strategies, Morgan needed the conceptual grounding that would allow her to understand that authentically collaborative learning is predicated upon fine-grained insight into individual students—of the nature of their Vygotskian "zones of proximal development," and, by association, of the sorts of instructional "scaffolding" most appropriate to their changing needs. So, too, did Morgan need to be encouraged toward the yet-elusive understanding that such learning is never unilateral, inevitably entailing a reciprocal influence, reciprocal advances in understanding. As she struggled to come to terms with her own ethnic ambivalence, to defend herself against a vociferous chorus proclaiming her "not black enough," Morgan had reason to take heart in Fannie's dramatic and rather trying process of transition. Had she thought to ask, Morgan would no doubt have been fascinated by Fannie's descriptions of this other cultural and linguistic context, with its very different perspectives on education in particular and the world in general. Most of all, perhaps, she would have been interested to know that Fannie was learning to inhabit both arenas, and in so doing, enacting a negotiation of admirable complexity—a negotiation different in degree, perhaps, but certainly not in kind, from Morgan's own.

Having tutored only one semester previously, Morgan was understandably eager to abandon her lingering doubts about her effectiveness, eager for a sure-footed sense that she was providing something worthwhile. Her idealism and good intentions were everywhere apparent—in her lengthy meditations on her work, in her eager enthusiasm at the CCCC, in her persistent efforts to try out new approaches, and in the reassurance she extended to me when I confessed that I'd be writing some fairly negative things about her vexed attempts to reach Fannie. Morgan had been offered relatively little by way of preparation and support: beyond a sprinkling of workshops and an occasional alliance with more experienced tutors, she was left largely on her own—alone with the substantial challenges and opportunities that students like Fannie presented, alone to deal with her frustration and occasional feelings of failure as best she could. Like all beginning educators, Morgan needed abundant support, instruction, and modeling if she were to learn to reflect critically upon her work, to question her assumptions about students like Fannie, to allow herself, even at this fledgling stage in her career, to become a reflective and therefore vulnerable practitioner. This is not to suggest that Morgan should have pried into hidden corners of Fannie's past, insisting that she reveal information about her background before she felt ready to do so; only that Morgan be respectfully curious, ever attentive to whatever clues Fannie might have been willing to offer, ever poised to revise old understandings in the light of fresh evidence.

Those of us who work with linguistic minority students—and that's fast becoming us all—must appreciate the evolving dimensions of our task, realizing that we have to reach further than ever if we're to do our jobs well. Regardless of our crowded schedules and shrinking budgets, we must also think realistically about the sorts of guidance new tutors and teachers need if they are to confront these rigors effectively, guiding them towards practical strategies informed by understandings from theory and research, and offering compelling reminders of the need to monitor one's ethnocentric biases and faulty assumptions. Most of all, we must serve as models of reflective practice—perennially inquisitive and self-critical, even as we find occasion both to bless and curse the discovery that becoming students of students means becoming students of ourselves as well.

Notes

1. "Fannie" was the actual name of this student's maternal grandmother. We decided to use it as her pseudonym to honor this lasting influence.

2. Morgan's assumption is also contradicted by published accounts of life among the Navajo, which from early on have emphasized the prestige and power of female members of the tribe. Gladys Reichard, an anthropologist who lived among the Navajos in the 1920s, reported that "the Navajo woman enjoys great economic and social prestige as the head of the house and clan and as the manager of economic affairs, and she is not excluded from religious ritual or from attaining political honors" (55). Navajo women often own substantial property, and children retain the surname of the matrilineal clan; the status accorded women is further reflected in the depictions of female deities in Navajo myths (Terrell 57; 255).

Acknowledgements

Special thanks to Sarah Warshauer Freedman for encouragement and sage advice throughout this project. Thanks also to Don McQuade, Guadalupe Valdés, and the members of my fall, 1991 writing research class at The University of Iowa.
This work was supported by a grant from the NCTE Research Foundation.

Crossing Lines

Carole Deletiner

In an interview with Gloria Watkins, bell hooks is asked, "Why remember the pain . . . ?" She says to herself:

> I say remember the pain because I believe true resistance begins with people confronting pain, whether it's theirs or somebody else's, and wanting to do something to change it. And it's this pain that so much makes its mark in daily life. Pain as a catalyst for change, for working to change. Sometimes working in the academic place I have found it's my peers not understanding this pain that has made for such a deep sense of isolation. I think that's why everywhere I am, my true comrades are often non-academic workers—who know that pain, who are willing to talk about that pain. That is what connects us—our awareness that we know it, have known it, or will know it again. (215)

In my job as an "outsider," an adjunct lecturer at Hunter College, where I am supposed to be "enacting authority," I find that my comrades are my students. We spend a lot of time reading, writing, and talking about pain.

A student approaches me after class; "Do you want to know why I wasn't here yesterday?" "Sure," I say. "I can't tell you," she whispers. Several days later, this same young Haitian woman is sitting in my office. She is crying quietly. She did not come to class because she was in a locked ward, under a suicide watch, after swallowing a bottle of antibiotics. "My family treats me like shit," she says. "They're crazy." Two years ago her father tried to kill them all with a machete. Her boyfriend, a graduating senior at another college, just dumped her. School is ending and there's too much pressure. The only way out of all of this pain is to die. I sit there listening and recall what an analyst friend of mine told me, "Suicide is a way of solving a problem you don't have."

I don't have a particularly good relationship with this student. Eviarna is hostile and manipulative, always asking me, "Is my work good?" I know that it does not matter what I say and wonder if she would feel more at home if I told her that her writing was mediocre (it wasn't). After she reads selections from *Incidents in the Life of a Slave Girl* and *Narrative of the Life of Frederick Douglass,* all of her writing centers on slavery, cruelty, and oppression. The essay assignment for these readings asks students to "compare the slave narra-

College English, 54 (November 1992), pp. 809–17. Copyright © 1992 by the National Council of Teachers of English. Reprinted with permission.

tives you have read by Harriet Jacobs and Frederick Douglass." Eviarna writes that Harriet Jacobs

> tried to make her readers take the oppression of slave women personally so to see it as a threat to their own sense of themselves as women; also, to touch their hearts, she told her story in a way anyone could identify himself or herself with.

And I have to ask, who is she really writing about?

In his first paper, a narrative describing a single important educational event, Jeff writes about his parents' divorce. His father left his mother for another woman. He writes that he has learned that the world is divided into predator and prey and he always has to watch his back because someone is just waiting to do him in. He writes, "You can't trust anyone and that is a good thing to know, because it makes you independent." Jeff comes to class late, when he comes at all. He has lots of excuses for why he doesn't do the work. He is always apologizing, always asking if I'm going to drop him from the class, always saying that he will do better. I just listen.

When I can't take his hostility anymore, I tell him what walking into class late means. It's an act of aggression, a way of saying "Go to hell" to everyone in the room. I ask him if he knows that he is angry, that he sets himself up for others to be angry at him. I ask him if he knows what self-destructive behavior is. He looks at me in bewilderment; his eyes cloud over, but I know he knows.

I tell him that he is my school project for the semester, that no matter what he does, he's going to get at least a B in the class. I say that sometimes people, especially those who feel they don't deserve anything, need to have something good happen to them. At the end of the semester Jeff manages to hand in a completed portfolio. He has fulfilled the requirements of the course; his writing is imaginative and perceptive; his essays are neatly typed. On the day of the final exam he tells me that after four semesters in college, he is about to be expelled because of his barely passing grades. He waited for four hours to see his academic counselor and wound up screaming at her. His father is about to throw him out of his house. My class is the only one he attended with any regularity this semester. And, oh yes, he tells me that he now knows what self-destructive behavior can do. He writes me a letter:

> Even if I fail this class, I don't care. I will never forget the way you treated me this semester. Even though I can't figure out why you are so nice, I guess some things in life should not be analyzed, you're just a cool, wonderful and weird teacher. I say weird because any other professor would have said, "Get the hell out of my class!" I guess you like me for some bizarre reason.

The instructor who reads his portfolio gives him a B. I give him an A in the course.

Several weeks after classes end I read Jeff's final exam. He writes about his identification with Adrienne Rich in her essay "Split at the Root." It seems that no one in Jeff's family, including his mother, ever bothered to tell him that she was a Jew, and according to Jewish law so is he. His father's family rejected his mother's side, so he never met any of his Jewish relatives. He, like Rich, struggles to come to terms with his identity and writes.

> One must know one's self or you're not real. You must become a unified person. You must blend the two halves together. You must mix the two chemicals together and get a positive unified identity solution. You must respect and know both sides, and be that person.

His essay is filled with his rage and sense of loss; however, he never uses the word "I."

Is this what I've taught him, to acknowledge his anger and pain? Is this a good lesson to learn? Or should I just point out the comma splices and run-on sentences, as some of my colleagues do? "You mean your students write drafts?" a senior faculty member asks at a staff meeting for composition teachers. Should I write that this kind of personal writing is not appropriate for college? His essay is brilliant, but who else would know that? Am I going to cross the line and write to him to tell him how moved I was by his final essay? The line gets blurred between professional and personal when people open themselves up to you in this way. The departmental description of English 120 covers none of this.

All of this makes me think about my experiences as a student. I remember my sixth-grade teacher, Mrs. O'Connell, taking me to task for talking to myself. She was an anti-Semite and used to read selections from the New Testament at assemblies and in our class, and her eyes once met mine as she talked about "those people who killed Christ." She had a special lesson just for me. In high school, I disappointed Mr. Bortnick by not doing as well on the SATs as he had expected. I spent four years as a silent (or should I say silenced?) undergraduate student who never raised her hand in a single class. At the one compulsory conference I had with my freshman composition teacher, I was so filled with feeling that I sat down, burst into tears, and was unable to say a single word. I now teach freshman composition and sometimes students cry when they come to talk to me. Sometimes, we cry together.

When I return to graduate studies after a twenty-year hiatus, to finally conquer school, one of the many remaining demons in my life, I think that everything will be different; well, at least I know I am different. And in some ways things have changed. I make myself speak in each of my classes. As I now tell my silent students, it is a way of marking my territory and leaving my scent. It is the only way to make myself feel as if I belong.

However, I encounter all too many of the attitudes I thought had been left behind. In a Contemporary British and American Poetry class, there are no women poets on the reading list. The response to a query about this omission is, "I did them last year." In my first semester in a doctoral program in English Literature, the academic adviser asks me if I have followed a traditional course of study for my master's degree, or "Have you taken modern dance?" My field of interest, nineteenth-century women's fiction, is characterized as "sub-literary." I complain to the head of the department, and he, mistakenly assuming that we are peers, says, "He talks that way to me too." And yet I persist, at least for a while.

I think about the paper I have written on mothers and mothering in a seminar on Henry James. Regarding James's remarks about his mother, I write: "It is comforting to be so 'taken care of,' but I think it would be rather oppressive and frightening not to know where my consciousness ended and my mother's began." My professor has crossed this sentence out and has written in the margin, "This is well put but perhaps a little too personalized for this forum." And later on more and more of my feelings are crossed out and the margin is cluttered with: "Occasionally you create a tone and use locutions that are probably too familiar and personal for a professional essay" and "This seems stylistically and tonally jarring, probably because it's too direct, too personal!!" That particular remark is followed by a series of exclamation points, just in case I don't get it.

My student Orietta writes about the years her father physically abused her mother. She does not speak to him and wishes he were dead. Geraldine's parents are compulsive gamblers. Hillary worked in a sweatshop at the age of twelve. Her father had been a professor of literature in China and cannot support his family on his salary as a stockboy in a Chinatown hardware store. Eighteen-year-old Andrew writes about waiting for a subway in Brooklyn: "Everyone stared at me. Am I really that eccentric? Did they sniff out the faggot, and if so, was I going to be pushed in front of the next train to glide by the platform?" In the margin on his paper I write, "It hurts to read this." And when he reads this "Crossing Lines" essay, he responds in my margin, "It hurts to feel that way too, but I grew callous after a while unfortunately." And I write back, "I don't believe this."

A graffiti artist writes to me about a crew that went bombing in Brooklyn and murdered a homeless person who had built a fire near the exit to their evening's handiwork. When I tell him that I have no words to describe how appalled I am at this act of meaningless brutality, he responds casually. "Carole," he says, "there are people who think hitting other people over the head with hammers is fun."

And they keep on writing like this. It's only a few weeks into a new semester and I know who the recovering addicts and alcoholics are; I know who's been battered and sexually abused; I know who's ashamed of being Salvadoran or Russian, of being from a welfare family; who had a child when she was fifteen; who dropped out of high school and has never told her husband.

They don't/won't/can't stop writing (and I don't want them to) and the feelings and the pain drip off the edges of their pages, only stopped by the comments I write where I tell them about my own experiences as an estranged member of a dysfunctional family, a terrified student who never spoke in four years of college, a student now grappling with whether or not I can take another day in a graduate school that feels just like the unaccepting home in which I grew up. My fear, rage, and comradeship tumble out onto the margins of their papers in the comments I write to them. This makes some of my colleagues nervous. It even made one cry.

Sometimes students write responses to the comments I make in the margins of their essays. They write essays *for* me, but these communications are written *to* me. Occasionally an innocent question, never a demanding "Tell me the most intimate and personal details of your life" will lead to unforeseen consequences. Responding to Richard Rodriguez's essay on the "scholarship boy," Claudia writes about freedom and the process of assimilation:

> I have a proud Hispanic heritage and I have learned from difficult experiences
> of life that freedom is an essential instrument in our life.

In the margin I ask, "Can you write about one of those experiences?" In her second draft, this appears:

> In my country we (my family) were not free to do or to say what we want. . . .
> One of my uncles was an exile from my country. He worked for the government. . . . During the 70's every person who worked for them was supposed to
> do everything as they please. My uncle was a mechanic, but one day he was
> asked [by] the government to do a very special mission. This time he was supposed to go to a small village in one of the very important cities of Guatemala
> and kill over 100 people. There were grandparents, parents, sons, daughters,
> children, grandsons, etc. This was a massacre and my uncle could not do such
> a thing. So he refused to do it and he deserted his job. The government sent
> other people to do the mission and also they were supposed to kill my uncle.

Not only was her uncle forced to flee, but the entire family had to seek asylum. Could I ever have expected such a response? Was my "innocent" question intrusive? Should it not have been asked?

Do *I* elicit these personal revelations from students? Or is it something about the process of writing itself that unleashes the anger and the pain that appear in my students' writing, as well as in my own? Writing about our lives, writing in a personal voice, enables us to communicate, but not necessarily with one another. Writing lets us talk to ourselves.

Each semester I ask my students to write a critique of the course. Many students respond that I treat them as people, as fellow writers, not students, that I share myself with them, and that although this makes some of them uneasy, my class is a different experience from any other they have taken.

Nick, after thanking me, writes, "What I have just told you in my first paragraph, I would find impossible to tell you to your face. When I try to speak the thoughts get lost travelling from my brain to my mouth." He is able to express himself on the page and he docs it beautifully, although, throughout the semester, he continues to write about his lack of ability. My ultimate reward comes in Nick's last sentence, "You made me into a confident writer and I appreciate that very much."

Marvin, one of the student readers of this paper, wrote the following comment to me:

> Not only did I enjoy reading your essay but I admire you for your honesty, the way you open up yourself to the reader. It's true that in school teachers are teachers and students are students. There's this imaginary wall separating them. In this class, Carole, there is no wall. When I wrote my essay on assimilation, "The Loss of Identity," you understood because you have experienced it yourself. I thank you for sharing that with me but what I'm saying is that if it weren't for your comforting, warm comments I don't know whether I would feel even more secure about myself now than I did when I began writing it. We both speak and write English but you as a teacher speak *our* language, the language of the student. You understand us and know the way we feel as if you yourself are one. The students are lucky to have you, someone who is as we are. Your comments are very helpful both in the essays but also in our lives. Don't stop! I have had teachers who have given me advice but not one who speaks from the heart, from experience.

Sometimes students begin to correspond with me outside of the required writing assignments. After class, Steven, a recovering alcoholic and cocaine addict, hands me a letter:

> . . . I find I'm having a difficult time right now in my life. Doing the next "right" thing is difficult and I sometimes feel overwhelmed by the complexity of life. . . . Anyway, I'm frightened I guess. Simply frightened. I wonder where my life will lead me (where I will lead my life). What will I do with myself after school? . . . I cry over this stuff. Like I'm beginning to cry now. I don't cry like I used to. The tears come few, usually with no sound from my body (like now). I used to wail away, loud and clear. I wish I still could, don't really know for sure why I can't. . . . I don't want you to feel that you have to write back. A look and a smile would be enough. It would say I read your letter and I understand the feelings.

But of course, I do write back. And this is where the line is crossed. Am I an effective teacher because I do cross that line? If I moderated my self-exposure, kept my vulnerability a secret, would students respond to the class in the same way? Would they produce the kind of writing they do? Would Raphael have written a twelve-page paper about being sexually abused at the age of four if I had not written, in response to a research paper topic loop writing exercise, "Did this happen to you? You don't have to answer this question, but I feel the need to ask." In whose interest would it be if I insulated myself from the feelings and the histories in the room?

In his critique at the end of the semester, Steven warns me:

> Sometimes I wonder Carole if it's a good idea to be quite so revealing of yourself to the class—not me!—but I sometimes wonder what some of the "kids" in here think—not that it necessarily matters, but the more you give away for free, the more vulnerable you leave yourself.

And I write back to him:

> You say that by giving myself away for free, I make myself vulnerable, that I'm likely to be hurt. So what is life about Steven? Being alive is being vulnerable and the more we defend ourselves by not allowing ourselves to feel, the closer to death we come. The things you value in me—my sensitivity, searching and questioning—are in you too. Don't deny or be afraid of them. They're the best things about us and they don't preclude just being in the moment and enjoying life and the world around us. They give us access to life. They are the life force.

A senior faculty member who observes my class asks me how our discussion of Harriet Jacobs's life will teach the students about writing. I don't know what to say, so I lie. "Naturally we discuss the form of an essay, the introduction, the developing paragraphs in which we supply supporting details, and of course, how to write a conclusion." I feel like a traitor to everything I believe in.

A different semester, another observation. The class takes part in an exercise on stereotypes, an exercise that I have been doing for ten years. I am called at home by the observer who tells me that he has judged my performance as "mixed." He writes in his report that I have allowed anti-Semitic remarks to go unchallenged. He notes that the students call out these remarks with relish. He does not remark on the anti-black, anti-Hispanic, anti-Asian, anti-woman, anti-gay, anti-poor people statements that also go "unchallenged." I am devastated.

If this is what has transpired in my classroom, if students have been injured by things that I have allowed to be said, if this is how they feel (the way I do at the moment I listen to the observer's voice), I should never be allowed to teach again. I find myself reading this observation report over and over, like picking on a wound so that it can never heal.

I am required to attend a meeting with the chairman of the English Department and the observer. I try to defend myself, but I sit there in tears, mortified and furious. I manage to articulate some of what I feel, some of what I believe about the need to confront the hatred, about the point of the exercise, the way people feel comfortable until the slurs are aimed at "their" group.

Ultimately, my observation is emended. I am no longer a bad teacher who has wasted class time by answering student questions. I am not encouraging anti-Semitism. This is especially ironic considering that I have written the required essay on stereotypes along with my class. They have read my essay, in which I, for the first time, write about being a Jew and how I kept that fact a secret for the first seven years I taught.

I am transformed from an "inexperienced teacher" who made a "major mistake" into an "excellent teacher" who made a "minor error in judgment." There is an unexpected benefit from this experience. This incident binds the class together (because, of course, intentionally making another error in judgment, I tell them all about what has happened; I need to know if they were in the same class as the observer). I also learn much later that this faculty member has attacked adjuncts before, in precisely the same way. In the course of writing this paper, I finally throw the observation report away.

But still my own insecurity prevails, for after all, although I do "real" work, this is not a "real" job. I am a "part-timer." Maybe the professor who said that reading about the life of an enslaved woman has nothing to do with writing is correct. Maybe I shouldn't encourage students to write about their lives.

At the end of each semester I write an essay for my classes. Each essay is a response to a theme or issue that emerges over the course of the semester: "Plagiarism—What's wrong with our words?" "What are we afraid of when we sit down to write?" I write about my own struggles as well as reflecting on theirs. My feeling is that the students write for me, week after week, draft after draft, and I owe them something in return. Maybe it is the interest on their accounts in *my* Freirean educational bank. I owe them a piece of writing that I have worked on and anguished over. I've written three of these essays, and the class response is always the same. Many of the students are uncomfortable. When I hand out copies of my essay, the room is silent. They are not used to the teacher crossing the line. I am saying, I am vulnerable too, and we are all in this enterprise together; I trust you with myself, with my words.

I gave a copy of last semester's essay to a colleague and it was returned to me without comment. The theme, which came out of the experience of teaching two classes in which students were extremely open in their writing but refused to speak out loud, was, "What are we afraid we'll say if we speak in class?" After reading my students' portfolios, this same colleague asked, "Aren't they shocked to read the things you reveal about yourself?" Why should they be shocked? Is it just because I am "The Teacher"? What is so special or different about me or my life? I've known joy and pain, and I can't not identify and respond when I encounter the feelings I know in anything I read. All of the books that are important to me are marked up with my marginal jottings. After so many years of self-imposed silence, I can no longer stem the flow of words or feelings.

In the cover letter for his final portfolio, Chuck writes:

I've never done so much writing in such a short period of time as I have in this class. I both hated it and liked it. I hated this class because it took up so much time and energy. Never have I taken such a time consuming class, ever. Some of the writing assignments in this class, which we were to select from, cause me to think about particular aspects of my life that were emotionally sensitive and pain evoking.

For some of the same reasons as above, I enjoyed the writing assignments. It was very self analytical, motivational and insightful for me. From one revision to the next, I saw my thoughts and ideas come together in a more clear picture on the pages. With my pen in hand, at times I felt that I was on the couch at the therapist's office. Just as it's hard work confronting realities once they're dredged up, I found those similar difficulties while writing about myself.

And that is precisely the point. Pain is the thing that we all know so much about and are so reluctant to reveal and share with one another. As I wrote to a student who was having difficulty with the final essay assignment—an "Identity/Self Analysis" paper, the only truly personal piece of writing that students are asked (but not required) to do:

You write that your life is "fucking depressing." The therapist I saw twice a week for seven years used to tell me that the goal of therapy was to learn that I was part of the common misery, that it was not mine alone, that I shared it with others. The grandiosity of the narcissist wants all of the pain in the world for her own. Only I am worthy of suffering this much. What purpose does pain serve? It joins us. I want to do something to take your hurt away, but I know I can't. I'd be stealing something from you. I can just listen and let you know that I hear you and that I battle the same demons. We aren't alone. There are lots of us who speak the same language and curiously enough (or maybe not) we spend a lot of time laughing. Crying and laughing together. That's what it's all about.

Stick with your writing. Don't fight it. Write the pain. It does make it go away. I promise you that. The resistance is the desire to hang onto the anguish. It's the only companion many of us have ever had. We know it. We love it. Don't worry, there's an infinite amount of pain in the universe—you/I won't run out. Know that there are people (almost strangers—like me) who care about you and don't want to say goodbye when the semester is over (crying yet? I am). You're O.K. Gregg. Write your paper.

Work Cited

hooks, bell. *Yearning*. Boston: South End Press, 1990.

Part Three

Fluency, Flow, and Wonder

My first impetus to write came from a sixth grade English teacher
who filled us with feeling that writing was a good thing to do and
that there was something noble about the English language.

—Anonymous

Motivation is the first lesson in learning to write. Without it, writing runs the
risk of being sterile or mindless. Motivation calls for the attention of all writing teachers, the teacher in the primary grades, the professor in the graduate
course, the tutor in the writing center. Motivation is not merely a lesson learned
at some point in time, but a continuing concern throughout the whole of the
educational enterprise. Generally speaking, motivation may be categorized as
extrinsic, e.g., rewards, punishments, grades, or *intrinsic*, the satisfaction derived from some specific activity. The emphasis in this section is on intrinsic
motivation, and the essays included here speak to the ways in which joy, satisfaction, personal identity, even a sense of wonder, may grow out of an activity
as demanding as writing.

Motivation suggests those invisible dimensions of the writing process, especially all that we associate with the word *desire*. But how does a teacher
know whether desire is present? Or what its roots are? Certainly it can't be measured or quantified or even taught directly in the traditional sense. Yet it remains an important, if not the most important, part of our teaching. Knowing
the proper form or the right rule is not enough. Without the energy to drive the
process, the form remains empty and lifeless.

Knowing that the sources of motivation are subtle and capricious, teachers
of writing rely on not only what they *do* but what they *be* in order to encourage
its presence. The essays in this section speak of both *doing* and *being*, pointing
the way toward fluency and depth in the writing process.

In the first essay, Gina Briefs-Elgin applies the principles of a well-known
text, *Flow: The Psychology of Optimal Experience*, to the writing classroom.
The author explores the roots and common misconceptions of happiness, arguing that "happiness may be found not in relaxation and freedom *from* difficulty but in growth-producing encounters *with* difficulty" (81). The connections between flow and fluency have profound implications for the teaching of
writing.

The connections between dance and writing are powerful, suggests Sherry Swain in her essay, "Entering Wonder." In describing that special moment of creation in dance, the author uses phrases such as "feeling of surrealism," "sacred space," and "crystal pool of magic." So too the writer sometimes comes upon such moments when everything is perfect: consciousness is suspended and the words flow, seeming to come from some place other than oneself. The reader should observe that these first two essays come from different grade levels—Briefs-Elgin from the college level and Swain from the first grade—and yet both suggest a subtle mystical presence in the learning process.

Patience, inner stillness, conscious awareness—these are insights in Donald R. Gallehr's "Wait, and the Writing Will Come: Meditation and the Composing Process." When the natural rhythms of the body are in harmony, then the writer can see the path ahead more clearly. Meditation, the author tells us, makes us whole and brings the whole person to the writing process.

Because we are so close to the events of daily life, their being so fresh on our mind, we do not see them for what they are. "What I Learned from Verle Barnes" is full of memory, and in memory there is perspective, and in perspective pattern. The river, the mythic town, the Bay and the morning sunlight, the beloved barrier island, the incessant rhythm of the sea are all elements of the pattern. Discovering the pattern leads toward understanding, which itself may be the jewel buried at the bottom of the sea, the one for which we have to dive deep and bring to the surface.

In "Focusing Twice Removed," Lesley Rex shows how someone can find a subject for writing by making "a list of personal experiences that somehow changed you or your life so that you were not the same after they happened" (122). The reader of this essay is spellbound as Linda, a student in the author's class, describes the experience of childhood rape. The author goes on to describe a sequence of steps that leads toward a completed piece of writing and draws explicit connections between literature and good student writing.

Ultimately we come to the place where desire and knowledge coalesce. In this place, where both the desire to write and an understanding of the principles of rhetoric come together, the writer dwells in paradox. "It is neither this nor that," Meister Eckhart tells us, reminding us that solutions are often found not in the extreme but in the energy generated by tension between the two extremes. Perhaps he would say that it is both *both* and *neither,* and that our proper role in the universe is always ambiguous.

Happiness and the Blank Page

Csikszentmihalyi's Flow in the Writing Classroom

Gina Briefs-Elgin

If, then, there is some end of the things we do, which we desire for its own sake (everything else being desired for the sake of this) . . . clearly this must be the good and the chief good. Will not the knowledge of it, then, have a great influence on life?

—Aristotle
The Nicomachean Ethics

In his *Letters to a Young Poet,* Rainer Maria Rilke (1908/1993) advised his disciple to "hold to the difficult." If he did this, what he most feared would be transformed into great happiness: "How should we be able to forget those ancient myths that are at the beginning of all peoples, the myths about dragons that at the last moment turn into princesses . . . ?" (p. 69). Rilke's advice to this young writer is not new. Throughout time, teachers have tried to convince young people of the apparently absurd and certainly unsettling proposition that happiness lies in seizing the difficult. I would like to suggest that recent developments in psychology may help us as writing teachers (particularly as developmental composition teachers) in this struggle.

For a long time, psychology wasn't much interested in happiness. The study of mental illness preempted the study of mental health. But in the past two decades interest in the phenomenon of happiness has blossomed (Swanbrow 1989, pp. 37–38) At the center of this endeavor is University of Chicago psychologist Mihaly Csikszentmihalyi, "the father of flow psychology." In *Flow: The Psychology of Optimal Experience* (1990) which crystallized for the lay person twenty years of research in the field, Csikszentmihalyi used the tools of modern psychology to provide statistical evidence for what thoughtful people have generally maintained: that happiness may be found not in relaxation and freedom *from* difficulty but in growth-producing encounters *with* difficulty. He examined what happens during individual encounters with difficulty: episodes

Journal of the Assembly for Expanded Perspectives on Learning, 3 (Winter 1997–98), pp. 70–79. Copyright © 1997 by the Assembly for Expanded Perspectives on Learning. Reprinted with permission.

of "flow," an enchanted state we enter when we engage in any meaningful, difficult activity that stretches us to the limits of—but not beyond—our skills so that we are poised perfectly between boredom and anxiety. He demonstrated that, while some activities, such as rock climbing and chess playing, are naturally conducive to flow, any activity, through our decision to make it our own and to tease meaning from it, can be transformed into a flow activity, and he invited us to create the conditions of flow in work and in leisure.

Because the theory of flow involves issues at the heart of teaching—difficulty and mastery—its interest to educators should be obvious. Reed Larson (1985), Csikszentmihalyi's coauthor of studies on adolescent development, demonstrated that students in flow write better than students who are anxious or bored and that successful student writers instinctively monitor their processes to achieve a flow-producing balance between anxiety and boredom, and S. McLeod (1987) called for research into the ways Csikszentmihalyi's theory of flow can guide writing task design.

I would like to suggest that flow theory can also be valuable to improve student motivation to write. I believe emphasis on the rewards of engagement with difficulty can be useful to all teachers and particularly to those who teach English composition, the subject many students consider most difficult.

What has composition got to do with happiness? Students would no doubt respond, "Very little." Recently, I surveyed my basic writers on their attitudes towards writing papers. One question had them number these activities in order of preference: writing a five-page paper, painting five rooms, digging a ditch, or undergoing root canal. Writing a five-page paper came out first on only 17 of the 71 surveys. Painting five rooms beat writing a five-page paper 33 times. Digging a ditch beat writing a five-page paper 28 times, and at least 10 students chose the root canal over the five-page paper.

We don't need surveys to tell us that many students don't enjoy writing papers. They dread it because writing can be a laborious task involving complex performances and—worse—riddled with unknowns. "The maker of a sentence," wrote Emerson (1834/1960), "launches out into the infinite and builds a road into Chaos and Old Night" (p. 59). Surely, since time immemorial students have approached writing assignments unhappily, scowling over their clay or wax tablets, making despondent ink blots in their *cahiers*. But in the late twentieth century there are new wrinkles. Because they live in the thick of consumerism, students are less experienced in the challenge of making things from scratch than were young people formerly; what's more, our consumer culture actively discourages them from including "difficult-making" in their definitions of happiness.

Our country's success has depended on each individual's energetic productivity. Children were raised with the uncomfortable notions that idle hands were the devil's workshop and that happiness lay in accomplishing difficult tasks. They learned from their parents the rewarding work of wrestling raw matter and data into shape—often into complex patterns. Jefferson's Monticello, at the plutocratic level, and the *Foxfire* series, at the popular level, remind us that our predecessors were intimate with difficulty and with the exhilaration of difficult making.

But contemporary culture affords scant opportunity for what Irving Stone once called "the agony and the ecstasy" of creating. The Industrial Revolution took away our need and ability to create manually—our own houses, furniture, food, clothing—and the media revolution has virtually taken away our ability to create mentally—ideas, music, stories, images, entertainment, adventure. In a society where agribusiness, corporations, and the media meet every need, making is severed from any relationship to necessity and reduced to mere hobby. Our country's economic success seems to depend on passive consumption and has redefined it as happiness. We are assured that if we are free of the labor of making things (not just dinner but plans and love), if we are carefree, we will be happier. And so, as Charles Reich notes in his perennially relevant *The Greening of America* (1970), we are "sold artificial pleasures and artificial dreams to replace the high human and spiritual adventure that had once been America" (p. 40).

"We have a new joke on the reservation," the shaman tells author Richard Erdoes (Fire & Erdoes, 1972), "What is cultural deprivation?" Answer: "Being an upper-middle-class white kid living in a split-level suburban home with a color TV" (p. 110). Our adolescent students are particularly bombarded with the media credo that happiness lies in consuming someone else's products, images, dreams.

Besides disparaging hard work and promoting consumption, TV swallows the hours students might otherwise dedicate to the pleasures of carpentry or gardening, of making models, clothing, poetry, or art. A 1995 government report on adolescent use of time offered these statistics: "American adolescents aged 12–17 spent an average of two-and-a-half hours per day watching television, but only 27 minutes a day doing homework, . . . and 9 minutes a day pursuing hobbies or arts and crafts . . . weekday and weekend days combined" (Zill et al., p. 7).

For students with little experience in creative difficulty and ample experience with passive consumption, it is easy to understand the misery of freshman writers, slumped like a question mark at midnight over the white page of an open notebook. That blank white page might as well be a blank cassette or a TV screen with snow—because composition, more than most other college subjects, requires the anguishingly difficult and ultimately exhilarating creation of something from nothing, the very opposite of consumption.

Unless we're sadists, we don't enjoy this image. We want our students to want to write, to be happy, that is, motivated to write. We find some useful methods to ease students into writing: journals, prewriting techniques, engaging topics. But no matter how valuable, such strategies for easing the writing process ultimately hit a brick wall. We can't eliminate the difficulty—but by taking a page from Csikszentmihalyi, we can tackle the other end of the problem: helping our students reject "the strongly rooted cultural stereotype" (1990, p. 160) of happiness as ease and redefine it to include difficulty.

Let us take a closer look at Csikszentmihalyi's research. He began in the seventies to look for the answer to a simple question: "When do people feel most happy?" He felt that if people knew the answer, they could shape their lives in more satisfying directions. With the help of an international network of colleagues, he interviewed people from dozens of countries and every walk of life—collecting over one hundred thousand records—to discover when they felt happiest. From this data, Csikszentmihalyi composed the first scientific profile of happiness (or as he also calls it, "optimal experience" or "flow"). His central findings (1990, 1994) were:

> Contrary to what we usually believe, moments like these, the best moments in our lives, are not the passive, receptive, relaxing times—although such experiences can also be enjoyable, if we have worked hard to attain them. The best moments usually occur when a person's body or mind is stretched to its limits in a voluntary effort to accomplish something difficult and worthwhile. Optimal experience is thus something that we make happen. (p. 3)

Regardless of circumstances or background, people all over the world—chess players, telephone operators, shepherds, CEOs, weavers, pilots—offered descriptions of their flow experiences which Csikszentmihalyi found astonishingly similar. Using their reports, he compiled a list of the major components of enjoyment:

1. Tasks are manageable
2. Environment is conducive to concentration
3. Goals are clear
4. Feedback is immediate
5. Involvement is deep but effortless
6. Individuals feel in control
7. Individuals are free from sense of self
8. They lose an awareness of time
9. A stronger self emerges after the experience.   (p. 49, 71)

These optimal experiences "are not necessarily pleasant at the time they occur," wrote Csikszentmihalyi:

> The swimmer's muscles might have ached during his most memorable race, his lungs might have felt like exploding, and he might have been dizzy with fatigue—yet these could have been the best moments of his life. Getting control of life is never easy, and sometimes it can be definitely painful. (pp. 3–4)

We see how different this definition of happiness is from the definitions of many of our students (and even our own!). This happiness has nothing to do with ease. Rather, it has difficulty at its very heart. And yet, it is crucial that our students understand this: that the happiness Csikszentmihalyi is talking about is no sacrifice-and-struggle-someday-you-will-thank-me sort. No, this is upfront happiness, happening as they do an arduous, perhaps even painful, thing — or immediately after — like the runner's high.

The issue is how to achieve the biggest rush of happiness, or, in Csikszent-mihalyi's term, flow:

> In fact, when we struggle against entropy, we do get an immediate and very concrete reward from our actions: we enjoy whatever we are doing, moment by moment. The self is flooded with a sense of exhilaration. . . . In those moments we feel that, instead of suffering through events over which we have no control, we are creating our own lives. (1994, p. 175)

Csikszentmihalyi believes this sense of exhilaration is one "that becomes a landmark in memory for what life should be like" (1990, p. 3).

And the most enduring rush of happiness. As did Maslow (1968), Csikszentmihalyi pointed out that pleasures such as food, drink, shelter, and relaxation do not satisfy for long because they do not lead to the growth of self. Homeostatic experiences merely eliminate an organic need and restore the self to its previous condition. But the happiness that arises out of our conscious engagements with difficulty endures, according to Csikszentmihalyi, because each occasion of flow adds "complexity to the self" (1990, p. 46). What Csikszentmihalyi's research thus demonstrates is that difficulty is, in fact, an essential condition, which, over a lifetime, adds up to self-actualization.

An exploration into the paradoxical inner workings of happiness can help students discover its rich realities. But we must clear the air of a question. If flow occurs naturally when human beings engage with difficulty in a personally meaningful endeavor, what does it matter whether students learn about the psychology of happiness? What does it matter whether or not they redefine happiness to include difficulty? A good question, particularly since writing assignments based on sound composition theory meet all of Csikszentmihalyi's conditions of flow: they challenge students to nudge what Larson (1985) calls their "performance envelope" (p. 40).

Not necessarily. According to Csikszentmihalyi, being involved in a flow activity is no guarantee of a flow experience: "How we feel at any given moment of a flow activity is strongly influenced by the objective conditions; but consciousness is still free to follow its own assessment" (1990, pp. 75–76); a professional football player, for example, might be bored in the middle of a game most people would rank high among flow activities.

No matter how carefully we design for flow, many students may fail to experience it in writing because the powerful myth prevents them from noticing the evidence from their senses. People's workday experience exemplifies this phenomenon. Certainly, one reason people are reluctant to get out of bed on Monday mornings is because many jobs are neither self-generated nor personally meaningful. But Csikszentmihalyi noted:

> On the job people feel skillful and challenged, and therefore feel more happy, strong, creative, and satisfied. In their free time people feel . . . their skills are not being used, and therefore they tend to feel more sad, weak, dull, and dissatisfied. Yet they would like to work less and spend more time in leisure. (1990, pp. 159–160)

An observation of Maslow (1968) further illuminates this point. He described the central role of perception in a person's ability to have "peak-experiences":

> My experience is that whenever I have lectured approvingly about peak-experiences, it was as if I had given permission to the peak-experiences of some people, at least, in my audience to come into consciousness. (pp. 88–89)

What I am recommending, then, is a little benign tinkering with our students' definitions of happiness. By sharing Csikszentmihalyi's findings with them, we can help students recognize what actually does make them happy rather than what their cultural programming tells them will make them happy. Csikszentmihalyi can teach them to anticipate flow in their laborious work so that they will embrace rather than dread writing assignments and (using Alice Brand's apt term) "recruit" (1983, p. 441) emotion into their encounters with the blank page.

Each of us can think of ways to include these new/old discoveries about the nature of happiness in our pedagogy to help our students approach even the most arduous project as a source of happiness. What follows is a miscellany of projects that I have used in basic writing, freshman composition, and research classes.

The first has students examining media definitions of happiness, thinking about their elders' definitions and articulating their own. Later projects introduce students to Csikszentmihalyi's findings on happiness and ask them to examine their own lives in light of flow psychology.

As classes began, I told my students that happiness would be a recurring topic during the semester. I made Aristotle's point, in Book 1 of his *Nichomachean Ethics,* that happiness is the mother of all motivations, and added that for this reason I consider it a central educational issue. In another project, I asked my students to bring in and present three images or artifacts representing aspects of the media's definition of happiness. Among their exhibits the following week were Bud bottle caps, copies of *Sports Illustrated,* dollar bills, Marlboro and Camel coupons, autographs of sports heroes, a *Star Wars* video game, CDs, and ads for a wedding dress, a strip club, and Absolut Vodka.

As students presented their items, I asked them to look for recurring themes. For example, advertising images mimic sensations in flow—the refreshment of novelty ("NEW!"); heightened senses of color (camera/film ads) or sound (stereo ads); and the sense of being lighter than air (bubbly soft drink ads and those using images of sailing and ballooning). Advertisers market sensory simulations of flow/happiness in lieu of the Real Thing, which, of course, is not for sale but can be obtained with ease by engaging with difficulty. This assignment prepared students for further discussion of the idea of happiness by making visible the narrowness and easy glitz of the media's definition.

Another definition exercise provided a sharp contrast. One day I put two columns on the board: "happiness for our elders" and "happiness for us." Then I asked students to compare the way they and their grandparents find happiness. After filling the two columns, my students concluded that for the older generation central ingredients for happiness were work, family, religion, cultural traditions, and patriotism. An important insight was the connection between happiness and work. "In our free times, we watch TV," commented one student. "But my grandpa, he'll go to work. He loves to work." When students recognize how free the elderly can be from media stereotypes of happiness, it may be easier for them to relinquish these stereotypes.

After my students had examined their definitions of happiness and those of their elders, they wrote their own. Most felt happiness lay in loving relationships, financial security, relaxation, entertainment, and sports. A large number defined happiness as the absence of difficulty: happiness was having "no worries," no troubles," "no problems," "feeling carefree." Certainly, loving relationships are central to happiness and the "no worries, no problems" definitions might reflect the serious health, family, and financial crises our students so often face. The disheartening thing is that of the 67 students responding, only 17—one quarter—included challenging themselves or pursuing goals anywhere in their extended definitions of happiness. And yet we'd want every university student to say, I feel like I'm walking on air when I take on a really laborious project, struggle with it, and make it my own. What is a university if not a place for people who find happiness in the rigors of discovery and creation?

Once my students had consciously defined where in their lives they expected to find happiness, I hoped that exposure to Csikszentmihalyi's *Flow* would help them expand those definitions. At every opportunity I brought into the classroom—under the guise of diagnostics, essay prompts, exercises, and even grammar drills—passages from Csikszentmihalyi that addressed the connection between difficulty and happiness. Productive essay prompts may be found throughout *Flow*, for example: "Periods of struggling to overcome challenges are what people find to be the most enjoyable times of their lives" (p. 6) and "[e]njoyable events occur when a person has gone beyond what he or she has been programmed to do and achieved something unexpected, perhaps something even unimagined before" (p. 46).

A unit on paraphrasing and summarizing provided an occasion for students to work closely with important passages from *Flow:* I teamed Csikszentmihalyi's "contrary to what we usually believe" (p. 3) quotation with Rilke's on "dragons that in the last moment turn into princesses." Students paraphrased the passages and then wrote about times in their own lives when they had experienced its truth (sports excluded!)—a job, volunteer work, a chore, or a challenging project they had set for themselves.

Like much of the wisdom we wish to pass on to young people, the truth of this unglitzy message may not be immediately apparent. It may be years before students actually stretch to experience this truth. Or it may be the next day. Or it may never be. As composition teachers, we can only remind students, over and over again and in different ways, of this expanded idea of happiness, give them opportunities to push their performance envelopes, and wait.

The research paper class may be what we wait for. The terrifying rigors of this first serious, professional paper, the sense of its importance, the terrific sense of accomplishment any student even half successful feels on printing out the crisp white final pages—these make the research paper a perfect candidate for a first conscious experience of flow in writing. In the first weeks of this class, I reiterated the formula: At the thought of this paper you may experience terror and despair; but you will seize the bear by the ears and you will be surprised by happiness, flow. I alerted them to all the masks their fear would take: the sudden domestic obsession that leads to starched tablecloths or investments in semigloss paint, the compulsion to crawl under the bed with a quart of Chocolate Death Ripple. And I used their dry-run papers, written from controlled sources, to immerse them in the new findings on the psychology of happiness. I provided them with excerpts from, and reviews of, *Flow* and articles on the psychology of happiness, drawn from *The New York Times, Psychology Today,* and the *Utne Reader.*

As students began their work, they kept process journals, recording not only their discoveries and library strategies, but also their emotional states as they worked their way through their laborious project. And I entertained them with purple passages from my own process journals.

Process journals are useful for drawing students' conscious attention to their emotional states during writing; surveys are useful for drawing attention to their emotional states after writing is over. We think of surveys as serving the survey-giver; but it's likely that they serve the respondents more. What is a survey if not an invitation to examine and reflect on one's experience? Students completed surveys at two points during the research paper class. I gave them an informal survey the day they handed in their first draft and a formal survey the day they handed in their final paper. With their first drafts, I wrote these survey questions on the board: "During the days before you started writing, how did your body/mind feel? During the writing process, did you experience any strong positive feelings like excitement, exhilaration, happiness? Did you ever experience any of these eight characteristics of flow that Csikszentmihalyi identified?"

Eighteen out of twenty-three students reported feeling flow.[1] Typical before-and-after responses were

During the days before I started writing, my body felt anxious. . . . My mind felt overwhelmed, disorganized. . . . During the writing process I felt . . . over-joyed, . . . I lost track of time;

Before I started writing, my body felt very horrified . . . I felt so weak. . . . Yes, I did experience "flow"—I felt very challenged and I feel a great sense of ac-complishment now that I've met my challenge;

[Before writing I felt] submerged in an Arctic-like body of water. . . . When the words . . . began to just fly right out of my head, down to my hand and onto my paper. . . .

The day my twenty-five researchers turned in their final papers, I passed out an anonymous survey that I would see only after grades were in. I intro-duced several survey questions with key passages from *Flow*. The survey opened with the already-familiar passage about the best moments of our lives occurring when our minds or bodies are voluntarily stretched to their limits. "Does this passage relate at all to your experience working on your research paper?" I asked. Three students responded No, and 22 students responded Yes: "Yes, it comes very close to what I was feeling"; "Yes, . . . when I accomplished what I thought was difficult, I was proud of myself"; "Yes, I feel like this is the way I see life, so I am rather enthused by this passage."

"Overcoming a challenge inevitably leaves a person feeling more capable, more skilled" wrote Csikszentmihalyi (1990, p. 41). I asked my students if they felt stronger, more skilled having completed their research paper? Twenty-one out of 22 responded Yes. I then asked, "As a result of our study of flow/happiness, do you feel that you are more aware of your feelings before, during, and after writing than you were before you took this class?" One said No; 19 said Yes. One wrote, "I have more courage now." I asked, "In the future, will you approach difficult writing projects with less dread and more anticipation?" One student responded No and 18 responded Yes.

The purpose of these surveys was not, of course, to gather data demon-strating to me that arduous writing brings happiness. The purpose was to demonstrate it to my students. Reading these results to students—how one writer after another began in misery (the termites, the horrified body) and ended in elation—is perhaps the best way to drive home the point that difficulty and happiness go hand in hand.

Csikszentmihalyi's theory of flow can unmask the fraudulent images of happiness foisted on our students. Such an act is liberating for all students: our

1. Two prep school students showed some pleasure at the prospect of the research paper, suggest-ing that their backgrounds had programmed them to anticipate happiness from laborious encoun-ters and supporting my belief that exposure to the psychology of happiness has particular utility for developmental students.

poor students, humiliated by the media equation happiness = spending power, and our affluent students, surfeited and betrayed by material possessions and consumer entertainments. Csikszentmihalyi can help our students experience the existential difference between consuming and making, between the shopping mall and the blank page. The mall offers unnumbered products, experiences, and emotions to consume—none of which requires a spark of creative spirit or effort. The mall says, "You can relax. I have everything. Everything depends on me." But the destructive subtext is "You are nothing." On the other hand, working on a difficult writing project is anxiety-producing. "You better worry," says the blank white page. "I have nothing. Everything depends on you." But the constructive subtext is "You are everything."

References

Aristotle (1984). *The Nicomachean ethics.* (D. Ross, Trans.) New York: Oxford.

Brand, A. (1987). The why of cognition: Emotion and the writing process. *College Composition and Communication, 38*, 436–443.

Csikszentmihalyi, M. (1990). *Flow: The psychology of optimal experience.* New York: HarperCollins.

Csikszentmihalyi, M. (1994). *The evolving self: A psychology for the third millennium.* New York: HarperCollins.

Emerson, R. W. (October 18, 1834/1960). Journal entry, New York. In R. N. Linscott (Ed.), *Journals of Ralph Waldo Emerson.* New York: Random House/Modern Library.

Fire, J. F., & Erdoes, R. (1972). *Lame Deer, Seeker of visions.* New York: Simon & Schuster.

Larson, R. (1985). Emotional scenarios in the writing process: An examination of young writers' affective experiences. In M. Rose (Ed.), *When a writer can't write.* (pp. 19–42). New York: Guilford.

McLeod, S. (1987). Some thoughts about feelings: The affective domain and the writing process. *College Composition and Communication, 38*: 426–435.

Maslow, A. H. (1968). *Toward a psychology of being.* New York: Van Nostrand.

Reich, C. A. (1970). *The greening of America.* New York: Random House.

Rilke, R. M. (1908/1993). *Letters to a young poet.* New York: Norton.

Swanbrow, D. (1989, July–August). The paradox of happiness. *Psychology Today,* 37–38.

Zill, N., Nord, C. W., & Loomis, L. S. (1995). *Adolescent time use, risky behavior, and outcomes: An analysis of national data.* Washington, DC: Department of Health and Human Services.

Entering Wonder

Sherry Swain

Recently, while waltzing to the music of a five-piece orchestra, I was overcome by a feeling of surrealism. Conscious thought dissipated; a sense of wonder filled my being. Following my partner's lead required no effort; I had but to focus on his face, and somehow my feet knew the steps and turns of the dance. Lights whirled and blended into a fluid pallet. Faces of the other dancers and patrons melted into a universal smile. Life's complexities spun themselves into perfect harmony during those moments. In this trancelike dream, joy and dance became one, each equal to the other.

Describing that dance experience to a friend, I commented that other patrons of the restaurant as well as the musicians had applauded and asked for more. Unaware of the presence of others during the dance itself, I surprised myself by enjoying the attention it generated. "Is it okay to enjoy the applause?" I asked my partner.

"You can thrive on it!" he assured me. The music began for the next dance; I slipped easily and naturally back into the surrealistic space. And so it went for the remainder of the evening. During the hiatus between dances, I sipped wine and chitchatted with friends. But with the first step of each new dance, I entered the sacred space once again. It was as if the dancing itself were a crystal pool of magic. The music surrounded me like gentle waves, and when it paused, I floated to the edges and remained suspended, waiting for the music's invitation to reenter the mystical pool.

"You were in 'the zone,'" my friend explained, "the magical place that athletes strive to enter—the state in which they can do no wrong." Suzanne Langer writes that dance is "an apparition of active powers, a dynamic image." It is not so much the music or flowing garb or rhythm or steps themselves, but rather the display of interacting forces that creates the aura. "Two people . . . seem to magnetize each other; . . . to be animated by one single spirit, one Power" (Langer 1957, 10). It was this Power, this sense of wonder, that consumed me that evening on the dance floor. And it was this Power that brought forth insights for my classroom.

The Spiritual Side of Writing: Releasing the Learner's Whole Potential. Edited by Regina Paxton Foehr and Susan A. Schiller. Portsmouth, NH: Boynton/Cook-Heinemann, 1997. Copyright © 1997 by Boynton/Cook Publishers, Inc. Reprinted with permission.

A few years ago I heard Donald Murray say, "Writing that is easily written is easily read." Similar thoughts rushed through my mind during the dance that evening and continue even now as I reflect on the experience.

Easy dancing is beautiful dancing.
What is easily danced is easily, joyously observed.

Is this true of all art? Are paintings easily painted the artists' masterpieces? Is music easily composed joyously received? Is teaching that comes through wonder, naturally and spontaneously, the best teaching?

I had entered the place of wonder once before on a mountainside in North Carolina. I was writing, not dancing, on that day. The following excerpt is from my journal.

10/19/91

I am perched on a large flat gray stone that emerges from the mountainside. Below me a tiny gurgle of water flows over stones and sticks and under the ivy-covered footbridge I crossed to get here. I can hear the voices of tennis players and the few cars moving around the hotel parking lot, but I am ignoring them. Behind me, I imagine the family of squirrels I disturbed with my noisy scramble up the hillside is watching me, wishing I'd go away.

Now the wind rises, pushing leaves to the ground as it moves through the painted forest. The cool gray stone feels hard; the honest smell of the earth permeates the air; a King cab pickup truck chugs across a rustic one-lane bridge. Small trees, hugging the forest floor appear half lemon, half lime. The dark red leaves are missing this year, replaced by brilliant rose-colored leaves that move with the wind like Spanish dancers. Far above my head, the giants' tufts of dark green, gold, and brown are framed by the china blue sky.

Before me a graceful dogwood spreads a salmon canopy that reaches over the stream in one direction and back this way almost to my rock. Behind me, further up the mountain, its twin displays slightly darker foliage. And I marvel at the idiosyncrasies with which God has blessed us—that two of the same species growing on the same mountainside can be so nearly alike, yet distinctly different.

If man had created the world, every dogwood would look exactly the same. Not only does God alone have the power to create life, he has infinite appreciation for the diversity of life. With the exception of a few people of spirit, mankind spends lifetime after lifetime trying to standardize the diversity God created. Is it not blasphemy to paint and saw and bend and tie one dogwood so that it is outwardly identical to the other?

Oh, God, what are we doing to our children? Must they all master the same body of knowledge to be loved by fellow humans? Must they all read the same books, spell the same words, and write on the same topics to be valuable?

A few days later, taking part in reading workshop with my first-grade students, I reflected in my journal on the need for a classroom environment in which students can enter a place of wonder.

10/22/91

Saturday I spent several hours sitting on a rock on the side of a mountain writing. It was wonderful being still, being aware of the smell of earth, the play of squirrels, the colors of leaves, the sound of bubbling water. I value silent time in the classroom also, time for turning inward and reflecting. In *Living Between the Lines,* Calkins writes of a teacher who attempted to capture true writing silence for her classroom. She had wondered if it were really possible. I, too, wonder. I have no trouble filling these pages during our special journal writing time, but is the depth of reflection and thinking that was with me on the mountainside with me here?

Is it possible to bring children close enough to the mountainside in the classroom so that they will search out their own cool gray stones when they leave here?

How do we bring the mountainside and the apparition of dance into our classrooms? How do we invite our students to enter the zone, the place of wonder where insights become illuminated, where the difficult becomes easy, where complex details melt into wholes? I've heard a colleague talk about "educating the deep place," but he advises that we must teach to it indirectly, obliquely, and that unless a student decides to share an insight or experience with us, we may never know for sure that we have been successful. Sometimes my colleagues in secondary and college education share anecdotes of times their students have tapped into that place of wonder. As a teacher of first-grade children, and as a teacher of teachers in graduate courses, I am sometimes asked by those colleagues whether or not it is possible to reach that deep place in little children or, indeed, whether or not such a place exists in children.

My response to their query is an emphatic "Yes!" My students are whole, complete people—still growing and developing as we all are—but whole and complete nevertheless. And they possess that deep spiritual core that defines all humanity. To the extent that it is nurtured, it will grow. Suzanne Langer describes this feeling core as a sense of life that exists, like a waterfall, only if it continues its motion (1957, 48). Like my colleagues who teach older students, I must offer my students mountainsides and music, allowing personal connections to take hold obliquely and indirectly and then move along. This theory speaks to my teaching of graduate students as well as primary students. It's not the age of the student that invites wonder; it's the process that allows students to enter the illuminated zone. Three possibilities for classroom experiences rooted in academics, yet filled with openings for students to enter their own spiritual spaces, include silence, sky journaling, and reflection.

Silence

Silence in my classroom is a part of the daily routine of reading workshop. First the children and I (and sometimes guests) read for twenty or so minutes. I, of course, read silently, but the children, while engaged personally, can often be heard inventing voices for the characters in their books. "Mama, I've come for your youngun," Victoria reads from Molly Bang's *Wiley and the Hairy Man.* Her voice is deep and raspy; her head nods emphasis on every word. Then a high-pitched voice in reply, "You can't have him, Hairy Man!" Across the room Ben rests his chin in his palm, pushing his gold-rimmed glasses a little higher as he reads yet another book about the human body. Gerilynn and Greta read Ogden Nash's poetry. Jackson and his friend Christopher read *The Boxcar Children* together on the small porch outside the classroom. Occasionally they confer, giggle, and reread a passage together before going on. So silence in this case doesn't mean physical silence but metaphorical silence, an exclusive time for swimming around in text, a time for shutting out all that is not reading.

Physical silence does, however, permeate the twenty or so minutes of time set aside for journal writing. On a videotape depicting the whole process in my classroom, viewers see and hear children reading aloud from their books; yet after the children begin writing in their journals, viewers usually ask me to turn up the volume. "I haven't changed the volume," I reply. "There is total silence in the classroom." The children write; I write; any visitors present also write. When the timer signals an end to the writing time, a few children stop writing; some ask for more time; most just continue writing. They have found their deep places and are reluctant to leave. Just as adults can write into their places of wonder through doors of silence, children can come to know their reflective inner selves through silence and writing.

The following entries from Jerry, one of my first-grade students, show that young children can indeed use moments of silent writing to explore the wonder of the inner self.

In this entry Jerry unconsciously uses the rhetorical device of contrast, exploring antithetical elements such as winning and losing and then culminating with his real question of wonder: Why do parents cry? Jerry, an only child who lives with his grandparents rather than his parents, enters the silence with surface issues, first addressing winning and losing, overcoming a fear of darkness, and learning to swim. Then after writing five sentences about family members, Jerry allows his real question to flow onto the page. It is as if Jerry descends a stairway into a deep well, and when he touches its depths with his question, he quickly ascends, scrambling to the surface with the argument about how fast or slow he runs.

On one page of his journal, Jerry played with his initials, *J. T.*, arranging them into various shapes that might become his logo. Working in the silence of the classroom and finally deciding on the shape in the upper right-hand corner, one that reminded him of an ice cream cone, he wrote a rationale and in so doing

Jerry—"Reflections"

My cousn lost the champusihp.
Rut he got o crafy. I usr to
be sekrd of drdk. I'm hot
sckrd now I cuo dn't svim. I
no . how now. Hong is Thais
sustr. I do not have a sustr. I
have a uckole, and, a unt. Jake
has brutre named frichly. Trey
has a sustr. Why do pinrti cry
Trey told Tim that Jerry ran
slwoe. But he don't. I am
a swimer.

3/8
My cousin lost the championship.
But he got a trophy. I used to
be scared of the dark. I'm not
scared now. I couldn't swim. I
know how now. Hong is Thai's
sister. I do not have a sister. I
have an uncle and an aunt. Jake
has (a) brother named Frenchy. Trey
has a sister. Why do parents cry?
Trey told Tim that Jerry runs
slow. But he don't. I am
a swimmer.

Jerry—Logo

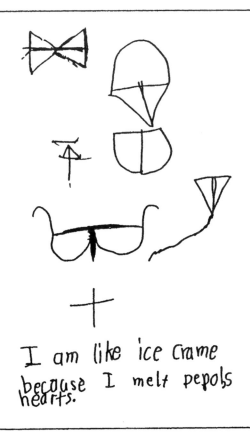

I am like ice crame
because I melt pepols
hearts.

3/28
I am like ice cream
because I melt people's
hearts.

created knowledge of himself. He made himself aware of his connection with other people, with an unseen yet felt spiritual life in which he has the power to affect those around him.

In the following poetic entry, Jerry writes from his own experience and seems to embrace the river as an archetype for his own actions and feelings.

Unaware of the history of rivers as sources of spiritual wisdom, Jerry follows his intuition as it leads him to the river as a personal place of wonder. In the daily routine of silent journal writing, Jerry is writing his way into that deep inner well, asking and answering his own questions on his journey.

Journal-writing, or *freewriting,* to use Elbow's term for uninterrupted writing in silence, tends to begin with jabber, noise, static, nonsense. Yet somehow

Jerry—River

8:35 am. ～～～～～～ 4/10

River, River
If a River could talke?
what would it say? I
wonder. Maybe it will tell
a story, or cry. If it
Was alive what will it do?
Sit, walke, run; I don't
know what it will do. Do
you?

4/10
River, River
If a River could talk?
What would it say? I
wonder. Maybe it will tell
a story, or cry. If it
was alive what will it do?
Sit, walk, run; I don't
know what it will do. Do
you?

this cacophony of internal noise makes room for thought and insight expressed in the true voice of the writer. Graves refers to silence as the "first teacher of writing" (Graves 1994). Students like my student Jerry show us over and over again how silence and writing combine to create insights and windows through which we catch a glimpse of them.

Sky Journaling

Once my students have experienced sky journaling, they clamor for it often. Since it requires a warm day, dry ground, and an absence of pesky insects like fire ants and honey bees, we're lucky to sky journal three times in the spring.

We begin in the classroom by connecting to earlier studies of the universe and atmospheric conditions. We discuss the miracle of one sky that covers all people of the world. Children tell about friends and family members living in other parts of the country, and together we marvel that Kelley's father and step-sister in Texas are being warmed by the sun at the same time we are. Finally, each child collects a journal and writing instruments and we walk quietly outside. As we stroll the large playground of our school, the children stop one by one and nestle into private nooks to look at the sky and write. Ethel curls up in the exposed roots of a magnolia tree. Orlicia finds the base of a crepe myrtle. Jereme chooses a square on the sidewalk. Leif sinks into a clover nest. I too find a quiet place where I can appreciate not only the beauty of the sky but also the beauty of twenty-three children connecting with the universe and with themselves.

Although initially observing the physical beauty of the sky, we are free to let our minds dance off in any direction, guided by the images above or the sounds around us. We write and write and write. After about thirty minutes, I catch the eye of one or two children, and we begin to collect ourselves quietly. Often children who have joined the group open their journals again, squat on the ground surrounded by their friends, and continue their writing. Back in the classroom, we sit in a circle on an area rug while volunteers share their journal entries and thrive, as I did after the waltz, on the responses of their classmates. Skywriting allows them to tap into something spiritual, something surreal. Most children have several pages of text, so we respond by helping each other identify the kernel of meaning in each entry. The children recopy these kernels on cloudlike shapes and post them in the hallway. A selection of these kernels follows.

> It seems as there is a king that
> rules the white clouds.
> And it seems as there is a king
> that rules the gray clouds.
> The sky owns the clouds.
> —Bryan

> I see clouds.
> I see the sun.
> I see the color white
> up in the sky.
> I see the color blue.
> I miss my friend Will.
> —Ethel

> It feels like the wind is blowing.
> It sounds like the birds are singing. They are
> up in the sky.
> I feel like dancing with the clouds.
> —Orlicia

It makes me happy to see
the sun.
God is in the sky and
Angels are in the sky.
                    —Danielle

I want to know
How the sun looked
When it was a baby.
                    —Jereme

The sky looks like it
is waving to me.
I see an eye.
It seems to be
Looking at me.
                    —Peter

Look again at the last line of each child's poetry. Even as adults, we can leap with them from the reality of the situation to the place of wonder their words reveal. They were not asked to write poetry, just to enjoy the sky and to write whatever came of the experience. They wrote from places of wonder, allowing their inner voices to surface and create what Langer (1957) labels as poetic image or *semblance,* that which need not correspond to actual things or experiences. Poetic creation as Langer describes it is more like a virtual object, a composed apparition of a new human experience (1957, 148). I wish I had thought to ask how the sun looked as a baby.

Reflection

Clarissa Pincola Estes on her tape *The Creative Fire* discusses the phenomenon of artists inspiring each other. The creative energy of the art or the artist at work generates more creative energy. If your creative fire has dimmed, she advises, go where someone is creating something—anything. Just being in the company of an artist who is creating can inspire you to create in your own form (Estes 1991). I've seen her theory at work in my own life. In fact, this article was inspired by the dancing I mentioned at the beginning. I've also seen it at work dramatically in one of my students.

Jackson was a natural poet. His first journal entries, as well as many later ones, consisted of line after line of syllables arranged rhythmically. He wrote with fervor. Naturally reflective, he read quietly, discovering what he had written as he read, almost unaware of his audience of classmates. Often he would pause and giggle at some joke or play on word sounds known only to himself or perhaps to himself and his inner self. Jackson knew about his own deep place before coming to my classroom. I had only to allow him to enter that place and to teach to whatever erupted from it. One of my supreme joys was in discussing

Jackson's work with his parents, who understood and valued what they called his "rich inner life."

Jackson was born into a reflective family; his father, an artist, keeps journals in which he connects his own spirituality with his paintings. His mother, a dancer, often uses her talents to celebrate her own spiritual beliefs. In late spring, Jackson's family took him out of school to attend a gallery showing of his father's latest paintings in Memphis, a breathtaking series featuring Jackson and his mother emerging from a primeval forest. Upon the family's return, Jackson's father shared his son's trip journal with me. He had carefully transcribed each of Jackson's entries on index cards, but he also shared the original wire-bound notepad that contained the tiny lettering I'd come to recognize as Jackson's. I was overwhelmed with the volume and variety of writing that Jackson had completed over a single weekend. The experience of the gallery showing, the gala surrounding the event, the public applause of his father's work, and the powerful subject matter of the paintings themselves had combined to inspire the poet in Jackson. The following transcriptions represent a small portion of the writing that flowed from this seven-year-old boy in the span of a few hours after immersing himself in his father's art.

The Party

Tonight I went to Dad's party. We saw Dad's painting of me and Mommie. Many people were there. They looked at Dad's painting. They applauded when Dad gave a speech. He read from his journal and he read poems by [Rainer Maria] Rilke. [Jackson's experience at the party led him to create the following poems.]

Cat Eyes

I can hardly
See them glow—
They turn so slow
I can hardly
See the middle
It's as dark as the
black fiddle—
You can see they're
Wonderfuller
Than me—
I just can't believe!

One Everything

One man
One house
One castle
One horn
One you
One me
I can be most anything!

"16"

2 + 2 is 4
4 + 4 is 8
8 + 8 is 16
That is as far as
I can go—Now it's
Your turn to
Help me.
Count now:
1 2 3 4 5 6 7 8 9
10 11 12 13 14 15
16

Splashing Rain

I told my friend Dustin
I don't know why the
Rain came so suddenly.
Dustin said why don't
You ask your mom and
Dad so I did and my
Dad said, "I don't know."
My mother said the
same old thing—I just
Couldn't figure it out so I
Told Dustin and Dustin
said he heard all about
It. I said, "You did?"
We did and the sun
Came out!

Teachers and students can follow Jackson's example, using reflection to generate creativity. Whether I'm teaching graduate students or first graders like Jackson, I ask my students periodically to reflect upon their writing. This means deliberately perusing journal entries or other reflective writings and contemplating them in a metareflective mode. Through this process, they generate reflections on reflections as they look through their journal entries for signs of growth in reading or writing or simply to discover whatever they might about themselves as writers or human beings. The results sometimes suggest something spiritual, like the reflection on page 102 written by Laura after studying three notebooks of her own journal entries.

Laura is in a state of wonder contemplating having seen her inner self as a person apart from age and time. Her own growth is a personal miracle that leaves her without words. Her expressions "inside to outside," "miracle," and "can't believe" hint at the spiritual wonder this seven-year-old is experiencing as she reflects on her own journal entries.

Laura—Journal Evaluation

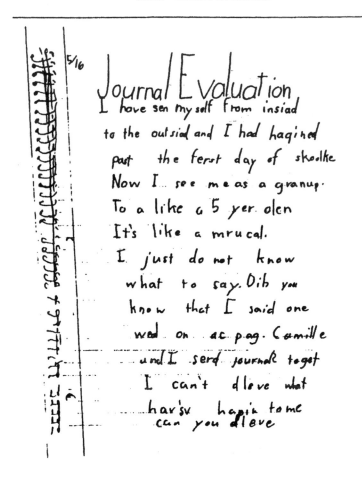

Journal Evaluation

I have seen myself from inside
to the outside and (all that has) happened
past the first day of school.
Now I see me as a grownup
to like a 5-year-older.
It's like a miracle.
I just do not know what to say. Did you
know that I said one
word on a page. [Laura explained orally that she wrote only one
word in her first journal entry.] Camille
and I shared journals together.
I can't believe what
has happened to me.
Can you believe?

Another student, Bryan, had struggled with minor depression when his good friend and neighbor moved away early in the school year. Subsequently, Bryan came to love our student teacher very much. On her last day, while his classmates lamented her leaving, he wrote a humorous journal entry chiding her for choosing to attend graduate school at a rival university. During our reflection process, Bryan reread his humorous entry, smiled, and announced, "I've learned that when someone leaves, I don't have to be sad."

I've found that by celebrating some children's reflective self-discoveries in the classroom, others become inspired to take the risk of introspection. After hearing Laura's journal entry and Bryan's announcement, many students pulled out their journals and began active searches for truths about their own inner growth. Our classrooms are fertile ground for becoming reflective communities. As we adult teachers share our own reflective lives, we invite our students to share their discoveries. But we must be honest in our reflections, in our writing, and with our sharing. A first-grade teacher who attempts to write like a first grader is fooling no one. Students respond to genuine writing, to real spiritual connections with others; they are not people under construction, waiting to participate in life. Students, whatever their ages, are already living their lives, already searching for spiritual connections with others, ready to respond to others' searches for connections with them. In a classroom that is also a reflective community, students like Laura's and Bryan's classmates are nourished spiritually and creatively by the spiritual and creative acts of their friends.

Somehow we must find pools where we, along with our students at any level, can immerse ourselves in the deep place, the zone, the place of wonder that illuminates insight and inspires creation. We must dance the easy dances, not just the technical steps but the divinely inspired apparitions. We must write the easy writing and compose the music of our feelings. We must seek out the silence that will open the doors to our spiritual places of wonder. We must look to the sky and to rivers and to the earth to nurture our wisdom. We must deliberately reflect on our own spiritual insights and wisdom. And when our creative pools run dry, we must learn to seek out and draw from another's pool. We must nurture the Jerrys who wonder, the Lauras who see themselves from the inside, the Jacksons who feast on the creativity of another artist. In our classrooms, we must teach the easy lessons, naturally and obliquely, celebrating easy, natural growth and wonder as the consequence.

Works Cited

Estes, Clarissa P. 1991. *The Creative Fire*. Sounds True Recording.

Graves, Richard L. 1994. "Writing Is Like Breathing." *Conference on College Composition and Communication*. Nashville, 18 Mar.

Langer, Suzanne K. 1957. *Problems of Art*. New York: Charles Scribner's Sons.

Wait, and the Writing Will Come

Meditation and the Composing Process

Donald R. Gallehr

> Do you have the patience to wait
> till your mud settles and the water is clear?
> Can you remain unmoving
> till the right action arises by itself?
> —*Tao Te Ching,*
> Stephen Mitchell, trans.

I am standing in my backyard, bow drawn, staring at an archery target seventy-five feet away. I am about to release my ninth arrow. The previous eight have hit the bull's eye. My mind is fluttering: I don't want to blow it. I want to hit all ten. My breathing is erratic, my left hand tired and shaking. I lower the bow and breathe abdominally, letting go of my fears and hopes. When calm returns, I again raise the bow. This time I think of snow sliding off a leaf at just the right moment. I draw the bow, wait for the moment, then release the arrow. Bull's eye.

My neighbor has been watching and calls over, "Good shot." To him, I am playing. He smiles and waves. He does not know that I am practicing meditation, the focusing of my whole body and mind on one point. If I were to sit cross-legged on a cushion, he would think me odd. He also does not know that I use this and other forms of meditation as an integral part of my writing. I do not know what he would think of my joining writing and meditation, but I know what my students think. For them it makes considerable sense.

Over the years I've been fascinated by the complementary nature of writing and meditation. Writing empowers meditation; meditation empowers writing. Insights derived from meditation are the material for writing, and vice versa. And some of the results seem identical—a sense of rejuvenation and control, a centering accompanied by courage, a clearer mind. Even the recent Western histories of writing and meditation seem to complement one another.

An earlier version of this article was published in *Life-Studies*, 4 (Winter 1988), 24–29.

Presence of Mind: Writing and the Domain Beyond the Cognitive. Edited by Alice Glarden Brand and Richard L. Graves. Portsmouth, NH: Boynton/Cook-Heinemann, 1994. Copyright © 1994 by Boynton/Cook Publishers, Inc. Reprinted with permission.

Until the 1950s, for instance, knowledge about the inner lives of writers writing was limited largely to conversations and correspondence between them. With the publication of the *Paris Review* interviews starting in the 1950s some of the secrets were finally out. In writing education this was followed by the pioneering studies of Janet Emig and Donald Graves, as well as the perceptive texts by journalist Donald Murray and teacher Ken Macrorie. Unlike their predecessors, these scholars, writers, and teachers described what they saw—the actual writing practices of writers.

At about the same time Eastern methods of meditation found their way West. This movement was led by the Japanese scholar D.T. Suzuki, whose works appeared in the late forties and fifties, and included practical, psychological, and philosophical aspects of Buddhism (1956, 1964). Suzuki influenced young Englishman Alan Watts (1955) as well as the Beat Generation of writers and poets, including Gary Snyder, Jack Kerouac, Philip Whalen, and Alan Ginsberg.

In the sixties and seventies, a number of individuals established highly influential meditation centers, including that of Soto Zen master Shunryu Suzuki, whose talks were published as *Zen Mind, Beginner's Mind* (1970); Chogyam Trungpa, the Tibetan Rimpoche who established Dharmadatu centers in several major cities and published such works as *Meditation in Action* (1969); Tarthang Tulku, who established a famous center in Berkeley and was the first to bring Tibetan practices to the West (see Anderson 1979); Dainin Katagiri, Japanese Zen Master in Minneapolis, author of *Returning to Silence* (1988), and teacher of Natalie Goldberg; and Vietnamese peace activist Thich Nhat Hanh who headed the Vietnamese Buddhist Peace Delegation to Paris and whose works such as *The Miracle of Mindfulness* (1987) introduced readers to meditation. And, of course, Hindu Marharishi Mahesh Yogi, who not only influenced hundreds of thousands through his Transcendental Meditation techniques, but also medical researchers such as Herbert Benson and Miriam Klipper (*The Relaxation Response,* 1975). The arrival of meditation in the West was also accomplished by Americans who journeyed to the East to study meditation and later returned to establish centers and training programs for laity and monks alike: in Massachusetts, Joseph Goldstein wrote *The Experience of Insight* (1976), and with Jack Kornfield wrote *Seeking the Heart of Wisdom* (1987); Philip Kapleau in Rochester, New York, wrote *The Three Pillars of Zen* (1965), and *Zen: Dawn in the West* (1980); and Walter Norwick in Maine described by Janwillem van de Wetering in *The Empty Mirror* (1973) and *A Glimpse of Nothingness* (1975).

This parallel disclosure of the practices of writers and meditators resulted in a wealth of "how-to" books and instructors. Some were reputable; others were not. The American hunger for a quick fix led to outrageous claims for learning writing or meditation in incredibly short periods of time, and for those who followed such paths, the disappointment and failure were certain and swift. "I tried it and it didn't work," or "I tried it for a while and use it from time to time," became by-products of these fast food approaches.

Fortunately, some Americans took the long road and wrote or meditated on good days and bad, deepening their understanding and broadening their abilities. A few continued to practice both, including James Moffett, the best known meditator/educator whose "Writing, Inner Speech, and Meditation" (1981) continues to serve as the theoretical foundation for practicing both writing and meditation.

Before connecting writing and meditation, let me briefly describe the activities involved in each. First, writing. Although composing is not linear, it has direction and form which hold true for most writers. Donald Murray was among the first to identify three stages: prewriting, writing, and rewriting, with the following subcategories:

Prewriting: collect, connect, rehearse
Writing: drafting
Rewriting: develop, clarify, edit

Later he revised the seven-step list to five: collect, focus, order, develop, and clarify. Betty Flowers (1981) took another approach by describing writing in metaphoric terms:

Madman
Architect
Carpenter
Judge

Regardless of the way individuals cut the pie, writing involves ideas, emotions, and language which change recursively over time, through reordering, adding, deleting, substituting, and reconceptualizing.

Like writing, meditation provides alternative approaches, but most contain the following: *Posture, Breathing, Awareness, Letting Go, Concentration.*

Posture

The posture for meditation is usually a sitting position, often on a cushion on the floor with legs crossed. When practiced in a classroom, students sit in chairs with their feet on the floor and their backs balanced, leaning neither forward nor back. Their hands are folded in their laps and their chins are tucked in slightly. Their eyes are either open or closed: if open, they rest on a point some six to nine feet in front of them.

Breathing

Several approaches to meditation begin by focusing attention on breathing, with meditators watching their inhalation and exhalation. Some proceed to breathing exercises which deepen the breath and concentrate the attention.

Awareness

As thoughts and feelings occur—as they invariably do even if meditators are trying to stay focused on breathing—meditators become aware of them, neither clinging to nor running away from them.

Letting Go

In some approaches meditators note or label their thoughts or feelings before letting them go, a mental decision which is often accompanied by physical relaxation.

Concentration

Letting go may be followed by a period of concentration in which thoughts cease. For most beginning meditators, it is a brief period lasting only seconds. Continued practice enlarges this period and allows it to recur several times during a twenty- to thirty-minute meditation.

When writing and meditation are joined, they produce four qualities of mind: *Awareness, Concentration, Detachment,* and *Balance.*

Awareness

Awareness of feelings and thoughts occupies a large portion of a beginner's meditation. Some call it witnessing, that is, watching thoughts and feelings as they arrive: watching as they stagger, strut, and bump into one another; and watching as they leave, some scurrying away, some shoved off the stage by more powerful thoughts and emotions. During meditation there is no jotting down but there is a noting—a rise of language to label and recognize, even, at times, to recall afterwards. Obstacles to this witnessing such as desire, aversion, sleepiness, restlessness, and skepticism, make it difficult to stay seated or to let go of thoughts and feelings.

Writers are involved in a similar process of awareness. For instance, Peter Elbow talks about nausea which may overcome writers during revision: "Revulsion. The feeling that all this stuff you have written is stupid, ugly, worthless—and cannot be fixed. Disgust" (Elbow 1981, 173). Successful writers, of course, know they can acknowledge and let go of disturbing thoughts and feelings until their mind once again clears. They also know that they will survive nausea, joy, doubt, or anything else their minds throw at them.

Janwillem van de Wetering travelled to Japan in the fifties to learn Zen meditation from a Zen master. Even though he was discouraged from reading about meditation on the premise that he would be tempted to compare his experiences to the "texts," he and others kept notes on their experiences. A similar technique employed by those using language to learn is called note-taking/note-making. It refers to *taking notes* on one side of the page about what happened, and making observations about those notes on the other or *note-making* side of the page. The activity is strikingly similar for both writers and meditators: awareness, reflection, and letting go.

In addition, successful writers and meditators know that hindrances, problems, and struggle are part of the territory. By treating them as old friends rather than enemies, they disarm them.

Based on my practice of meditation, I have added two awareness exercises to my advanced nonfiction writing classes. The first I call the worry sheet which uses mapping to discharge thoughts that bother students. In the center of a blank page we write the word WORRIES, circle it, then map words and phrases that represent our worries. After approximately ten minutes, we do a progressive relaxation exercise, letting go of our worries as we relax each part of our bodies, much as I let go of my fears and hopes before releasing the arrow in archery. Students say that increased awareness enables them to write for longer periods of time without interruption.

The second awareness exercise is based on the Steppingstones technique developed by Ira Progoff. Students jot down twelve events in their lives as writers—such things as writing letters to family, receiving particularly good or bad grades on a school writing assignment, and learning how to write in a new form (research paper, report, resume, proposal, etc.). They then choose one steppingstone and write the story of that event.

We differentiate between active and inactive steppingstones—between those that do or do not play a role in the students' current composing practices. Inactive steppingstones are merely memories. By "sitting with" active steppingstones, students deactivate them. Awareness of these steppingstones enables students to develop their identities as writers. Releasing these memories frees them to write.

Concentration

Among several forms of concentration, two relate to writing and meditation: focusing on one object; and focusing on objects as they occur. In meditation the mind can pay attention to a candle, mandala, artistic configuration, archery target, or any object of significance. Or the mind can focus on thoughts and feelings as they arise. The same is true of writing. The writers' mind can focus on an object or focus on a succession of events, ideas, or things. In both activities concentration works when we relax and hold the mind steady. Tightening up, of course, tires the mind.

Concentration allows us to see in detail. Betty Edwards, in *Drawing on the Right Side of the Brain* and *Drawing on the Artist Within,* sees this as a shift in hemispheric dominance that occurs when artists draw. We notice the stripes of the tulip, the lines around the eyes, the space that forms the backdrop of the portrait. Concentration also allows us to move beyond preconceived thought and cliché. As the veil of language drops, we see the object of our concentration clearly.

In the middle of my advanced writing course we develop our abilities to concentrate by practicing drawing exercises developed by Betty Edwards. We turn Picasso's line drawing of composer Igor Stravinsky upside down, then we draw it as we see it. Relaxed and attentive, we move our eyes and pencils slowly and carefully. I watch students, guiding them to draw only what they see, not what they imagine.

We also concentrate on listening without thinking, letting go of thoughts as they arise, working toward an uninterrupted attention to sound. We also practice with our other senses. When we eat, we just eat; when we touch, smell, and think, we notice the temptation of the analytical mind to distinguish one sensation from another: to compare, contrast, compartmentalize, and categorize. We acknowledge the presence of the discriminating mind, and make an appointment with it for later. We train our minds to concentrate for longer and longer periods, to observe in greater detail, and thus bring to our writing a rich collection of experiences.

We talk about the ability of the mind to observe itself (Sekida). For instance, we *observe* the computer screen with a story on it, we *reflect* on our observation, and we are *aware* of ourselves reflecting. We see that distractions from one-pointed concentration—that is, focusing on a single object—come not only from skipping from one object of observation to another, but also from shifting from observation to reflection to self-awareness. We notice that the power to concentrate is only one side of the coin; the other is the power to let go. When we try hard to concentrate, the trying gets in the way. The observation, for instance, has a smudge on the lens, the smudge of trying. So we let go of the trying. We wait for the mind to settle until we are attentive without effort.

Detachment

Donald Murray says of writers, "They must detach themselves from their own pages so they can apply both their caring and their craft to their work" (1982, 68). He then cites Ray Bradbury's practice of putting a manuscript away for a year before revising it, acknowledging that not many writers have the discipline or time to do this.

Beginning writers not only have problems with deadlines, they must also struggle with topics they identify closely with. Most writers, beginning and experienced, in fact benefit from being able to detach themselves because it helps them move more quickly from writer-based to reader-based prose before their drafts are due. Detachment in meditation comes from adequate attention to thoughts and feelings arising in us. It also comes from an ability to practice letting go. For beginning meditators, letting go is rarely final. Strong thoughts or feelings in particular return repeatedly in the same meditation or in subsequent meditations. Over time, however, meditators develop the "big mind" as Shunryu Suzuki describes it, a form of detachment that sees from a distance and places things in perspective. In addition, continued meditation reveals a dynamic rather than a static world, a world in which previously perceived solids are seen as consisting of moving parts. This is true on the physical level (as in atoms in motion) as well as in the world of thought collections of interrelated ideas.

When writers perceive a writing problem as a solid entity, they are apt to deal with it as a total rather than as parts and connections. Writers' block, for instance, is not a monolith but a combination of actions and reactions to discrete writing problems. By becoming aware of and letting go of these different pieces, writers can move on.

Zen, one form of meditation, uses koans or word puzzles to trick the mind into detaching, much as the upside down picture does in drawing. Koans cannot be answered logically. The question, "What is the sound of one hand clapping?" does not have a logical or rational answer. To practice detachment, I adapted the Zen koan to ask questions about writing which can be answered only intuitively. For instance, "What does this writing want to become?" forces us to move away from a rational identification with the writing to a detached intuition.

Answers to koans do not come immediately. We relax and wait, and waiting is one of the most difficult parts of both writing and meditation. Doubt begins as niggling and annoying, and as we wait the doubt grows and grows. I encourage my students to trust themselves, to relax and observe the question just as they observe the drawing.

Answers to koans have certain characteristics. They are *holistic*. Even if they are working on a segment of writing, they take it as whole unto itself. They are *surprising*. Because koan answers are not a product of the analytical mind, our intuitive mind is "surprised." Koan answers are *delayed,* that is, they take a period of time to arrive (Zen koans, which deal with issues as large as the meaning of life, may take months or even years to answer). Students who receive quick responses to koan questions say they have thought about the koan over a period of time, sometimes in response to a question previously posed by another student. Koan answers arrive *suddenly,* not in drips but in a gush. And koan answers appear *when least expected and often while writers are physically in motion.*

In the latter part of the course, we custom-make koans or questions about a particular work. For example, Irene spent her early childhood in Cyprus until her parents brought her to the United States. As a college student, she visited her relatives in Cyprus over the summer. When she returned to the United States she found herself writing about whether she should make Cyprus or the United States her permanent home. Analytical thinking to answer her question, "Where should I live?" was giving her usual, logical pros and cons. She couldn't decide. Nor could she complete her writing until she asked the koan question, "Where do I belong?" Then her answer was, "I'm an American." She had become not only a U.S. citizen but also an American. Where she lived at any given point her life seemed less important than knowing her national identity. In addition she felt she was not ready to make a lifelong decision on where to live; for now, she would stay in the United States with her friends and, after graduation, look for a job.

Balance

I think of balance as scales. When the needle hits the middle, the scales are balanced. For instance, writing from too little or too much information is imbalance. Similarly, revising too early leads to nit-picking, revising too late restricts writers to sentence-level changes. Gauging the right moment is balance.

In meditation, sitting without leaning forward or back, watching thoughts and emotions without clinging to or rejecting them, develops balance. Meditators find that too busy a schedule distracts. Too much sleep leads to sluggishness. Too much excitement results in overload. Balance is in the middle.

Students who let go of praise and criticism, maintain balance. Students who let go of the wish to get an "A" keep their focus on writing. Students who wait until distracting thoughts leave, proceed with their minds clear.

Applying meditation to writing in its most secular sense serves several purposes. It preserves the connection between meditation and its Eastern heritage. It refuses to reduce this profound and complex practice to gimmicks. And it is an enlightened response to the question of how to bring *all* our abilities to bear on writing that instructors have long sought.

References

Anderson, Walt. 1979. *Open Secrets: A Western Guide to Tibetan Buddhism.* New York: Viking Press.

Benson, Herbert, and Miriam Z. Klipper. 1975. *The Relaxation Response.* New York: William Morrow.

Edwards, Betty. 1979. *Drawing on the Right Side of the Brain.* Los Angeles: J. P. Tarcher.

———. 1987. *Drawing on the Artist Within.* New York: Fireside.

Elbow, Peter. 1981. *Writing with Power.* New York: Oxford University Press.

Flowers, Betty S. 1981. "Madman, Architect, Carpenter, Judge: Roles and the Writing Process." *Language Arts* 58 (7) (October): 834–36.

Goldstein, Joseph. 1976. *The Experience of Insight.* Boston: Shambhala.

Goldstein, Joseph, and Jack Kornfield. 1987. *Seeking the Heart of Wisdom: The Path of Insight Meditation.* Boston: Shambhala.

Kapleau, Philip. 1980. *Zen: Dawn in the West.* Garden City, NY: Anchor Books.

———. 1989. *The Three Pillars of Zen.* Anchor, NY: Doubleday.

Katagiri, Dainin. 1988. *Returning to Silence.* Boston: Shambhala.

Moffett, James. 1981b. "Writing, Inner Speech, and Meditation." In *Coming on Center: English Education in Evolution,* 133–181. Portsmouth, NH: Boynton/Cook.

Murray, Donald M. 1982. "The Maker's Eye." In *Learning by Teaching: Selected Articles on Writing and Teaching,* 68–71. Portsmouth, NH: Boynton/Cook.

Nhat Hanh, Thich. 1987. *The Miracle of Mindfulness.* Rev. ed. Trans. by Mobi Ho. Boston: Beacon.

Suzuki, D. T. 1956. *Zen Buddhism: Selected Writings of D. T. Suzuki.* Edited by William Barrett. New York: Anchor Books.

———. 1964. *An Introduction to Zen Buddhism.* New York: Grove Press.

Suzuki, Shunryu. 1970. *Zen Mind, Beginner's Mind.* New York: Weatherhill.

Trungpa, Chogyam. 1969. *Meditation in Action.* Berkeley, CA: Shambhala.

Van de Wetering, Janwillem. 1973. *The Empty Mirror: Experiences in a Japanese Zen Monastary.* New York: Washington Square Press.

———. 1975. *A Glimpse of Nothingness: Experiences in an American Zen Community.* New York: Washington Square Press.

Watts, Allan. 1955. *The Way of Liberation in Zen Buddhism.* San Francisco: American Academy of Asian Studies.

What I Learned from Verle Barnes

Richard L. Graves

"I wonder how many of you—or anyone in the organization, for that matter—would like to go on a sea turtle patrol?"

I thought I had missed something. The occasion was the fall business meeting of the officers of the Southeastern Conference on English in the Two Year College. The setting was a conference room in an Atlanta hotel. Sea turtles? Had my mind wandered momentarily?

"You see, the sea turtle is an endangered species. We need people to watch where they lay their eggs, and then put wire mesh around the eggs to protect them from predators."

"The island is uninhabited, just off the coast of Florida," he went on. "You can't imagine how beautiful it is, there in the Apalachicola Estuary. One of the best kept secrets of the Northern Hemisphere."

"Sorry, sea turtles are not on the agenda," the chair reluctantly stated.

I didn't hear anything else about sea turtles until the following February at the annual convention, this one in Jackson, Mississippi. There on the program under the general heading of "Creative Writing/Reading" was the title: "The Apalachicola Estuary: An Overview." The speaker was Woody Miley, manager of the Apalachicola National Estuarine Reserve. Also at this same session was—you guessed it—Verle Barnes[1]: "Earth, Water, and Good Writing: The Making of a Natural History Book." I couldn't resist; I went to the session. In a little less than an hour I learned a lot about the Apalachicola Estuary, but even more important I relearned a valuable lesson about the teaching of writing which I hope will remain with me for life. This lesson is so important and so profound that it touches the professional lives of writing teachers everywhere and determines in large measure how much our students learn. Yet it is so subtle that it is routinely overlooked and taken for granted. First, though, more about the estuary.

Apalachicola Estuary

From the session and from later conversations, I was able to piece together why Verle Barnes was so interested in the Apalachicola Estuary. In the early 1970s, while a graduate student in English at the University of Florida, he became

Teaching English in the Two-Year College, 15 (February 1988), pp. 20–24. Copyright © 1988 by the National Council of Teachers of English. Reprinted with permission.

interested in a series of articles appearing in the Gainesville and other news-papers. A battle was raging between the Corps of Engineers, who wanted to dam the Apalachicola, and a group of environmentalists who wanted the river to remain free flowing. Always something of an environmentalist himself, Verle followed the story throughout that spring, generally siding with those who wanted the river left as is. In order to see the situation firsthand, he decided on a memorable day in 1974 to visit the town where the river comes into the bay. Little did he realize that the experience would profoundly alter the rest of his life.

> *Friday, May 3, 1974: I come to the town of Apalachicola for the first time. You arrive from the east, along Highway 98, following the Gulf coast. You cross the bridge, and there's the town.*
>
> *Clean in the morning sun. Hint of salt spray in the air. Old. Quaint. Unpainted but clean. Everything is slow. Time stands still.*
>
> *To the left, across the bay, hazy in the morning sun, are the barrier islands. In the distance to the right are the fish houses and shrimp boats.*
>
> *But here immediately before me is the river. The river joins the bay, fresh water and salt intermingling, and I am overwhelmed. Sunlight everywhere is mirrored on the surface. Sun and river and bay, and I am here, breathing slow. I see and understand this holy place.*

It has been almost fifteen years since Verle first came to the Apalachicola. During that time he has spent many hours, many days, in the region, and even when he could not be there physically, his mind was filled with it. He has canoed the length of the river; spent time on the barrier islands which provide a haven for the endangered sea turtle; studied the estuary and surrounding flood plain; met local merchants, fishermen, townspeople; become acquainted with others who love the estuary with equal intensity; studied the plant and animal life of the region; speculated about the impact of hurricanes and other natural phenomena; read voraciously everything he could find about the history and ecology of the area. On several occasions he has conducted field trips, first with his journalism students, taking them from eastern Tennessee to Florida to study and write about the Apalachicola, and then later with other faculty members to protect the sea turtle. On a trip last summer, one of the students, Torrey Fields, fell in love with the beauty of the region, and then later became Verle's wife.

It is only natural that a book should grow out of this long-standing love affair with the estuary. Just off press, the full citation is Verle Barnes, *Portrait of an Estuary,* Corpus Christi, Texas: Helix Press, 1987. The publication is a story in itself. The book was originally conceived in 1979 as a chronicle of the struggle between the Corps of Engineers and the environmentalists. Over the years, however, it evolved into what the title suggests, a portrait of the estuary.

Finally, in the fall of 1986 a contract was signed with Helix, and the book became a reality.

The Lesson I Learned

As interesting as the estuary is, the lesson I learned most vividly is not so much about a place in Florida as it is about writing, and about teaching and learning. In all this, I have been eloquently reminded that the first lesson in teaching composition is that the writer must find his or her own subject. If young people do not care about what they are writing, if they do not own their work, or better, if their writing does not *possess* them, then it profits little to lecture on parallel structure or rhetorical strategy or whatever. If our students are ever to understand what writing really is, then they must come face to face with their own subjects, "A good subject is like a jewel buried in the bottom of the sea," I tell them. "You must dive deep, hold your breath, scrape away all the sand and mud and debris, take the jewel in your fingers, and bring it to the surface." I cannot give another person my subjects, for good writing has its origins and roots in the writer's soul. The kind of class I want is one where the discovery experience occurs routinely and where writing grows naturally out of that experience, taking its own direction, finding its own form, reaching its own audience.

What I really want is to bring Apalachicola into my classroom. That is, I want my students to discover a topic which captivates them in the same way the Apalachicola Estuary captivated Verle Barnes. I realize, of course, that Verle's experience is extraordinary and that my students may not experience anything with an equal intensity or that has such a long-standing effect. Still I want them to experience *some* of it. I want them to get perhaps a taste of it, to experience the quality of it directly.

This kind of discovery experience is not found in an English textbook. Indeed, the kind of experience I am describing is not an intellectual experience at all but rather an emotional response. It is not something you can put into a syllabus. You don't talk much about it, especially to department heads or deans or basic skills people. They wouldn't understand. But it's there, always in the back of your mind. You don't experience it directly but wait for it to happen. Perhaps you call it "creative energy," but it's not something you control directly. It's like an early morning fog. The more you try to capture it, the more it eludes you. So you lie back, and watch and wait for it to come, and then, Bingo! it happens. You sense its presence, nod silently, and pray that it becomes epidemic. Sometimes it does, but there are no guarantees.

What I am describing is not found in Aristotle or Quintilian or the standard writers, but rather in Carl Jung or Daisetz Suzuki or Meister Eckhart. More than likely they would phrase it this way: "The writer must become one with the subject." This concept of oneness or wholeness has been generally characterized by Walter T. Stace as "undifferentiated unity" and for centuries has permeated the literature of both east and west.

> Undifferentiated unity is necessarily thought of by the mystics as being *beyond space and beyond time*. For it is without any internal division or multiplicity of parts, whereas the essence of time is its division into an endless multitude of successive parts, and the essence of space is its division or parts lying side by side. Therefore the undifferentiated unity, being without any multiplicity of parts, is necessarily spaceless and timeless. Being timeless is the same as being eternal. Hence Eckhart is constantly telling us that the mystical experience transcends time and is an experience of "the Eternal Now." (25)

Being beyond time and space, this concept of undifferentiated unity is exceedingly difficult to explain. Once at the conclusion of a discourse on the topic, Eckhart told his audience, "If anyone does not understand this discourse, let him not worry about that, for if he does not find this truth in himself he cannot understand what I have said" (232). In other words, if you did not already understand it before I told you, you wouldn't understand it anyway. The clearest and perhaps most vivid illustration of the concept can be seen in a recent movie. The final scene of *Places in the Heart* is both breathtaking and puzzling. Because of the final juxtaposition of the characters, the viewer's sense of time and space is distorted. There is no dialogue, just music, and the viewer is left with a feeling of peace and wholeness. It is indeed a beautiful and gripping cinematic portrayal of what Stace calls "undifferentiated unity."

A classroom in which this kind of discovery experience happens is one in which there is much freedom. Not surprisingly, the idea of freedom occurs over and over throughout Eckhart's work. Eckhart's concept of freedom was revolutionary; at the time of his death, he was being tried by the Church for heresy. Although the following passage comes to us from a theological perspective, it takes little effort to see how the idea itself applies equally well in a pedagogical setting:

> Some with attachment cling to prayers, to fastings, to vigils, and to all kinds of exercises and mortifications. Attachment to any of these deprives you of the freedom to serve God in this present now and to follow him alone in the light by which he instructs you what to do and what not to do, free and new in each now, as if you did not possess (anything), nor desire (anything), nor indeed could do anything else. (208)

Eckhart could just as easily have been talking about the creative process. As long as we rigidly follow preconceived rules or principles or guidelines or whatever, we will miss out on the opportunity to reach that level of excellence in our writing that comes through the freedom to create. When rules are foremost in our minds, then our primary concern is the fear of making a mistake. When rules are foremost, we find ourselves in a passive stance, like someone in a game of dodgeball. Our primary concern is reacting to someone else (in the composition class, to the teacher) rather than finding our own way. So the lesson of freedom is important in the composition class. It requires intelligence but also courage. When our students fully understand this, they will likely say, "It's scary."

But as important as freedom is, it must be tempered with discipline, or it will remain mushy and accomplish no good end. The important thing, I believe, is that discipline must grow naturally out of freedom, and not vice versa. It is only after our students have tasted the ecstasy of writing their own subjects that we can demand excellence. Only then will they understand and be willing to endure the tedious work of editing. This is why Verle persevered year after year to find a publisher. This is why no is never really No. This is the creative energy that motivates and compels the writer to do the difficult work that writing is.

Someday I hope to go out on that barrier island in the Apalachicola Bay and maybe even put wire mesh around turtle eggs. I'll think of Verle. I'll think of writing. I'll wonder if I can communicate to my students what Verle's experience communicated to me. Will my students have the courage to seek out those subjects buried deep and lying dormant within their own experience, to bring them to the surface, to look them full in the face and to write? I will listen to the waves come in, and wonder.

Note

1. Verle Barnes taught at Roane State Community College, Harriman, Tennessee, before he died in an automobile accident in 1993.

References

Barnes, Verle. *Portrait of an Estuary*. Corpus Christi: Helix Press, 1987.

Blakney, Raymond B. *Meister Eckhart: A Modern Translation*. New York: Harper, 1941.

Stace, Walter T. *The Teachings of the Mystics*. New York: Mentor Books, 1960.

Focusing Twice Removed

Lesley Rex

"Before I read this I need to tell you that when I was seven I was raped." These words of warning were my freshman student's apprehensive introduction to her shocking account of being attacked by the neighbor's gardener's son. Taken completely by surprise, the class and I listened as she read the description she had been given ten minutes to write. Though its details were not particularly graphic, we were riveted. Her classmates were impressed and appalled by her open sharing. I was taken back by the unexpected intimacy of her subject. She had chosen to write about her rape knowing that she would be reading it to the rest of the class and that I would follow up with questions. Bravado was not her intent; her hands shook, her voice quavered, and her eyes welled up as she recalled the experience. Later I asked her how she had been able to write about such a painfully personal experience. "You told us that the one experience we didn't want to face, the one we felt in the gut, was the one that could potentially yield the best writing," she said. "I wanted to start with something that could really be good."

As startling as it seemed to me then and as shockingly insensitive as it may sound now, this was exactly the kind of experience that I had wanted her to write about when I asked her to volunteer. The late Robert Kirsch, writer and literary critic, had advised his students to "write from the gut" when selecting their topics. I had found this advice invaluable and passed it on to my students. This quarter, as usual, I had fortuitously asked the right student to share her "gut-level" prose. I chose Linda because she was the first student to show up for class that day and because she was a self-possessed participant in class discussions. This was only the third week of classes, so I had had nine sessions with my students—not enough to find out who would be best suited for this type of public soul-baring. For indeed, that was really what I had asked for and hoped would happen. The exercise's success depended mainly upon the sensitivity and openness of the student guinea pig.

This barbaric-sounding exercise was one that I used each quarter with my freshman literature students. It seemed to me that my students took for granted the insight and skill of published writers like E.B. White, George Orwell, and Joan Didion (the essayists with whom they were beginning the quarter). With typical freshman critical aplomb, they berated the themes, the style, and the

Freshman English News, 14 (Spring 1985), pp. 1–4, 8. Reprinted by permission of the publisher.

tone of these professionals. For them, criticising a piece of literature meant saying why they didn't like certain things, which meant identifying those elements which didn't fit their worldview, their experience, or their personal expectations for style and form.

I like to think that one of the reasons I am teaching literature, though certainly not the main reason, is to sophisticate my students' critical perceptions of literature. I spent quite some time pondering which word to use before I settled on "sophisticate," and even then I looked it up to make sure Webster thought it meant what I had intended. He said it means, among other things, to deprive of simplicity, to disillusion, to make worldly wise. That's what I was after. I wanted my students to see, appreciate, and absorb some of the wisdom they encountered in literature so that the rather simple view they have of themselves and of the world would expand—much like when the f-stop on a camera opens to allow more incoming light. What I wanted was a perceptual and intellectual transformation from an f-stopless Kodak instamatic mentality to a Canon with its changeable f-stop aperture and compatible film speeds. As the Canon is more sensitive to the light, producing more perceptive photographs, changing snapshots into art, I wanted my student readers more sensitive and sensible. For this to occur, they needed to willingly open themselves up, which, as Webster points out, requires an initial disillusionment with their present view of the world. They had to be willing to endure self-questioning, uncertainty, and confusion to be receptive to the complexities of the human condition and the artistry with which it is portrayed in literature. They had to open themselves to the *affect* and *effect* literature has on them: its power to lay hold of them, to impress them, and then to change them so they can truly see what literature has to say and the way in which it is said.

Dilation began the first day of class because my students arrived having read few engrossing essays and having written even fewer. Using the text *Eight Modern Essayists* (Wm. Smart; St. Martin's Press; 1980) we read and discussed a half dozen essays of three very different professional essayists which had come directly from the author's personal experiences, for example, E.B. White's "Walden," "Once More to the Lake," and "Death of a Pig"; George Orwell's "Shooting an Elephant," "How the Poor Die," and "Marrakech"; and Joan Didion's "On Morality," "On Going Home," and "Goodbye to All That." Far from being intimidated or even impressed by the professionals, the students were blasé. They had no idea of what was involved in writing an engrossing essay in the manner worthy of such critical attention. Pursuing my goal to sophisticate them, we read what the writers said about their own work, including the interesting comparison between Orwell's and Didion's respective renderings of "Why I Write." They listened to my laudatory analyses and strove to adopt the language and logic of the literary critic, but they were simply trying on the accoutrements of literary appreciation; they were not yet engaged closely in the text, not yet seeing it for themselves. While they were beginning to understand what they should be looking for and how they should be looking, they still had not read carefully and closely enough. Few of them could comprehend beyond a surface reading of the text that elicited the author's general meaning and intent. Of even more importance to the exercise I am presenting in this article was my observation that hardly any students had ever written an essay of the kind they were reading. They had not been asked to write about a critical personal experience that made the demands on their thinking and writing the professionals had made upon themselves. Another means of developing their appreciation had not been used. They couldn't understand what the essayists had accomplished by reading their texts, and, furthermore, they had not tried writing personal analyses themselves to find out what the professionals were up against to produce essays with power to engage, depict, and persuade.

I do not mean to suggest that their high school English teachers were remiss, though more often than not I find myself working with students who have written less than five essay-length papers throughout their four years of high school. While I advocate the use of this exercise in high school, the level of analytical sophistication it could produce would probably be less than what I expect from my college freshmen. Nevertheless, in principle the effect should be the same: becoming more aware of the difficulties involved in personal analysis and more sensitive to the accomplishments of those who master it intelligently and artistically with written language.

I had other reasons for choosing this kind of writing assignment in place of the traditional literary analysis essay. I thought it would make my students more mature writers as well as more sophisticated readers. Indeed, my freshman writers preferred the view that they were in the process of maturing rather than suffering from inadequacies. With exercises like this, I intentionally shifted my teaching to promote their maturity, whereas my former approach was to inform them of what they had somehow missed learning and needed to acquire to catch up. Seeing them as the pupa still at work in the chrysalis and not the fully formed, but crippled, butterfly gave both of us more leverage to experiment and explore possibilities that would not have presented themselves before.

Reading and writing, the prospective and the introspective, aligned in a more meaningful and useful way for the students when they did the focusing exercise. First they read the mature thinkers and writers who used their significant personal experiences as the gist from which they dramatized, narrated, analyzed, and theorized about life. Their probing reflection spun persuasive essays with the dramatic immediacy of fiction and the convincing urgency of real life actions and issues. E.B. White's pig's death took on farcical and tragic proportions as he recaptured the events of the pig's passing. We tittered as he recounted his much interrupted telephone conversation with the vet, sniggered as he described his pet dog licking the suds from the pig's enema bag, and fussed along with White about the intimate bonds that are broken by death. Speculations about the implications of loss and unmet expectations continued to reverberate within us long after we had put the essay aside.

Next, I wanted my students to ponder the causes of these reverberations and attempt to duplicate them in a writing assignment. After pointing out the levels of abstraction which manifest in various discourse modes within each essay (e.g. recording, reporting, explaining, classifying, advising, speculating), I explained James Moffett's manner of depicting the relationship between a writer and his/her subject (*Universe of Discourse* p. 35). Having synthesized several of Moffett's writer-subject progressions into a single chart for my students, we practiced finding evidence in the texts of the various relationships the writers had with their subject matter.

Recording what is happening	Dramatization	Sensory ongoing perceptual selection
Reporting what happened	Narration	Chronologic memory selection
Generalizing what happens	Exposition	Analogic of class inclusion and exclusion
Inferring what will, may, or could happen (or be true)	Logical Argumentation	Tautologic of transformation and combination

When they arrived, some of my students wrote almost entirely in the narrative mode; others were clinically analytical. None of them incorporated all modes in a single text. The dramatic impact and persuasive engagement of the professional essayists eluded them as long as they continued to write in a mode that restricted how they approached their subjects. I wanted them to write a three-page essay incorporating a variety of abstraction levels so they might expand and play with the many relationships they could have with their subject matter.

To generate their first drafts, I led them through an exercise I adapted from one that Cherryl Armstrong, a member of the South Coast Writing Project, had published in one of their newsletters. She had observed Keith Caldwell's Bay Area Writing Project presentation of "Focusing" at the South Coast Writing Project's Summer Institute and written her slightly modified version. You could say that my exercise is "Focusing" twice removed, and probably bears little resemblance and relates only slightly to the exercise Caldwell developed. I was after more than focusing from my students' writing, although that was an essential starting place. I wanted them to work their thinking and writing from description that put the writer in the critical moment of a significant personal experience through the modes of narration and exposition to persuasion, stopping short of blatant argumentation. After several trials, I had honed the steps of the exercise and my methods of delivery to the point where, in hindsight, students remarked about how satisfying and engaging their writing had been. They were also more appreciative of what the authors they were reading had accomplished.

Nevertheless, at its start each exercise was another shot in the dark, and as such could miss entirely. Before class I asked one student, Linda, if she would mind volunteering to read a piece of personal writing to the rest of the class. I identified the topic, explaining that it would be a descriptive piece everyone would write according to my instructions which I would then question her about while the class looked on. The other class members, after seeing our model, would group in dyads and question each other. Our purpose was to model the questioning procedure for the rest of the class.

Linda agreed and, along with the class, began following my instructions to generate the first draft. First, make a list of personal experiences that somehow changed you or your life so that you were not the same after they happened. They do not have to be major events. They could be something that the rest of us might consider insignificant (e.g. E.B. White's pig's death). However, they should be events that caused a shift in your perception of yourself, of life, or of "reality." You were not quite the same after these events happened. Those vivid memories that frequently crop up, especially those that flashed in your mind as I was giving these instructions, are the ones you want to write down. After generating a list of four or five, select one that you would be willing to write about. The best choice is usually the one that gives you a gut reaction when you recall it, the one that you definitely do not want to write about. Those are the incidents from which previous students have produced their best writing. Hearing these instructions, Linda changed her topic to her rape.

Second, after getting a vivid mental picture of the incident, jot down the colors and sounds that seem to stand out. Perhaps there was a particular smell or feeling that you had at the time; what was it? List the people who were involved and their distinguishing characteristics. Be brief. Next, listen to the dialogue that occurred if there was one. Write down key snatches of dialogue that would unlock the whole conversation.

Third, writers have to decide where to begin and end the episode they will write about. They have to arbitrarily cut a manageable chunk out of the whole story which may have its beginnings in early childhood and still be reverberating in their lives. However, they only want the most interesting piece, the part which is the context for the actual experience. Do this now: choose an appropriate manageable beginning and end for your experience. Remember that you are only writing a three-page paper and not a novel. (When students find it difficult to arbitrarily choose a starting point, I suggest they proceed by saying, "Once I was _____ when _____ " which forces them into a storytelling mode.)

Fourth, draw a linear time line on your paper. Place the first action of your story's plot at the left end and the last action at the right. As you mentally recall the actions in between, fill them in on the time line. Again, don't try to include every action, only the ones significant to the plot. Survey the actions you've plotted and pick the critical moment, the exact moment at which students have said they "shifted," "cracked," "realized," "knew," "changed" or "decided." Put an X on the time line at that spot. I usually interrupt the instructions at this point to provide an example out of my own experience. I tell them a story, hastily plot the event for them on the board, and mark a big X at the strategic moment. I then wax dramatic and describe the crucial seconds in vivid detail, including my own physical and emotional conditions along with the action and color of the moment.

Shifting their attention back to their own critical moments, while trying to maintain the sense of significance and intensity that has developed in the room, I give the next direction. Fifth, as you keep that critical moment clear in your mind's eye, begin writing it down, describing it so completely that it provides a language photograph of that moment for the reader. It puts the reader in the moment and allows him/her to recreate your experience. Write for about ten minutes.

By this time all the students were writing vigorously in the emotional fervor of the moment. Unfortunately, limited by time, I had to drag most of them away from their papers after ten minutes, turning their attention to Linda. Drenched by the emotional recall of their own triggering moment, they were primed for Linda's recounting of the moment of her rape.

> He threw me down on the floor, forcing me with his body to lie down. He pushed up against me. I was only seven years old, but I had guessed what he was going to do to me. I knew I had to try to get away. He hit me in the face, punched me in the stomach so I couldn't move. He started touching me in ways that I _____ . He ripped off clothing and starting fondling me. At this moment I felt a horrible feeling of disgust. I could not believe he was doing this to me. I started screaming louder and louder. He told me to shut up or he would kill me. So I did. Then he raped me, a seven-year-old child, shivering, terrified under his weight.

On other occasions students have recounted witnessing deaths of loved ones and complete strangers, divorce announcements, all types of accidents, and incidents involving animals. They, like Linda, had often completely forgotten about the incident until recently and had not discussed the moment with a mental health professional. Often, a recent event had brought the earlier incident to their attention. After Linda finished reading I asked her one of several versions of the question I eventually repeated ten times: "So what?" I softened the stark effrontery of it by saying instead after a respectful pause, "So Linda, what do you want to say to us about your rape?" Struggling to a more objective view of the experience so she could go on with the exercise, she said in a whisper, "That it is terrible to be raped when you are seven years old." She had leapt immediately to the point she wanted to make. Now I had to lead her back to fill in the explanation she knew but had not put into words. My next question was obvious. "What is so terrible?" She replied, "The pain, the fear, and the disgust." Wanting to provide a narrative context for the description she had given us and the analysis and explanation that was to come I asked her, "What happened that created the pain, the fear, and the disgust?" She began a narrative recounting of the events surrounding the critical moment she had described. By saying, "Then what?" I urged her narrative on to give us a chronological context of what had happened. When she had given us enough narration I moved her on by asking, "So what?" She responded by shifting into prose that was analytical and advisory. As though she were talking to another seven-year-old, she analyzed her feelings and actions. For a long time she had been afraid of men, including her father. She went on to explain her present difficulties with intimate relationships. She did not like to be touched. Moving from emotional saturation to mental engagement, the class was beginning to see the enormity and complexity of what Linda had meant by "it's terrible."

Even though I had ended the exercise by thanking Linda for being such a powerful model and releasing the rest of the class to perform the same "so what" exercise with their partners, Linda did not want to stop. She wanted to explain more about the incident and ask the same question that the rest of the class asked after I dragged them away from their partners: How do we write this up? What do we do next? My instructions sent them off to find writing havens as the next class entered: Write about your significant personal experience in such a way that you include description that puts us in the moment, narration that gives us a context, explanation that reflects insightful analysis, and a touch of persuasiveness that is speculative but not argumentative. The power of your recreated moment and your accompanying explanation should move the reader to adopt your point of view, or at least accept its validity. This essay is not meant to be objectively and logically argumentative. By this I mean that we are not trying to construct a logical argument for or against an issue (in Linda's case, rape) which could stand alone if the writer's personal experience were removed. We are not working to remove the writer's subjective authority from the issue. Rather we are working to draw the reader into the writer's subjective frame of reference. We want to use the writer's emotional expression to entangle the reader's sensibilities, and in so doing persuade the reader to adopt the writer's point of view, putting the reader in the writer's position where she/he experiences the crisis through the writer's eyes.

As one would expect, Linda's first draft, while gripping in its reporting of a shocking moment, is not a well-written depiction. I directed Linda away from concerns about graceful writing on this first draft. A series of refining and polishing drafts would follow, but for now the exercise had another objective—to affect the class so that its members would relate to each other and their writing in a different manner. I wasn't disappointed. Linda's exercise did more than rivet the class's attention; it changed the working atmosphere, the kinds of writing the students would do, and their attitudes toward their work. From now on they would not write what James Britton calls "dummy runs." The stakes were much higher than simply completing the assignment. Linda had put her heart into the ring, and the others knew they had to follow her lead to produce writing the rest of us thought worth reading. They now expected more from themselves. They were challenged to find something truly meaningful to write about. Several students moaned that unfortunately nothing dramatic had ever happened to them, so they had nothing of equal value to write about. Interestingly enough, these students, who thought they had lived uneventful lives, often wrote better essays for this assignment. Without the shocking impact of a significant crisis to rely upon, they had to wring more subtle and often sensitive significances out of their mini-traumas. Deeply reflective and perceptive essays were written about a decision to forgive a family member, the first shot on a hunting trip, and a father-daughter conversation.

Class members also expected more from each other—more openness, more personal commitment, more honesty, or else they felt disappointed. They were also more curious about each other. Effervescent and gregarious, Linda did not seem like a childhood rape victim. We carry stereotypes of how such people should look: withdrawn, anxious and tentative. If Linda had such a secret, what about the others? Was their jocularity a cover for equivalent psychic traumas?

At the end of the assignment, reading the polished drafts, class members were engrossed and often moved by the detailed authenticity and depth of their classmates' writing. They felt the power of such personally committed writing. This experience, and the individual redrafting and writing group work that led up to it, allowed them to realize that no secret formula (known only to teachers and professional writers) exists for writing effectively; student writers could see that they carried the essay "in them" and hard work was required to get it out and onto the paper. Furthermore, as more accomplished writers, they could now begin to understand the process by which professionals write about their experiences, and to have more respect for the results.

But you may be more concerned about Linda, about all the Lindas who came before her and who made themselves vulnerable in such a potentially damaging way. As teachers are we not responsible for the repercussions? To that question I unerringly answer "yes." We have to hold ourselves responsible. Exercises such as this which deal with our students' most intimate and intense memories require us to use care and skill in administering them. Linda's willingness to share her terrible moment was a tacit statement of trust and a plea for it to be returned in kind. She had taken my request seriously and asked me to do the same. While challenging her to enrich and analyze her depiction, I had to keep in mind that this had other implications beyond a writing exercise. The temptation to capitalize upon the high drama of this pedagogical moment has to be tempered by constant vigilance. By remaining sensitive to what Linda was going through as she relived her memory, I could be more certain she would benefit as much as the class from the exercise. In this way, as with all classroom lessons that are basically personal and confrontive in nature, we can ensure that our students will not only be willing to continue with them, but will find them valuable. If we don't manage such exercises well it seems to me that we will be forever doomed with "dummy runs" and essays in which no one is at home. And we will be missing an opportunity for students to come to appreciate literature in a wholly personal way.

Part Four

Perspectives 2000

Within the new paradigm, old terms, concepts and experiments fall
into new relationship with one another.

—Thomas S. Kuhn
The Structure of
Scientific Revolutions

At the present moment we are standing on an important threshold in the teaching of writing. During the past forty years or so, we have seen writing emerge as a serious academic study at the college level and as the premiere component of the English language arts curriculum in the public schools. During this time several ideas have been advanced, some of which have lasted only for a brief while, others continuing on into the present moment. Now is the time to take stock, gather up that which seems good, discard that which is no longer useful, and look to the road ahead. This section, Perspectives 2000, advances insights that appear useful for the journey ahead.

It should be noted that this section is not a collage of recent ideas but a collection of insights to inspire and guide us in the future. Many worthy ideas and practices emerge, find their way into the curriculum, and become a part of the mainstream. Two such recent examples are the uses of the portfolio and the computer in the writing classroom. Neither of these practices is described here because, having become a part of the mainstream, they are no longer current, even though some older members of the profession may continue to think of them as current. The essays in this section embody *living insights* capable of enhancing the quality of the experience in tomorrow's classrooms. Some of the voices in this section are respected authorities in the teaching of writing. Others may not be so well-known, and yet their message is rich and their eloquence deserves our attention.

In what ways do dance, art, and other creative activities contribute to growth in literacy? This is one of the questions addressed in Ann Alejandro's essay, "Like Happy Dreams—Integrating the Visual Arts, Writing, and Reading." The answer Alejandro provides could revolutionize traditional viewpoints about literacy learning. The reader might also consider in this essay the impact of the teacher's personality in the acquisition of literacy. Although the children in the author's classroom were impoverished and were learning English as a second language, they showed remarkable growth in reading, writing, and social development.

In "Are Today's Students Better Writers?" Mary M. Licklider describes an alternate way of assessing writing. Recognizing that the National Assessment of Educational Progress assessment of student writing did not conform to her own intuitions of what it should be, the author set out to discover the truth for herself. She says that the NAEP assessment of writing is comparable to "assessing naval officers according to proficiency in a canoe" (Zorn 1986). Both these teachers, Ann Alejandro and Mary Licklider, raise significant questions about the assessment of writing, which is one of the important problems we face. More important, they suggest that classroom teachers possess a kind of intuitive wisdom that should be heard in any effort to create valid and reliable national norms.

Not everyone comes to the task of writing the same way. Among the students we see daily, some are handicapped physically, some emotionally, some intellectually. John R. Corrigan teaches us what it means to be dyslexic, and in doing so reminds us of the variety of possible handicaps we may encounter. His essay "Teaching Writing to Dyslexic Students: A Guide for the Composition Instructor" speaks to the question of dyslexia from the inside and offers valuable insights for the teacher.

The next three essays represent a variety of cultural viewpoints, Italian American, Afro-American, and Jewish American. All are rooted in personal history, revealing the rich intermingling of one's personal and professional life. Although the perspectives come from different cultures, they are all written with a quiet reverence that pays homage to personal roots and at the same time celebrates the power of the written word.

All three writers explore how certain common objects or scenes reverberate with strong overtones. For Tom Romano it was a small, hand-carved wooden pony. For Es'kia Mphahlele it was the memory from childhood of tending cattle on the African savannah: "The darknesses, the silences, the sounds of day and of night, the open vastnesses, landscapes teeming with daylight, shimmering distances of subtropical heat, savannah lying low and biding its time under the winter spell . . ." (167). For Nancy Sommers it was coats, coats from her father's dry goods store in Terre Haute, Indiana. Mphahlele articulates so well a truth that runs through all three essays: "Our humanism is essentially spiritual, recognizing the Vital Force or the Supreme Being at the center of and integrating human, animal, and plant life and the inanimate elements of the universe" (167).

The influence of gender and all that gender entails—power, sexual perspective, values, personal interests, and behavior—are explored in Lad Tobin's essay "Car Wrecks, Baseball Caps, and Man-to-Man Defense: The Personal Narratives of Adolescent Males." Although Tobin deals with male gender issues in the writing classroom, his essay suggests rich possibilities in the study of a broad range of gender issues. How writing and literacy learning are interwoven with gender remains a major concern at all levels of the composition curriculum.

The final essay in this section is a classic, Patrick Hartwell's "Grammar, Grammars, and the Teaching of Grammar." During the twentieth century, several experimental studies have addressed the issue of the influence of grammar on growth in writing ability, and yet the question has remained unresolved for many teachers of writing. Patrick Hartwell offers an amazingly simple and lucid explanation of the issue, though the issue itself is exceedingly complex.

The resolution, Hartwell suggests, ultimately lies in the teacher's concept of what a writing classroom should be. Is the writing class a place where young people grapple with real problems of writing each day, i.e., a workshoplike environment, where issues of grammar and style are addressed as they arise? Or is it a place where the teacher systematically lectures about grammar and style and where student writing, presumably, occurs outside the classroom?

Hartwell argues that literacy grows out of "a rich and complex interaction of learner and environment . . . an interaction that has little to do with sequences of skills instruction as such. Those who defend the teaching of grammar tend to have a model of composition instruction that is rigidly skills-centered and rigidly sequential: the formal teaching of grammar, as the first step in that sequence, is the cornerstone or linchpin" (200).

With one exception Hartwell's essay appears here exactly as it was printed in *College English* in 1985. For the sake of brevity, as well as readability, the extensive list of references (forty-two footnotes comprising five pages of small type) has been deleted. Those who are interested in pursuing the references may readily find them in the originally published essay.

Like Happy Dreams—
Integrating Visual Arts, Writing, and Reading

Ann Alejandro

Not only are the arts not a fringe in the curriculum, but they may
also represent a unique hope for getting beyond the skill-and-drill
curriculum that is so often imposed on children from poor and
"non-mainstream" backgrounds.

Wake-Up Call

In 7 years of teaching English and writing at a junior college and state university that shared the same campus, I somehow missed the reveille of public
school reform in the state of Texas. Higher education had urgencies of its own,
and as director of the writing lab and instructor of various freshman writing
classes, I was in the thick of the burgeoning divisions of developmental education that had sprung up everywhere in response to disproportionate numbers of
severely underprepared students entering colleges and universities.

On some campuses across the state, more students were enrolled in developmental English, reading, and math classes than in regular freshman fare. Anybody who spends time teaching college freshman, either in standard Composition and Rhetoric or in developmental writing courses, recognizes with some
levity that teaching freshmen English students is often a process of *waking up*
18-year-old kids who've coasted joylessly or a little smugly through the last
few years of high school classes. I can still see their bright, clean faces and fat,
curly handwriting. Press hard enough, and usually these students at last find
articulate voices. Like the lights shooting sparks at the end of Malamud's
The Natural, the work gives joy.

I took what I thought to be a year's leave of absence and spent some time
doing poetry workshops in my son's second-grade classroom where I realized,
"Hey, *this* is where the magic is. These kids are *awake*." Along with many other
parents, I became alarmed at the amount of homework time our children were
spending filling out bubble-dot worksheets instead of reading and writing

Language Arts, 71 (January 1994), pp. 12–21. Copyright © 1994 by the National Council of
Teachers of English. Reprinted with permission.

wonderful stories. The worksheets, as it turned out, were practice blurbs for the Texas Assessment of Academic Skills (TAAS) test all third-, fifth-, seventh-, and ninth-grade students would be taking at the beginning of the next year.

Our district was on the verge of hysteria, not because of parents like me who hated the curricular emphasis on the test, but because the Texas Education Agency was using its results as the means to target and reform "low-achieving" schools and districts; and our students weren't performing well on it, particularly Hispanic, low-income, or otherwise "at risk" populations. After working with the second graders and seeing the extraordinary writing an ordinary classroom could produce, this TAAS test seemed to me an inaccurate measure of how young children really master their language. I spent that year getting my elementary certification, and I haven't taught college since. Instead, I've built two reading-writing communities with primary students in two districts. I've been their teacher, and they've been mine.

Twenty Miles South: Third Grade, 1992–93

This year, we are: 33 third graders in two language arts blocks, 12 of whom began the current school year reading at the readiness or first-grade levels. We are all Hispanic: 26 are classified as "at risk"; 19, limited English speakers; 17, the children of migrant farm workers; 2, learning disabled; 1, emotionally disturbed; and 31 are receiving public assistance. According to the 1990 census, 60% of the community respondents said that they did not speak English "very well," 76% of those 25 or older did not graduate from high school, nearly 65% of school-aged children lived below the poverty line, and 16.4% of the adult population were unemployed. Once a week for the last 3 weeks, someone in our community has been killed. We have a population of 1,500, three gas stations, one cafe, no public library, and a postage-stamp-sized post office open from 9:00 until 10:30 and 11:30 until 4:00. All you can see from anywhere you stand in our town are farmed fields, tumble-down shacks and implement sheds, a cotton gin, a chemical supply, and an airstrip for the cropdusters. Our families have worked on these farms and ranches, sometimes for generations, and now the jobs are fewer and farther between.

We work together in this state that has threatened to close its public schools unless compromises can be reached about how to distribute education funding fairly and, for the last few years, has demanded that public schools address and fix the crises of high drop-out rates, gang violence, and terrible standardized test scores, particularly among minorities. When our local administrators responded to the threats of the governing state education agency (both of which demanded that we get "back to basics"), we were nearly denied the privilege of out-of-town field trips (for which we ourselves had already raised the money at school fairs and carnivals) because such a reward, our administration felt, should be earned by performing well on the TAAS tests.

"Art" has been relegated to a nonbudgeted craft activity involving paper plates and Popsicle sticks. For music, the children sing to records once a week for 25 minutes. Since we don't have sinks in our classrooms, painting is trouble and cleanup impossible, especially on the days we have no running water. Since our district lives under the gun of what the Education Agency will do to us unless we get our scores up in reading, writing, and math and "cover" all the test objectives, art and beauty are frivolities in which we just cannot indulge our students.

When I began working with primary-age children in our area, I doubted whether any of them had really seen, heard, or read anything truly beautiful in their lives. They'd missed it, even when it was around them, because nobody had shown them how to see it. Sometimes a crop flowering or ready to harvest is beautiful, and a scraggly rose bush in a grandmother's yard or even the chickens bred for cockfighting can be beautiful. But the students didn't recognize the beauty. The school library has many beautiful art books, but most of them stayed on the shelves. At the beginning of the school year, none of my students had ever seen a real painting or sculpture or stained-glass window, and most had never seen a real Christmas tree.

Twenty Miles East: Second Grade, 1991–92

I had begun to use art extensively in my language arts instruction the previous year with second graders in a different district, 20 miles from the district where I work now, but with parallel populations and situations of difficulty. Because I believe that most writing is visually dependent, I am convinced of the parallels between teaching children how to draw and teaching them how to read and write. In all cases, students need to learn *how to see,* to interpret data from the world, the canvas, and the page. We see whole texts in paintings, in the scenes of life around us, and in the books we read. I believe children can understand thematic wholes as they look back on the events of books, the composition of paintings, and the unfolding autobiographies of their own lives. Conversely, I recognize that when we analyze the small components of paintings—dots, circles, curved lines, straight lines, texture, angles, genre or media, use of color, mood, atmosphere, and even conflict of character or plot—we use thought processes similar to those involved in creating or analyzing components of the text we read and write. Sounds, words, sentences, punctuation, spelling conventions, genre, paragraphs, poetic language, metaphor, character development, and style provide an interplay of parts that contribute to a harmonic, full-blown whole. I believe that immersion in art can parallel and enhance immersion in text: When we read and write, we use the same critical thinking and decision-making brainpower that we use when we paint or respond to paintings. Probably the same comparisons among musical, sculptural, and printed compositions can be made; it's a theory I haven't had time to test yet.

Ironically, my art-centered classroom began as a direct response to the state-mandated reading, writing, and math test these second graders would be taking in October of their third-grade year, a test which would measure their second-grade "skills mastery." Every teacher in the state was given enough worksheet preparation materials for this test to reforest the Amazon River Basin. The idea of the writing test was simple: Students would be given a "prompt" and then would generate a draft of a process-analysis, a description, or a narrative from that prompt. Their papers would then be scored holistically by two or more state-trained readers. Based on these writing samples, combined with scores on the objective (bubble-dot) components of the writing portion of the test—capitalization, punctuation, spelling—students would have either "mastered" or "failed to master" the test objectives, and their teachers and districts would be held accountable for the results. A student could compose a decent writing sample and still fail the writing test; likewise, it was very possible to master the objective component but freeze up or compose "off the prompt" on the writing sample and fail. My students would be all of 8 years old when they took it, after months of summer vacation and then 7 weeks of cramming for it, in another grade, with another teacher.

The Lure of Paintings

These writing "prompts" consisted of cartoon-line drawings, the quality of which was insulting to the imagination of any child who ever held a crayon. As I thought about inviting the children to write descriptively, I threw away the prompts and invested in a set of slides and transparencies of famous paintings and a set of slim, inexpensive paperbacks in the *Art for Children* series (Raboff 1988a, 1988b, 1988c, 1988d). I also stole all my mother's art books, set them in stacks on the tables in our classroom, and watched my students change. During small-group reading sessions, I shared little bits of two lovely books by Gladys S. Blizzard: *Come Look With Me—Enjoying Art With Children* (1990), a volume of portraits accompanied by engaging, thought-provoking questions like, "What do you think the little girl is staring at so intently?" and *Come Look With Me—Exploring Landscape Art With Children* (1992), with similar questions and situations inviting children to imagine, pretend, and immerse themselves in the landscapes. Because all these treasure books were out on the tables all the time, my students came to the classroom early and stayed late, gathering around the books, laughing, talking, showing, and exclaiming, or sneaking off to corners to look at books all by themselves. They couldn't wait to finish assignments to explore the books in the free time I gave them, and for several days, I mostly watched, listened, and offered a few comments when students brought me pictures to look at.

When it was time to become art critics, we began looking at slides in whole-group settings, observing colors, background, foreground, different media, and mood. The children began to observe character and plot, and we talked about how "every picture tells a story." Brainstorming, we imagined names, feelings, and relationships among the subjects painted. They noticed that each painting had its own time of day, source of light, and weather, and they soon made comparisons between paintings and artistic styles. Quickly, they observed contrasts between cool and warm colors, and they made comments like, "It's very hot in this scene, and the men are very tired" (in response to a Frederic Remington desert scene) and, "Renoir likes to paint in the springtime."

They had no interest in relying on the text descriptions even when they could read them; nobody needed to explain these pictures to any of these little people. On the day I decided it was time to let them choose their favorite painting to describe, no child could be dissuaded from the painting he had chosen, the one that elicited the strongest emotional response. Although some of my cowboys would have no truck with anything but Remingtons, and most girls grabbed for the books of Renoir, Cassatt, and Monet, I was very pleased that many boys were drawn to Da Vinci portraits of women and Millais's drowning "Ophelia," and several girls loved Van Gogh's portraits of peasant men and the "Bedroom at Arles."

The 7-year-olds drafted their descriptions, and, that night, when I read them to my mother, she was able to identify each artist whose work the children had described. They had enabled an adult to "see" what they had described in words.

Children As Art Critics

In the following days, we revised our drafts for correctness only because the students had already found plenty to say. We prepared our descriptions for publication. Responding to Michelangelo's stylized, early "Doni Tondo," Cynthia, whose only pair of shoes were so tight they made her cry, wrote in her final draft:

> This is a round picture. Joseph is holding God. And God is pulling Mary's hair and she is reaching to get God. Mary and Joseph are very proud of baby Jesus. Baby Jesus has curly hair and he is looking at Mary and Mary is looking at baby God. Mary has an ovl chin and a ovl face. and Mary has on pink and blue and green. Joseph has oringe and gray and a mustache. And there are some men fighting in the background. There are some mountains in the background.

It was the most she ever wrote in the entire year and one of two discourses she ever completed.

Lorraine, an award-winning artist who turned all she read, wrote, or painted into love stories, was especially drawn to the rich colors and fairy-tale qualities of the paintings of Marc Chagall. She combined two rough drafts as she completed her interpretation of Chagall's "The Three Candles":

A Desciption of the Tree Candles

> In this painting there is a woman and a man getting married. It seems like thay like each other. In the Backgrownd thar are green leaves and three candles and a goat and two people are out of the house that is red. This is a picture of angels flying in the sky. Thar is six houses and one car and flowers are by the angels. White rings are floting arownd. There is a clown standing on the tints.

The people at the botum of the bride have a magic wone and thar pontin it to the air. And the air is red. And thar is earth all over. The magic angel is floting in the sky making drems come true for the woman and a groom. And thay lived happile ever affter.

The End

Responding to the same painting, "The Cowboy," by Remington, Rigo and Daniel took different angles. Remembering to describe in detail, Rigo wrote:

I see a wonderful picture by Frederic Remington. I see one man riding on a strong horse and I see 46 rocks on the ground. The hores is slipeen off a mountain and I can see 4 horses, and the man has a hat on his head and he has a gun and bullets and he is wereng broun. He has a brown hat and brown short pants. The Shadow is broun and the background is blue, brown, and gray and I see that it is in the evnen. . . .

Daniel really was a cowboy who worked on a ranch with horses and cattle every day after school, and he'd had a few spills and close calls that became part of his description-turned-narrative: "This is a picture of a man riding as fast as he can on his horse on a very hot day. He's very tired. He is hitting his horse with all his fears. He doesn't care if he Fall's down. . . ." Daniel was a talented clay sculptor of horses and cowboys. Later in the year, he also won an award for one of his paintings in the annual area-wide creative arts contest sponsored by our junior college. All dressed up in a western suit, he showed up at the awards ceremony at the college with his parents, who spoke very little English, beaming for him, shaking my hand, and asking, "Es good boy? He give you no trouble?" Yes, I said, he was a very good boy and never any trouble. A few days after school let out for the summer, Daniel's parents got into an argument, and his father killed himself in front of the children. I have no idea what became of Daniel. There was speculation that his mother may have moved the family back to her people in Mexico. I'm holding on to the arts magazine in which his painting was printed, in case I ever see him again.

Dana had a twin sister in the other second-grade classroom, and they were always dressed exactly alike—like princesses. Dana also had a younger sister, and her narratives were always characterized by beautiful girls or young women who had, specifically, no brothers, sisters, husbands, or children. Although she had not read any of the written description of the painting, her final copy appeared on my desk like this:

**A Description of Diego Rodriguez
De Silva y Velasquez's "The Infanta Margarita"
by Dana Tristan**

This is a painting of a beautiful little girl. She is wearing a beautiful blue dress. She looks like a princess. She has a white face and a silver necklace on her neck. She has an olive green bow on her hair. The background is mostly black.

She has a blue bow in front of her dress. She has gold on her dress, too. She feels so wonderful that she is a princess. It looks like she lives in a beautiful red orange castle. She is rich. She has black beautiful eyes. She has long light blond hair. She made that beautiful leathered dress that she worked on it for several days. She is in a dark room that there's no light in. She is not married. She does not have any kids or brothers or sisters.

She has a lot of jewels. She is sweet and thoughtful. She wears a lot of gold on her dress every day. She wears a little bit of makeup and lipstick. She cares for everybody. She is always happy. She looks like she lives in France.

I copied all the pictures, typed all the text, made book covers, and bound our volume of art criticism to present as Mothers' Day gifts. All year long, the children were more excited on "Authors' Day," when their bound books come to the room hot off my presses, than they were at Christmas parties or Easter egg hunts. They were just as delighted to read their classmates' words in print as they were their own, a consistent response each time I brought completed copies of one of the seven class sets of chapbooks we published that year. After the children pored over their anthologies for a long time, we had Author's Chair in the reading circle, and each author read his own contributions. Then they autographed copies for each other, the school library, the principal, and the superintendent.

Combining Paintings to Tell Stories

A few days later, I cut out quality artwork from calendars, magazines, old date books, catalogues, and journals; and I laminated them for the next series of "prompts," the narratives. Before school, I covered all the desks and much of the floor with these prints of paintings and sculptures. The students already knew that narrative structure required characters, a setting, a problem to solve, and the solution to the characters' problem; but before we began using paintings and sculpture as the stimulus for writing, all these elements had to come out of their own heads, and some of the stories had an uninspired sameness as the young writers borrowed ideas from each other. When they walked into the room filled with art, I asked them to pretend to be in an art gallery, looking quietly and carefully at each print, taking plenty of time, and then choosing four prints to incorporate into a story. I instructed the students to pick one or two character pictures; a setting picture; an event picture (if they had only picked one character picture); and one picture they absolutely did not like because it bothered them, scared them, or made them feel uneasy.

They chose their four pictures with great care, frequently changing their minds. The room stayed very quiet as they frowned, walked, picked, rejected, and finally chose. For prewriting, they began to take notes and wanted me to come to their assistance: "What do you think his name could be, Miss?" "Where do you think this picture is?" "Why don't this person's eyes match?"

"Is this a lady or a man?" I answered all of them, "You decide." The resulting narratives were rich and complex, and I am convinced that the element of tension created by the one "disturbing" picture lifted these stories out of the trite, bland, and predictable. The students truly had wrangled with the resultant conflicts, and not one "formula" story came out of this assignment. We were all convinced that we were wizards.

Test Results

My principal resigned under pressure due to the campus's previous years' low state-test scores, and over the summer, the administration hired a new principal who would whip us all into shape and make those scores come up. After spending 20 minutes with him and hearing his plans to push me back into basal readers and "preparing for the tests," I resigned. The second graders from that school came back as third graders and, 7 weeks into the new school year, took the all-important state test, the results of which were published in December. Third-grade writing had moved from 38% mastery the previous year to 88% mastery. Reading scores went up from 28% student mastery in 1991 to 80% in 1992. The school received a $30,000 bonus from the state for significant improvement, and the superintendent attributed the gains to the strong new campus leadership. Nobody knew that, in second grade, my students had hardly ever heard a mention of that test. I never had told them we were preparing to "master test objectives." We had been too busy loving what we read and what we wrote.

Coming Home

I applied to teach elementary school in my own home district, where I had always attended school and previously had taught at the high school before moving to our junior college to work in the writing lab. My criteria for teaching assignments were exclusive: My students could not consider themselves too big to sit in my lap or hold my hand, and they had to believe in Santa Claus. When no calls came, I prepared to homeschool my own children and those of my relatives and a few friends who, like me, felt our kids were being robbed by the district's emphasis on mastery of basic skills and test-taking practice. But 2 days before inservices for the academic year began, the principal from the school where I now work called. (The campus was 20 miles from me in the other direction, 4 miles from the farm and ranch which had more or less supported my father's family all through my childhood, and less than 300 yards from some of my brother's cotton fields. I was, in many ways, back home.) This tiny community is part of our local school district and has one school serving Grades Pre-K through 8. The principal offered me kindergarten but asked me to take third grade, which I did, taking all my art books, posters, slides, videos, prints, paintbrushes, and clay with me to the new classroom where I would be obliged to prepare the incoming third graders for their early October testing.

Boot Camp Art and Writing

Astonished and overwhelmed by my students' "deficiencies," their lack of experience in reading, writing, and especially *seeing* (connecting language to visual stimuli and sensory experience), I began the same processes using the art slides and prints, having 7 weeks to give the children the tools with which to compose narratives, descriptions, or process analyses. This didn't include reading "skills" measured by the test, so we dived deeply and hardly came up for air as we struggled for words, descriptors, sense, rudimentary organizations, and structures for ordering language. I only remember four things about those 7 boot camp weeks: I brought huge buckets for watering horses to use as sinks, and we filled them with water from the hose outside, passing it through the window whenever we needed water for painting, making, or cleanup, and for our process-analysis. Instead of describing "How I Clean Up My Room" or "How I Get Ready for School in the Mornings," we cooked clay dough on hot plates and colored it with dry tempera powder. As their hands turned wonderfully red and green and purple while they squeezed and kneaded the magic goo, the students didn't know they were prewriting. The next day, our hall bulletin board was covered with baggies of brightly colored play clay and sentence strips completed by small groups describing the process stages for "How to Make Your Own Clay Dough and Injoy it With Your Frends." My principal said, "I see," and asked some of my students to write down the recipe so he could make the clay with his preschool daughter.

Pope Julius and the Texas Education
Agency Have Their Standards

I showed the students pencil-sketch studies (prepainting?) and the resulting Sistine Chapel frescoes, asking the children to make the connection between vision—the beginning work, the germinating idea from the artist's eye—and revision—literally, seeing again, making the final product ready for the eyes of an audience. We talked about the kinds of changes we must make as we move from writer to reader of what's written. Using transparencies of their own writing, I taught them how to score writing holistically, using the same measures which their test evaluators would use. Within hours, they could evaluate accurately the strengths and weaknesses of their discourses. "See it in your head," I kept telling them. "When you read, don't depend on looking at somebody else's pictures of what you're reading. There won't be any pictures on the reading test. When you write, see it in your head like it was a movie or a painting. Let your readers know exactly how you see what you see. Don't leave any white spaces on your canvas."

It's Not Cute. It's Messy. It Has Misspelled Words.

When I look back, I think the most important part of those first weeks stemmed, once again, from my aversion to "canned" methodology. It seems to be a necessity that an elementary school bulletin board, usually teacher-made, must be "cute," the product of some preprepared activity from a cute teacher magazine, with little precise worksheets to duplicate, color, cut out, and write in response to seasonal or thematic caricatures about "spring" or "puppy love." Grown-ups walk down the halls and say, "Oh, isn't that a cute idea?" Most cute ideas make for lousy reading and writing experiences, completely lacking in authenticity of students' voices and passions. I think groups of students should design, make, and caption their own messy, error-plagued, crooked bulletin boards. Because I honestly felt that about a third of my students stood a chance of mastering their reading and writing test objectives, I took that third to the library during our enrichment period at the end of the day, as my miracle-working, full-time aide kept the others for reading or completing final copies of their writing; pulled out the grown-up art books and set them beside my own collection; invited small groups of students to research their favorite artists and compile examples of their work from magazines (again, stolen from my mother, who parted with them for the good cause); and directed the groups to compose teaching bulletin boards for the rest of the students in the classroom and the school. When the bulletin boards were complete, each member of the different groups would explain different aspects of the artists' lives and work to the rest of the class.

The groups chose Michelangelo and Da Vinci (spin-offs of which resulted in brief studies of scientific invention, Biblical history, architecture, and the Renaissance), Georgia O'Keeffe, and Marc Chagall. The resulting scratched-out, messy bulletin boards they made were the project's crowning glory, and little Debbie Gauna, who is almost too shy to speak above a whisper and who has shingles activated by the stress of major state-mandated tests, concluded her part of her group's bulletin board caption with the statement, "Marc Chagall's paintings look like happy dreams."

Deliverance

All Texas students took the same standardized tests on the same days. I felt riding on me the hopes of my last year's students, now third graders, and my new group, with whom I had worked these 7 weeks. Our school's third graders' reading scores rose from 48% of the students passing the previous year to 66% passing. Writing rose from 20% to 55%. The district thought the achievement was significant. Having read the results of what my last year's 7-year-olds in the other district had accomplished, I didn't. We merely had done the best we could, limited by our ill-prepared circumstances, in 7 weeks that left me bone-weary. I was furious at a state that measured my 8-year-olds' skills and my own teaching ability by the standard of one yardstick which had little or nothing to do with the real, always emerging literacy experiences my students and I needed, wanted, and loved.

The Consequences of a Day

The pressure of that test off, the real fun and the authentic learning could begin. Preparing for our upcoming field trip to the San Antonio Museum of Art, where our students could view one of the best Hispanic folk-art collections in the nation, we spent a few weeks looking at and talking about the difference between the artistic expressions and media of everyday people from cultures all over the world and those of the trained artists, Michelangelo and Da Vinci. We talked about flatness versus real, three-dimensional perspective; about the differences between painted wood and polished marble, and about children's toys compared to hammered gilt altar pieces. Our generous librarian supplied us with carts of Post-It tagged books showing the masks, weavings, furniture, and religious idols from cultures all over the world. When we went to the museum, we had a context that ranged from Hispanic folk art to masterful, prized examples of Phoenician glass and pottery; Greek and Roman statuary; Native American ceremonial robes; stone-carved Mayan and Aztec cooking utensils ("My grandma has a *molca jete* just like that for grinding her chiles"); and pioneer American quilts and crocheted bedspreads. The Lure of The Mummies hit them hardest (and me, too). The children kept gravitating back to the second coffin of some minor pharaoh's third cousin, wanting to touch it, to open it, to understand the hieroglyphs, and to see the mummy, which was not there.

For lunch, we went to the Japanese Sunken Gardens, where the children, in the rain, raced, screaming among the secret paths, pagodas, bridges, waterfalls, and ponds in which giant goldfish went into bread-crumb feeding frenzies. A lady asked me if I was a sponsor of a Christian school because the children, even in the ecstasy of exploration, had remembered to say, "Excuse me, ma'am." She had even overheard one of them chanting to herself, "Oh, thank you, Jesus, for letting us come here"—somewhere beautiful, away from the sheds, the windblown grit, the tin sheds, the Quonset hut cotton gin, the flat fields, and the thorny mesquite trees.

The day never left us as we continued to read and write all year long; the students continually made connections between what they saw that day and the material we explored and made back in the classroom. For Halloween, their three-dimensional papier-mache masks harkened back to the ceremonial masks they had seen either in books supplied by the library or on the field trip to the art museum; and it was clear that their own sculptures drew from those they had seen as examples of the masks of China, India, Africa, Native America, South America, and Mexico. These creations were of such high quality that they drew crowds to the lobby of one of our biggest area banks, where they were displayed several weeks. As we spent weeks in January and February reading the myths and creation stories of various worldwide cultures and religions, the students reminded me of the Buddhas, urns, *retablos,* totems, and carvings of gods and goddesses they had seen during their 2-hour tour of the art museum. When we read "Pygmalion and Galatea," several reminded me of the memorable marble sculptures from the classical age. Our observation of the quiet textures and description of the small hospital courtyard, so valuable because of its comfort to the protagonist of *Sadako and the Thousand Paper Cranes* (Coerr 1977), led the students to make comparisons with the serene composition of the Japanese Sunken Gardens they had visited. And, finally, when we read *The Day of Ahmed's Secret* (Heide & Gilliland, 1990), the children were able to identify the setting (country and city—illustrated in water colors with teeming, emotive detail) when they recognized the pyramids of Giza in the background of one of the pages.

Phrases like, "It looks like . . . " and, "It reminds me of . . . " consistently appeared in their oral language and descriptions of their own story settings, which became more descriptive and visual. Their handmade Big Books became rich volumes of detailed print and vividly painted illustrations. Without my teaching them the literary definitions of schemes and tropes, many of the students began using poetic language in their journal responses to the questions I posed, as well as in their own descriptions and stories. Natural-born metaphor makers, the children now had fairly rich artistic backgrounds to draw from as they painted with words—and with color.

Painting and Writing Who We Are

Throughout the year, I've periodically used lessons from *Drawing With Children* by Mona Brookes (1986) to give my students formal, sequenced instruction in the use of line, color, perspective, and drawing what they really *see*. I'm hard to please. I never saw blue clouds shaped like wads of cotton candy, I know that trees aren't rectangles topped off by loopy ovals, birds aren't upside down letter *m*'s, people's bodies aren't shaped like sticks, and houses don't float on spaces of white air. To teach my children to draw what they see instead of careless, dim representations of what they vaguely remember having seen, I've had temper tantrums: "You go outside, and you look at those cars, and you break them up into lines and ovals and circles and dots, and you make me a car that looks like a car!" "Look out there at that playground and that sky! Do you see any white spaces? Does the sky start 7 inches above the ground? Is all the grass one flat color, like a carpet? Give me a background!"

Challenged by people who have wondered if I interfere with my students' personal creativity by giving them formal art instruction with high critical standards, I've answered that creativity, like any natural potential, is a capacity that either levels off and becomes ordinary or is challenged to achieve higher and higher planes of expression. Some creativity survives in some rare children in spite of the ways schools attempt to kill it; but most creativity in most children has to be elicited and then channeled toward a set of culturally accepted standards. (Why else do we teach?) Otherwise, our language wouldn't have any conventions of spelling, punctuation, semantics, or pronunciation, and nobody would understand anything anyone else ever said or wrote.

In other words, I know my students are geniuses, but I won't tell them that until they show me that they are. Our whole academic year works toward their recognition of genius in themselves and their ability to go out independently like the people in the Nike commercials, and "Just do it." Approaching the end of this school year, most of them have taken on the attitude of, "Sure. I can do that. What do you want next?"

To make memories of who we are right now, we read an English-Spanish book written and illustrated by a young woman raised not 200 miles from us, who experienced almost exactly the same childhood traditions as ours—county fairs, eating *nopalitos,* cakewalks at parish festivals, religious pilgrimages to the Rio Grande Valley, *posadas* at Christmas, *piñatas* for *cumpleaños, sandía* on summer evenings, and *tamaladas* for New Year's Eve. Using Carmen Lomas Garza's *Family Pictures/Cuadros de Familia* (1990) as their springboard, my students painted and then wrote vignettes describing their favorite family and cultural traditions. We displayed them all over the room and out in the hall. "This lady's from Kingsville, Miss? I been to Kingsville. We went to the beach, too. Just like that author."

We will wrap up this third-grade year with one more reading-writing-art book we'll make ourselves after reading and thinking about Leila Ward's (1978) lyrical portrait of the inherent wonders in the life a Kenyan child opens her eyes upon every day: *I Am Eyes/Ni Macho.* With simple, subdued illustrations by Nonny Hogrogian, a two-time Caldecott medalist, *I Am Eyes* teaches *seeing* as well as classifying beginning, ending, or rhyming sounds of words with pages that read, "I see sunflowers and skies, . . . stars and starlings, . . . donkeys and monkeys, . . . kites and Kilimanjaro, . . . And everywhere/where I am eyes, I see butterflies."

This past summer, my "at-risk" exiting third graders responded to *I Am Eyes* by describing either the world they inhabited or the one they want to inhabit someday, covering their pages with tempera-paint illustrations and leaving just enough unpainted space to print their final copies of "I see." From the perspective of being in the starry purple space and looking down on the blue-and-brown planet Earth, partly covered with swirls of white clouds, Effain wrote:

I See a Lot of Things

I see my family at the river.
I see my brother and me playing in the backyard.
I see my brothers and sisters swimming.
I see the earth from out space.
I see the Milky Way.
I see my whole family at the beach.
I see the sky torning into blue berries.
I see the trees at my house so beautiful.

I see my mom baking a cake for my teachers.
I see New York City turnin into popsides.
I see my teachers famous.
I see my whole friends and teachers
singing at school in the library.

Postscript: Dwelling in Possibility

Reform continues. The future of public education in our state is out there and looking pretty ragged. Our district, with a capital base of per-pupil wealth at $65,523 compared to the state average of $178,277, has just lost more than a million dollars in state funding and fired 43 of its support personnel—many of whom worked every day in the classrooms with us, with our students. They were vital. Eight people on our campus lost their jobs, and probably more will have to go next year. The legislature removed the possibility of merit pay raises for all teachers who had not already achieved "career-ladder" status. On the last day of work on our campus, everybody cried as we waited and watched our co-workers get axed. Our principal, red-eyed, said it was the worst day of his life. We left the campus for summer vacation feeling kicked in the teeth.

In response to these worst-case events and data like the classroom profile that I received at the beginning of this year (the statistics compiled by the census bureau, the lice, the impetigo, the handicaps, the single parents and poverty levels, the simultaneous mandates for change and back-to-basics, the insanity and threats over district- and statewide scores, the programs piled on programs, the goal of minimal skills proficiencies), I take comfort from the knowledge that my students and I can always fall back on Boticelli and Picasso, on tribal masks and Homer.

We can always keep the quest for understanding beauty and making beauty at the heart of our curriculum, as long as we don't tell anybody that's what we're doing, and we can always strive for meaning that matters to us. I can keep throwing away most of those practice test worksheets, or using them for rough sketches or drafts; and at least for the time being, we can still take one field trip that transports us from where we are, where we live. We can imagine anything for ourselves. I can keep screaming at my district, "*Never* remediate. *Always* enrich. Treat students as if they were all gifted and talented, and they will show you that in some way or in many ways, they are." Maybe someday, somebody will believe me. Meanwhile, like Debbie Gauna, we can think about reading and writing and painting a world we can make "like happy dreams."

References

Blizzard, G. (1990). *Come look with me—Enjoying art with children.* Charlottesville, VA: Thomasson-Grant.

Blizzard, G. (1992). *Come look with me—Exploring landscape art with children.* Charlottesville, VA: Thomasson-Grant.

Brookes, M. (1986). *Drawing with children*. New York: St. Martin's.

Coerr, E. (1977). *Sadako and the thousand paper cranes*. Illustrated by R. Himler. New York: Putnam.

Garza, C. L. (1990). *Family pictures/cuadros de familia*. San Francisco: Children's Book Press.

Heide, F. P., & Gilliland, J.H. (1990). *The day of Ahmed's secret*. Illustrated by T. Lewin. New York: Morrow.

Raboff, E. (1988a). *Diego Rodriguez: De Silva Y Velasquez*. New York: Harper & Row.

Raboff, E. (1988b). *Frederic Remington*. New York: Harper & Row.

Raboff, E. (1988c). *Marc Chagall*. New York: Harper & Row.

Raboff, E. (1988d). *Vincent Van Gogh*. New York: Harper & Row.

Ward, L. (1978). *I am eyes/ni macho*. Illustrated by N. Hogrogian. New York: Greenwillow.

Are Today's Students Better Writers?

Mary M. Licklider

The Nation's Report Card on Writing issued by the National Assessment of Educational Progress (NAEP) in June 1990 left me frustrated and confused. I could not tell whether students' writing had declined or improved since 1970. From the tone of the report I suspected the former. As an English teacher, I thought I might be more effective selling shoes.

Not yet willing to accept that verdict, however, I turned to the 1969–70 NAEP reports on writing, hoping to compare scoring guidelines and sample papers from assessments twenty years apart (Eleanor L. Norris, et al., 1970, *National Assessment of Educational Progress Report 3 1969–1970 Writing: National Results,* Washington: GPO; Eleanor L. Norris, Charles Gadway, et al., 1971, *National Assessment Report 5 1969–1970 Writing: Group Results for Sex, Region, and Size of Community,* Washington: GPO). I found it impossible to make objective comparisons because the reports for the two assessments did not provide me with sufficient information.

I could find only one instance in which writing samples from somewhat similar assignments were provided by both reports. In 1969–70, students were asked to "write a story" in response to a photograph of an old woman holding a package of tomatoes (Norris, et al. 1971, B-41). The prompt for narration in 1988 was to "write a good scary ghost story" (Arthur N. Applebee, et al., 1990, *Learning to Write in Our Nation's Schools: Instructions and Achievement in 1988 at Grades 4, 8, and 12,* Princeton, NJ: Educational Testing Service, 80). In 1970, 14 percent of seventeen-year-olds wrote papers at least as good as this:

> She looks around to see if there are any clerks or other store authorities who would apprehend her for shoplifting those tomatoes. There is a 50-50 chance that she will be discovered and then charged with a misdemeanor. She might be using five-finger discount because it gives her a thrill. This seems more true than if she was stealing because she didn't have the money because I can tell by her appearance that she is not poverty stricken. (Norris, et al. 1971, B-42)

English Journal, 81 (February 1992), pp. 34–39. Copyright © 1992 by the National Council of Teachers of English. Reprinted with permission.

In 1988, 50.6 percent of thirteen-year-olds wrote papers at least as good as this:

> One dark, and silent night, some high school kids were walking along a long, narrow road that led to a graveyard. The kids were drunk from a party in which they were. One girl said "Let's check out that graveyard!" The group agreed and soon they were traveling down the narrow path. When they reached the gate, it was open. Usually, at night, someone locks it. Opening the gate made a loud screech. They entered through the gate. The kids walked a bit further to a newly laid grave. To their surprise there was no name or date of death. While they were studying the grave they heard a moaning like noise. Suddenly, a gray foglike smoke arose from the plot. It was a deformed creature. One girl fainted at the sight of it. Her boyfriend picked her up and carried her off. The ghost had opened the gate so that the kids could get in easier. The weird ghost started to chase them out of the yard. When the kids were gone the ghost made a laughing sound and slammed the gate shut. He then locked it. The creature slowly floated back to his resting place. (Applebee 83)

The 1970 sample represents the best writing of the oldest students; the 1988 sample represents "adequate" writing of eighth graders. In my judgment, the 1988 sample is better. Compared with the sample from seventeen-year-olds, it represents greater fluency; it's about twice as long. It is more fully developed and has a clearer sense of plot, including a beginning, a conflict, and a resolution of sorts. The language of this piece—"a gray foglike smoke arose," "a deformed creature," "newly laid grave"—strikes me as being at least as sophisticated and interesting as that of the 1970 sample. The sentence structure of the two is pretty close. Both tend to rely upon simple sentences, and neither seems to be entirely in control of the more complex structures attempted.

If these papers are indeed representative, they suggest that only fourteen percent of 1970's seventeen-year-olds could write at least as well as over half of 1988's eighth graders. Perhaps I didn't need to look into selling shoes just yet. At this point, I suspected that the reason we are continually pounded with negative reports of our students' abilities has more to do with the statistics than with writing. Holistic scoring makes comparisons *within* the batch of papers to be scored; no external criteria are imposed. Score points, then, describe the range of papers presented by a given assessment. If the whole range improves, presumably the standards described in the scoring guides also rise. Thus, comparisons of statistics from one assessment to another are not valid.

So far as I can tell from the 1990 report, the 1988 assessment was not based on "registered" holistic scoring, which is an attempt to adjust scoring criteria to make score points comparable to those of other years. The number of score points used by NAEP over the years has varied from four to eight. The 1970 assessment used general impression scoring, whereas the most recent used primary trait scoring. Considering these differences and in the absence of anything to the contrary in the 1990 report, I infer that the meaning of the score points in each of the assessments is relevant only to that sample.

Comparing Local Samples, 1980 and 1990

I was left with my original question: Are today's students writing better than the students of twenty years ago? Those single writing samples from the national reports didn't provide enough evidence to draw confident conclusions, but they pointed me toward comparing samples as a possible means of answering my question. I turned for samples to literary magazines I had sponsored at Oakland Junior High in 1980 and in 1990. I confined my "study" to magazines from Oakland because the characteristics of the students involved would be essentially the same. Oakland's population has grown, but it is not demographically very different from what it was in 1980. Since the first magazine had included only ninth-grade work, I looked only at the ninth-grade pieces in the 1990 issue, even though it included seventh- and eighth-grade writers as well. While both magazines included poetry and prose, I decided to focus exclusively on the prose selections.

The selection procedures hadn't changed much in eleven years. Individual students still decided which (if any) writings to submit. Independently completed as well as assigned writings were welcomed. Students were given class time to choose and, in 1980, to revise chosen writings. Writings were then numbered to make them anonymous, juggled between classes to maintain anonymity, and evaluated by ninth graders during their English classes. I printed what the students chose and added any pieces (three or four each year) which the students overlooked but which I felt deserved publication. In 1980, I did quite a bit of proofreading as I typed. In 1990, I did none. A committee of volunteer students did it.

The two magazines provided me with more material than the NAEP reports for judging "how well students use writing to accomplish a variety of purposes," "manage the writing process," and "value writing and what has been written" (Applebee 98). The magazine selections represent what the students consider to be their own and their peers' best work. Further, they represent the results of students' genuine writing processes more accurately than do the timed writings of the NAEP assessments. As to whether students "value writing and what has been written," I can cite the commitment of volunteer students in 1990 (but not in 1980) to proofread some 125 pages of text. The 1990 issue boasts two selections that were recognized in state, regional, and national writing contests. The 1980 issue had no contest submissions, let alone winners. In 1990, nearly three-fourths of the student body purchased magazines, a concrete demonstration, I'd argue, that they value writing.

The biggest difference between the selections in the two magazines, the difference that fairly leaps off the pages, is that the 1990 issue is fun to read. These students had a sense of audience that the 1980 students sorely lacked. About half the prose pieces in 1980 were descriptive paragraphs; the other half were narrative paragraphs. Only two selections, narrating childhood memories, could even loosely be called "stories." The modes and topics of the 1980 selections included descriptions of fictional and real people (one-fourth), descriptions of places and things (one-fourth), and brief narratives describing stressful situations (one-half), most of these written in response to an assignment. There was also one piece which contrasted a female character's spoken dialogue with her interior monologue throughout a less-than-successful date. This piece and the two childhood memories were the only selections that seemed to convey a sense of audience—a sense of the author communicating purposefully with student readers of the magazine.

The 1980 selections served their purposes fairly well—to describe and to narrate an incident. But those purposes were much less ambitious than those of the 1990 selections. About half of the 1990 prose consists of short stories and vignettes. One-fourth were parodies: one of adolescent love, one of our school's emphasis on learning-styles research, and one on television cooking shows. One 1990 piece was a fictional monologue to comment on peer pressure and drug abuse. Another is the story of a terrorist attack on the local McDonald's, which turns out to be staged for a movie. In one vignette, a composer struggles with a difficult commission: Death has ordered a requiem. An essay traces the development of the word "frisbee" and comments on the constancy of change in our language. A plotless short story muses on mortality and memory.

These students have things to say to their readers and their own ideas about how to do so. The most sustained and heated argument about what to include in the 1990 magazine occurred when eighth graders discussed "Herbert and Wilma."

> [T]here lived a man named Wilma and a woman named Herbert. Wilma was thirty-one years old and he went to plumbing school at the age of seventeen. He graduated at the age of twenty-one. (It was only supposed to be two years but he kept flunking.) Now he is a professional toilet cleaner. . . . One day while they were walking to the dumpsters to find Wilma's toothbrush that he had lost the day before, they saw a BIG . . . HUGE . . . UGLY . . . Cockroach! They put it on a leash and took it home and named it Lester. . . . That night for dessert, they had what Herbert called "Lester Pie." She said it had her "secret touch."

The gist of the discussion was not about the quality of the piece. The students agreed that this writing contains extraneous details and numerous mechanical errors which needed attention. Some students were certain that, for these reasons, it should not be published. The other half adamantly urged publication, maintaining that there is an element of the junior high audience for whom "Lester Pie" would be great fun. They argued that those readers deserved to have at least one such piece in the magazine. I remember no such sophisticated discussions in 1980.

Even the evolution of the magazine's title reflects increased confidence. In 1980, all the students could come up with was a rather sheepish *Ninth Graders Are Creative, Too.* By 1990, the magazine had for some years been known as *Hot Lead and Burned Erasers.*

Fluency and Use of Dialogue

Not only are the themes and modes more sophisticated and varied in 1990, but the writing itself is more fluent and complex. The average number of words in a 1980 selection was 191; in 1990, 1,089. The average number of words per sentence in 1980 was 11.7; in 1990, 18. This 45 percent increase was even more striking to me when I calculated that 39 percent of the sentences in 1990 contained dialogue compared to only 4.6 percent in 1980. Dialogue pulls the average sentence length down because of exchanges like these:

> "Gary?"
> "Hey guy. How's it going?"
> "Fine. Do you think I should go out with Gwen?"
> "Gwen, huh? Hey, go for it."
> "Thanks."
> "Sure."
>
> "You know Sarah, Charlie is pretty cute."
> "I know, he has great eyebrows and a nice . . ."
> "Yeah, I know."

The extensive use of dialogue in the 1990 magazine is another sign of increased sophistication. It's much easier and often much less effective to *tell* what happened or what a character is like than to *show* those details through dialogue. Look at how much characterization Jeremy accomplishes when he introduces the reader to Sarah (from the piece quoted above) with a deliberately run-on sentence:

> "Hmmm. Oh hi, Charlie. How's it going? I mean with me it's going O.K. but with other people you never can tell you know I mean what if someone in your family had died or something I mean my God that would be awful but it hasn't happened or anything like that, you know?"

Patrick says a great deal about the relationship between his two characters, Dr. Wraithbone and Death, reinforces the mood, *and* moves the plot along in just three lines of dialogue:

> "Are—are you there?"
>   "I am indeed," came the sonorous answer from the darkness. "I am waiting to hear my requiem."
>   "Ah . . . I see," replied Dr. Wraithbone. "I can only play the piano reduction, you see, with what is at my disposal—and there is no soloist."

The Abstract and the Concrete

Besides their more extensive use of dialogue, the authors of the 1990 magazine seem more comfortable and less self-conscious in moving between the abstract and the concrete within a given writing and in using figures of speech such as similes and metaphors to achieve their purposes. The details of the 1980 selections often tend to exist for their own sake:

> I have sat behind this young, flat-headed, slump-shouldered boy since the beginning of the year. Tom Murley is his name. He has hair about the color of a cup of coffee that's been sitting for twenty-four hours.

When generalizations are included, often they are not related as closely to the details intended to support them as one might hope:

> We know everything about each other. He'd sit there with his cigarette hanging out of his mouth and just talk away. In ways Ronick looked very tough. But deep down inside, he was as sweet as could be.

The 1990 authors don't seem to struggle as much to move from the general and the abstract to the specific and the concrete:

> For four months Charlie had liked Gwen. For four months he had blown very lightly on her neck in English to see if she would turn around. For four months he had written "I Love Gwen" in eraser on his desk.

> It all starts out one nice and breezy day when your husband returns home from work at 5:17 and informs you that he has promised seventeen co-workers, his softball team, his seven poker buddies and the entire group of Royal Water Buffalos to a three-course meal if they're here by six. You now have forty-three minutes to decide what you're going to fix and fix a three-course meal for eighty-two people, or you could file for a divorce.

Figures of speech, too, are used more naturally by the 1990 authors:

> The last rays of the sun played over the tin roof and in through the grimy windows of the old gas station as shadows crawled out from where they had been resting.

> At the wake there is a gloomy gray feeling in the air. My coffin is blanketed with a musty smell.

Beginnings and Endings

Conclusions were difficult for the 1980 authors. Some pieces just stop, mid-detail; others attempt endings that tend to be obvious or too simple.

> This is what anger is, but no one understands it.

> Wakka Island is a fairly nice place to live, to vacation, and just to see.

Opening lines caused fewer problems than endings did in 1980, but the results were still somewhat mixed:

> She's a blonde, but not a dumb one.

> A lump rose in my throat as I noticed the forever long track.

> Ronick was a great person.

The openings of the 1990 selections much more consistently pull the reader into the piece:

> Sitting stiffly on an old ripped up chair, James shifted his weight for the sixth time and wiped off the sweat that trickled from his forehead.

> He was hunched by the large wooden pillar with his old gray hat covering his thin face.

And endings are smoother and more meaningful:

> But even as the memories fell to individual shards and eventually absolute mockery of life, the house was not alone.
>   In the living room sat the old man and the young boy.

> Words influence our life, and we influence words. As we grow old, so do they.

> [T]he car pulled out of the station. He didn't even think about it really. His old life was something he didn't miss. The sun had set, and he picked up his cat and started inside.

My Continuing Questions

At Oakland Junior High, students appear to be writing much better now than ten years ago. I find this heartening; at least, I can postpone entering the shoe business. But on a number of levels my original question persists. The students published in the literary magazine represent the most accomplished writers each year. My analysis of their writing is only a start. I'd still like to know if a sample including the whole range of our students would show similar gains.

How the skills of students today compare to those of students ten and twenty years ago at the national level is a question that NAEP dodged this time. It is worthy of attention if only for the sake of teachers' morale. And even if the answers were to prove positive, other questions would remain, questions about students' relative strengths and weaknesses and about how much progress can be reasonably expected. NAEP's average response method (ARM) of scaling scores, in which all of a given student's writings are reduced to one number, is intended to provide "an estimate of average writing achievement for each respondent as if he or she had taken all of the writing tasks given" (Applebee 107). In a critique of the 1986 assessment, Jeff Zorn likens this to assessing naval officers according to proficiency in a canoe. My analogy is to the thirty-second "sound bites" used by the media to make complicated issues amenable to television news.

Surely, the extensive resources of NAEP, including a massive data bank covering two decades, might yield information that teachers need if they are to become better teachers of writing. And teachers need that information readily available to them. It seems to me that the NAEP reports are directed less to teachers than to "legislators, educators, and others concerned with improving education in this country." I feel somewhat shortchanged by the reports I have read; and I have been unable to obtain essential NAEP documents even with the help of interlibrary loan operating through our local public library and reaching out of state as well.

NAEP is in a unique position to help teachers through information and discussion of how and why and how much of our students' writing is or is not progressing. Discussion of questions that the 1990 NAEP report neither asks nor answers would be far more useful to me as an English teacher than a 122-page report containing 53 pages of graphs and tables and only 21 actual writing samples. I suspect that others among NAEP's professed audience of "legislators, educators, and others" might also appreciate a professional analysis of trends in student writing over the years that would render unnecessary the limited and clumsy comparison I've reported here. That "study," though, has served a purpose. I'm still teaching, not selling shoes.

Teaching Writing to Dyslexic Students

A Guide for the Composition Instructor

John R. Corrigan

Introduction

I always hated school. Dreaded it. Looking back, I know why. Reading, writing, math. I couldn't get it. I'd try, then try harder. Every time I went to read aloud—I'd stutter and stammer, in an effort to make out each word—I'd hear the snickers and laughter.

My earliest memory of school is a spring day in 1975. I was in kindergarten and the class was writing the lowercase letter *d,* while I continuously scrawled *b.* Time and time again. Embarrassed, frustrated, eventually humiliated, I left school that day in tears. It would not be the last time. My teacher had written a note, sealed the envelope, and asked me to carry it home and deliver it to my parents. I had been singled out for poor academic performance for the first time. For me, days like this were all too frequent, and they continue to be for many children growing up with dyslexia.

Later, in the fourth grade—after failing math and continuing to struggle in my other courses—my mother requested a meeting with school officials, during which she was told to just accept the fact that her son was "slow."

Thankfully, she did not. My parents took me to the Boston Children's Hospital. I was diagnosed as having a learning disability. Later, when more was known about dyslexia, an education specialist appeared at my elementary school and said, according to the symptoms of that specific disability, I was a poster boy. I have grown up with the disability and persevered.

I no longer dread school; in fact, as a teaching assistant and an MFA candidate in the creative writing program at the University of Texas at El Paso, I instruct two sections of basic composition. Here I want to draw on my research and experiences with dyslexia and offer suggestions for instructing dyslexic students to write.

Teaching English in the Two-Year College, 24 (October 1997), pp. 205–211. Copyright © 1997 by the National Council of Teachers of English. Reprinted with permission.

What Is Dyslexia?

Dyslexia is a learning disability, believed to stem from a neurophysiological flaw in the brain's ability to process language. It is not a disease. It is a disability which can be overcome. The disability afflicts many individuals possessing above-average intelligence (Simpson 41). Dyslexia is believed to be inherited and to affect 5% of the American population (Brachacki, et al. 297).

For many, the pitfalls of dyslexia do not end with one's ability to process language. Generally, the disability hinders one's ability to process information and, in most cases, lasts a lifetime. Dyslexia is typically first spotted when a child begins to read, because reading and recognizing the letters of the alphabet are the central activities of early schooling. But many dyslexic students score poorly on standardized tests measuring competency in subjects such as math. Dyslexia, then, not only hinders one's ability to read, or process language, but can affect several areas of a person's education and life.

Symptoms

Students who managed to get by in high school may not know they possess the disability when they enter college. Instructors of composition can look for several warning signs. Many dyslexic students will have difficulty with grammar, spelling, and reading comprehension—language in general. Composition teachers see these problems in many essays, though. Many times dyslexics' oral abilities do not match their written work. For most students, their speech resembles their writing. But many dyslexic students will be able to explain orally a writing assignment and what they would like to do but struggle when they try to put those same ideas into clear form on paper. A thoughtful, in-depth discussion can translate into an unorganized, rambling essay. The opposite is true as well. For me, it is a constant struggle to express myself orally. I find my expressive venue on the written page. Strategies can be developed to help in this area, however, as discussed below.

A dyslexic student might also incur *information-processing difficulties*. I struggled to follow successive informational steps in processes growing up and, to this day, must constantly write notes to myself. This can be an obvious problem for dyslexics learning to write since writing is process-oriented. Often, dyslexics can see where they are and where they want to be, but not how to get from where they are to where they want to be. This problem is not limited to writing, but can occur when walking across campus. (I tend to get lost easily.) A helpful assignment for this problem is outline development. Outlining ideas to be presented in an essay is particularly helpful to the dyslexic.

An additional problem with the disability is that it is often misdiagnosed and mistreated at the elementary and secondary levels. This can lead to a variety of emotional traumas such as stuttering and low self-esteem. There is no in-class exercise to cure this. Many students are deemed "slow" by teachers or said to be simply "not trying." Many dyslexic students spend much of their elementary and secondary years in remedial classes, or in resource rooms, or clumped with children suffering from retardation and disciplinary problems. The effect on one's psyche is obvious—it is no wonder some dyslexic children grow up with anxiety problems. I remember being a big, shy eighth grader who spent each afternoon in the resource room of my junior high school. Others in the room included students who had recently returned from drug rehabilitation and the mentally retarded. Other students were quick to stigmatize.

Such sideline problems can lead to many troubles when students reach college composition courses. Dyslexic students might be tentative to speak in class, for fear of looking "stupid." Many times the worst thing an instructor can do to these students is to force them to speak. To this day, I fear reading aloud; I have difficulty processing and transferring information from page to eyes to brain. Being asked to read aloud makes the process much more difficult. As I mention later, if a dyslexic student fails or is embarrassed, the loss of confidence can affect their entire college career.

Help for Students

The best thing instructors can do if they suspect that a student is dyslexic is to suggest testing. Once a student is diagnosed as dyslexic, various doors are opened. For a onetime nominal fee, a student can take advantage of over 80,000 textbooks on four-track tapes offered through a nonprofit organization called Recording for the Blind and Dyslexic. If the organization does not have the desired text, the student can mail the text to the office, and it will be taped free of charge. For further information, contact Recording for the Blind & Dyslexic, 20 Roszel Road, Princeton, NJ 08540; Phone: 800-221-4792; Fax: 609-987-8116; Web Page: http://www.rfbd.org. For a list of dyslexia test locations, contact: The Orton Dyslexic Society, Suite 382, Chester Building, 8600 LaSalle Rd., Baltimore, MD 21286-2044; phone 410-296-0232; fax 410-321-5069; E-Mail: info@ods.org; Web Page: http://ods.org.

Instruction for Dyslexic Students

Despite growing up with many of the problems mentioned above, I learned to read and write. The process was not easy. It involved a lot of extra work on my part and for my instructors. Now, as a composition instructor, I want to share some strategies with colleagues who suspect they have dyslexic students in their classes.

- One-on-One: For a dyslexic, for whom individual attention is many times a must, classrooms set in large auditoriums with hundreds of other students might prove difficult—if not impossible. Typical universities and colleges are not designed for dyslexic students, so the students and their teachers must find ways to cope.

The best method is one-on-one help. Instructors should suggest that the dyslexic student schedule weekly teacher-student conferences to seek extra help and go over assignments. If an instructor cannot find time for this, it should be suggested that the student look into available tutorial programs. If institutions offer specially designed services for the learning disabled, the student should be encouraged to seek that help. Basic writing instructors must insist students master their course, for in reality the students chances of succeeding at the collegiate level without possessing a solid writing background are significantly diminished.

- Study Skills: The basic writing teacher can serve dual capacities here, because many reading assignments are given throughout the semester in most basic composition courses. The ability to read efficiently, then write on specific topics is essential to virtually all college courses, and because most dyslexics read slower than many students and struggle to retain information, learning how to read and take notes become vital.

Giving and grading note-taking assignments can help dyslexic students. Composition instructors can assign a reading, then require a written paragraph summarizing the material. Also the instructor can check textbooks for highlighting and notes taken in the margins. Both parts of such an assignment should be graded. Assignments like this encourage the development of valuable study skills, which all students, but especially dyslexics need.

To best teach these techniques, a composition instructor should model these skills. I have always found it beneficial to see what is expected. During in-class readings, composition instructors have the opportunity to teach dyslexic students how to read most effectively by demonstrating how to locate the main point of a text and explaining that most academic tests focus on the main points of reading material. Instructors can also show students how to skim a text to locate key words, key phrases, and topic sentences. These skills are necessary for dyslexic students who read at a slower pace and who struggle with retention.

The ability to gain the most important information from a text in the most time-efficient manner is vital for dyslexics. Basic writing instructors can help them gain these skills by using the semester's reading assignments for these purposes.

- Individual Strategies: In many cases, an instructor and student can develop specific learning strategies to help the dyslexic student achieve success. Strategies can range from taking advantage of various government programs designed to help dyslexics—by providing textbooks-on-tape—to finding out the time of day students work best and suggesting they set a daily routine accordingly. For example, I still wake each morning at

5:00 a.m. to write. In college, I realized this was when I worked best. I also found a hallway beneath the main floor of the library, and I would go there from 7:00 to 9:00 p.m. several nights a week to read in silence.

Another strategy I developed as an undergraduate and continue to use now in graduate school regards classroom participation. I know that I struggle to comprehend what I read, so many times I will skim assigned reading materials, but I attend all classes and participate as much as possible—asking questions and offering my opinion. I find this participation—because it is oral—is much more beneficial than wasting an hour reading 15 pages from which I retain little.

Books-on-tape can also serve dyslexics well when they are trying to develop writing skills. If one reads slowly and struggles to get through each sentence, how will he or she see what the author is doing or discover what the author is trying to say? As a developing fiction writer, I am constantly purchasing novels on tape and studying them. A dyslexic student may benefit greatly from audio material.

A valuable assignment is to have dyslexic students use a handheld recorder to tape highlights of a class or lecture—push-button note taking—then listen to the tape later and write a summary. The instructor knows the most important segments of the class and can look for those points in the written summary.

- Step-by-Step: Many times a dyslexic simply takes longer to master things. Most composition instructors carefully check the final draft of each writing assignment, looking for patterns, and inform students of mistakes and how to correct them. Dyslexic students can thrive on this personal attention, but may need it more frequently than just on final drafts.

Some students can sit down and turn out a first-rate essay with little or no prewriting. In the case of a dyslexic student, this is not likely. The process of writing—from brainstorming, to outlining, to drafting, to final product—must be emphasized and repeated to be mastered. The step-by-step process must be emphasized. If the process is broken into small assignments, dyslexic students will see the product take form and better understand how it was accomplished. As I have stated previously, many dyslexics see where they are and where they want to be, but not how to get there. For them, concentrated work on each step in the writing process is more important.

A good way to place emphasis on the process is to design homework assignments focusing on only one element of the writing process at a time. An example is to have the student hand in a written brainstorming session. The instructor can review it, marking strengths and weaknesses. The same can be done with each successive step.

With the need to emphasize the writing process, many dyslexics require more time to organize an essay. They are capable of a finished product equal to that of nondyslexic students, but may need more time. Composition teachers may want to notify dyslexic students of upcoming assignments or give them extra time to complete the prewriting stages of an essay.

- Less Is More and Breaking Down Assignments: What I suggest here should be taken case-by-case. If the composition instructor knows a student is dyslexic and reads slowly or needs additional time to organize an essay, the instructor may consider cutting the number of assignments that particular student is responsible for—while demanding excellence in all facets of the writing process.

  I am not saying lessen the dyslexic's workload. What I am suggesting would probably add to it. If the composition class is to write five essays during the semester, I suggest having the dyslexic student write three. But, for the dyslexic, each phase of the writing process—prewriting activities, outline, rough draft, and final draft—should be graded. While the rest of the class receives the topic and is more or less on their own, the dyslexic is assigned each step to be written in detail and turned in for a grade.

  The same can be done with reading assignments. Cut the list of readings for the dyslexic, but demand notes be taken, highlighting be done, and an overall solid comprehension of the material be demonstrated in the form of a written paragraph. Along the same lines, instructors may also want to consider breaking larger reading assignments into small chunks to allow more time. Again, I am not suggesting any load-lightening here. The dyslexic student should do several highlighting and note-taking assignments on each reading segment. This will give the dyslexic additional time to read the material and will offer repetition and an opportunity to master reading comprehension techniques.

- Oral Discussion: In order to write well, one must understand the concept of standard English. Many good writers don't always use proper spoken English, but know how to if they so choose. It is essential for dyslexic students to see and grasp the ability to use standard English—whether speaking or writing. Composition instructors can help dyslexic students improve their writing skills by insisting on the use of proper spoken English and correct sentence structure in classroom discussions—and certainly by modeling that in their own speech. If students grasp the idea of proper sentence structure when verbalizing thoughts, grammar problems will decrease and overall writing will improve.

  Aside from improving sentence structure, discussion allows dyslexics to verbalize ideas and orally plot what they are trying to do. One must remember, most dyslexics learn best from hands-on and oral approaches, not from reading. An oral-driven atmosphere is one in which I have always thrived, and many dyslexics gain the most from oral approaches.

  Instructors can add oral discussions to their classrooms in several ways. An easy way for an instructor to help dyslexic students is to consider thoroughly discussing all assignments. Always happens, right? Wrong. In some composition classrooms, assignments are simply typed and handed out with very little discussion. If students need elaboration, it is up to them to seek it. Since many dyslexic students grasp ideas and information orally better than on the written page, teachers should consider taking one or more classes to explain and discuss each assignment. In my composition classes, we spend one entire class meeting orally discussing the essay assignment and each student's thesis statement. If a student has a weak thesis or doesn't understand the assignment, a class member is usually there to offer ideas.

In-class peer-group collaboration to discuss each member's essay proposal—from original ideas, to outlines, to rough and final drafts is valuable. This teamwork approach offers an oral atmosphere that dyslexic students can benefit from greatly. Composition instructors teaching dyslexic students should consider discussion an integral part of their course.

- Select Topics of Interest to the Student: Many dyslexics have a one-track mind. They find one thing and focus only on it. As a youngster, I would only draw, write, and read about hockey. To this day, I am the same way, now focusing on creative writing. Such limited focus can give teachers headaches, but it can also lead to success and greatness in a particular area. Woodrow Wilson, Leonardo de Vinci, Tom Cruise, Albert Einstein, W. B. Yeats, Gustave Flaubert, and Bruce Jenner are all dyslexics. With hard work and inner drive, they overcame obstacles to achieve success (Seekins 2).

With this in mind, whenever possible, composition instructors should give dyslexic students the opportunity to write on topics of their choice. Dyslexics will have a better chance to excel under these circumstances. In many cases, an assignment a dyslexic student is interested in will lead to all-out effort and an unmistakable passion in their writing.

- Questions to Build Confidence: If an instructor suspects a student is dyslexic and sees that the student suffers from a lack of confidence—asking opinion-based questions can promote in-class participation.

Because many dyslexics go through various stages of their education with low self-esteem, this lack of confidence tends to make them tentative in the classroom. Especially in the first year of college, with a new atmosphere, an unfamiliar teacher, and a roomful of new peers, the dyslexic student might hesitate to participate. As I have said, for me, in-class participation is essential. For other dyslexics, some coaxing may be necessary. Confidence-building questions can be a good tool to get a student involved. And students should always be complimented after giving an answer.

Conclusion

Dyslexia afflicts many college students, and composition instructors must be aware of it and know that there are ways to help them. I have suggested many ideas which I find helpful. The strategies I mention have been tested through years of personal trial and error, and they work. Dyslexia is a lifelong disability, and coping techniques learned in the composition classroom can serve a dyslexic well far beyond the college years.

Works Cited

Brachacki, Gregory, W. Z. Roderick, I. Nicolson, and Angela J. Fawcett. "Impaired Recognition of Traffic Signs in Adults with Dyslexia." *Journal of Learning Disabilities* 28 (1995): 297–301.

Seekins, Brenda. "Different Doesn't Mean Dumb." *Bangor Daily News.* 14–15 Oct. 1995: A1.

Simpson, Eileen. *Reversals—A Personal Account of Victory over Dyslexia.* Boston. Houghton, 1979.

John R. Corrigan holds the MFA degree in creative writing from the University of Texas, El Paso. He has written two novels and published poetry, as well as worked as a newspaper reporter and freelance writer. He is currently teaching composition, AP literature, creative writing, and journalism at the Maine School of Science and Mathematics, Limestone, Maine.

Family Stories and the Fictional Dream

Tom Romano

Late one evening my daughter, Mariana, stepped into the room where I sat before the computer. She was eighteen then, in the last month of her senior year of high school.

"Will you listen to my story?" she asked.

Closing in on some writing of my own, I turned my head to her but kept my fingers at the keyboard. Mariana wore sweats. Her blonde hair was clipped back from her forehead. Her contact lenses were soaking in a heat sterilizer for the night. Her glasses had slid halfway down her nose; she pushed them into place with a forefinger. She looked weary. Track practice had been longer than usual.

Mariana held a dozen sheets of ragged-edged notebook paper she likes to write on with soft-leaded pencils. I knew those pages were the draft of her final paper for senior English. She had been thinking about this assignment for months, researching here and there, gathering information and impressions, asking me questions about my family. Since a late supper of microwaved leftovers, she had been in her room bent over a desk, filling pages with her looping handwriting.

For this assignment Mariana's teacher had asked the students to research particular years or eras and then—instead of composing traditional research papers—to write short fiction that incorporated details from their research. Mariana had made the assignment her own, had chosen to research Ellis Island and 1914, the year my father, then a boy of nine, immigrated to the United States from Italy.

Mariana dropped to the floor and sat cross-legged to read me her story. I removed my fingers from the keyboard and swiveled around to face her. She began, turning the pages sideways at times to read words written in the margins, looking closely other times to make out words she had squeezed between lines.

"Felice felt he was drowning in the ocean of people," she read. "He closed his eyes and tried to breathe. He could feel the small wooden pony against his heart and remembered Luca. Tears welled in his eyes but he swallowed them this time. Giuesseppe would call him *bambino* again and hit him. Felice wanted

English Journal, 82 (September 1993), pp. 34–36. Copyright © 1993 by the National Council of Teachers of English. Reprinted with permission.

to be strong too, and he wanted to be able to stand up to Papa like Giuesseppe said he was going to."

Elbows on my knees, chin resting in my hands, I gazed down at my daughter, then let my eyelids close. I entered the fictional dream Mariana had woven of my father, his two brothers, sister, and mother as they shuffled along in a crowd, moving off the ship that had brought them across the Atlantic Ocean. Filomena, the youngest child, slept in her mother's arms. Antonio, the youngest boy, cried and held his mother's skirt. Giuesseppe, the oldest child, carried himself bravely, almost disdainfully, as he moved toward American soil. Felice, my father, was between his brothers, but closer to Antonio's tears than Giuesseppe's defiance. The wooden pony Felice kept in his shirt pocket had been carved and given to him by his friend, Luca, before the family left the village near Naples.

In her short story Mariana explored a mystery she'd been aware of for years—the great influence on our lives of my father, then dead twenty-five years, the mythlike story of his family's immigration to an America decades away from fast-food restaurants, designer jeans, and alternative rock music. She conjectured in her fiction, too, inventing detail, action, and characterizations that have not been documented in family stories but that carry the illusion of reality, nevertheless.

Mariana's research in books had not been extensive. A half-dozen times, however, she had watched the opening of Francis Ford Coppola's The Godfather II (1974, Paramount), the scenes when the Italian immigrants enter New York harbor, are awestruck by the Statue of Liberty, and disembark at Ellis Island. These images had shown Mariana early twentieth-century America and the look of frightened, hopeful immigrants. The images spurred her imagination, bringing new vividness to the stories told and retold by members of our family, stories I'd heard my father and aunts and uncles tell when I was a boy sitting at the dining room table after a traditional Christmas Eve supper, stories that rolled from their tongues in the quiet fullness after the meal, stories that sparked further stories and drew my beloved relatives into debates about events, people, and memories.

During those fleeting hours of storytelling, I sat transfixed, asking questions that prompted an uncle or aunt to retell some incident or maybe, just maybe, reveal some bit of information I'd never heard before. And when my uncles and aunts and father slipped into the assured rhythms of reminiscence, I hoped that the telephone would not ring and that no one would knock at the door. Carefully, quietly, I refilled the small glasses with the dry red wine my uncle made each year. I wanted nothing—not an empty glass, not an unexpected call, not a glance at the clock—to break the spell of telling.

Mariana leaned forward, reading slowly, treating her language with great respect, adopting a colloquial tone when she read dialogue. Her sincere, urgent voice rolled up to me from the floor and entered my very bones. I'd never imagined my father as a boy at the moment he arrived in America, never imagined that he may have left a best friend in Italy, that his sister may have slept and younger brother may have cried. Because of "The Wooden Pony," Mariana's fictional dream woven of image and story, language and imagination, I would never think of my father in the same way again. Mariana read the final lines.

> Felice looked past Mama and met the gaze of Giuesseppe. He watched two tears roll out of his older brother's eyes and make their varied path down his face.
>
> The two brothers stared at each other, expressionless.
>
> Felice grinned. "*Bambino,*" he whispered.
>
> They laughed silently together. Felice patted his heart and thought about the future.

Mariana looked up to me and saw my eyes filled with tears.

A day or two after that evening I thought of buying Mariana a carved wooden pony for her high-school graduation. I had no luck finding such a present in area stores. I remained optimistic, though, since I was traveling a good deal. On trips to Calgary, Toronto, Montana, and New York, I found wooden bears, raccoons, wolves, seals, whales, moose, but no wooden ponies. Not even wooden horses.

My mother-in-law saved the day. She knew a wood carver, a longtime friend, who agreed to whittle a wooden pony for me. I sent him a copy of Mariana's short story so he could generate his own vision. Before he began his woodworking, however, he suffered a heart attack and underwent triple-bypass surgery.

Two months later I learned that he still wanted to carve the pony, that he and his wife, in fact, thought the work would be good therapy for him. By this time it was midsummer.

"Are you getting me something for graduation or not?" Mariana asked.

"Be patient," I told her.

The following year, ten months after she had written "The Wooden Pony," Mariana was home from college for spring break. The day before she headed back to school she and her mother went shopping. When they were gone, a small package arrived in the mail. I opened it and pulled out an object wrapped in tissue paper: a stiff-legged, blockish wooden pony. I turned it over in my hands, touching the ears, running my finger along the smooth back. I stood the pony on the kitchen counter. I was disappointed; it looked amateurish.

I found a note from the wood carver's wife. "Merle wasn't happy with the way this turned out," she wrote, "but our ten-year-old grandson loves it and wanted to take it home. We thought it might be just the thing Luca would have carved for Felice."

Precisely, I thought.

Mariana arrived home from shopping in a flurry, dropping plastic bags to the floor and plopping down to open them. I sat reading in a chair.

"Open the package on the counter," I said to her.

Mariana was busy removing skirt, sweater, and shoes from the bags.

"What's in it?" She laid the sweater against the skirt on the floor and eyed the combination.

"Just open it. Please."

"I will in a minute," she said, her voice colored with annoyance. She spent a moment or two more with her new clothes, then walked to the refrigerator and opened a can of soda pop. Finally, she turned to the package. Her eyebrows were pursed, troubled, as I had often seen my father's. From the package Mariana lifted the object. The tissue paper fell away. She held the wooden pony in both hands, her eyebrows raised in startled surprise. She glanced across the room to me. And this time, it was her eyes that filled with tears.

Writing, reading, storytelling. Some truth. Some fiction. And always our lives. These elements were woven together in Mariana's research and subsequent short story. Her fictional dream had taken me to a place I'd never been, enabled me to imagine my father as a boy, wearing a coarse, woolen cap and high-topped, black leather shoes.

"The Wooden Pony" went far beyond the classroom, much farther than the teacher could have imagined. Mariana's uncles, aunts, and cousins, great uncles, great aunts, and grandmother read the story and talked about it and read it again. The story triggered further stories. In a small town in northeastern Ohio, a retiree recovering from open-heart surgery used the images he envisioned from reading "The Wooden Pony" to guide his hand, eye, and brain in shaping his own creative response.

Mariana's fiction reached back seventy-five years, took readers to a moment when an immigrant child stepped ashore at Ellis Island. America and his life lay before him. And years later, one of his granddaughters, a girl born seven years after his death, thought long about this grandfather she knew only through family stories and photographs, wondered further about a magical day in October 1914 that her relatives had talked about ever since she could remember. Powerful images took shape and language stirred. Setting became real. Characters spoke and moved. Mariana wrote a fictional dream. And we who entered that dream were never the same.

Educating the Imagination

Es'kia Mphahlele

It has been my fate to be a teacher and writer. The imagination is my regular beat as it is also the workshop of my mind; the territory of ideas, knowledge, thought, and emotion is my hunting ground. To use another metaphor, I have grown up alternately grappling with hard and almost intractable concepts, and then relaxing to make a pole-vault leap into the realm of the imagination. Yet the concepts keep trailing behind me, as it were, keeping me in contact with the real concrete world. Like a kite a person keeps on a string no matter how high it flies, feeding it more line and still more.

I come from a country where for virtually two centuries the people of color have, as a deliberate policy, been denied the freedom of association, assembly, thought, inquiry, and self-expression. For this reason I have treasured and savored every moment when I could snatch any one of the freedoms. We are still reeling from the nightmare life has been for the majority population— the oppressed and dispossessed. The wounds are still too raw for us even to begin to appreciate the loosening up of some of the racist laws. Especially because fundamental inequalities still exist: economic, social, and political structures, some of them centuries old, still stare us in the face. This in spite of the fact that the present government possesses the absolute instruments for the immediate dissolution of white supremacy without our assistance, even before we start talking.

I spent the earlier part of my childhood in a pastoral environment as a boy tending cattle and goats. I was, during those seven years, a pupil of nature. It was only in later years that I realized what schooling nature had put me through. I learned even as a seven-year-old that I should monitor a goat or cow giving birth, carry the small kids home at sunset, track down lost animals. I learned to hunt rock rabbits in the moonlight, to carry wood from the wilds for making the communal fire where we would listen to the men tell stories. The fascination words have always had for me is an echo of the music of language that registered on my ears in those days as it conjured up a strange world. A strange world recreated out of familiar things, events, people. The line between the natural and the supernatural often blurred.

College English, 55 (February 1993), pp. 179–86. Copyright © 1993 by the National Council of Teachers of English. Reprinted with permission.

Those days, as I came to discover later, I was thrown upon myself, so that I could contemplate and feel and imagine. There was plenty of time to do this. The darknesses, the silences, the sounds of day and of night, the open vastnesses, landscapes teeming with daylight, shimmering distances of subtropical heat, savannah lying low and biding its time under the winter spell--all these and others provided for me good training ground from which to launch the odyssey of the imagination.

But this was not to be the journey of typical modern western man or woman alienated by industrialization and urbanization, an allegory of innocence lost and never to be regained. For those folk tales taught the social relationships and family allegiances that informed a morality we associate with African humanism: I am because you are, you are because we are. It was not the intellectual odyssey that became a cult in western humanism from the Renaissance on. Our humanism is essentially spiritual, recognizing the Vital Force or the Supreme Being at the center of and integrating human, animal, and plant life and the inanimate elements of the universe. It is a simple faith free of the tyranny of theology and intellectual argument. This is the measure of the imagination's investment in the power of oral expression.

Since our encounter with Europe, we the colonized communities of the world have been the ones to shoulder the task of synthesizing the west and "ourselves." The west has always felt superior and culturally self-sufficient, with no need to learn anything from anybody else. The fierce drive of the intellect buttressed by economic advancement has reinforced that sense of supremacy even more today than ever before.

This is where the imagination's task lies in child-raising in Africa, Asia, and their diasporas today. Right at the crossroads of two main streams of consciousness: the western, which has pushed the science of manipulating the material world and the environment to the outer frontiers of possibility, and "the other," which holds on for dear life to that great and splendid pursuit of enduring spiritual values rooted in social relationships, in the integrated personality. I am not in the least suggesting that "the other" has a monopoly on transcendental wisdom and intuition. I only wish that the west could begin to reeducate itself towards a conscious synthesis, and that "the other" could assimilate and synthesize on its own terms, not those of the "master" race.

The unfolding of the collective imagination through folklore, proverbs, and allegory was something we took for granted, without a grasp of its spiritual dimensions. All I knew was that my imagination was constantly at work. Nature led me through its own rugged and smooth paths according to its integrated curriculum. I imagined that by repeatedly singing a ditty, "Cloud do not blind the sun, waste away, cloud stay out of the sun's way," I could cause a cloud to dissolve into the blue. It did. I believed that the power of the spoken word had done it. I spoke aloud to trees and other inanimate things. I imagined that I heard them respond. This kind of education, observe, was a way of growing up, of living, rather than a conscious preparation for later life, which we are often told is the overall aim of formal schooling.

My recurring dreams ever since my mother removed us from the rural area to an African ghetto outside Pretoria city have to this day revolved around my early rural childhood experiences, the cruel and the benign.

By the time Mother came to fetch us, urban ghettos were mushrooming all around as a result of industrial expansion. The white man badly needed labor. But the influx of Africans had to be contained by means of the "pass" system, which not only checked migration from the rural areas but also herded us into ghettos. Segregation, apartheid, euphemistically called "separate development," was the underlying ideology.

Our people had long been dispossessed of their land. Millions woke up one day soon after the Land Act of 1913 without any land of their own. They had to leave their sharecropper shacks in droves for rural ghettos, now referred to as "homelands." The areas set aside for the Africans were small, often with poor water supply and poor soil. Those who had been living here for centuries could only do so because the land was unsuitable for white farming. Poverty, together with its companion malnutrition, stalks the rural areas today. Landlessness has become a permanent condition. Even when the land laws are repealed, Africans will not be able to afford to buy land. They do not possess any farming skills either. The drift to the towns seems irreversible for now.

Until the 1930s, people grew the food they ate. Today they buy their food from the nearby store—in small miserable quantities, absurdly overpriced. In most rural areas women still carry firewood from the bush. They still carry water on their heads from the river or communal pump. This used to be a way of growing up for an adolescent girl, a rite of passage. Just as it was for her male counterpart to go hunting, tilling the soil. Today they carry wood and water for sheer harrowing survival.

Yesterday ploughing time, the first spring rains, the time of harvesting brought out of the people rituals that replayed their poetry, song, and dance. Today, no land, no ploughing or harvesting, no rituals, no poetry. Older men and women who can still recite praise songs are dying out. They have no heirs left. We are carriers of a disinherited mind. Time has been dislocated. What poetry exists is woven out of urban life and the political predicament. Or it comes through in the work songs of the city.

When I came to live in the urban areas at the age of twelve, survival dramatized itself in other and harsher ways. The poverty, the muck, and the stench of slum conditions filled every day and night of our lives. Above all, we had to try to survive white racism and its police force. (In the country, we rarely saw a white person. When one did appear, we watched from the security of the bushes.)

I felt an inner compulsion to improve my education. At thirteen I was at a level in school equivalent to the American fourth grade. Because I tended cattle and goats in the country, my schooling had been erratic. In my new setting, I read every scrap of paper I picked up. There were no newsstands in the ghettos of the thirties. I relied on neighbors to give me newspapers, no matter how old, to read. My mother's employers in white suburbia gave me their old magazines and books to read—the adventures of white girls and boys, "love and romance," that kind of stuff. By a stroke of luck my hunting expeditions yielded from a pile of discarded books Cervantes's *Don Quixote*. I still cannot forget the thrill of discovery I experienced reading it.

As I went on to a mission high school and later to a mission teacher-training institution, both of which had libraries, the unending quest led me through progressively better reading. From guzzling chunks of printed matter ripe, raw, and rotten, I moved to the higher plane of discriminating reading habits. Books were my refuge from living conditions that were created expressly to frustrate our self-realization.

An irrepressible moviegoer, I reveled in the silent films of the day. I saw the movie industry change to talkies. My imagination was taking on experiences that were totally different from rural life.

Urban poverty and slum life presented challenges of another order. Whites kicked or pushed us off sidewalks. Most train coaches, entrances into stations, platforms and waiting rooms were out of bounds for us. Police raids, roadblocks, and curfews were an integral part of our lives.

The rural and urban zones of my being are locked in a neverending dialogue. They constitute together a landscape of my being on which is enacted a story that has no ending. As far as my limited understanding goes, it has no beginning either. Maybe one is always at the starting point.

A woman is sitting by the roadside, suckling a baby—a commonplace scene typical in the developing world. A flight of birds enacts a ballet up against the blue, carefree, far away from human concerns, far away from trucks and other vehicles that chew up the road and leave clouds of dust in their wake. The woman waits and endures as so many other women of the world do: waiting and enduring, like the trees she's sitting under. Massive concrete inhabitants of the city behind me heave themselves up into space, as if they were jostling for attention.

The poetic essence of this scene lies in the relationships the mind intuits between the disparate elements. The mind and sensory perceptions recreate new or familiar relationships, perceiving things as an organic whole. Poetry is a way of perceiving. There is an inner compulsion for the imagination to create a picture that will harmonize and establish a rhythm in the relationships between phenomena. Poetry is always there. What we need to do is pluck it from the tree. Recreate it. Refine it as we write it, or speak it, expressing vigorous feelings with vigorous words.

Surely, in order to educate the imagination, the creative person has to learn how to deal with the world of things, events, people, open up all the pores of the body, bombard the sense organs until they cannot help but register impressions that press against them and must try to make meaning out of them. We are forever seeking meanings in the world around. Because these meanings of the external world help us discover meanings of ourselves at every stage of our growth.

Early in a person's life his or her social environment, in combination with his or her inner resources or character, creates a disposition to inquire, search, yearn to discover, respond acutely, probe relationships. All over the world the child is exceeding adults' traditional expectations of what it should know at certain stages. But South African children who grow up on the dark side of the color and racial divide live about eighteen years in a space of ten. At fifteen they are much more mature than their white counterparts. But it is a desperate maturity, which is often a severe handicap in their formal schooling. They are angry, afraid, reckless, daring, because they are under siege: police and military surveillance are forever with them. And the educational system was never designed to make self-emancipation possible. It was intended to enslave them, incapacitate them. They possess knowledge from life's experiences, but they have not the ability to mobilize this knowledge into a coherent, disciplined force that will illuminate meanings.

"Bantu Education," as it came to be called, is a product of Afrikaner nationalism and apartheid ideology. Before 1953, when Bantu Education became law, although facilities were separate and unequal, curricula and syllabi were the same for black and white; the new curricula and syllabi compelled teachers to instruct their children how to *be* and *feel* inferior. The rationale was to lower the quality of education for the Africans so that we did not aspire to pastures set aside for whites. The State insisted on mother-tongue instruction from elementary through high school, knowing full well that English textbooks were not going to be translated. It was hoped that the new system would counter political activism: the Mandelas, the Sobukwes, and their fellow activists had been educated in the earlier system. The frontiers of the imagination would thus be limited, because ideas that come with education were blocked.

Artists respond to political and social upheaval through their own kind of sensibility—the written word or body movement or sculpture or song—as well as through the activism society demands of them. At such times of upheaval, there may seem to the artist to be nothing, but *nothing,* as important, as sacred, as freedom. Writers become completely absorbed in the predicament of their community, which in turn almost swallows us up. We begin to program the imagination, channel it so that it serves our ideals, our vision of a glorious future. In the process we pump energy into our diction, and more and still more until we imagine that words themselves are like missiles. We invest words with the mystical power that can bring ramparts tumbling down. We speak with the tongues of prophets, priests, gurus. We invoke the presence of our ancestors, especially the spirits of our heroes. We often imitate oratory in our drama and poetry. Poetry becomes theatre. (If the poetry and drama of the Black world have anything in common, it is this aptitude to recapture the resonances of oratory.)

I feel constrained at this point to say something that is quite unpopular in my country. We are at that stage in our history when we lose all patience with those who do not embrace our own tactics toward liberation. We would like all people to think alike, speak and act alike. Some groups even kill for their beliefs. This is the point I want to put across for what it is worth: that in situations of political conflict and violence we can rescue the imagination, at least for an interim period, from the kind of programing that compels us to repeat ourselves. We must surely realise that there is a certain kind of repetitiousness that spells stagnation. The imagination begins to atrophy. For this is when we live on borrowed passion, heroics, certitudes. The imagination may well retreat a bit at this point, reorganize itself, sharpen focus, and restore the fullness of its landscape. The imagination then becomes our sanctuary.

One of the ways of salvaging the imagination, I suggest, is through this very method of recapturing with the written word the power of incantation, of oral delivery, of the ancient inner magic of language as metaphor. Another way is to provide as full a context for protest as possible, if protest there must be. Myth-making, context, lend resonances to our creations. The myth is that never-ending story of life: children are still being born, women still wait and endure, men still betray one another, we still dream, idle and meaningful dreams. . . . And we must keep trying to negotiate the meeting point between art and history: an effort that is itself the enduring purpose of life.

Gwendolyn Brooks has said in a foreword to an anthology of poetry compiled by Langston Hughes and published in 1964:

> At the present time, poets who happen also to be Negroes are twice-tried. They have to write poetry, and they have to remember that they are Negroes. Often they wish that they could solve the Negro question once and for all, and go on from such success to the composition of textured sonnets or buoyant villanelles about the transience of a raindrop, or the gold-stuff of the sun. *They* are likely to find significances in those subjects not instantly obvious to their fairer fellows. The raindrop may seem to them to represent racial tears—and those might seem, indeed, other than transient. The golden sun might remind them that they are burning. (13)

During the fifties, when a crop of writers including myself emerged around *Drum* magazine in Johannesburg, I wrote bitter stories. I choked on the stuff and the heartburn it was releasing. The bitterness left me emotionally drained. I knew that I could not sustain the anger without doing myself harm. I went into exile, to teach in Nigeria. With my exit came my release. Even though I continued to write mainly about the life I had left behind, I had the freedom to learn to tame my bitterness with language. Words hammered out on the anvil of life itself, words lifted out of the fire of imagination and reordered into the shape of poetic truths.

It may often appear that the poet in an environment of political conflict and tyranny simply revels in predicting doom for the oppressor. Especially when it is just possible that he may not heave himself up to do anything of such apocalyptic dimensions as he says he or the people are planning. But the anger hurts badly. It can be corrosive if sustained and if we do not tame it with words.

Although I felt discontented and restless in the last three of my nine years in the United States, just raring to return home, I realized more than ever before that I had come a long way from my small-village and slum beginnings. During my twenty years' exile I had enjoyed the freedom to move in and learn from a diversity of cultures—here, in Africa, in Europe.

I have learned, too, that even in open democracies such as the American and Western European there are pockets of bigoted morality operating under the banner of Christianity, just as we have witnessed in the case of Islam in some states. This often places the imagination in a state of siege. Indeed it has become impossible to talk meaningfully about the imagination without reference to culture, its breeding ground: belief, ideology, education, values, and so on.

Bigots will continue to thrive, a price we have to pay for the democratic ideal. This ideal promises us the right to be what we will and still ensures that we do not claim any right to violate another human being—physically, or by blackmail, or by setting up barricades around that person's freedom to be.

The battle is on. The mind is straining at the chains in order to break them. The children are still angry. Their kind of anger readily finds expression through the destruction of school property—something tangible, destructible, something that symbolizes white authority.

Educators are faced with the daunting task of setting up structures in which the intellect must find a humanistic environment to regain its right to learn, to attain the farthest reaches of the imagination possible.

The beauty of this adventure is that the imagination does not wait for the day when we shall have rid ourselves of tyranny. It overarches history and may get there long before the event. The imagination reorganizes reality where there was chaos before; the artist rebels against disorder. Now. Jean Toomer captures the breathless urgency of the creative imagination in the same dramatic terms that spell out the exhortation toward freedom:

> Come, brother, come. Lets lift it;
> Come, now, hewit! roll away!
> Shackles fall upon the Judgment Day
> But lets not wait for it.
>   "Cotton Song" (25)

Credit

Lines from "Cotton Song" excerpted from *Cane* by Jean Toomer. Introduction copyright © 1975 by Darwin T. Turner. Copyright 1923 by Boni and Liveright. Copyright renewed 1951 by Jean Toomer. Reprinted with permission of the publisher, Liveright Publishing Corporation.

Works Cited

Brooks, Gwendolyn. Foreword. *New Negro Poets U.S.A.* Ed. Langston Hughes. Bloomington: Indiana UP, 1964. 13–14.

Toomer, Jean. *Collected Poems of Jean Toomer.* Ed. Robert B. Jones and Margery Toomer Latimer. Chapel Hill: U of North Carolina P, 1988

The Language of Coats

Nancy Sommers

The colors—those are what I remember most vividly about the nightly ritual of the ticket game. Sometime in the early evening, while my mother cleaned up the kitchen and my brother counted his baseball cards, my father and I would sit at our dining room table, sorting and organizing tickets from the coats he had sold that day. Tickets were laid out by size—green upon green, orange upon orange—then by manufacturer's style number, and then by price. As manager of the coat department in my uncle's department store, my father needed to know which styles and sizes had sold that day in order to know which coats needed to be reordered and which shipped back to the manufacturer.

While my brother took great pride in knowing, to the decimal point, the batting averages of Mickey Mantle and Roger Maris, I prided myself upon recognizing the range of colors and sizes of the tickets—the tangerine-colored size 16, the pale green size 18, or the violet size 24½—reciting with my father the vocabulary of coats: cashmeres, camel hairs, tweeds, with rabbit, squirrel, raccoon, or muskrat collars, sewn-on or detached.

Aside from these tickets, my father didn't have much emotional or financial security. An immigrant from Europe, he had lost contact with his language and culture, and found himself in Terre Haute, Indiana, a town where people lived generation after generation, growing up in the houses their great-great-grandparents had built. We had our modest ranch house at 134 South 23rd Street, but no ancestral home, no family reunions, no burial plots. People in Terre Haute thought my father exotic; they couldn't place his dark, Semitic looks, often asking him where he came from, or if he knew or was related to Ricky Ricardo.

Even though he had just survived Hitler, my father said that nothing had ever happened to him, that he was a simple person—"no one famous." His experience in Germany in the thirties taught him to stay inconspicuous, avoid controversy, never wear or say anything out of the ordinary. Such a modest profile was perfectly suited for the department store business, a business in which it was best if a manager was never observed driving too fast or speaking too loudly, such actions reflecting poorly upon the character of the store.

"The customer is always right," my father would tell us—even if the customer returned coats, tried on every size 18 available but bought nothing, or

College English, 60 (April 1998), pp. 421–25. Copyright © 1998 by the National Council of Teachers of English. Reprinted with permission.

asked my father to open the store early or stay late while she decided between the full-length fur-lined tweed coat and the three-quarter length fur-collared and cuffed camel hair.

On a good day, in season, my father might sell forty coats; the day after Christmas, three hundred. But then there were the days when the sales clerks quarreled or were sick, the competition undersold him, or customers wanted herringbone-tweed and he had only plaid. Those were the days in which he didn't make his day. "Making your day" was department store language for selling the amount of merchandise you predicted you could sell, based on previous years' sales. Despite rain, sleet, hail, markdowns, and willful customers, a manager was expected to make or exceed his day, every day, day after day. Meager raises or Christmas bonuses, money my father needed to establish some roots in Terre Haute, depended on him making his day.

As a child, I didn't know much about what it meant when my father did or did not make his day. My only desire during those evenings we spent at our dining room table was to see how high we could pile the tangerine or violet tickets. But I knew that the ticket ritual could end abruptly. Maybe I said the wrong thing or put a ticket in the wrong place; maybe my mother, in the kitchen baking apple kuchen, kneading hope into our life, day by doughy day, might have expressed too much optimism. My father, seeing that he hadn't made his day, would erupt into a bewildering rage. During such moments, I fixed my eyes above the dining room table, at the painting of two green peppers, while behind me the man who had been so tightly controlled for the customers bellowed Germanic curses. What I wanted at those moments was simply for the words to stop. I wanted a still life.

But still life never claimed me. Instead, like my father, I worked. I spent my teenage years working at the family store, extending my knowledge of the vocabulary of coats into a study of the store's entire language—its diction and syntax, its style and structure—until I knew even idioms and metaphors. First, sorting hangers, stocking shelves, then selling men's furnishings and women's foundations; later, being the store spy, checking the prices of the competition, and, finally, selling coats myself. Working in the store, I learned something firsthand about the intimacy of work, its romance and its danger, its myths and rituals, its pulsating pleasures and disappointments, the ways in which work can feed a family and color a life.

Now, at age forty-five, I have defined my life's work as a teacher and director of a writing program, work which is simultaneously exhilarating and exhausting, days folding one into the next, overlapping deadlines, breathless dashes from meeting to memo, from conference to classroom, each day an unfinished draft. Arriving home, always late, unburdening, deflating my body with long, ponderous sighs, the family chiming "no more excuses." A quick dinner, and the thread of work continues. My husband, a computer architect, returns to his silicon world of chips, micro processors, and semiconductors. I sit at the kitchen table with the children, a nightly ritual. They write their compositions; I read my students' drafts and revisions. No one's at the stove baking apple kuchen. There are no tickets to count; I have no way to know if I am making my day.

I calculate that my father sold around 350,000 coats during his forty years at the store. By now, after twenty years of teaching writing, I have probably read about 3,500 student drafts, a similarly mind-boggling number. I keep thinking that when I hit my 4,000th draft it will be like my fantasy—the great fortune of being the hundredth customer of the day, the one for whom the bells and whistles ring as she dashes aisle by aisle for ten minutes of free shopping. Something should come to me; some gift, freely given, some clarity of vision, some way of doing my work better after all these years.

It is peculiar work, this teaching writing. In a heavy semester, I myself write nothing except that genre we call "comments" or "responses" to student writing. My comments ask students to be specific, to provide evidence, to ana-lyze, explain, define, argue, counterargue, interpret, and to do it all vividly, con-cisely, eloquently. The vocabulary of teaching reveals the ways in which we size and label our students' writing, responding to what is on the page. And yet what we desperately desire, and what our language leaves us searching for, are ways to show students how to consider what is not on the page, a new frame for their ideas, a real revision—another way of being, of creating, a structure that may not—should not—already exist as a pattern for dozens of other essays. Unlike my father, I must sometimes convince my customers, my students, to take an interest in a coat whose pattern they haven't imagined.

As I sit at my kitchen table, trying to summon my own words to show a student how to animate a moribund thesis, I sometimes wonder if I have made my day. Sometimes I feel like I haven't, and I yearn again for a still life, one without words. Those are the moments when I feel as if I can't do enough for my students—our fifty-minute class period over just as it begins, the semester ending just as the students arrive at a place where they dare to take risks with their writing. At the end of a class or a semester, I am still trying to get many of my students to move beyond the dull gray tweed and at least try on the blue cashmere with the squirrel collar. This is something my father might not under-stand—a coat is a coat, a single ticket, the customer gets what she wants. But so much in teaching writing is about what we can't size or label and involves, at first, not always giving the customers what they want.

After teaching for so many years, I tend to dwell on the students I can't reach, the tough customers, and wonder what kind of vision might have helped me teach them better. Hannah, for instance, a student in my class last year, had a habit of arriving just as the class began. She announced her presence by stretching her hand out on our seminar table, then spending most of our class time drawing intricate Escher-like worlds within worlds on the palms of her hands and in the webs of her fingers. What I wanted to say to Hannah was "Stop writing on your hands; start writing on the page." She turned in breathtaking prose when she wrote, but for most of our assignments she struck a Bartleby pose of "I prefer not to." She teased me with paragraphs that left me begging for more. She was her generation's next great essayist, I imagined, but no matter if I pulled up or extended the deadline, opened up or limited the assignment, Hannah could never write enough to pass the course. In the end, we both felt as if we hadn't made our days.

I am often struck, when interviewing candidates for teaching positions in our program, by the range of answers given to one of my most important questions—how do you know if you have been successful in teaching your students to write? Some newly minted teachers, raised on theories of student empowerment, tell me that they know they have been successful when they don't need to be present in the classroom and their students begin to teach themselves. If I, as a newly minted teacher twenty years ago, had been asked to define success, I probably would have taken refuge in the professional slogans of the 1970s, saying something about the importance of teaching "process not product," about process being our most important product.

We need such professional stories about empowerment and process because the very ways universities measure and count teaching success are so limited, so threadbare and worn out. Our student evaluations—that moment when the marking pen is handed across the desk and the student ranks, on a scale of 1–5, a range of skills from the teacher's ability to stimulate discussion to her use of the blackboard—are imprecise at best in showing us if we have taught our students to write. Even from teachers with some of the highest student evaluations, I too often see bland, trendy student writing which makes me wonder whether it would have been any worse if those students hadn't taken a semester of expository-writing. I often think that student evaluations do a better job of ranking how students feel about the grades they were given, or how they liked the clothes or personality of their teacher, than what they learned about writing.

Yet student evaluations do matter, as all writing program directors know, when our deans measure if we have made our day. A program average of 4.38, an impressive number for a required course, suggests that we must be doing something right. To the university, "the customer is always right," and the price tag of education, a brightly colored costly one—about eight times more than it cost to get a college education in the 1970s—forces us to keep asking ourselves and our students if we are doing enough to prepare them for the demands of college writing.

That's a legitimate and necessary question to ask. But reading and critiquing a student essay is *not* like the vocabulary of coats—although the tickets, those numerical scores, do speak to others. Teaching writing is such all-consuming, challenging, and intimate work because in order to show students how to revise, to reimagine, to do something completely different in the next draft or in the next essay, as opposed to "giving the teacher what she wants," we need to climb into their heads and they into ours. Teaching writing is entering into the actual space of the work, and into the yardage itself—the basic fabric of the student's ideas and capacities— and then assisting in the very design and cutting and stitching of that work. It's learning the language in full, so that communication between teacher and student grows and evolves and is finally made present in the essay itself, so clearly that someone from outside, someone who does not work in the classroom, can see and feel it, and the essay can go out into the world like a new coat, something useful, beautiful, made to last.

Retired for ten years now, my father has gracefully moved from forty years of selling coats to becoming a newly minted ESL tutor at the Terre Haute Public Library. Volunteering as a tutor is his way of giving back to a language he loves and to a town which raised his children, protected him, gave him a home. Our family store has gone the way of most locally owned businesses, bought by one corporation, sold to another, becoming part of a conglomerate which doesn't care much about individual stores, employees, or even customers. The tickets in these stores are all white, printed, coded, and scanned by computer. "The coat business has lost its soul," my father tells us. Still, I often find myself almost magnetically drawn to the coat departments of large department stores. Even in the sweltering heat of summer, I love to touch the wool coats, be claimed by soft cashmere, press my palms and run my fingers through the fur collars, remembering the squirrel and rabbit of home. Sometimes I think of my father and Terre Haute. And sometimes, in coat departments, I think of my students.

If I were asked these days to define success in teaching writing, I might use the language of coats. Instead of talking about helping students find the appropriate evidence, arguments, or interpretations, I might talk about the ways in which students—our customers—aren't always right when they enter the classroom. Some don't want to be noticed, are afraid to stick out their necks to say anything gutsy, wild, or risky. Some enter nervously, hiding behind the racks of quotations and surplus footnotes they find in the storage room. Such students need to be encouraged to take chances, to try on something new, to make a bold statement. Others have to be shown the false, commercial side to their choices: if they think college writing involves a puffed-up voice or strings of obscure jargon-filled abstractions, they will look pretentiously overdressed. Some may even need Thoreau's advice to "beware of any enterprise that requires new clothes."

Students, all writers, need to learn how to design for themselves garments that fit. These days I feel as if I make my day when I can show students how to be designers, not customers, when I can show them how to value, maybe even love, the work they do as writers; to have something at stake, personally, in the language they claim, as if the world depended upon their every word—that they can know the beauty, elasticity, and power of language in the palms of their hands and in the webs of their fingers, and on the white page spread before them.

Car Wrecks, Baseball Caps,
and Man-to-Man Defense

The Personal Narratives of Adolescent Males

Lad Tobin

As soon as Tim Flanagan skipped the second class of the semester, I had him pegged as a problem to be endured rather than a student to be taught. "Hey professor" (he missed the day when I asked them to call me by my first name), "Professor, you're probably wondering where I was Thursday? *Third* row tickets to U2 Wednesday night. You couldn't expect me to give that up, could you?" I should have asked right then what Wednesday night had to do with Thursday morning or joked about lowering his grade for not getting me a ticket to the concert or said that, yes, I did expect him to give it up if he couldn't make it to class otherwise. But, for some reason, I just shrugged, smiled sickly, and muttered, "No, I guess not."

I did decide on a strategy for dealing with Tim: I would just ignore him, plow ahead, and make him the first volunteer in my personal struggle to stem grade inflation. "I asked you to bring in your first drafts of your personal narratives. Would anyone be willing to read your essay aloud so we can discuss it in a workshop?" To my surprise, Tim was the only one who raised his hand. I didn't think that he had even written an essay. "I'll read mine but . . . [here he paused to smile] . . . is it OK if my essay is about something illegal?" I responded with that same inarticulate shrug, mumbled "I guess," and waited for another of those male narratives that I have come to hate—another "why I should be admired for getting drunk and getting into a near-fatal car crash" or "what was so funny about that time me and my friends played a great Halloween prank on the class nerd." And, sure enough, my first impression of the opening paragraph of Tim's narrative about his success as a shoplifter was that it seemed self-congratulatory, vaguely antisocial, and stylistically Hemingwayesque; that is, it seemed embarrassingly male:

> It was a game we played. I'd show up about a half hour after school. Never
> sooner, never later. Those were the rules. He'd be there, usually hanging
> around the register, stuffing bags or authorizing checks or just waiting, I'd
> stroll in through the automatic doorways. I'd pause to read the announcements

College English, 58 (February 1996), pp. 158–75. Copyright © 1996 by the National Council of Teachers of English. Reprinted with permission.

on the bulletin board. That's rule #18 of shoplifting. I did it so he could see me and prepare for the game. I knew he was watching. I knew that he was probably wishing that I was older so he could punch the shit out of me. But he had to stay within the rules. His own rules. The rules he established and the rules he lived by. We rarely made eye contact but we are always aware of each other's presence. He the stern store manager and me the young hoodlum.

Now, as I reread this, I can see that in many ways—in fact, in most ways—Tim's essay was not typical or conventional. It does not seem pat or predictable (there is a provocative and potentially powerful tension between the dangerousness of the situation and the jocularity of rule #18, for example), and it has a kind of consciousness and control in the narrative that most young male writers aim for but usually miss. Significantly, though, my first reaction was to read Tim's essay and the epic struggle he was setting up with Leo through the lens of so many other male "hero as antihero" narratives that I have learned or grown to resist.

But it wasn't just my problem with the genre that got in the way. I was not ready or able to see much of the honesty, skill, or promise in that paragraph because I was not ready to see much of the honesty, skill, or promise in Tim. And that goes back not only to what he did—skipping one class, coming into the next one five minutes late, and then, without worrying that he had missed anything significant, theatrically volunteering to read his illegal narrative—but also to problems that I have had with certain male students throughout the years. Like many teachers, I find I often have trouble with male students because they are either too aggressive or too passive; but unlike many teachers who feel this way for personal and perhaps unfair reasons, I resented Tim Flanagan for perfectly legitimate ones:

- He almost always wore a baseball cap.
- I heard from a colleague that he was obnoxious.
- He was a sophomore who—because he had transferred into our university after his first year—was now disrupting the usual classroom dynamics of my freshman class.
- I knew he was in a fraternity because one day I saw him, wearing a blue blazer, red tie, and satisfied expression, make another student, wearing a clown outfit, do fifty pushups.

And so as I listened to Tim read his narrative, I listened for error rather than for potential. And when he got to the second paragraph I started to find some evidence to support the negative conclusion that I had actually already reached:

His name was Leo. I know because his picture hung above the service counter entrance. "Store Manager" was his title although I just thought of him as the enemy, the establishment, the order. He was Italian in name and looks. He had that dark complexion and black hair. I remember his face: stern and unfriendly, almost angry. He always wore the same ugly clothes. A brown tie and oxford and brown pin striped pants. He had a slight belly and slouched shoulders. He always carried a small notebook and pen in his ear.

I remember being put off by what I took to be the snotty, self-satisfied, middle-class portrait of Leo's working-class, Italian status—and by the way Tim's portrait of "the enemy" reminded me of other narratives written by other problematic male students—narratives about overcoming impossible odds and performing with grace under fire, narratives that start, for example, like this one:

> The game had more meaning than the average championship match because we had lost to the same team one year earlier. Once again we were billed as the underdogs, and it seemed as though we were out to prove something more because the other team was stacked with so many good players. Their forwards were the fastest in the whole league and they had two huge defensemen who would smash you against the boards any chance they got.

In other words, they are narratives which focus in clichéd language on acts of machismo. And though there are many male students who do not write in this form and some female students who do, there seems to be a general understanding in the field, supported by most of the published literature, that these narratives constitute a common genre of adolescent male writing: Geoffrey Sirc in his analysis of "male topic features" observes that these essays often deal with the author's mastery of an "epic" experience—often a "quest or mission"—in the "apocalyptic" tone of "pulp" fiction (5); Linda Peterson, borrowing one of her student's descriptions, refers to young men's stories of "wild canoe trips" that have "the fine echoes of Miller's beer commercials" (175); Elizabeth Flynn maintains that many male narratives, such as a description of a solo airplane flight or of a high school swimming career, "are stories of individual achievement or frustrated achievement and conclude by emphasizing separation rather than integration or reintegration into the community" (429); and almost everyone writing on this topic notices that these narratives almost never include female figures but quite often include strong male figures that the isolated male narrator must react against.

The usual professional response to these conventional narratives—after pointing out that essays that uphold gender stereotypes are problematic whether they deal with male or female roles, whether they are written by men or women—is to suggest the need for more class discussion of gender difference and behavior (Flynn 432); for designing and evaluating assignments in ways that do not privilege one sex over the other (Peterson 175); and, perhaps, for encouraging students to experiment more in their writing with cross-dressing (Peterson 178) and code-switching (Sirc 10).

Though I, too, have noticed these patterns and endorsed similar suggestions, I still worry about positing notions of gender that seem fixed and monolithic, notions that by ignoring class, culture, race, ethnicity, sexual preference, and individual difference seem to move inevitably towards essentialism. Once we begin with the assumptions, for example, that men do not value intimacy or connection or that women have trouble acting independently or assertively, our readings of student texts can easily become reductive and self-fulfilling prophecies. In an insightful extension of the previous literature on this topic, Don J. Kraemer suggests that our usual coding or identification of essays according to gender categories is often misleading or simplistic. In his readings of two essays—one by a male and one by a female—he shows how conventional readings overlook the complexity and subtle code-switching that occurs. In other words, an essay about the schoolboy football victory may focus on an act of achievement and success but may also contain significant indications of doubt and insecurity.

Still, the fact that a male writer may choose to write about doubt or insecurity or about the desire for intimacy by writing about football or shoplifting *is* significant—and, I think, problematic. For my sense is that many composition teachers—*male as well as female*—have largely negative reactions and particular resistances to the conventional male narrative. I know this resistance through my own personal experience as a writing teacher—I've always found the men who write about car wrecks, sports, and male bonding to be among the most difficult I teach and I've always found their rough drafts among my least favorites in the class—but I also know it through the stories, reports, and questions of the teachers who work in the writing program that I direct. At our annual "Papers From Hell" staff meeting—I invite faculty to bring in the kind of essays that they least like to read—there is always a wide range of dreaded genres represented, including the author-vacated research paper, the politically incorrect persuasive essay, and the plot summary response to a literary text, but each year the conventional male narrative is right up—or down—there with the worst of them. (Such negative reactions may go far to explain the documented gender discrepancy in grades: in "Gender and Teacher Response to Student Writing," Duane Roen cites eight separate studies demonstrating that "our grading, especially at the secondary level, has tended to favor females over males" [127–28].)

Some of these males' essays are conventional success stories—like scoring the winning touchdown or run in a big high school game—which seem to the instructor to have no insight or point beyond the narrator's desire to say "Look at this great thing I did before I came here to college." That seems, surprisingly enough from a middle-class adult perspective, anyway, to be the same motivation for the conventional delinquency papers—the narrative in which the narrator and his buddies "got ripped and trashed a golf course—just for the hell of it" or the time the narrator and his friends decide to get back at a cranky middle-aged neighbor who complained that their music was too loud by tipping over his car. These stories are told with pride and (though I read them in a grim and tight-lipped way) a sense of humor. Reductively, I plugged

Tim's essay into this genre, though as I look back now at his draft I see how difficult it is to reduce:

> I always walked around the store one time before the game actually started. It wasn't very big but it was big enough. Sometimes when he lost me I would sneak into the produce section and look though the one way mirrors at him. It was the only safe haven in the store where I could see him and he couldn't see me. I could look in his eyes. He tried to look unobvious and relaxed, talking to customers but he was always sweating and constantly scanning the aisles. I used to think about him a lot then. Was he married? Did he have kids? Was he happy? I could have almost felt sorry for him but emotions weren't part of the game. They could make you lose your touch and that could be dangerous.

Tim's provocative questions about Leo should have led to provocative questions of my own: was this a narrative about shoplifting? About mastery? About individuation? Or was it about Tim's relationship to Leo? About what connects and isolates men from each other? Instead, because I was irritated by his tone and the fact that he made Leo sweat, I listened with my arms tightly crossed and my jaw clenched. I have run into this problem before: several years ago, I published an article in *College English* about the problems that I had with several passively aggressive eighteen-year-old males whom I identified by their baseball caps, high-topped sneakers, smirkiness—and by their self-congratulatory writing. I suggested that I felt inappropriately angry at these males and that my anger kept me from reading their essays with generosity, creativity, or enthusiasm. Though that part of my essay was admittedly quirky and confessional—and though I attributed much of the problem to my own neuroses and insecurities—I received a number of letters, phone calls, and email responses from male and female teachers suggesting that I was not alone in my experience or response: apparently, these passively aggressive herd-instinct young men who write about sports successes, acts of delinquency, and conquests of nature populate composition courses across the country and, apparently, they create anger, frustration, and resistance in a significant number of college writing teachers.

So why *are* these essays so difficult for so many of us to read and like? And why do so many of us resist the details, ethos, and worldview they present and represent? When I asked that question of faculty members who teach in our first-year writing seminar, they offered three common explanations: first, they suggested, these essays just are not very good—predictable, superficial, and unsophisticated. Second, since male authors are often more difficult to work with—less open to negotiation, more resistant to revision—a writing teacher anticipates trouble and, thus, reads these drafts with conscious and unconscious anxiety and anger. And, finally, since these essays often focus on acts of machismo, often glorify aggression, competition, and male bonding, and usually fail even to acknowledge the existence of women, the teacher-reader encounters a text which seems to reflect, support, and promote an androcentric and, to some extent, misogynist agenda.

While all of these explanations sound reasonable, I think that they reveal as much about our limitations as about the limitations of our male students. To say that these male narratives are predictable, superficial, or unsophisticated only begs the question. Most first drafts by first-year students—whether written by males or females, whether dealing with an experience as a volunteer in a homeless shelter or a star of a high school football game—initially seem, well, like first drafts by first-year students: predictable, superficial, unsophisticated. In most cases, however, we use our skill, experience, and imagination to read (or misread) these drafts in productive ways; that is, we have learned to listen to what is not yet being said and to read through the text for meaning, nuance, tension, potential.

However, because we are bothered by the implicit and explicit politics of characteristically male essays, by the ethos that is being created and exalted, we become resisting readers, unable or unwilling to read behind and beneath the conventions that these men choose or are chosen by. We are often too quick to imagine in male narratives a lack of ambiguity, complexity, or doubt. Or put another way: we too often read male narratives as fixed, reifying our own interpretations, acting as if the meaning of a text can somehow be read right off the page. What I'm suggesting is that our readings ironically reproduce the problem: in the face of these male narratives and their authors, we, too, become passive aggressive; that is, we too hold back and become predictable, superficial, unsophisticated.

Though most of us are usually expert at "reading for discontinuity" (Kraemer 331) in student texts, we often fail to do so when confronted by heavily gendered drafts—and I think that this is particularly true when we are dealing with these male narratives. I did not, for example, look at first for discontinuity or potential in Tim's essay because he is exactly the kind of student I do not normally read with much empathy or openness: male, aggressive (or passively aggressive), cocky (a word, like "strident," that carries strong gender connotations), and (not insignificantly, I think) baseball-capped. It is not simply a matter, however, of saying that many of us have trouble with these narratives *and* we have trouble with the students who write them; rather, many of us have trouble with these narratives *because* we have trouble with the male students who write them.

Certainly that was part of the reason that I read and listened to Tim's narrative in such an unimaginative way; how else could have I have failed to notice how important this game was to Tim?

> He knew I always went for the candy aisles. What else would I want? Tuna fish? Spam? Jelly beans. Those were my favorite. The trouble was that they tend to make a lot of noise. So they usually ended up down my pants. It was the only place I could put them where they wouldn't move and where Leo

could never check. It wasn't very comfortable but it was very efficient. Now I could have gone straight out the door but that was way too easy. First I had to get his attention and get him to follow me. Then I had to lose him and then I would walk out. I was surprised at how many times this worked. It was almost as if he tried to be stupid. How could he not know that I was about to rip him off? Maybe Leo gave me permission. Maybe he didn't want the game to end.

These suggestive references—to what is down Tim's pants, to what Leo could never check, to why Tim almost wanted to get caught, to why Leo almost wanted Tim to get away—seem significant to me now. In retrospect, it all seems so clear to me—that Tim is struggling here with his own masculinity, with his relationships with older, powerful men, with his anger at the power that I had as his teacher—that I wonder how or why I failed to see any of that then. Of course, even if I *had* seen all of this at the time, I would not have said so to Tim. After all, it is one thing to tell ourselves that we see more in our students' texts (and lives) than they see themselves; it is another to tell our students about what we take to be their sexual anxieties or dysfunctional family relationships. Still, if I had been more open to Tim and his essay, I would have read and responded to his essay more generously and imaginatively.

But if he was in some largely unconscious way resisting my authority, then I was in some largely unconscious way resisting his resistance. Normally I would be willing and able to read for discontinuity or, to use my friend Bruce Ballenger's poetic advice, to find the line or passage in the student's text that "dips beneath the surface." That at first I was unwilling or unable to do so— that I was somehow still convinced that Tim's essay was another "typical male narrative"—is, I think, significant not only in what it might say about my own resistances but in what it also might suggest about how gender operates in the writing class. For when I reread that essay now I am struck by the fact that, though Tim keeps trying to make it a conventional male story about what he takes with him out of the store, he can hardly keep out the suggestions that this essay is really about what he did not have when he entered.

> I remember how much that game meant to me, though I'm still not sure I understand why. Every time I walked out of the store with something stuffed down my pants or in my pocket, it was the one place I experienced victory. It was a win. Rack one up for the angry, young rebellious kid with the red hair. I never really thought about what might have happened if I got caught or if the game stopped being a game. That would have to wait for another round with an authority figure who had a little more power than Leo.

Who was that authority figure? And why was the store the *one* place Tim ever experienced victory? The fact that his essay was turning into something more than he may have originally intended is not surprising; after all, we often think we see more in a student's narrative than the student seems to see. This becomes especially tricky, though, when a student author, like Tim, hints at a problem which he then immediately dismisses or ignores. Or when a student author sums up an unresolved problem in a pat and unconvincing way. For example, after describing a drunken near-fatal car wreck in great detail or a summer volunteering at a homeless shelter, student authors are apt to conclude, "I learned never to take life for granted again." Or after writing five pained pages about a mother who always expects the impossible or a father who was never emotionally available when needed, we will read, "Sure, my mother is different, she's different in a good way" or "All I know is how much I love my father." Tim's essay offered an odd version of this "everything is fine" ending: after hinting that his shoplifting may have been connected to deeper, personal problems, particularly problems at home, problems in his relationships with male authority figures, he returns in the final paragraph to the moment at hand and to the odd jocularity he had established in the introduction:

> I rarely saw Leo after I had possession and he had lost sight of me in those mirrors. I could just walk out without even worrying about getting caught. That's good. Rule #355 for shoplifters: don't steal something every time you go into a store especially when they know you are doing it. Rule #356: always, however, look like you had. It's times like that you pray that the clerk accuses you because then you will make them look real bad, piss them off big-time, and give yourself tremendous leeway the next time you walk in that store. If you do all that, you can become a successful shoplifter.

Tim's attempt to bring the essay back to its lighthearted "how to shoplift" tone makes some sense; after all, that has been a strand throughout the essay and, like many other student writers, Tim is driven by an understanding (or misunderstanding) that every essay needs a neat resolution at the end. Though these "false resolutions" ("My brother's death did teach me to make the most out of every single day") often seem ludicrous, they should not surprise us: many students are not yet ready to deal with the ambiguity or unresolved tension that they themselves have identified, and these pat resolutions may provide them with a means of dealing (or not dealing) with problems that are simply too painful. That is, whenever these problems present themselves, these students rely on long established coping mechanisms and ego defenses which allow them to complete the narrative (and, perhaps, to fall asleep at night) by telling themselves "This is really OK."

It is also not surprising that we are never quite sure what to do in these situations. Do we point out the inconsistency between the narrative and its (lack of) interpretation? Do we push the student to deal more fully with the complexity of the issues? Do we take this to be a problem of organization? Of psychological development? While this is always a tricky situation, it is especially complicated when we are dealing with these conventional male narratives, for two reasons: first, blinded by our own conventional reading and response to the sports or delinquency narrative, we may fail even to recognize the seriousness of the conflict that the student has introduced but then quickly dismissed and, second, we may refuse to pay attention to that unresolved conflict because we are afraid that what is beneath the surface will be even worse than what is there on the page. In other words, if the manifest content—a football game, a Halloween prank, a drunk drive—suggests a degree of carelessness, hedonism, violence, or misogyny, what must the latent content look like? That is, we may, therefore, refuse to follow male narratives beneath their surfaces because we read them intertextually against our worst nightmares of male culture and male violence.

Here, too, I am drawing on my experience as a writing program director who each semester sees dozens of essays that our instructors, for one reason or another, find problematic. Though the bulk of these essays involve matters not directly related to gender (plagiarism or second language problems, for example), there is a small but steady stream of essays each semester written by male students, usually for female teachers, which involve sexually explicit material; many of these also include some threat or even graphic description of violence. While it seems only fair and reasonable to distinguish between a male narrative which reproduces certain cultural codes—about, say, sports, driving, or the value of individual achievement—and a male narrative which seeks to provoke, control, or even threaten its (typically) female subject and female reader, these distinctions are often blurred by our own unconscious associations. Just as my intertextual reading of Tim's essay lead me to see it in misleading and reductive ways, here, too, we may too easily connect the dots that separate the somewhat innocent male delinquency essays from the dangerous, misogynist ones.

And here, again, I do not mean to suggest that this is exclusively or even primarily a problem for female teachers. My own sense is that, while many of us make this leap from the traditional adolescent male to the worst incarnations of male violence, we often do so unconsciously. The other day, for example, I was walking with my thirteen-year-old daughter through the college town where we live. As we passed a fraternity where a group of shirtless young men in baggy shorts and backwards baseball caps were playing whiffle ball to the loud rap music coming from the speakers in their windows, Lucy said, "I'd like to live in a house like that when I go to college."

I explained that fraternities were only for men and—though I realized even at the time that I had no idea if I was right about this—that I disliked fraternities because they still discriminated on the basis of race, religion, sexual preference. Lucy looked skeptically at me and at the boys on the lawn.

"Do all of them do that?"

"I'm not sure."

"Well, if they don't, I'd like to at least go to one of their parties; they look like they're fun."

"Yeah, it does *look* like fun in a way," I started in response, "But . . . " And, though it *did* look like fun and though I could clearly see what was attractive about these boys, the next thing I knew I had launched into a lecture about fraternities, drinking, and date rape. Lucy again dragged me back to facts and evidence.

"Did that happen in *this* fraternity?" I realized that when I read those newspaper stories that I never bothered to distinguish between the Greek letters.

She asked again: "*All* fraternities are like that? I can't believe that *all* those boys are like that."

I couldn't either, really, but I was not quite ready to give up the point: it only takes one, I thought glumly.

So what do we do?

(1) We pay more attention to the cultures of adolescent males.

At first I was reluctant to think along these lines. After all, it is only in the last twenty years or so that we have finally begun to think about the role that women play in the classroom and university. "After two thousand years of concentrating on men," a colleague who teaches Women's Studies told me, "the last thing we need now is Men's Studies." It seemed useless to point out that my interest in studying adolescent males and their cultures is really a logical and inevitable outgrowth of Women's Studies. The problem, as I see it, is that for too many of those two thousand years, too many male scholars acted as if their studies were gender-neutral, implying that what they discovered in their research about men applied to women as well. This is precisely why studies of psychological and cognitive development by Freud, Piaget, William Perry, and many others have been rightfully and effectively criticized by feminist scholars. It is also why men's studies scholars argue that research on the construction of masculinity is consistent—rather than competitive—with feminist scholarship. In "A Case for Men's Studies," Harry Brod explains, "Like women's studies, it too attempts to emasculate patriarchal ideology's masquerade as knowledge. Women's studies explores and corrects the effects on women and our understanding of them—of their exclusion from traditional learning caused by the androcentric elevation of 'man' as male to 'man' as generic human. Men's studies similarly looks into the, as yet, largely unrecognized effects of this fallacy on men and our understanding of them" (264).

By studying the ways that masculinity is constructed for men in the larger culture, we could begin to understand the ways that male students struggle to construct themselves in our classrooms. As Barrie Thorne points out in *Gender Play,* her study of boys and girls in school, this problem of male sexual anxiety begins long before adolescence:

> When asked about the gender situations they find most troubling, teachers and
> parents of young children often talk about boys. The troubling behaviors lie
> at opposite ends of a continuum. At one end is the aggressive masculine bond-
> ing in evidence when groups of boys disrupt classrooms, derogate girls and
> invade their play, and make fun of subordinated "weaker" boys. Boys who en-
> gage in this sort of behavior take center stage in many school ethnographies:

in fact, as I earlier observed, their style is often equated with masculinity itself. At the other extreme, adults express concern about boys who do not uphold dominant notions of masculinity, who avoid the tough and aggressive, don't like sports, and are therefore vulnerable to ostracism, teasing, and being labeled "sissy," "nerd" and "fag." (167–68)

It is within this context and continuum that our adolescent male students struggle to compose their narratives and their identities. That so many of those narratives are so troubling should not surprise us or tempt us to respond with censure and self-righteousness. But even more important, the fact that so many of these narratives are so unsettling to our students and ourselves should not be used to support the argument that autobiographical writing should be kept out of the curriculum. In fact, the opposite point could be made: since it is so often the central site of conflict, confession, and catharsis, the personal narrative gives us a unique opportunity to help students negotiate the borderlands between home and school, past and present, self and other.

But we will be of little help in this negotiation if we do not know our way around this territory. As feminist theory and scholarship have helped us to read the signs and to listen to the silences of female voices, narratives, and texts, gender and men's studies could help us to read the "troubling behaviors" and personal narratives of adolescent males. I have in mind, for example, the sort of reading that Susan Glaspell models in her short story, "A Jury of Her Peers." In that story, rescued and reinscribed by Annette Kolodny and other feminist critics, Glaspell shows how men read women's texts in limited and limiting ways, oblivious to the nuances and ignorant of the culture that produced them. In Glaspell's story, a group of men fail to solve a murder that has occurred at an isolated farmhouse because they do not know how to read women's text—in this case, the condition of the kitchen, cooking stove, sewing needles, house pets.

I think that we often make the same mistake when we—male and female academics—try to read the narratives of adolescent males. We often look in the wrong places and miss the central point because we do not know enough about the culture of, say, sports victories, car wrecks, and sexual anxiety in which it is embedded. Consider, by way of example, the trouble many of us have reading those baseball caps. Now I am not suggesting that all wearers of caps are problematic nor that all problematic students wear caps—only that there is a correlation and intersection of some imperfect kind—and that understanding the cap as a problematic text might help us to understand our response to these essays and their authors. When I mentioned in my earlier *CE* essay that all of the problematic men in my class wore baseball caps, I intended very little in the way of heavy symbolism. I mentioned it only because it seemed to be a detail that I hoped was somehow symbolic of the status of these male students.

In the intervening years, though, I've noticed a busy intersection between the caps, talk about the caps, the identification of problematic male students, and the resistance of many teachers to male narratives. One of my older, more traditional colleagues has actually included a note on his syllabus "No baseball caps in class—ever"; another asked the other day in exasperation, "What am I doing—teaching a writing class or coaching a little league team?" Part of the strong response some of us have to these caps is created in part by the complex of contradictory functions the caps serve and by the ways they trigger our resistance to what we take to be the male student's passive resistance, while at the same time suggesting the aggression that most of us find problematic in these students.

On the one hand, the bill of the cap conceals and protects, sometimes making it difficult to see the student clearly. At the same time, the bill juts out, intrudes, even threatens, not only in its physical sense but also in its reference to cross-racial or cross-class identity. By referring to physical activity (sports or rap music or farm work), to powerful organizations (a professional team, a major university, a rap group, a street gang, a motorcycle manufacturer) the cap allows the wearer to identify and align himself with a power and prestige outside the classroom. Most of all, though, the cap is performative: by wearing the cap during class, the student crosses certain lines of decorum, propriety, and control, and thereby asserts his individuality; ironically, though, since most of his peers are also wearing caps, it at the same time allows him to efface or erase that individuality, and to identify with the group. In that sense the male student may wear the cap not so much to individuate or threaten but to connect and conceal.

Of course, here, too, I need to point out that the day is long past when the only students wearing caps in class were males. Yet when female students wear baseball caps, as when female students write about winning a big sports game, there may be a certain welcomed degree of originality and code-switching that is absent when these acts are performed by male students. When males wear these caps or when they write mock-heroic essays, we may miss the specific gestures and meanings and respond instead to what we dislike in general about male group behavior, about patriarchy, about male violence.

Or about, say, those car wreck narratives. If we want to learn how to read these celebrations of drunk driving, destructiveness, and self-destructiveness, we need to know more about the experience and consciousness of adolescent males in much the same way that we need as readers of eating disorder narratives to know more about the experience and consciousness of adolescent females. We can find some of this cultural and psychological information in scholarly journals and some of it, like this paragraph from a revision I recently received, between the lines of the conventional male narratives themselves:

> My parents keep telling me that it is stupid to hang around with someone like Tommy who is always messing around with cars and drugs and drinking. I know they're right but that is part of the reason we all like to hang around with him. It's weird that when you are doing something that could get you killed that's when you feel like you are most alive.

I have also found it helpful to look to feminist literature and research, for it is there that we find the most compelling justification and strategy for reading texts that uninformed readers might find inaccessible, trivial, confusing, or objectionable. Admittedly, there is an irony in borrowing from feminist theory designed to help us hear the voices of silenced women to help us hear the silences behind the voices of aggressive men. But I am not suggesting that we stop trying to hear the silenced voices of women students or that we let these male voices silence others. Nor am I suggesting that we strive to be sympathetic to or supportive of every single essay regardless of its quality or politics. In other words, I am certainly not suggesting that we can or should be sympathetic to and supportive of essays which are misogynist, racist, homophobic, or otherwise objectionable. And while I am on the subject of disclaimers, let me state that I do not mean to suggest that we should privilege gender above all other factors, including class, race, ethnicity, sexual preference, personal background.

What I *am* suggesting is that we need to become more informed and open-minded readers of texts—including, in this case, the conventional male narrative—that may at first glance or on initial visceral reaction seem inaccessible, facile, or even objectionable. We need, in other words, to stop reifying our own interpretations of these male narratives, to realize that our readings are often retellings of our own unconscious associations, and to remember that behind every story is another story. What adolescent male students give us in first draft personal narratives is just the manifest content, the starting point, the conventional story. Our job is to help them to go further, by helping them to hear what they have not quite said, what is lurking in the background. And if we do not understand that culture or if we find it inherently dull or reprehensible, we will not be of much help in that process.

(2) Since any reading of a student essay is also a rewriting, we need to work harder to sort out the role our own biases and unconscious associations play in our interpretation of and response to any heavily gendered narrative.

Any heavily gendered narrative is bound to trigger strong personal and unconscious responses in its reader. In my own case, I have long struggled against conventional male narratives that remind me of males that I competed against during my own adolescence; on the other hand, I have a tendency to overidentify with narratives that are consistent with my own politics, experiences, or philosophy. I am not suggesting, though, that we should (or that we *can*) keep our own unconscious associations out of our readings and responses. In fact, our own free associations are often our best tools in this process. When, for example, I reread Tim's essay I had two strong associations: First, I sensed that the authority figure with more power that he referred to was his father and that in some significant sense he was trying to write about that relationship. Second, I felt that on some level the essay was also about Tim's relationship with me. I am not sure how or why I knew that. I suppose that it could have been the description of Leo (I am also dark, short, and ethnic looking) or maybe it was the notebook he carried and the pencil behind his ear. But more likely it was the nature of the relationship, the fact that Tim was trying to get away with something, that Leo was trying to catch him, and that they both were ambivalent about these roles.

Though both of those associations felt useful to me as a reader, I needed, at the same time, to be careful about imposing them on him as a writer. In our program, we have formed a group of writing teachers and personal counselors who meet occasionally to read narratives of this sort in order to help work out some of these boundary issues—and to try to sort out our issues from theirs. I have been accused, for example, by one of my colleagues of thinking that *every* male narrative is, finally, a story of Oedipal struggle. "Sometimes," he will argue, "a cigar is really just a cigar. And sometimes a story of a Halloween prank is just the story of a Halloween prank." Though my first impulse is to say, "So, Ralph, why are you so threatened by the psychological aspect of these essays?" I need instead to think about how my readings and responses to these kinds of narratives can overdetermine my students' revisions. I need, in other words, to think about how my own experiences—my relationship with my own family, my own sexual orientation, my own construction of masculinity, for example— might help and hinder me as a reader of male narratives.

Though some composition theorists, including Linda Peterson (175), have suggested that male narratives may give female teachers more trouble while female narratives may be more problematic for male teachers, we found in our group, anyway, that our responses and experiences are more complex and idiosyncratic than that. For example, I did play high school sports so that may be a shared territory with many students (male and female), but the truth is that I have hardly participated in all sorts of conventionally male experiences (for example, the sorts that have to do with getting drunk, fighting, fast driving, talking with other men about women's bodies, working with my hands, taking it like a man), while I have been included by my wife, my daughters, my mother, my women friends, in all sorts of conventionally female activities. So when I read a male student's narrative of "the night me and my fraternity brothers got drunk and went cow tipping," I am not necessarily any more likely than my female colleagues to share the writer's experience or point of view; then again, I have always felt more comfortable (or less uncomfortable) reading and responding to a student narrative about a messy and painful interpersonal relationship than one about a kayak trip or a trusty dog.

(3) We need to change the pattern of response to these male students.

My own tendency, when confronted by a male student who seems particularly obnoxious and resistant, is to try not to waste much thought and energy on him—and to remind him and myself that eventually, at grading time, I will be able to get even. Although this response is punitive and unproductive, I have sometimes clung to it in anger and frustration. Recently, though, I found myself on the other end of this man-to-man defensiveness and realized how unpleasant it was to have my own work and person read unsympathetically by a more powerful male. It happened in an unlikely setting: I was on my way to a conference in Britain. As I rushed off the plane to catch my bus, a customs agent stopped me and motioned me over to a side room: "Just a security measure. It shouldn't take long." As I stewed in silence at the customs table, the guard went through, first, my passport, and then my suitcase. I found myself growing increasingly nervous and agitated but, in spite of my irritation, eager to please. "It's an international conference. I've always wanted to visit Wales and, since I'll be presenting a paper, my university in the States agreed to pay my way."

He cut me short with a wave at my suitcase. "Mind if I look at what's inside your briefcase, then?" he asked as he unzipped it. He began taking out the overheads for my conference presentation. He held up the first one and frowned. "What?" I asked. "Is there a problem?" Still no response. His silent disapproval goaded me on. "This isn't a final paper or anything . . . but the whole project is being funded by a grant from the federal government." He seemed enormously unimpressed. Which by now was making me angry. I mean who was he to act so haughty, to be so contemptuous of something which I had put time into, something I cared about. I wanted to say, "Who the hell are you to be critiquing my work? You're so damn brilliant?" But since he had the power to make things uncomfortable—maybe even miserable—for me, all I said was, "In America there is a lot of interest in these issues. You don't have Freshman Comp here, but in the States it really is very big." I was on the verge of telling him why the project was so difficult, why I hadn't had time to accomplish what I wanted, what I still might do. But it hardly seemed worth it. He just didn't seem very interested in my work.

I know that this is a long way for me to make you travel to introduce what I want to say about how men teach or fail to teach other men to write. But I can't help thinking that something about the way the customs agent treated me is very much like the way I sometimes treat my male students. I know that many of them resent my authority, resent the fact that I make them show me their work in conferences and class, and resent the way I grudgingly dole out compliments and suggestions. I know that many of them think that they are on their way to more important things than I—a comp teacher—am doing with my life. I know that some of them resent the fact that I keep reaching into their private memories and political beliefs. And I know that I sometimes resent their resentment and enjoy my own authority for its power to control.

Though it goes against my first instinct, I find that I can be more successful if I encourage these students, if I push myself to find points of identification, and, most difficult of all, if I seek to nurture them. Maybe I could begin by unfolding my arms and suspending my sense of judgment. When, for example, I read an essay about male aggression, I often find it difficult to conceal my sense of disgust, let alone find a way to understand and encourage the writer. But if I can be patient enough to withstand the initial angry response many male students have to my authority and the initial angry response that I in turn have to their behavior, I often find that a different student and different narrative emerge. Because these students both scare and anger me, I am surprised each time that one suddenly decides to trust me, the class, and himself enough to admit weakness, doubt, vulnerability.

I was not prepared, for example, when Jerry, my most aggressive and least favorite student—the one most apt to challenge my authority in class or to act insensitively toward another student in workshop—brought to his latest conference a narrative about the strange man who showed up at his college dorm room one day, announced that he was his father, explained why he should be forgiven for walking out on Jerry, Jerry's mother, and his familial and financial responsibilities sixteen years before, and then had the nerve to ask, "Don't you think it's time the two of us got a fresh start?" Suddenly it dawned on me that maybe Jerry and I needed a fresh start, too.

Rather than confronting these male students, male teachers may need occasionally to disarm them with empathy. In some sense, I think that this is the corollary to the advice of some feminists, including bell hooks and Susan Jarrett, that female students may benefit more from "an oppositional world view" than from the "safe and nurturing classroom" that most female teachers try to provide (Jarrett 120). In my own experience, I have found that most resistant male students are much less resistant in one-to-one conferences than they are in class. When I met with Tim in conference, for example, and told him what I liked about his writing and how interested I was in his comments about struggling with authority, he began to relax and open up. When I asked him, with curiosity and without judgment, "Why did you always and only steal from Leo?" he said that he did not know but that he was interested in writing more about that. Then to my surprise in a revision he followed his comment about his troubles with authority figures with a confessional anecdote about an argument with his father that had almost led to a physical beating. The precipitating incident had been his father's refusal to let him wear shorts and a tee shirt to his first day of high school. Tim refused to change; his father refused to back down.

> "Dad, it's pretty hot outside, I think the only way I'll be comfortable is if I go to school like this."
> "Tim, I just spent a lot of money on you for new school clothes and you plan to go like this." Danger. We were already setting up a battlefield without giving much attention to peace talks.
> "Dad, I really want to wear these to school today. EJ's wearing shorts, why can't I?" I hated to bring my brother into this but I was losing ground fast.
> "EJ's been in high school two years. This is your first day. Now march upstairs this second and change into those new clothes."

I didn't even look at him. I had lost him. Come on, Dad, why don't you just say it, fucking say it! What the hell does that mean? He's been in high school two years and THAT'S why he can wear shorts and I can't. That makes sense. Let's see, where can I find that rule, Dad? Oh here it is, Rule #445: One has the privilege of wearing shorts after two years at the school in question.

"I want to wear these clothes."

"I don't care what you want to wear. Do as I say!" And that's when I lost it as much as I always try to keep my composure and calm . . . I lost it.

"Fuck you Dad," I screamed.

EJ was horrified. I'll never forget the look on his face as he saw me dash up the stairs with my Dad close behind. I was faster but it didn't matter. There was no place to go. I jumped on my bed. There was some room to maneuver. He tried to grab me. I pulled away. He swung and missed. I had never seen my Dad raise his hand to anyone.

"Go ahead and hit me. HIT ME! Is that what you want? Do it!" I screamed. He didn't say anything. He stood there, his face stern and un-friendly, almost angry. He walked down the stairs.

I put on those new school clothes over my shorts and walked downstairs past him without saying a word. When I got in the driveway, I took off the school clothes and left them on his car. I walked to the bus stop in my favorite t-shirt and shorts. That was the way to play the game.

Although I had felt or sensed that there was some connection between Leo and Tim's father, I did not expect that connection to be so direct as the talk about the rules of the game and the "stern and unfriendly" face suggested they were. I was surprised by the depth and complexity this anecdote added to my sense of the narrative—and of Tim. That impression was strengthened still further when I asked him in his next conference if he planned to write more in his essay about the connection between Leo and his father. His response was that he thought that his shoplifting was part of his general rebelliousness and that he would like to try to write about that. But when he handed in his final portfolio, he included this note: "I tried to write more about why I was such a rebellious kid but I couldn't fit it into my shoplifting essay. I did decide to include it in the portfolio, though." And he did:

My parents separated when I was 10 and Dad moved out of the house. The fights and the threats and arguments started long before then so it was no real surprise when they finally decided to call it quits. I rarely saw my Dad after that. It was an awkward situation to say the least. He obviously didn't feel com-fortable leaving home. My mom worked as a waitress to support us. That meant that she left for work soon after I got home from school and didn't come home till late at night. It was then that I began to question things. If having a mother and father and family meant that I could count on them and learn and be happy, then how come I didn't have any of that? If learning to be a man meant I needed my father, then why wasn't he around? If I was supposed to listen to other people and if I was supposed to be a good little boy, then why did it feel so good when I wasn't?

The thing is my mom moved out of the house when I was in 8th grade. It was a horrible situation. The end result was my father had to come live with us. My brother and I hadn't really experienced much of my Dad after the breakup and then four years later he is our parent. No one ever talked to us. It was just assumed that it would be OK with us for my Dad to move in. We would accept him and he would accept us. It was also assumed that it would be OK for my Mom to move out.

I'm not entirely sure how to fit this in *my* essay, either. It doesn't have much to do with the ways that I have typically read my male students and their texts. But, like Tim, I think that it needs to be included.

Works Cited

Brod, Harry. "A Case for Men's Studies." *Changing Men: New Directions in Research on Men and Masculinity.* Ed. Michael S. Kimmel. Newbury Park, CA: Sage Publications, 1987. 263–77.

Flynn, Elizabeth A. "Composing as a Woman." *College Composition and Communication* 39 (Dec. 1988): 423–35.

Jarrett, Susan C. "Feminism and Composition: The Case for Conflict." *Contending with Words.* Ed. Patricia Harkin and John Schilb. New York: MLA, 1991. 105–23.

Kolodny, Annette. "A Map for Rereading: Gender and the Interpretation of Literary Texts." *The New Feminist Criticism: Essays on Women, Literature, & Society.* Ed. Elaine Showalter. New York: Pantheon, 1985: 46–62.

Kraemer, Don J., Jr. "Gender and the Autobiographical Essay: A Critical Extension of the Research." *College Composition and Communication* 43 (Oct. 1992): 322–39.

Peterson, Linda H. "Gender and the Autobiographical Essay: Research Perspectives, Pedagogical Practices." *College Composition and Communication* 42 (May 1991): 170–83.

Roen, Duane H. "Gender and Teacher Response to Student Writing." *Gender Issues in the Teaching of English.* Ed. Nancy Mellin McCracken and Bruce C. Appleby. Portsmouth, NH: Boynton/Cook–Heinemann, 1992. 126–41.

Sirc, Geoffrey. "Gender and 'Writing Formations' in First-Year Narratives." *Freshman English News* 18 (Fall 1989): 4–11.

Thorne, Barrie. *Gender Play: Girls and Boys in School.* New Brunswick, NJ: Rutgers UP, 1993.

Grammar, Grammars, and the Teaching of Grammar

Patrick Hartwell

For me the grammar issue was settled at least twenty years ago with the conclusion offered by Richard Braddock, Richard Lloyd-Jones, and Lowell Schoer in 1963.

> In view of the widespread agreement of research studies based upon many types of students and teachers, the conclusion can be stated in strong and unqualified terms: the teaching of formal grammar has a negligible or, because it usually displaces some instruction and practice in composition, even a harmful effect on improvement in writing.

Indeed, I would agree with Janet Emig that the grammar issue is a prime example of "magical thinking": the assumption that students will learn only what we teach and only because we teach.

But the grammar issue, as we will see, is a complicated one. And, perhaps surprisingly, it remains controversial, with the regular appearance of papers defending the teaching of formal grammar or attacking it. Thus Janice Neuleib, writing on "The Relation of Formal Grammar to Composition" in *College Composition and Communication* (23 [1977], 247–50), is tempted "to sputter on paper" at reading the quotation above (p. 248), and Martha Kolln, writing in the same journal three years later ("Closing the Books on Alchemy," *CCC*, 32 [1981], 139–51), labels people like me "alchemists" for our perverse beliefs. Neuleib reviews five experimental studies, most of them concluding that formal grammar instruction has no effect on the quality of students' writing nor on their ability to avoid error. Yet she renders in effect a Scots verdict of "Not proven" and calls for more research on the issue. Similarly, Kolln reviews six experimental studies that arrive at similar conclusions, only one of them overlapping with the studies cited by Neuleib. She calls for more careful definition of the word *grammar*—her definition being "the internalized system that native

Professor Hartwell wishes to thank Wayne Edkin, Camden (New York) Public Schools; Michael Marler, Brigham Young University-Hawaii; and Ron Shook, Utah State University, for discussing these issues with him, and particularly to thank his colleague Dan J. Tannacito for references and discussion.

College English, 47 (February 1985), pp. 105–27. Copyright © 1985 by the National Council of Teachers of English. Reprinted with permission.

speakers of a language share" (p. 140)—and she concludes with a stirring call to place grammar instruction at the center of the composition curriculum: "our goal should be to help students understand the system they know unconsciously as native speakers, to teach them the necessary categories and labels that will enable them to think about and talk about their language" (p. 150). Certainly our textbooks and our pedagogies—though they vary widely in what they see as "necessary categories and labels"—continue to emphasize mastery of formal grammar, and popular discussions of a presumed literacy crisis are almost unanimous in their call for a renewed emphasis on the teaching of formal grammar, seen as basic for success in writing.

An Instructive Example

It is worth noting at the outset that both sides in this dispute—the grammarians and the anti-grammarians—articulate the issue in the same positivistic terms: what does experimental research tell us about the value of teaching formal grammar? But seventy-five years of experimental research has for all practical purposes told us nothing. The two sides are unable to agree on how to interpret such research. Studies are interpreted in terms of one's prior assumptions about the value of teaching grammar: their results seem not to change those assumptions. Thus the basis of the discussion, a basis shared by Kolln and Neuleib and by Braddock and his colleagues—"what does educational research tell us?"—seems designed to perpetuate, not to resolve, the issue. A single example will be instructive. In 1976 and then at greater length in 1979, W. B. Elley, I. H. Barham, H. Lamb, and M. Wyllie reported on a three-year experiment in New Zealand, comparing the relative effectiveness at the high school level of instruction in transformational grammar, instruction in traditional grammar, and no grammar instruction. They concluded that the formal study of grammar, whether transformational or traditional, improved neither writing quality nor control over surface correctness.

> After two years, no differences were detected in writing performance or language competence; after three years small differences appeared in some minor conventions favoring the TG [transformational grammar] group, but these were more than offset by the less positive attitudes they showed towards their English studies. (p. 18)

Anthony Petroskey, in a review of research ("Grammar Instruction: What We Know," *English Journal,* 66, No. 9 [1977], 86–88), agreed with this conclusion, finding the study to be carefully designed, "representative of the best kind of educational research" (p. 86), its validity "unquestionable" (p. 88). Yet Janice Neuleib in her essay found the same conclusions to be "startling" and questioned whether the findings could be generalized beyond the target population, New Zealand high school students. Martha Kolln, when her attention is drawn to the study ("Reply to Ron Shook," *CCC*, 32 [1981], 139–151), thinks the whole experiment "suspicious." And John Mellon has been willing to use the study to defend the teaching of grammar; the study of Elley and his colleagues, he has argued, shows that teaching grammar does no harm.

It would seem unlikely, therefore, that further experimental research, in and of itself, will resolve the grammar issue. Any experimental design can be nitpicked, any experimental population can be criticized, and any experimental conclusion can be questioned or, more often, ignored. In fact, it may well be that the grammar question is not open to resolution by experimental research, that, as Noam Chomsky has argued in *Reflections on Language* (New York: Pantheon, 1975), criticizing the trivialization of human learning by behavioral psychologists, the issue is simply misdefined.

> There will be "good experiments" only in domains that lie outside the organism's cognitive capacity. For example, there will be no "good experiments" in the study of human learning.
>
> This discipline . . . will, of necessity, avoid those domains in which an organism is specially designed to acquire rich cognitive structures that enter into its life in an intimate fashion. The discipline will be of virtually no intellectual interest, it seems to me, since it is restricting itself in principle to those questions that are guaranteed to tell us little about the nature of organisms. (p. 36)

Asking the Right Questions

As a result, though I will look briefly at the tradition of experimental research, my primary goal in this essay is to articulate the grammar issue in different and, I would hope, more productive terms. Specifically, I want to ask four questions:

1. Why is the grammar issue so important? Why has it been the dominant focus of composition research for the last seventy-five years?

2. What definitions of the word *grammar* are needed to articulate the grammar issue intelligibly?

3. What do findings in cognate disciplines suggest about the value of formal grammar instruction?

4. What is our theory of language, and what does it predict about the value of formal grammar instruction? (This question—"what does our theory of language predict?"—seems a much more powerful question than "what does educational research tell us?")

In exploring these questions I will attempt to be fully explicit about issues, terms, and assumptions. I hope that both proponents and opponents of formal grammar instruction would agree that these are useful as shared points of reference: care in definition, full examination of the evidence, reference to relevant work in cognate disciplines, and explicit analysis of the theoretical bases of the issue.

But even with that gesture of harmony it will be difficult to articulate the issue in a balanced way, one that will be acceptable to both sides. After all, we are dealing with a professional dispute in which one side accuses the other of "magical thinking," and in turn that side responds by charging the other as "al-chemists." Thus we might suspect that the grammar issue is itself embedded in larger models of the transmission of literacy, part of quite different assumptions about the teaching of composition.

Those of us who dismiss the teaching of formal grammar have a model of composition instruction that makes the grammar issue "uninteresting" in a scientific sense. Our model predicts a rich and complex interaction of learner and environment in mastering literacy, an interaction that has little to do with sequences of skills instruction as such. Those who defend the teaching of grammar tend to have a model of composition instruction that is rigidly skills-centered and rigidly sequential: the formal teaching of grammar, as the first step in that sequence, is the cornerstone or linchpin. Grammar teach-ing is thus supremely interesting, naturally a dominant focus for educational research. The controversy over the value of grammar instruction, then, is inseparable from two other issues: the issues of sequence in the teaching of composition and of the role of the composition teacher. Consider, for example, the force of these two issues in Janice Neuleib's conclusion: after calling for yet more experimental research on the value of teaching grammar, she ends with an absolute (and unsupported) claim about sequences and teacher roles in composition.

> We do know, however, that some things must be taught at different levels. In-sistence on adherence to usage norms by composition teachers does improve usage. Students can learn to organize their papers if teachers do not accept pa-pers that are disorganized. Perhaps composition teachers can teach those two abilities before they begin the more difficult tasks of developing syntactic so-phistication and a winning style. ("The Relation of Formal Grammar to Com-position," p. 250)

(One might want to ask, in passing, whether "usage norms" exist in the mono-lithic fashion the phrase suggests and whether refusing to accept disorganized papers is our best available pedagogy for teaching arrangement.)

But I want to focus on the notion of sequence that makes the grammar is-sue so important: first grammar, then usage, then some absolute model of or-ganization, all controlled by the teacher at the center of the learning process, with other matters, those of rhetorical weight—"syntactic sophistication and a winning style"—pushed off to the future. It is not surprising that we call each other names: those of us who question the value of teaching grammar are in fact shaking the whole elaborate edifice of traditional composition instruction.

The Five Meanings of "Grammar"

Given its centrality to a well-established way of teaching composition, I need to go about the business of defining grammar rather carefully, particularly in view of Kolln's criticism of the lack of care in earlier discussions. Therefore I will build upon a seminal discussion of the word *grammar* offered a generation ago, in 1954, by W. Nelson Francis, often excerpted as "The Three Meanings of Grammar." It is worth reprinting at length, if only to reestablish it as a reference point for future discussions.

> The first thing we mean by "grammar" is "the set of formal patterns in which the words of a language are arranged in order to convey larger meanings." It is not necessary that we be able to discuss these patterns self-consciously in order to be able to use them. In fact, all speakers of a language above the age of five or six know how to use its complex forms of organization with considerable skill; in this sense of the word—call it "Grammar 1"—they are thoroughly familiar with its grammar.
>
> The second meaning of "grammar"—call it "Grammar 2"—is "the branch of linguistic science which is concerned with the description, analysis, and formulization of formal language patterns." Just as gravity was in full operation before Newton's apple fell, so grammar in the first sense was in full operation before anyone formulated the first rule that began the history of grammar as a study.
>
> The third sense in which people use the word "grammar" is "linguistic etiquette." This we may call "Grammar 3." The word in this sense is often coupled with a derogatory adjective: we say that the expression "he ain't here" is "bad grammar." . . .
>
> As has already been suggested, much confusion arises from mixing these meanings. One hears a good deal of criticism of teachers of English couched in such terms as "they don't teach grammar any more." Criticism of this sort is based on the wholly unproven assumption that teaching Grammar 2 will improve the student's proficiency in Grammar 1 or improve his manners in Grammar 3. Actually, the form of Grammar 2 which is usually taught is a very inaccurate and misleading analysis of the facts of Grammar 1; and it therefore is of highly questionable value in improving a person's ability to handle the structural patterns of his language. (pp. 300–301)

Francis' Grammar 3 is, of course, not grammar at all, but usage. One would like to assume that Joseph Williams' recent discussion of usage ("The Phenomenology of Error," *CCC* 32 [1981], 152–168), along with his references, has placed those shibboleths in a proper perspective. But I doubt it, and I suspect that popular discussions of the grammar issue will be as flawed by the intrusion of usage issues as past discussions have been. At any rate I will make only passing reference to Grammar 3—usage—naively assuming that this issue has been discussed elsewhere and that my readers are familiar with those discussions.

We need also to make further discriminations about Francis' Grammar 2, given that the purpose of his 1954 article was to substitute for one form of Grammar 2, that "inaccurate and misleading" form "which is usually taught," another form, that of American structuralist grammar. Here we can make use of a still earlier discussion, one going back to the days when *PMLA* was willing to publish articles on rhetoric and linguistics, to a 1927 article by Charles Carpenter Fries, "The Rules of the Common School Grammars" (42 [1927], 221–237). Fries there distinguished between the scientific tradition of language study (to which we will now delimit Francis' Grammar 2, scientific grammar) and the separate tradition of "the common school grammars," developed unscientifically, largely based on two inadequate principles—appeals to "logical principles," like "two negatives make a positive," and analogy to Latin grammar; thus, Charlton Laird's characterization, "the grammar of Latin, ingeniously warped to suggest English" (*Language in America* [New York: World, 1970], p. 294). There is, of course, a direct link between the "common school grammars" that Fries criticized in 1927 and the grammar-based texts of today, and thus it seems wise, as Karl W. Dykema suggests ("Where Our Grammar Came From," *CE,* 22 [1961], 455–465), to separate Grammar 2, "scientific grammar," from Grammar 4, "school grammar," the latter meaning, quite literally, "the grammars used in the schools."

Further, since Martha Kolln points to the adaptation of Christensen's sentence rhetoric in a recent sentence-combining text as an example of the proper emphasis on "grammar" ("Closing the Books on Alchemy," p. 140), it is worth separating out, as still another meaning of *grammar,* Grammar 5, "stylistic grammar," defined as "grammatical terms used in the interest of teaching prose style." And, since stylistic grammars abound, with widely variant terms and emphases, we might appropriately speak parenthetically of specific forms of Grammar 5—Grammar 5 (Lanham); Grammar 5 (Strunk and White); Grammar 5 (Williams, *Style*); even Grammar 5 (Christensen, as adapted by Daiker, Kerek, and Morenberg).

The Grammar in Our Heads

With these definitions in mind, let us return to Francis' Grammar 1, admirably defined by Kolln as "the internalized system of rules that speakers of a language share" ("Closing the Books on Alchemy," p. 140), or, to put it more simply, the grammar in our heads. Three features of Grammar 1 need to be stressed: first, its special status as an "internalized system of rules," as tacit and unconscious knowledge; second, the abstract, even counterintuitive, nature of these rules, insofar as we are able to approximate them indirectly as Grammar 2 statements: and third, the way in which the form of one's Grammar 1 seems profoundly affected by the acquisition of literacy. This sort of review is designed to firm up our theory of language, so that we can ask what it predicts about the value of teaching formal grammar.

A simple thought experiment will isolate the special status of Grammar 1 knowledge. I have asked members of a number of different groups—from sixth graders to college freshmen to high-school teachers—to give me the rule for ordering adjectives of nationality, age, and number in English. The response is always the same: "We don't know the rule." Yet when I ask these groups to perform an active language task, they show productive control over the rule they have denied knowing. I ask them to arrange the following words in a natural order:

French   the   young   girls   four

I have never seen a native speaker of English who did not immediately produce the natural order, "the four young French girls." The rule is that in English the order of adjectives is first, number, second, age, and third, nationality. Native speakers can create analogous phrases using the rule—"the seventy-three aged Scandinavian lechers"; and the drive for meaning is so great that they will create contexts to make sense out of violations of the rule, as in foregrounding for emphasis: "I want to talk to the French four young girls." (I immediately envision a large room, perhaps a banquet hall, filled with tables at which are seated groups of four young girls, each group of a different nationality.) So Grammar 1 is eminently usable knowledge—the way we make our life through language--but it is not accessible knowledge; in a profound sense, we do not know that we have it. Thus neurolinguist Z. N. Pylyshyn speaks of Grammar 1 as "autonomous," separate from common-sense reasoning, and as "cognitively impenetrable," not available for direct examination. In philosophy and linguistics, the distinction is made between formal, conscious, "knowing about" knowledge (like Grammar 2 knowledge) and tacit, unconscious, "knowing how" knowledge (like Grammar 1 knowledge). The importance of this distinction for the teaching of composition—it provides a powerful theoretical justification for mistrusting the ability of Grammar 2 (or Grammar 4) knowledge to affect Grammar 1 performance—was pointed out in this journal by Martin Steinmann, Jr., in 1966 ("Rhetorical Research," *CE*, 27 [1966], 278–285).

Further, the more we learn about Grammar 1—and most linguists would agree that we know surprisingly little about it—the more abstract and implicit it seems. This abstractness can be illustrated with an experiment, devised by Lise Menn and reported by Morris Halle, about our rule for forming plurals in speech. It is obvious that we do indeed have a "rule" for forming plurals, for we do not memorize the plural of each noun separately. You will demonstrate productive control over that rule by forming the spoken plurals of the nonsense words below:

thule   flitch   plast

Halle offers two ways of formalizing a Grammar 2 equivalent of this Grammar 1 ability. One form of the rule is the following, stated in terms of speech sounds:

a.   If the noun ends in /s z š ž č ǰ/, add /ɨz/;

b.   otherwise, if the noun ends in /p t k f Ø/, add /s/;

c.   otherwise, add /z/.

This rule comes close to what we literate adults consider to be an adequate rule for plurals in writing, like the rules, for example, taken from a recent "common school grammar," Eric Gould's *Reading into Writing: A Rhetoric, Reader, and Handbook* (Boston: Houghton Mifflin, 1983):

> *Plurals* can be tricky. If you are unsure of a plural, then check it in the dictionary. The general rules are
>
> Add *s* to the singular: *girls, tables*
>
> Add *es* to nouns ending in *ch, sh, x* or *s: churches, boxes, wishes*
>
> Add *es* to nouns ending in *y* and preceded by a vowel once you have changed *y* to *i: monies, companies* (p. 666)

(But note the persistent inadequacy of such Grammar 4 rules: here, as I read it, the rule is inadequate to explain the plurals of *ray* and *tray,* even to explain the collective noun *monies,* not a plural at all, formed from the mass noun *money* and offered as an example.) A second form of the rule would make use of much more abstract entities, sound features:

a.   If the noun ends with a sound that is [coronal, strident], add /ɨz/;

b.   otherwise, if the noun ends with a sound that is [non-voiced], add /s/;

c.   otherwise, add /z/.

(The notion of "sound features" is itself rather abstract, perhaps new to readers not trained in linguistics. But such readers should be able to recognize that the spoken plurals of *lip* and *duck,* the sound [s], differ from the spoken plurals of *sea* and *gnu,* the sound [z], only in that the sounds of the latter are "voiced"— one's vocal cords vibrate—while the sounds of the former are "non-voiced.")

To test the psychologically operative rule, the Grammar 1 rule, native speakers of English were asked to form the plural of the last name of the composer Johann Sebastian *Bach,* a sound [x], unique in American (though not in Scottish) English. If speakers follow the first rule above, using word endings, they would reject a) and b), then apply c), producing the plural as /baxz/, with word-final /z/. (If writers were to follow the rule of the common school grammar, they would produce the written plural *Baches,* apparently, given the form of the rule, on analogy with churches.) If speakers follow the second rule, they would have to analyze the sound [x] as [non-labial, non-coronal, dorsal, non-voiced, and non-strident), producing the plurals /baxs/ with word-final /s/. Native speakers of American English overwhelmingly produce the plural as

/baxs/. They use knowledge that Halle characterizes as "unlearned and untaught" (p. 140).

Now such a conclusion is counterintuitive—certainly it departs maximally from Grammar 4 rules for forming plurals. It seems that native speakers of English behave as if they have productive control, as Grammar 1 knowledge, of abstract sound features (± coronal, ± strident, and so on) which are available as conscious, Grammar 2 knowledge only to trained linguists—and, indeed, formally available only within the last hundred years or so. ("Behave as if," in that last sentence, is a necessary hedge, to underscore the difficulty of "knowing about" Grammar 1.)

Moreover, as the example of plural rules suggests, the form of the Grammar 1 in the heads of literate adults seems profoundly affected by the acquisition of literacy. Obviously, literate adults have access to different morphological codes: the abstract print -s underlying the predictable /s/ and /z/ plurals, the abstract printed -ed underlying the spoken past tense markers /t/, as in "walked," /əd/, as in "surrounded," /d/, as in "scored," and the symbol /Ø/ for no surface realization, as in the relaxed standard pronunciation of "I walked to the store." Literate adults also have access to distinctions preserved only in the code of print (for example, the distinction between "a good sailer" and "a good sailor" that Mark Aranoff points out in "An English Spelling Convention," *Linguistic Inquiry,* 9 [1978], 299–303). More significantly, Irene Moscowitz speculates that the ability of third graders to form abstract nouns on analogy with pairs like *divine::divinity* and *serene::serenity,* where the spoken vowel changes but the spelling preserves meaning, is a factor of knowing how to read. Carol Chomsky finds a three-stage developmental sequence in the grammatical performance of seven-year-olds, related to measures of kind and variety of reading; and Rita S. Brause finds a nine-stage developmental sequence in the ability to understand semantic ambiguity, extending from fourth graders to graduate students. John Mills and Gordon Hemsley find that level of education, and presumably level of literacy, influence judgments of grammaticality, concluding that literacy changes the deep structure of one's internal grammar; Jean Whyte finds that oral language functions develop differently in readers and nonreaders; José Morais, Jésus Alegria, and Paul Bertelson find that illiterate adults are unable to add or delete sounds at the beginning of nonsense words, suggesting that awareness of speech as a series of phones is provided by learning to read an alphabetic code. Two experiments—one conducted by Charles A. Ferguson, the other by Mary E. Hamilton and David Barton—find that adults' ability to recognize segmentation in speech is related to degree of literacy, not to amount of schooling or general ability.

It is worth noting that none of these investigators would suggest that the developmental sequences they have uncovered be isolated and taught as discrete skills. They are natural concomitants of literacy, and they seem best characterized not as isolated rules but as developing schemata, broad strategies for approaching written language.

Grammar 2

We can, of course, attempt to approximate the rules or schemata of Grammar 1
by writing fully explicit descriptions that model the competence of a native
speaker. Such rules, like the rules for pluralizing nouns or ordering adjectives
discussed above, are the goal of the science of linguistics, that is, Grammar 2.
There are a number of scientific grammars—an older structuralist model and
several versions within a generative-transformational paradigm, not to mention
isolated schools like tagmemic grammar, Montague grammar, and the like. In
fact, we cannot think of Grammar 2 as a stable entity, for its form changes with
each new issue of each linguistics journal, as new "rules of grammar" are proposed and debated. Thus Grammar 2, though of great theoretical interest to
the composition teacher, is of little practical use in the classroom, as Constance
Weaver has pointed out (*Grammar for Teachers* [Urbana, Ill.: NCTE 1979],
pp. 3–6). Indeed Grammar 2 is a scientific model of Grammar 1, not a description of it, so that questions of psychological reality, while important, are
less important than other, more theoretical factors, such as the elegance of formulation or the global power of rules. We might, for example, wish to replace
the rule for ordering adjectives of age, number, and nationality cited above with
a more general rule—what linguists call a "fuzzy" rule—that adjectives in
English are ordered by their abstract quality of "nouniness": adjectives that are
very much like nouns, like *French* or *Scandinavian,* come physically closer to
nouns than do adjectives that are less "nouny," like *four* or *aged.* But our motivation for accepting the broader rule would be its global power, not its psychological reality.

I try to consider a hostile reader, one committed to the teaching of grammar, and I try to think of ways to hammer in the central point of this distinction, that the rules of Grammar 2 are simply unconnected to productive control
over Grammar 1. I can argue from authority: Noam Chomsky has touched on
this point whenever he has concerned himself with the implications of linguistics for language teaching, and years ago transformationalist Mark Lester
stated unequivocally, "there simply appears to be no correlation between a
writer's study of language and his ability to write." I can cite analogies offered
by others: Francis Christensen's analogy in an essay originally published in
1962 that formal grammar study would be "to invite a centipede to attend to the
sequence of his legs in motion," or James Britton's analogy, offered informally
after a conference presentation, that grammar study would be like forcing starv-
ing people to master the use of a knife and fork before allowing them to eat.
I can offer analogies of my own, contemplating the wisdom of asking a pool
player to master the physics of momentum before taking up a cue or of making
a prospective driver get a degree in automotive engineering before engaging the
clutch. I consider a hypothetical argument, that if Grammar 2 knowledge affected Grammar 1 performance, then linguists would be our best writers. (I can
certify that they are, on the whole, not.) Such a position, after all, is only in ac-
cord with other domains of science: the formula for catching a fly ball in base-

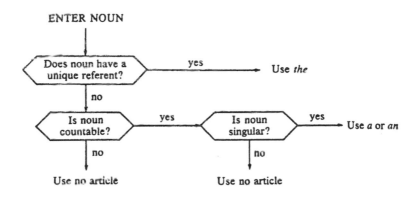

ENTER NOUN

Does noun have a unique referent? — yes → Use *the*

no

Is noun countable? — yes → Is noun singular? — yes → Use *a* or *an*

no → Use no article

no → Use no article

ball ("Playing It by Ear," *Scientific American,* 248, No. 4 [1983], 76) is of such complexity that it is beyond my understanding—and, I would suspect, that of many workaday centerfielders. But perhaps I can best hammer in this claim—that Grammar 2 knowledge has no effect on Grammar 1 performance—by offering a demonstration.

The diagram above is an attempt by Thomas N. Huckin and Leslie A. Olsen (*English for Science and Technology* [New York: McGraw-Hill, 1983]) to offer, for students of English as a second language, a fully explicit formulation of what is, for native speakers, a trivial rule of the language—the choice of definite article, indefinite article, or no definite article. There are obvious limits to such a formulation, for article choice in English is less a matter of rule than of idiom ("I went to college" versus "I went to a university" versus British "I went to university"), real-world knowledge (using indefinite "I went into a house" instantiates definite "I looked at the ceiling," and indefinite "I visited a university" instantiates definite "I talked with the professors"), and stylistic choice (the last sentence above might alternatively end with "the choice of the definite article, the indefinite article, or no article"). Huckin and Olsen invite nonnative speakers to use the rule consciously to justify article choice in technical prose, such as the passage below from P. F. Brandwein (*Matter: An Earth Science* [New York: Harcourt Brace Jovanovich, 1975]). I invite you to spend a couple of minutes doing the same thing, with the understanding that this exercise is a test case: you are using a very explicit rule to justify a fairly straightforward issue of grammatical choice.

> Imagine a cannon on top of _____ highest mountain on earth. It is firing _____ cannonballs horizontally. _____ first cannonball fired follows its path. As _____ cannonball moves, gravity pulls it down, and it soon hits _____ ground. Now _____ velocity with which each succeeding cannonball is fired is increased. Thus, _____ cannonball goes farther each time. Cannonball 2 goes farther than _____ cannonball 1 although each is being pulled by _____ gravity toward the earth all _____ time.

_____ last cannonball is fired with such tremendous velocity
that it goes completely around _____ earth. It returns to
_____ mountaintop and continues around the earth again and again.
_____ cannonball's inertia causes it to continue in motion indefi-
nitely in _____ orbit around earth. In such a situation, we could
consider _____ cannonball to be _____ artificial satellite,
just like _____ weather satellites launched by _____ U.S.
Weather Service. (p. 209)

Most native speakers of English who have attempted this exercise report a
great deal of frustration, a curious sense of working against, rather than with,
the rule. The rule, however valuable it may be for nonnative speakers, is, for the
most part, simply unusable for native speakers of the language.

Cognate Areas of Research

We can corroborate this demonstration by turning to research in two cognate
areas, studies of the induction of rules of artificial languages and studies of the
role of formal rules in second language acquisition. Psychologists have studied
the ability of subjects to learn artificial languages, usually constructed of nonsense syllables or letter strings. Such languages can be described by phrase
structure rules:

$$S \Rightarrow VX$$
$$X \Rightarrow MX$$

More clearly, they can be presented as flow diagrams, as below:

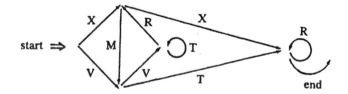

This diagram produces "sentences" like the following:

| VVTRXRR. | XMVTTRX. | XXRR. |
| XMVRMT. | VVTTRMT. | XMTRRR. |

The following "sentences" would be "ungrammatical" in this language:

| *VMXTT. | *RTXVVT. | *TRVXXVVM. |

Arthur S. Reber, in a classic 1967 experiment, demonstrated that mere exposure
to grammatical sentences produced tacit learning: subjects who copied several

grammatical sentences performed far above chance in judging the grammaticality of other letter strings. Further experiments have shown that providing subjects with formal rules—giving them the flow diagram above, for example—remarkably degrades performance: subjects given the "rules of the language" do much less well in acquiring the rules than do subjects not given the rules. Indeed, even telling subjects that they are to induce the rules of an artificial language degrades performance. Such laboratory experiments are admittedly contrived, but they confirm predictions that our theory of language would make about the value of formal rules in language learning.

The thrust of recent research in second language learning similarly works to constrain the value of formal grammar rules. The most explicit statement of the value of formal rules is that of Stephen D. Krashen's monitor model. Krashen divides second language mastery into *acquisition*—tacit, informal mastery, akin to first language acquisition—and formal learning—conscious application of Grammar 2 rules, which he calls "monitoring" output. In another essay Krashen uses his model to predict a highly individual use of the monitor and a highly constrained role for formal rules:

> Some adults (and very few children) are able to use conscious rules to increase the grammatical accuracy of their output, and even for these people, very strict conditions need to be met before the conscious grammar can be applied.

In *Principles and Practice in Second Language Acquisition* (New York: Pergamon, 1982) Krashen outlines these conditions by means of a series of concentric circles, beginning with a large circle denoting the rules of English and a smaller circle denoting the subset of those rules described by formal linguists (adding that most linguists would protest that the size of this circle is much too large):

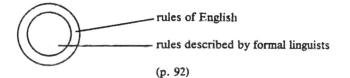

(p. 92)

Krashen then adds smaller circles, as shown below—a subset of the rules described by formal linguists that would be known to applied linguists, a subset of those rules that would be available to the best teachers, and then a subset of those rules that teachers might choose to present to second language learners:

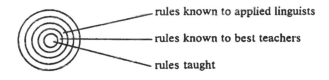

(p. 93)

Of course, as Krashen notes, not all the rules taught will be learned, and not all those learned will be available, as what he calls "mental baggage" (p. 94), for conscious use.

An experiment by Ellen Bialystock, asking English speakers learning French to judge the grammaticality of taped sentences, complicates this issue, for reaction time data suggest that learners first make an intuitive judgment of grammaticality, using implicit or Grammar 1 knowledge, and only then search for formal explanations, using explicit or Grammar 2 knowledge. This distinction would suggest that Grammar 2 knowledge is of use to second language learners only after the principle has already been mastered as tacit grammar 1 knowledge. In the terms of Krashen's model, learning never becomes acquisition (*Principles,* p. 86).

An ingenious experiment by Herbert W. Seliger complicates the issue yet further ("On the Nature and Function of Language Rules in Language Learning," *TESOL Quarterly,* 13 [1979], 359–369). Seliger asked native and nonnative speakers of English to orally identify pictures of objects (e.g., "an apple," "a pear," "a book," "an umbrella"), noting whether they used the correct form of the indefinite articles *a* and *an.* He then asked each speaker to state the rule for choosing between *a* and *an.* He found no correlation between the ability to state the rule and the ability to apply it correctly, either with native or nonnative speakers. Indeed, three of four adult nonnative speakers in his sample produced a correct form of the rule, but they did not apply it in speaking. A strong conclusion from this experiment would be that formal rules of grammar seem to have no value whatsoever. Seliger, however, suggests a more paradoxical interpretation. Rules are of no use, he agrees, but some people think they are, and for these people, assuming that they have internalized the rules, even inadequate rules are of heuristic value, for they allow them to access the internal rules they actually use.

The Incantations of the "Common School Grammars"

Such a paradox may explain the fascination we have as teachers with "rules of grammar" of the Grammar 4 variety, the "rules" of the "common school grammars." Again and again such rules are inadequate to the facts of written language; you will recall that we have known this since Francis' 1927 study. R. Scott Baldwin and James M. Coady, studying how readers respond to punctuation signals ("Psycholinguistic Approaches to a Theory of Punctuation," *Journal of Reading Behavior,* 10 [1978], 363–383), conclude that conventional rules of punctuation are "a complete sham" (p. 375). My own favorite is the Grammar 4 rule for showing possession, always expressed in terms of adding -'s or -s' to nouns, while our internal grammar, if you think about it, adds possession to noun phrases, albeit under severe stylistic constraints: "the horses of the Queen of England" are "the Queen of England's horses" and "the feathers of the duck over there" are "the duck over there's feathers." Suzette Haden Elgin refers to the "rules" of Grammar 4 as "incantations" (*Never Mind the Trees*, p. 9).

It may simply be that as hyperliterate adults we are conscious of "using rules" when we are in fact doing something else, something far more complex, accessing tacit heuristics honed by print literacy itself. We can clarify this notion by reaching for an acronym coined by technical writers to explain the readability of complex prose—COIK: "clear only if known." The rules of Grammar 4—no, we can at this point be more honest—the incantations of Grammar 4 are COIK. If you know how to signal possession in the code of print, then the advice to add 's to nouns makes perfect sense, just as the collective noun *monies* is a fine example of changing -*y* to -*i* and adding -*es* to form the plural. But if you have not grasped, tacitly, the abstract representation of possession in print, such incantations can only be opaque.

Worse yet, the advice given in "the common school grammars" is unconnected with anything remotely resembling literate adult behavior. Consider, as an example, the rule for not writing a sentence fragment as the rule is described in the best-selling college grammar text, John C. Hodges and Mary S. Whitten's *Harbrace College Handbook*, 9th ed, (New York: Harcourt Brace Jovanovich, 1982). In order to get to the advice, "as a rule, do not write a sentence fragment" (p. 25), the student must master the following learning tasks:

Recognizing verbs.

Recognizing subjects and verbs.

Recognizing all parts of speech. (*Harbrace* lists eight.)

Recognizing phrases and subordinate clauses. (*Harbrace* lists six types of phrases, and it offers incomplete lists of eight relative pronouns and eighteen subordinating conjunctions.)

Recognizing main clauses and types of sentences.

These learning tasks completed, the student is given the rule above, offered a page of exceptions, and then given the following advice (or is it an incantation?):

> Before handing in a composition. . . . proofread each word group written as a sentence. Test each one for completeness. First, be sure that it has at least one subject and one predicate. Next, be sure that the word group is not a dependent clause beginning with a subordinating conjunction or a relative clause. (p. 27)

The school grammar approach defines a sentence fragment as a conceptual error—as not having conscious knowledge of the school grammar definition of *sentence*. It demands heavy emphasis on rote memory, and it asks students to behave in ways patently removed from the behaviors of mature writers. (I have never in my life tested a sentence for completeness, and I am a better writer— and probably a better person—as a consequence.) It may be, of course, that

some developing writers, at some points in their development, may benefit from
such advice—or, more to the point, may think that they benefit—but, as
Thomas Friedman points out in "Teaching Error, Nurturing Confusion" (*CE,*
45 [1983], 390–399), our theory of language tells us that such advice is, at best,
COIK. As the Maine joke has it, about a tourist asking directions from a farmer,
"you can't get there from here."

Redefining Error

In the specific case of sentence fragments, Mina P. Shaughnessy (*Errors and
Expectations* [New York: Oxford University Press, 1977]) argues that such errors are not conceptual failures at all, but performance errors—mistakes in
punctuation. Muriel Harris' error counts support this view ("Mending the
Fragmented Free Modifier," *CCC,* 32 [1981], 175–182). Case studies show example after example of errors that occur *because of* instruction—one thinks,
for example, of David Bartholmae's student explaining that he added an -*s* to
children "because it's a plural" ("The Study of Error," *CCC,* 31 [1980], 262).
Surveys, such as that by Muriel Harris ("Contradictory Perceptions of the
Rules of Writing," *CCC,* 30 [1979], 218–220), and our own observations suggest that students consistently misunderstand such Grammar 4 explanations
(COIK, you will recall). For example, from Patrick Hartwell and Robert H.
Bentley and from Mike Rose, we have two separate anecdotal accounts of students, cited for punctuating a *because*-clause as a sentence, who have decided
to avoid using *because.* More generally, Collette A. Daiute's analysis of errors
made by college students shows that errors tend to appear at clause boundaries,
suggesting short-term memory load and not conceptual deficiency as a cause
of error.

Thus, if we think seriously about error and its relationship to the worship
of formal grammar study, we need to attempt some massive dislocation of our
traditional thinking, to shuck off our hyperliterate perception of the value of
formal rules, and to regain the confidence in the tacit power of unconscious
knowledge that our theory of language gives us. Most students, reading their
writing aloud, will correct in essence all errors of spelling, grammar, and, by
intonation, punctuation, but usually without noticing that what they read departs from what they wrote. And Richard H. Haswell ("Minimal Marking," *CE,*
45 [1983], 600–604) notes that his students correct 61.1% of their errors when
they are identified with a simple mark in the margin rather than by error type.
Such findings suggest that we need to redefine error, to see it not as a cognitive
or linguistic problem, a problem of not knowing a "rule of grammar" (whatever
that may mean), but rather, following the insight of Robert J. Bracewell ("Writing as a Cognitive Activity," *Visible Language,* 14 [1980], 400–422) as a problem of metacognition and metalinguistic awareness, a matter of accessing
knowledges that, to be of any use, learners must have already internalized by
means of exposure to the code. (Usage issues—Grammar 3—probably repre-

sent a different order of problem. Both Joseph Emonds and Jeffrey Jochnowitz establish that the usage issues we worry most about are linguistically unnatural, departures from the grammar in our heads.)

The notion of metalinguistic awareness seems crucial. The sentence below, created by Douglas R. Hofstadter ("Metamagical Themas," *Scientific American,* 235, No. 1 [1981], 22–32), is offered to clarify that notion; you are invited to examine it for a moment or two before continuing.

Their is four errors in this sentence. Can you find them?

Three errors announce themselves plainly enough, the misspellings of *there* and *sentence* and the use of *is* instead of *are.* (And, just to illustrate the perils of hyperliteracy, let it be noted that, through three years of drafts, I referred to the choice of *is* and *are* as a matter of "subject-verb agreement.") The fourth error resists detection, until one assesses the truth value of the sentence itself— the fourth error is that there are not four errors, only three. Such a sentence (Hofstadter calls it a "self-referencing sentence") asks you to look at it in two ways, simultaneously as statement and as linguistic artifact—in other words, to exercise metalinguistic awareness.

A broad range of cross-cultural studies suggest that metalinguistic awareness is a defining feature of print literacy. Thus Sylvia Scribner and Michael Cole, working with the triliterate Vai of Liberia (variously literate in English, through schooling; in Arabic, for religious purposes; and in an indigenous Vai script, used for personal affairs), find that metalinguistic awareness, broadly conceived, is the only cognitive skill underlying each of the three literacies. The one statistically significant skill shared by literate Vai was the recognition of word boundaries. Moreover, literate Vai tended to answer "yes" when asked (in Vai), "Can you call the sun the moon and the moon the sun?" while illiterate Vai tended to have grave doubts about such metalinguistic play. And in the United States Henry and Lila R. Gleitman report quite different responses by clerical workers and PhD candidates asked to interpret nonsense compounds like "house-bird glass": clerical workers focused on meaning and plausibility (for example, "a house-bird made of glass"), while PhD candidates focused on syntax (for example, "a very small drinking cup for canaries" or "a glass that protects house-birds"). More general research findings suggest a clear relationship between measures of metalinguistic awareness and measures of literacy level. William Labov, speculating on literacy acquisition in inner-city ghettoes, contrasts "stimulus-bound" and "language-bound" individuals, suggesting that the latter seem to master literacy more easily. The analysis here suggests that the causal relationship works the other way, that it is the mastery of written language that increases one's awareness of language as language.

This analysis has two implications. First, it makes the question of socially nonstandard dialects, always implicit in discussions of teaching formal grammar, into a nonissue. Native speakers of English, regardless of dialect, show tacit mastery of the conventions of Standard English, and that mastery seems to transfer into abstract orthographic knowledge through interaction with print. Developing writers show the same patterning of errors, regardless of dialect. Studies of reading and of writing suggest that surface features of spoken dialect are simply irrelevant to mastering print literacy. Print is a complex cultural code—or better yet, a system of codes—and my bet is that, regardless of instruction, one masters those codes from the top down, from pragmatic questions of voice, tone, audience, register, and rhetorical strategy, not from the bottom up, from grammar to usage to fixed forms of organization.

Second, this analysis forces us to posit multiple literacies, used for multiple purposes, rather than a single static literacy, engraved in "rules of grammar." These multiple literacies are evident in cross-cultural studies. They are equally evident when we inquire into the uses of literacy in American communities. Further, given that students, at all levels, show widely variant interactions with print literacy, there would seem to be little to do with grammar—with Grammar 2 or with Grammar 4—that we could isolate as a basis for formal instruction.

Grammar 5: Stylistic Grammar

Similarly, when we turn to Grammar 5, "grammatical terms used in the interest of teaching prose style," so central to Martha Kolln's argument for teaching formal grammar, we find that the grammar issue is simply beside the point. There are two fully articulated positions about "stylistic grammar," which I will label "romantic" and "classic," following Richard Lloyd-Jones and Richard E. Young. The romantic position is that stylistic grammars, though perhaps useful for teachers, have little place in the teaching of composition, for students must struggle with and through language toward meaning. This position rests on a theory of language ultimately philosophical rather than linguistic (witness, for example, the contempt for linguists in Ann Berthoff's *The Making of Meaning: Metaphors, Models, and Maxims for Writing Teachers* [Montclair, N.J.: Boynton/Cook, 1981]); it is articulated as a theory of style by Donald A. Murray and, on somewhat different grounds (that stylistic grammars encourage overuse of the monitor), by Ian Pringle. The classic position, on the other hand, is that we can find ways to offer developing writers helpful suggestions about prose style, suggestions such as Francis Christensen's emphasis on the cumulative sentence, developed by observing the practice of skilled writers, and Joseph Williams' advice about predication, developed by psycholinguistic studies of comprehension. James A. Berlin's recent survey of composition theory (*CE,* 45 [1982], 765–777) probably understates the gulf between these two positions and the radically different conceptions of language that underlie them, but it does establish that they share an overriding assumption in common: that one learns to control the language of print by manipulating language in meaningful contexts, not by learning about language in isolation, as by the study of formal grammar. Thus even classic theorists, who choose to present a vocabulary of style to students, do so only as a vehicle for encouraging productive control of communicative structures.

We might put the matter in the following terms. Writers need to develop skills at two levels. One, broadly rhetorical, involves communication in meaningful contexts (the strategies, registers, and procedures of discourse across a range of modes, audiences, contexts, and purposes). The other, broadly metalinguistic rather than linguistic, involves active manipulation of language with conscious attention to surface form. This second level may be developed tacitly, as a natural adjunct to developing rhetorical competencies—I take this to be the position of romantic theorists. It may be developed formally, by manipulating language for stylistic effect, and such manipulation may involve, for pedagogical continuity, a vocabulary of style. But it is primarily developed by any kind of language activity that enhances the awareness of language as language. David T. Hakes, summarizing the research on metalinguistic awareness, notes how far we are from understanding this process:

> the optimal conditions for becoming metalinguistically competent involve growing up in a literate environment with adult models who are themselves metalinguistically competent and who foster the growth of that competence in a variety of ways as yet little understood. ("The Development of Metalinguistic Abilities," p. 205)

Such a model places language, at all levels, at the center of the curriculum, but not as "necessary categories and labels" (Kolln, "Closing the Books on Alchemy," p. 150), but as literal stuff, verbal clay, to be molded and probed, shaped and reshaped, and, above all, enjoyed.

The Tradition of Experimental Research

Thus, when we turn back to experimental research on the value of formal grammar instruction, we do so with firm predictions given us by our theory of language. Our theory would predict that formal grammar instruction, whether instruction in scientific grammar or instruction in "the common school grammar," would have little to do with control over surface correctness nor with quality of writing. It would predict that any form of active involvement with language would be preferable to instruction in rules or definitions (or incantations). In essence, this is what the research tells us. In 1893, the Committee of Ten (*Report of the Committee of Ten on Secondary School Studies* [Washington, D.C.: U.S. Government Printing Office, 1893]) put grammar at the center of the English curriculum, and its report established the rigidly sequential mode of instruction common for the last century. But the committee explicitly noted that grammar instruction did not aid correctness, arguing instead that it improved the ability to think logically (an argument developed from the role of the "grammarian" in the classical rhetorical tradition, essentially a teacher of literature—see, for example, the etymology of *grammar* in the *Oxford English Dictionary*).

But Franklin S. Hoyt, in a 1906 experiment, found no relationship between the study of grammar and the ability to think logically; his research led him to conclude what I am constrained to argue more than seventy-five years later, that there is no "relationship between a knowledge of technical grammar and the ability to use English and to interpret language" ("The Place of Grammar in the Elementary Curriculum," *Teachers College Record,* 7 [1906], 483–484). Later studies, through the 1920s, focused on the relationship of knowledge of grammar and ability to recognize error; experiments reported by James Boraas in 1917 and by William Asker in 1923 are typical of those that reported no correlation. In the 1930s, with the development of the functional grammar movement, it was common to compare the study of formal grammar with one form or another of active manipulation of language; experiments by I. O. Ash in 1935 and Ellen Frogner in 1939 are typical of studies showing the superiority of active involvement with language. In a 1959 article, "Grammar in Language Teaching" (*Elementary English,* 36 [1959], 412–421), John J. DeBoer noted the consistency of these findings.

> The impressive fact is . . . that in all these studies, carried out in places and at times far removed from each other, often by highly experienced and disinterested investigators, the results have been consistently negative so far as the value of grammar in the improvement of language expression is concerned. (p. 417)

In 1960 Ingrid M. Strom, reviewing more than fifty experimental studies, came to a similarly strong and unqualified conclusion:

> direct methods of instruction, focusing on writing activities and the structuring of ideas, are more efficient in teaching sentence structure, usage, punctuation, and other related factors than are such methods as nomenclature drill, diagramming, and rote memorization of grammatical rules.

In 1963 two research reviews appeared, one by Braddock, Lloyd-Jones, and Schorer, cited at the beginning of this paper, and one by Henry C. Meckel, whose conclusions, though more guarded, are in essential agreement. In 1969 J. Stephen Sherwin devoted one-fourth of his *Four Problems in Teaching English: A Critique of Research* (Scranton, Penn.: International Textbook, 1969) to the grammar issue, concluding that "instruction in formal grammar is an ineffective way to help students achieve proficiency in writing" (p. 135). Some early experiments in sentence combining, such as those by Donald R. Bateman and Frank J. Zidonnis and by John C. Mellon, showed improvement in measures of syntactic complexity with instruction in transformational grammar keyed to sentence combining practice. But a later study by Frank O'Hare achieved the same gains with no grammar instruction, suggesting to Sandra L. Stotsky and to Richard Van de Voghe that active manipulation of language, not the grammar unit, explained the earlier results. More recent summaries of research—by Elizabeth I. Haynes, Hillary Taylor Holbrook, and Marcia Farr Whiteman—support similar conclusions. Indirect evidence for this position is provided by surveys reported by Betty Bamberg in 1978 and 1981, showing that time spent in grammar instruction in high school is the least important factor, of eight factors examined, in separating regular from remedial writers at the college level.

More generally, Patrick Scott and Bruce Castner, in "Reference Sources for Composition Research: A Practical Survey" (CE, 45 [1983], 756–768), note that much current research is not informed by an awareness of the past. Put simply, we are constrained to reinvent the wheel. My concern here has been with a far more serious problem: that too often the wheel we reinvent is square.

It is, after all, a question of power. Janet Emig, developing a consensus from composition research, and Aaron S. Carton and Lawrence V. Castiglione, developing the implications of language theory for education, come to the same conclusion: that the thrust of current research and theory is to take power from the teacher and to give that power to the learner. At no point in the English curriculum is the question of power more blatantly posed than in the issue of formal grammar instruction. It is time that we, as teachers, formulate theories of language and literacy and let those theories guide our teaching, and it is time that we, as researchers, move on to more interesting areas of inquiry.

Part Five

Attunement Through Shared Experience

Conversion to the people requires a profound rebirth.

—Paulo Freire
Pedagogy of the Oppressed

When in an academic discipline both theory and practice merge and support each other, that period might be described as a golden age. For whatever reasons, such does not seem to be the case in rhetoric and composition at the present time. Some of the most interesting and productive recent developments in the field have been associated with the *practice* of our discipline. It is as though a growing number of teachers have discovered the power of the written word and have reached out to others in order to make its benefits more accessible.

The title of this section is coined from Kurt Spellmeyer's powerful and moving critique of the profession, "After Theory: From Textuality to Attunement with the World." The author argues that theory, both postmodern and traditional, has lost its way and that the noblest goals of the profession lie not in texts but in "ordinary sensous life" and ultimately in "attunement with the world." "What our society needs most urgently is not another theoretical 'advance,'" writes Professor Spellmeyer, "but a better understanding of the practices though which everyone might enter. . ." (242). His admonition is eloquent: "Yet, in order to discover and protect such practices, English studies needs to undergo a change more profound than many people might like. We will need to become ethnographers of *experience* . . . , scholar/teachers who find out how people actually *feel*" (242).

The remaining essays in this section are examples of the ethnography of experience. In her essay "The Rhetorician As an Agent of Social Change," Ellen Cushman explores ways other than classroom activism to affect social change. The author argues that the reciprocal nature of such work enriches the life of the teacher-researcher as well as that of the student. In many ways Cushman's work is pioneering, showing us a way of teaching that challenges outworn and ineffective institutional conventions. Because the essay stands on its own merits, most of the author's extensive notes are not included here.

Susan B. Andrews' grueling childhood training as a ballet dancer seems far removed from her work as editor of Native American publications in

219

Alaska, yet the connections are there, as revealed by her essay "Writing As Performance." What made the connections possible was a shift in perspective from the desire to become a prima ballerina to a realization of the real joy in the amateur performance of dance itself. The shift made it possible for the author to immerse herself in the writing and culture of the Yup'ik, Athabascan, Tlingit, and other native peoples.

Susan Andrews teaches us to value all of life's experiences, both pleasant and unpleasant, no matter how far they may seem removed from one's present goals. The reader will observe, too, the thread of attunement that runs subtly through her work. It is "unself-conscious," she suggests, and its domain is corporeal, in specific people and cultures, in folk habit and custom, ritual and myth.

In "Kitchen Tables and Rented Rooms: The Extracurriculum of Composition," Anne Ruggles Gere traces the history of writing outside the formal curriculum. The author explores writing in self-sponsored events "undertaken by motivated individuals who frequently see it as having social and economic consequences, including transformations in personal relationships and farming practices" (271). Especially poignant is Gere's account of the women writers of the Tenderloin District of San Francisco. Mary TallMountain's sketch of Bilijohn, a fellow Native American, illustrates the intensity and vision generated in such writing groups outside the school setting.

Jane Juska's account of teaching her course, English 101: Reading and Writing Fiction, in San Quentin Prison is riveting. Her essay graphically details the conflicts and small victories of her inmate-students, who learn that writing is "not about spelling and punctuation" (286). The author knows that her pupils are indeed fluent, though they are not aware of it at the outset. The samples of writing included here speak eloquently about the power of the writing process.

After Theory

From Textuality to Attunement with the World

Kurt Spellmeyer

The hardest questions can be the simplest ones. For example, what was "theory"? In its heyday—the decade after 1968—theory could mean almost anything, from Deleuze and Guattari's "schizoanalysis" to Habermas's seemingly endless defense of "communicative rationality." No matter what the word might have meant at the time, however, people somehow sensed its importance, and they knew, if they knew absolutely nothing else, that theory had to do with "the text." But now, almost thirty years afterward, people somehow sense that theory is passé, and they know, if they still pay attention at all, that it has been displaced by any number of successors: by New Historicism, for instance, and by cultural studies, and by the eclectic mix referred to as "post-theory." While terms like "cultural studies" and "post-theory" circulate as loosely as "theory" did in its brief golden age, theory's successors all share among themselves at least one identifying feature—a commitment to descending from textuality into the particulars of everyday life.

Yet theory today is anything but dead, and it survives through the movements that claim to have left it behind. When Judith Butler in *Gender Trouble* sets out to rethink the logic of heterosexuality, she calls on Derrida. When Homi Bhabha, in *Redrawing the Boundaries,* starts to map the new terrain of postcolonial studies, he goes back to Barthes and Bakhtin. Although we tend to see ourselves as working in the era after theory, the truth may be far more complicated—and also far more troubling. We are, perhaps, *trapped* in theory, and trapped so inextricably that even our most careful efforts to escape keep returning us to the isolation that drove us from theory in the first place. And now, when the future of our profession has begun to look uncomfortably like a rerun of our past, the moment may have come for us to admit that theory itself brought us here. If the world is not a text, then when we treat it as one we soon lose the capacity to differentiate between actions that can lead to meaningful change and those symbolic practices that substitute for action all too easily. Worse yet, once we have surrendered to the siren song of "the text," nothing remains to call us back, since the failure of each new methodology—from Lévi-

College English, 58 (December 1996), pp. 893–913. Copyright © 1996 by the National Council of Teachers of English. Reprinted with permission.

Strauss's search for deep structures of the mind to Donald Morton's critique of "post-ality"—only lends a greater urgency to the whole enterprise.

Theory, in other words, has outlived its own "death," but its survival gives cold comfort to all the former converts who have irretrievably lost their faith. For those of us no longer charmed by the magic, by the myth, of the pursuit of signs—what other path remains if we want to be more than perpetually "post-"? What we need is nothing less than a paradigm shift: turning from the thread-bare ideology of "the text," we might start to explore an alternative so mundane that we have passed it over time after time in our scramble for sophistication and prestige. That alternative is ordinary sensuous life, which is not an "effect" of how we think but the ground of thought itself, or so I want to argue here. At this late hour, when theory's successors can teach us nothing really new, what prevents us firom returning to the idea of "the arts" by a long-forgotten path— the arts imagined as traditions of experience that intensify our sense of living in and with the world? If the humanities have, as I believe, very nearly lost the battle for the hearts and minds of our fellow citizens, then the future of English may well lie with those arts and the worlds they open up.

The Rhetoric of Theory: A Reading Lesson

The products of art and science owe their existence not merely to the effort of the great geniuses that created them, but also to the unnamed drudgery of their contemporaries. There is no document of culture which is not at the same time a document of barbarism.

Walter Benjamin (233)

What Walter Benjamin observes of culture in general holds true for theory in particular: although it may express the very noblest of hopes, it also perpetuates the legacy of an unacknowledged violence. And precisely because so many people working in English studies have encountered theory only as liberating, that hidden legacy has passed unnoticed—and unredressed. I can still remember my own first encounter with theory, which seemed to arrive at the moment of my greatest professional and personal need. But as theory itself has helped us recognize, such small conjunctions, multiplied many times, are what we mean by "history."

It happened on a January afternoon at a downtown Princeton bookstore where I went at the end of a uniquely unpleasant event. That event was the most recent meeting of New Jersey's Basic Skills Council, which our governor had charged with assessing the public schools, and on which I held a seat as the director of the state's largest college-level writing program. Fourteen years and many millions of dollars into a campaign of twelfth-grade exit testing, the council had assembled the data to "prove" that thousands of graduates from the poorest urban neighborhoods—Camden, Newark, and Jersey City—were functionally illiterate. But the data themselves were *all* we had; none of us knew why the scores were so low, and no one could explain with much clarity—although we were ostensibly the best in our field—how we should respond.

Our silence left me demoralized. As the snow piled up against the windows of the store, I found myself increasingly disturbed to think that we had measured the extent of "illiteracy" without ever knowing what the word really meant. Even more disturbing was the Council's public confirmation, carried everywhere by the local media, of deeply entrenched beliefs about New Jersey's "skills deficient" citizens—largely black or Hispanic, and almost always working class. After a decade in "remedial" education, I knew just how deep these beliefs could run, so deep that they shaped not only the policies of the state but also the canonical scholarship. One study I had been made to read when I was in graduate school spoke for much of the profession when it held that the children of the "culturally deprived . . . do not just think at an immature level: many of them do not think at all" (Bereiter et al. 107). And they could not think, this study maintained, partly because of their genetic heritage, which was cited in a footnote on selective black migration, and partly because their language lacked "the formal properties necessary for the organization of thought" (105, 113). A decade later, on that January afternoon, absolutely nothing had changed; from our data we expected to reach more or less the same conclusion, and the solution that the study had proposed long before was our state's solution as well: to begin instruction at the zero point, proceeding as if these "children" had "no language" of their own (113).

Like most of the Council's monthly meetings, the one in January dragged on so long that no one felt much relief when it wound down, and I spent what was left of the afternoon browsing numbly through the kind of "difficult" books I would otherwise have looked past. Somewhere in the store a string quartet was playing crisply on a compact disc, and it struck me as I stood listening that even if I traveled to the ends of the earth—to the Outback or Ulan Bator—I could not possibly be more distant than I was just then from the people we referred to as "skills deficient." Camden and Jersey City were a million miles away, but the book I bought that afternoon, with the enigmatic title *Truth and Method,* helped me understand what "reading" was and why no two human beings could *ever* read the same passage in quite the same way. And on another afternoon three months afterward, as I slogged through the book's last hundred pages or so, I realized that the author, Hans-Georg Gadamer—a protégé of Heidegger, not an instructor of "basic skills"—had given me the means to change nearly everything about what I did and who I was.

For the first time in my professional life, I found it possible to see the "skills deficient" differently, not as isolated individuals who had missed the chance for cognitive development, but as members of communities *strong* enough to survive despite enormous violence from outside. Although Gadamer himself would almost certainly disagree, given his commitment to the high culture of the West, his work still helped me recognize that people everywhere were historical beings no more capable of falling outside language and tradition than they were capable of falling outside time. Whether writing or thinking, speaking or acting, people are "always already" inside a linguistic world, and so thoroughly inside that we might say, as Gadamer did, not that we speak a language but that we ourselves are spoken (378, 549). Where the study I once read in graduate school had diagnosed a fundamental poverty, hermeneutic tradition revealed a plenitude to me; where the study called for a program of "no-nonsense" academic discipline, Gadamer invoked the vastly more humane ideal of learning as a journey and a conversation, an endless "fusion" of lifeworld "horizons" (306–7). Looking out from the horizon Gadamer opened for *me*, I recognized more clearly than I ever had before that teaching any subject was a self-defeating act unless all of those involved could find the means to enlarge their particular lifeworlds—worlds that were full and real in different ways but *equally* full and real. As Gadamer wrote in a passage that I am sure I will never forget, we always end our journeys by "returning home" (448).

Its detractors sometimes allege that theory changes nothing, but theory in my life has had far-reaching consequences. I acted on the insights theory offered me, and my actions touched the lives of many thousands of high school graduates whose experience at the university might have been more damaging than it turned out to be. For an entire generation in English studies, I believe, the encounter with theory followed a course like the one I have just retraced, an odyssey from silence, boredom, and paralysis to a sense of purpose and "empowerment," as we used to say. Yet it seems increasingly obvious now that something went wrong with theory. When the Frankfurt sociologist Max Horkheimer used the word in the 1930s, he had in mind a practice of immanent critique launched at institutions like the university, with their tendency to reproduce the status quo in supposedly objective and enabling routines (188–203). But theory in the decades after 1968 rapidly became the central pillar of orthodox practice in the humanities. When Robert Scholes observed in 1985— and quite approvingly—that teachers should "read theory to 'keep up,'" he reminded us, without meaning to, of just how far theory has traveled since the time when Horkheimer saw "keeping up" as a suspect idea (19). Once the margins had become prime real estate, who could be surprised to see *Paradise Lost* restored to its former stature as prophecy by showing how it anticipates Marx on class struggle? Instead of qualifying our statements, we were taught to put them *sous rature;* instead of saying that a character's behavior looks ambiguous, we learned to say that she "is placed"—never mind by whom— "under the sign of ambiguity." As the tool of a self-styled critical avant-garde, theory landed Yale High Church deconstructionists in a special section of *Time* magazine, while the founders of cultural studies, sporting silk Armani jackets, made fashion statements for the sputtering New York press. Trivial as these events might seem, they tell us something essential about theory and the movements that have followed it. For the first time since the quiz-show days of Charles van Doren, scholars who might have started their careers with books on Donne's debt to Plotinus or Trollope's comedy of manners saw the chance for something like celebrity by turning to the signifying practices of Bugs Bunny or 2 Live Crew.

Yet there has been, I think, more to theory's success than the lure of celebrity can explain—and this "more" has to do with the character of theory as a resource for preserving our profession's prestige. Like every other form of information dignified with the name of "knowledge" today, theory gets produced by specialists. But theory differs from a piece in *Harper's* or a report on the *CBS Evening News,* whose writers are no less specialized than we are, because theory is uniquely the discourse of privileged *and* declining institutions whose concerns have grown so distant from everyday life that a sense of crisis overtakes the specialists themselves. To justify the privileged status of their work, these specialists must show that their thinking is somehow *superior* to common sense—more inclusive, more penetrating, more rigorous. But theory wins the battle at the cost of the war, since the discourse that strays too far from the everyday world runs the risk of losing its lay clientèle as well as the confidence of neophytes, who no longer see themselves figured in its ghostly narratives.

Theory and its successors have taken shape in the space opened up by the conflict between our hunger for prestige and our loneliness in an age of mass communications; yet the purpose of theory as we have often practiced it, under a variety of names, is not to make intellectual life more open and democratic by enlarging the circle of participants, but rather to invest the culture of expertise with an aura of unalterable permanence. Theory makes a *weapon* of marginality by reversing the relations of power between ourselves and a public inclined to dismiss our achievements and concerns out of hand. And while every work of theory turns the tables on its readers, one work that points with unintended candor to theory's self-destructive contradictions is Gayatri Spivak's essay on "Breast-Giver," a short story by the Bengali writer Mahasweta Devi. Before looking closely at Spivak's essay, though, I should explain that the story can be read straightforwardly as an account of a woman's unhappy life when the crippling of her husband forces her to become a wet nurse. As Spivak herself concedes in a brief aside, Devi meant the woman to personify the troubled nation-state of India, from whom all its "children" take, giving nothing in return (244). But Spivak reads the story quite differently:

> Thought, as *jouissance,* is not orgasmic pleasure genitally defined, but the excess of being that escapes the circle of the reproduction of the subject. It is the mark of the Other in the subject. Now psychoanalysis can only ever conceive of thought as possible through those mechanics of signification where the phallus comes to *mean* the Law by positing castration as punishment as such. Although the point is made repeatedly by Lacan that we are not speaking of the actual male member but of the phallus of the signifier, it is still obviously a gendered position . . .

> . . . to call Mahasweta's preoccupation in ["Breast-Giver"] with *jouissance* in the general sense "writing like a man" is to reduce a complex position to the trivializing simplicity of a hegemonic gendering. . . .
>
> In ["Breast-Giver," the protagonist's body], rather than her fetishized deliberative consciousness (self or subjectivity), is the *place* of knowledge, rather than the instrument of knowing. (259–60)

To a reader unfamiliar with the conventions of high theory and its offspring, cultural studies, Spivak's interpretation is bound to seem like a parody of academic criticism at its worst. Readers have to make more than a modest reach, after all, if they want to trace out the connections between Devi's simple allegory and the grand themes that matter most to Spivak herself—writing, interpretation, reification, and the highly disincarnate form of ecstasy that the French, sad to say, call "*jouissance.*" But theory's advocates would probably reply that Spivak's tendentiousness is just what we need. Like every text that tells us more than we already know, she confounds our familiar point of view, and by doing so forces us to see not only the story but also ourselves in an unexpected light.

Such, at least, is the prevailing party line, but how true is it, actually? New ways of reading stories can be wonderful, yet over and above its novelty, Spivak's text subjects its readers to a violence that practitioners of theory and its "post" avatars take great pains to deny. Reading Spivak *hurts*—hurts beginners, anyway—precisely because her prose demands that we relinquish a large measure of our agency. But the reader's loss of agency does not follow simply from the convolutions of her prose. That loss of agency results, instead, from the double bind in which Spivak's rhetoric locks every reader generous enough to give her work a hearing. On the one hand, the text promises something like a mass emancipation from traditions that have failed to hear and understand people like Mahasweta's protagonist, the much-invoked global "subaltern." But Spivak's rhetoric, on the other hand, compels its readers to abandon Mahasweta's words in order to wander through the labyrinths of Foucault's, Derrida's, Volosinov's, and Lacan's. And the result is not emancipation but a forced admission on the reader's part that even when these eminent intellects make very little sense indeed, they still somehow think more usefully than the ordinary reader ever could. If there are any "subalterns" to be found in this particular study, one of them is surely the reader, insofar as Spivak's practice of theory does to that reader what educators do to the people they have stigmatized as "remedial." By refashioning the character of "literacy" itself, the practitioners of theory have learned to transform whole shoals of articulate PhDs into stammering "illiterates." But Spivak is no less diminished than we are, to the degree that she feels compelled to write about a parable of Indian political life in a language that makes India unspeakable. And, in fact, Spivak's largely Western audience comes away from her tour de force knowing something more about the Paris scene but absolutely nothing new about the people who live their lives in the villages and cities of West Bengal.

What disappears from Spivak's text is not just the reader's world, but also any sense of the world that produced Mahasweta's own narrative. And this violent act, which destroys and appropriates at the same time, is the quintessential gesture of both theory and remediation as they are typically practiced. In each case the motive is the same—the maintenance of a boundary between "ignorance" and "knowledge," mystification and enlightenment. Constrained as she is by the language of theory, Spivak has chosen to be heard at a certain cost to others—by speaking the argot of professionals and by laying claim to an insight that transcends the experience of absolutely everyone except a few cognoscenti like the ones she dutifully cites. While attempting to make room for the excluded and disempowered, the theorist continues to occupy a privileged place indistinguishable from the scientist's role as an objective observer, or from the philosopher's pretensions to pure reason. The theorist still plays Socrates, with the reader standing dumbly in as Glaucon, while the truth itself remains always somewhere else, far removed from the reader's here and now. If this displacement of the here and now is theory's greatest strength, it is also theory's greatest danger, since we can never know, looking up from Santa Cruz or down from Morningside Heights, how things appear to those positioned somewhere else. But the problem is more serious than our failure to see the lay citizen's point of view. Over the last fifteen years or so, theory's universalizing ambitions have given us the spectacle of upper-middle-class white North Americans using French philosophers (most of them males) to make sense of narratives by and about "Third World women." We can be sure, as well—and this strikes me as even worse—that at this very moment, college teachers from Cairo to Kuala Lumpur are busily stuffing their syllabi with readings that their counterparts in Paris would sniff at sourly as old news. Far from breaking with the legacy of colonization, this arrangement has simply reinstated it with a vengeance, so that the grandchildren of the Asian and African subjects who began their school day paying homage to "our forefathers the Gauls" now bone up on Derrida or Foucault. And the lesson we need to draw from this disastrous turn of events is that knowledge as we produce it in the academy—even when it takes the form of postcolonial critique—helps to perpetuate a truly global system of dependency.

The Knowledge-Class Professional: A Sociology of Theory

We will never understand the contradictions inherent in theory until we recognize a fundamental change in social life today, a change brought about by the passage from the relative coherence of premodern communities to the fragmentation of "postmodernity." Although we often want to fight the noble fight of "organic intellectuals," deeply rooted in the local scene just as Gramsci was in prewar Turin, when we speak *ex cathedra* to our fellow citizens, we speak as their masters, not as their friends; and as powerful authorities, not as fellow sufferers. The world within which we operate today is much less like the one evoked by Paulo Freire in *Pedagogy of the Oppressed* than it is like the one described by Gary Marx in an essay on his life as a sociologist:

> In 1970, there could not have been many sociologists just three years beyond the Ph.D. who were as professionally satisfied and optimistic as I was. . . . Immigrants, gold miners, and aspiring actors might head West, but as an ambitious academic born on a farm in central California, I had headed east to where I thought the real action was—Cambridge, Massachusetts.
>
> I had a job at Harvard with a higher salary and a longer contract (negotiated under threat of deserting to another Ivy League school) than the other assistant professors in the Department of Social Relations. I taught only one course and had a mammoth corner office, where I was protected from intruders by my own secretary in an outer office.
>
> My book *Protest and Prejudice* had sold fifteen thousand copies and had been translated into Japanese. Various chapters had been reprinted in more than twenty books. (261)

Even when we want to play an oppositional role, our disciplines continue to operate within a system carefully designed to preserve what Pierre Bourdieu calls our "distinction," our symbolic distance from the people below us on the ladder of prestige and opportunity (22–28). But the reality of this distance becomes obvious, as it does in Marx's narrative, only at the points of greatest tension between what we want to think about ourselves and what we actually do. Although Marx wrote a dissertation on insurgency, he completed his research with the aid of highly competitive fellowships; although he sided with landless peasants, he cut a sharp deal with Harvard; although he argued for cooperation and equality, he beat out his colleagues in the struggle for a big office. I cannot help thinking of another Marx, disenchanted with the academy, hounded across the English channel and living in London as his children died from illnesses that he lacked the money to treat. But to dismiss *Gary* Marx's behavior as hypocrisy—or to say only, as he does, that success went to his head—is to miss the essential point. Sociologists can write the most scathing critiques, or they can take on the more conventional role of Parsonian apologists for the status quo, but in either case they often leave unchallenged—and unchanged—the basic relations of production today, including the production of knowledge itself.

As the historian Samuel Haber observes, the modern professions in America grew up along with the industrial economy as a reaction to the social leveling that followed the decline of the old elites (xii–xiii). For a brief period at the end of the nineteenth century, one kind of labor had begun to look very much like every other kind, but in response to this leveling, doctors and lawyers, engineers and college teachers drew on the older ideology of "station" to create another hierarchy: doctors no longer "did work," they had a "profession." Yet the price that doctors paid for their privilege—ostensibly, if not always in fact—

was a life of unstinting service to the very people they perceived as their social inferiors. Things are no longer so simple, though, if they ever were. While
Haber identifies the *origins* of a profession like ours, his findings do not help
us understand how the professions operate today, when their power no longer
relies, as it once did, on the persistence of organic communities and the social
contract they once preserved. Gary Marx, after all, sounds less like a country
parson or a family physician than a film director or a courtroom top gun. Students and colleagues may have learned important things from his work, but no
one benefited from that work quite as tangibly as Marx himself, and we need to
consider why.

One account of the professions today would place them, over their protests
perhaps, in the context of the "information society," where they represent a
segment of the larger class of "knowledge workers." As another sociologist,
Bernice Martin, has observed, this new class "stands structurally between the
owners of capital and the proletariat," and the new class has raised itself above
the proletariat by not only its knowledge but its expertise as well: its capacity,
that is, to generate novel *kinds* of knowledge, virtually nonstop. Within premodern societies, the learned man was typically the master of information valued for its immunity to change; today, however, the value of most knowledge
rapidly decays once the luster of its novelty has dimmed. For this reason, the
power of the knowledge class lies in the production of *estrangement* rather than
in the preservation of stability—in the ability "to assemble a bricolage of . . .
symbols into customed packages that are in some sense [perpetually] unique"
(126). Advertising operates along quite similar lines, so that Ralph Lauren
never simply sells a line of towels but manufactures an entire artificial world
combining shirts and towels, ties and drapes to evoke nineteenth-century Nan-
tucket or Sante Fe in the spring. And this new economy of bricolage may account, as well, for the dizzying succession of movements and schools, positions
and counter-positions on parade at places like the MLA, where theory and its
successors enjoy preeminence. While we may someday discover that Ralph
Lauren's publicists get their ideas from Umberto Eco or Derrida, it seems to
me more likely that the tidal wave of change has overtaken *us*. Truth be told,
we could not have continued *credibly* to turn out knowledge of the older, pre-
theoretical sort—premised as it was upon the maintenance of tradition—when
"knowledge" meant the opposite everywhere else.

The restlessness and rootlessness of theory underscore our membership in
the knowledge class, but nowhere does the family resemblance become more
clear than in our conflicted attitude toward teaching. For our predecessors at the
close of the nineteenth century, the idea of a conflict between scholarship and
teaching would have seemed almost unthinkable, precisely because they saw
themselves as preservers of a culture that they *shared* with the young men
under their tutelage. By imbuing undergraduates with the sensibility of the
Anglo-Saxon elite, our predecessors reinforced the boundary between the ruling class, sequestered on the campus green, and the swelling ranks of the great

unwashed, more or less eternally debarred. Today, we draw the boundary at a different place, partly because the great unwashed have come in—literally millions and millions of them—and partly because we ourselves no longer serve the same "custodial" function that our predecessors did. And consequently, we no longer set out to make all our students into younger versions of ourselves; rather, we create within the university the distinction that most matters in the world at large—between the knowledge experts and the laity.

Charles Sykes's notorious exposé *Profscam* is clearly wrong about many things, but he points to trends that simply make no sense unless the university has indeed gone over to the new regime—trends such as the swelling ranks of "world class" faculty who never set foot in a lecture hall, or the burgeoning of quasi-independent research institutes throughout a decade of rising tuitions and decreasing teacher-student ratios. Sykes notes that in 1986, fewer than two-thirds of the faculty at the University of Wisconsin did any teaching at all, while at the same time the shortage of seats in required classes meant that the average student had to spend more than five vears en route to a bachelor's degree. Irving Shain, the former chancellor at Wisconsin, told Sykes a story that might apply, with a few variations, to almost any field today. "In the beginning," Shain recalled, "every biology student got to disembowel a frog of his own." But "because of insufficient [funds], the university had to cut back to one frog per class." Now they have "a movie of someone dissecting a frog and [they] show it over and over" (37). Compelling as this story seems—to me, anyway— I still think that we would be mistaken to accept Sykes's view that changes of this kind are primarily caused by the egoism of professors or the shortsightedness of deans. Rather, the decline of teaching points to the exclusionary character of the disciplines, whose power derives from their control of a specialized field and the things that define it, among them tenured positions, editorial boards, endowed chairs, and a body of primary material widely recognized as their *property.*

In an essay on the state of criticism today, one preeminent theorist, Jonathan Culler, openly expresses about teaching what many people think but hesitate to say. While admitting that a few of his fellow theorists have given their work a "pedagogical and democratic inflection," Culler represents their forays into pedagogy as distinctly "double-edged":

> For the most part, [the] appeal to teaching is a conservative, even reactionary gesture: the suggestion that thinking and writing about literature ought to be controlled by the possibilities of classroom presentation is usually an attempt to dismiss new lines of investigation or abstruse critical writings without confronting them directly. . . . Few would seriously suggest that physicists or historians should restrict their work to what can be communicated to 19-year-olds. (94)

Whatever we might think of Culler's priorities, he spells out with great precision the value system that obtains in the academy today, if not at every college and public university, then certainly at the preeminent schools that send quantities of newly minted PhDs across the continent. And yet, to argue against theory for the sake of teaching is still to misjudge the professional terrain, just as Marshall Gregory does when he writes, in the *ADE Bulletin*, about the mismatch between his training and his day-to-day professional life:

> As a student deeply immersed in nineteenth-century British studies and literary criticism, I certainly expected at the end of my doctoral labors to be effortlessly translated, like Enoch, into a higher kind of academic heaven-haven, levitated up and out of my library carrel at Chicago . . . and gently lowered into another library carrel at good old Research U, presumably in a beautiful city with a good symphony and affordable housing.

Gregory goes on to say that none of his professors at Chicago "ever suggested to me the reality that I would find in [an actual] classroom, much less helped me prepare for it" (20). But Gregory fails to understand that the system is working *properly* when it generates this contradiction—a contradiction that preserves a crucial hierarchy—just as the system works properly when students leave English 101 and never write again, or when they finish college without having learned where Paraguay might be, or when they wake up on the morning of their commencement wondering what in the world they can do with a degree in English, besides, that is, managing an Arby's and wishing they were back in Chaucer class. While it is certainly true that our current system of "public" education furnishes the professions with a venue for the recruitment and training of new members, the primary purpose of a course like Psychology 101 or Introduction to Political Science is not to disseminate expert knowledge but to ensure lay support for further specialized inquiry. The point is not to produce three or four hundred additional colleagues every semester—an economic disaster for any profession—but to persuade another generation of nonspecialists that the subject properly belongs to someone else.

And yet the worst casualties of this division of cultural labor may not be our students but ourselves, to the degree that our lives as professionals have been shaped as decisively by our isolation as by our structural privilege. If my own experience is typical, the first lesson we have learned on the path to the PhD is the obligation to play a role cut off from the worlds outside the university, since we share these mundane worlds with nonspecialists, while our knowledge is supposed to reinstate the crucial distinction between blind experience and the insight that flows from the practice of criticism. So completely have we come to presuppose that understanding and estrangement go hand in hand that even a person like Edward Said, though a tireless critic of professional isolation, still celebrates our state of homelessness as the hallmark of urbanity (Said 319–21, 333–36). It seems to me, however, that we cannot afford to take our own urbanity for granted.

At a moment in our history when many observers have commented on the accelerating breakdown of communities and the spreading mood of cynicism, we need to ask if learning as we now imagine it helps to strengthen our students' sense of agency and self-worth while replenishing the fragile sources of compassion and mutual aid. Or have our "projects" actually served to discredit local ways of life on behalf of the knowledge society? Positioned on the threshold between the specialists and the laity, teachers of undergraduate English might begin to explore these questions by openly acknowledging the divided character of their own situation. Nothing could be less helpful, in my view, than to embrace once again an image of academic intellectuals as representatives of "Culture" on the one hand or "the People" on the other. Instead, we need to understand that the triumph and persistence of theory, like the call to revive "books" in an age of television, is symptomatic of a widening gap between the concerns of elites who produce what counts as knowledge—Fredric Jameson and Gertrude Himmelfarb *both* belong to this new elite—and the needs of those to whom this knowledge gets strategically parceled out. Precisely because I believe, as John Dewey did, that a knowledge made for others is no knowledge at all, I want my students to use the work of specialists to complicate their own self-understanding, but I also want those students to preserve an attitude of profound skepticism toward the authorities whose job it is, no matter what the ideology of the day might be, to turn out properly tractable subjects (Dewey 93–97).

Of course, humans do not live by skepticism alone. The case can be made that the most important social changes of our time are not taking place inside the academy, but in the private lives of women and men who have begun to explore new and uncoercive forms of interaction—as couples, families, support groups, "salons," and congregations—and in our courses we too might explore interactions of this same uncoercive kind. That these experiments are still largely confined to the private sphere only shows how far the so-called public sphere—the classroom perhaps most glaringly of all—has to go before it might be regarded as "democratic" in any credible sense. And yet the openness that people have begun to pursue in their private lives they increasingly expect in the public sphere as well (Giddens, *Transformation* 184–204). The enormous popularity of Bernie Siegel, a physician who supports patients in the desire for more active control over their own medical treatment, testifies to a significant change in popular attitudes toward the system of professions. Since medicine has set the pace throughout this century for all the other kinds of expertise, we may have some small reason to be hopeful. But whether academic intellectuals, who have historically marched in the rearguard, will support a more equitable distribution of cultural power remains an open question. Labor reform, women's suffrage, and the civil rights movement—achievements the academy would like some of the credit for—each took root far from the campus and long before we snatched them up as badges of honor. Yet in deciding where to place our loyalties, we should remember that we have choices other than the two most obvious ones: continuing the legacy of theory-by-other-means or else turning in our resignations. If we want to start playing a different role, then perhaps we need to make a different kind of knowledge.

What this different kind of knowledge might concretely look like is anybody's guess, but our own profession's history may provide some unexpected clues. English in the bad old days was elitist without apology, but its faculty developed a culture of teaching designed to instill a *felt* sense of being at home in the world, a sense quite unlike the nervous style of our own times, with its penchant for abstraction, self-doubt, and critique. No matter how much smarter our work appears when we set it beside their amateurish scholarship, our knowledge is no more egalitarian—and in fact, it may prove much less amenable than theirs to any future culture of democracy. For all its truly vicious blindnesses, and I scarcely wish to downplay them here, the sensibility of our predecessors had its foundation in their class's claim to agency or "freedom" as a natural right, a claim I regard as spurious not because I see freedom as an illusion, but because those men retained it for themselves alone. What would happen, though, if we now set out to revive the "aristocratic" sense of the world as home while repudiating its exclusiveness? Wouldn't such an undertaking need to start where theirs did long ago: that is, with an attention to emotional, sensuous life, because our thinking and our acting have their origins in this crucial source? Or, to put my question just a little differently, at a time when knowledge rather than force of arms has become *the* instrument of domination, won't a democratic counter-knowledge need to take root deep beneath the arid surface of "the text"?

Reimagining Knowledge as Attunement with the World

I suspect that most of us began to value words long before our inclinations coalesced into a conscious loyalty. And now, when we try to justify our field and work, we may rush to the conclusion that we honor language best when we honor it in an unqualified way. We might prefer to believe, for example, that language shapes—directly or dialectically—all of our relations to the world. "In the Beginning was the Word," says the Gospel of Saint John; and now, as the Beginning grows more distant than it was, Derrida has arrived to reassure us, "There is nothing outside of the text" (138). Whatever Derrida might have intended to suggest—and he often seems to change his mind—many of his followers have taken him to mean that we never encounter the actual world but only its representations. This is a claim that has engendered some absurd debates, such as whether *vache* and *cow* can be said to make reference to the selfsame animal. A few theorists have even gone so far as to insist that the French- and the English-speaking worlds are essentially "incommensurable," though in response we may find ourselves roused to ask how those who speak some melange of languages, as my mother's Scots and French-Canadian parents did, manage to bridge this unbridgeable abyss. Of course, they bridged it easily because language is neither self-contained nor self-defining, but only one part of a more complex expressive universe sustained by all our senses and unified by our various forms of intelligence—emotional, aesthetic, spatial, linguistic, and so on. When a French-speaking boss, for example, wants to tell his Anglophone workers that it's time for "lunch," he can do so by raising his fingers to his lips—the universal signal for "Let's eat." While the fingers still count as what we call a "sign," there are linguists who suggest that such signs arise from a preverbal somatic "language" that is the legacy of our entire species (Bickerton 82, 148–49).

Yet behaviors like the hand-talk my grandfather used are not the only ones left unexplained by our idolatry of word and text. It would be hard to explain, for instance, music. We could always speak of music as nothing more than another *kind* of language, but the "language" of music clearly works in ways quite different from the languages we speak and read. While fair-minded people can be counted on to admit that musicians express *something* when they play, what in fact gets expressed is first processed by the parts of our brains that deal with sound as "sound" and not as "words." A wealth of research supports the argument that our brains process words and music quite differently, and in this sense at least, there is certainly something "outside the text." Some research has even documented that a reader's understanding of a text will change with changes in accompanying music. Given the appropriate music, trivialities can brim with pathos while moments of deep tragedy strike one as absurd. We might speculate that music has this effect because it structures feeling more deeply than words do: we might even speak of music as the language of feeling (Matravers 165–87).

Music, though, is scarcely the only case that calls into question the hegemony of the text. Painting and sculpture would also be quite hard to explain at all if Derrida's interpreters were right. As anyone knows who has studied the creative processes of artists, the language of words typically plays a peripheral role, when it plays any role at all, and many artists describe their process of creation as a matter of suspending the desire to explain. Although the textualist bias in our society has convinced us that the work of art conveys a verbal meaning or a "message" of the kind that art critics elucidate, the truth is that the painting or sculpture always *says* just what it *is*. This is why, of course, artists often leave their works untitled, and why Picasso, among countless others, could insist that "people who try to explain pictures," as he put it, "are barking up the wrong tree" (Goldwater 421). If the visual arts "speak" to us in some sense, they do so in the "language" of color and shape, texture and rhythm. Needless to say, the word "red" can never be red, unless we actually print it in red ink; the word "rough" can never be rough, or "dark" truly dark.

What holds true for art making holds true for science as well, unlikely as that may seem. While no one would dispute that scientists rely on the written word, the practice of science places language and sensation into conflict with each another, in order to revise the image of "reality" that language holds in place. If the inquiries that scientists undertake really were linguistically determined through and through, then experiments would be superfluous, as medieval philosophy supposed. Instead, the research done by scientists has expanded and reshaped language itself, often in quite radical and unforeseeable ways, as words like "quark" and concepts like "chaos" demonstrate. This revision of language by experiment has even reached the point that some fields now reach conclusions that strain against limits of expressibility: physics tells us, for example, that the universe is finite but unbounded, that certain objects have mass but no weight, and that single, moving particles can travel in more than one direction at a time. While those of us in English might shore up our self-esteem by replying that the basis of the sciences—mathematics—qualifies as a language too, it comes closer to a language of images than of words, a language of pure forms, as Einstein once observed.

The point I want to make is not that language doesn't count and that English departments ought to close up shop, but that changing our words, in and of themselves, may change much less than we have wanted to believe. Just as we make ourselves blind and deaf when we assume that words stand guard at the gates of all our senses, so we begin to look distinctly ridiculous when we suppose that words alone afford a transparent view into our own real complexity. When the poet writes in dejection, we have been schooled to assume that the poet *was* depressed. And when a theorist like Spivak makes her argument in prose more tortuous than the Labyrinth of Crete, we might mistake her representation of uncertainty for a truthful index of an actual struggle to traverse some conceptual wilderness. But the tangle of the prose remains a *fiction* of perplexity. As for what lies behind the fiction . . . from the words themselves we can never judge. This is the point that Stanley Fish once made when he confessed (or so I hear) that he often likes to watch television when he writes, and that he can recall, when he rereads his work, the specific program he was watching. Perhaps some reader somewhere might have guessed the truth, but there is, all the same, no necessary link between words and lived worlds, precisely because those worlds are made of more than words. Yesterday, after reading Michel de Certeau, I might have seen myself as a Nietzschean, and today, after working through a book by Paul Ricoeur, I might declare myself a Catholic, but very little in the scope of my actions will have changed, and not just in my actions but also in my perceptions and my feelings.

Words, to put it crudely, don't come to us alive; instead, we are obliged to enliven them. But how? Let's suppose for just a moment that things are as I have said—that each of the five senses has a language of its own, all speaking at the same time as the language of words. In that case, they would somehow come together in some "place," and that "place" *phenomenologically* is the body, which we should not make the mistake of reducing to the corporeal body alone—the hands I see in front of me, the skin I feel, and so on—since the body extends well beyond the skin into the sensible world. And at its center, the body is unperceivable, always *below* the reach of the awareness that the body itself orchestrates. Along these lines, we might understand both science and the arts as traditions of "orchestration," each with its respective limits but each drawn by the promise of connection with things.

Our words come alive—become embodied—when they help to realize this promise; when they help in their way to harmonize our many different forms of contact with the world, sentiment with sensation and reason with memory. But so long as we deny any of these forms, or insist on the subordination of one form to another, we forestall the convergence that gives language and culture their living force. I scarcely need to add that the privileging of particular forms of contact corresponds to the privileging of particular people, as the metaphor of the "body politic" implies. While a democracy of the senses—a democracy among our various "languages"—will not automatically transform society, we can be sure that the hegemony of the text has had far-reaching real-world consequences, personal as well as social. If the rise of theory is, as I maintain, the symptom of a worsening rigidification of knowledge, then perhaps we today can imagine knowledge differently only in our moments of true crisis when we need living words to bring ourselves back to life.

About ten years ago, a friend of mine, a physicist and astronomer, had flown from New Jersey to Arizona for the most important moment in his entire professional life. Many times at the start of his career he had applied for a week on a telescope in the hills, and then, once a panel had accepted his request, he patiently waited almost two more years before his special moment arrived. By then, of course, other things had happened to him: marriage and a child, and the slow and painful struggle for publication. Now the decision on his tenure was coming up. He was buying a house and he wondered about that; he had done some research, but he had his doubts. Still, the moment, *his* moment, was about to occur, and when it did, absolutely everything would take place as he had planned. To his amazement, though, absolutely nothing did. The weather turned bad; he waited. It got worse, and he waited, and he kept waiting until his five days were gone.

Along with his clothing and some technical notes, my friend took several novels and an anthology of poems—to read, he supposed, once the data came pouring in. But now that there would be no data at all, he picked up the anthology and tried to find some poetry that could put his mind to rest. The tension, as he described it, throbbed through his chest and arms, but then he found one poem that switched the current off. And the two lines of the poem that brought him the deepest calm are the ones he remembers even now, the lines almost every English major knows, about "the still point of the turning world . . . The inner freedom from the practical desire" (119). It was a poem about the tyranny of time, read by a man whose time had literally run out.

It goes without saying, however, that the way my friend spoke about T. S. Eliot's poem was not the way most critics handle poetry today. The salient features of a poem, they might insist, have no more to do with the reader's world—

with his perennial fears and his immediate desires—than they do with the poet's own intentionality. Some of us in English might say instead that what matters most is a poem's place within a *system* of conventions and codes—the same system within which we ourselves think our thoughts and look out at the world. The poem is a text and the world is a text, and even you and I are ensembles of texts, each of which keeps getting refigured in an endless circulation of signs and tropes. Granted, one reader might bring to the poem certain memories and feelings quite unlike another reader's; still, the theorist's appropriate concerns cannot lie with the particulars of an individual response but with the discursive constraints that define how everyone will respond more or less.

Yet something gets lost when we travel with these critics, something essential to much more than poetry. As a person who has never cared for Eliot, I have probably read *Four Quartets* fifteen times without finding solace in his rather bloodless evocation of the still point in a turning world. Other readers, I know, feel quite differently, among them my friend the physicist. But this distinction is precisely the one that gets lost in the flattening of our world into a text—the distinction between my friend's experience of the poem and my lack of any such experience. What gets lost in the semiotic universe is the crucial distinction between "codes" or "signs," which simply "signify," and the living words that foster a "felt" resonance between ourselves and the world.

The poem, we might say, "spoke to my friend": for him, it had a certain resonance. But what does it mean for words to resonate? One reason why no answer may lie ready at hand may be that our ideas about words have grown systematic and impersonal on the model of science, as though people can never think reliably except at an enormous distance from their sensations and emotions. I find it more than slightly ironic, though, that with all our attention to structures and codes, conventions and tropes, the *real* sciences keep telling us simple things we seem unwilling to hear. Many paleo-archaeologists now believe that language did not arrive on the scene at a single juncture in our prehistory, but gradually developed, as all forms of human culture have, through endless interactions with our habitat, renewed and refined over thousands of years. Yet the prehistory of humankind is something more than the idyllic narrative of our gradual "evolution." Language and culture begin, we are now told, with a *shift* of habitat—out of the trees and down onto the plains—a shift so drastic that it forced a fundamental change in almost everything we did: how we stood, how we moved, how we slept, even how we dreamed, perhaps (Campbell; Sheets-Johnstone). Our language and our culture start, in other words, as responses to the suffering brought about by this irrevocable change—by humankind's collective waking into a world that seemed confusing and dangerous. And although words enable us to transform the world—through the use of complex tools, for example—they primarily enable us to transform ourselves by reshaping what we do and how we do it.

But even to say this is still to remain under the spell of semiotic idealism, because many of the changes that language brings about occur on a level the "linguistic turn" cannot even start to address. So long as our language remains routine—*only* an array of "codes" and "signs"—its essential character is concealed from us, but when words begin to resonate, we undergo a bodily and emotional transformation. To be insulted, to be caught in an error or in a lie, to hear unexpectedly that a loved one has died, is to *feel* intensely even before we are able to *understand* exactly what has just happened. Your face flushes, your eyes water, your heartbeat picks up, the muscles in your stomach clench and unclench. We have all been carefully trained to dismiss these reactions as incidental to the dynamics of "textuality," but signification cannot occur without an experiential anchoring, since we know and remember only what has changed our immediate relations to the world. Such change can assume a negative form, as in the heightened sense of pain produced by the experience of challenge or frustration. Or, as in my friend's case, change can produce the pleasure that follows from a sense of connectedness—the sense that Shigenori Nagatomo calls "attunement with the world" (Nagatomo 197–202).

The roots of language lie in suffering, as I said, but the roots of the self lie in attunement and release. Our conviction that the self is enduring and real— is more than an ensemble of random events—depends on our ability to move past suffering, not once but again and again. It can scarcely be an accident that psychotics are often the childhood victims of a violence that fragments the self so completely there will never be a lasting synthesis. Nor is it merely coincidence that people who endure prolonged physical pain are often at a loss to describe their personal history, not because they have repressed it but because meaning follows from our connections with things—connections that intense pain erodes and erases. Shortly before his suicide, the writer Primo Levi recalled that the occupants of the concentration camp where he was imprisoned were exposed to such relentless pain that escape and resistance had become unthinkable: the world itself had vanished from their horizon of consciousness (11). It is only through our journeys out of suffering into pleasure that each of us can become a self. And it is only through these journeys toward coherence in ourselves that we can move beyond the self, as when a baby finds its parents' presence "transferred" to a blanket or a favorite toy (Winnecott 167–72). Repeated many hundreds, many thousands, of times, the transition from the parent to the blanket, and then from the blanket to the home and neighborhood, weaves together unconnected places and events into a coherent "life-world," a place where memory, meaning, and ultimately love become ever-present possibilities.

If the body, and not language, is the source of the self and the doorway into the living world, it is also the ground of all conviviality. With a spinal tumor blocking more and more of the signals sent from his arms and legs to his brain, the anthropologist Robert Murphy described his loss of motor functions as a "deepening silence." "As my body closes in upon me," he writes, "so also does the world. . . . To fall quietly and slowly into total paralysis is much like either returning to the womb or dying slowly. . . . This growing stillness of the body invades one's apprehension of the world . . . and I must continually fight the tendency for this growing passivity to overcome my thoughts." But "there is," Murphy adds, "a perverse freedom" in "such deep quietude" (193–94). Regrettably, this freedom is the only one that we in the academy now seem to recognize. Of course, our playful disembodiment, which is not the less destructive for pretending to be play, has a history that predates Derrida or Lacan. Plato inaugurates philosophy in the West by denouncing the senses as inimical to knowledge, which he equates with an abstract order that dissolves the knower's subjectivity. But the era of theory inaugurates a different and "postmodern" form of otherworldly knowledge, one that offers us a multitude of "subject positions" while persistently subverting their embodiment. We have many, many different *roles* but, increasingly, no *selves* because the formation of a self requires that our actions help to sustain a continuity between the present and past, and between feeling and thought.

Continuity, of course, is troublesome: continuity makes people far less tractable than they might otherwise be, and so it seems imperative that we ask ourselves if English studies has a vested interest in the current, disconnected status quo. Whether the venue is an essay by Judith Butler or an advertisement for Guess jeans, isn't the logic unnervingly similar? Each encounter with the text underscores the reader's lack—his failure to see what gender really is, her failure to be thin and tall enough. And this failure, this lack, initiates an ordeal of involuntary change that never leads us back to a still point in the turning world, but only, once again, to a sense of insufficiency. As the philosopher Susan Bordo maintains, social power in our time often operates by colonizing the self, first evacuating and then reconstructing it, as we see in mass pathologies like anorexia and bulimia (45–69). The eighteen-year-old girl who learns from the ad that she looks somehow wrong can stick a finger down her throat five times a day. But a similar dynamic may be at work when a frightened student or a younger colleague feels compelled to talk the current lit-crit talk. In both cases, the novice learns to accept a condition like the one that Murphy describes, in which the world sustained by experience withdraws. Night might be day; right be left, with everything displaced and put *sous rature*. Under these conditions, however, texts no longer speak to us. Instead, when they insist that we permit ourselves to "be spoken"—as Gadamer once claimed approvingly and as I once believed—they actually demand that we *remake ourselves* in conformity with the project of the theorist. And our reward for submitting to this painful regimen is seldom the renewal of connections to actual others, the people we happen to know in daily life. Don't we learn, instead, to serve an anonymous "they"?: for the graduate student, something called "the profession"; for the anorexic girl, an admirer in whose radiant gaze she will be real at last. When a baby turns to the blanket as a surrogate for a parent's arms, the transitional object "works" because the blanket provides a *genuine* satisfaction—a continuity in the baby's felt life. But in the culture of postmodernity, the objects of desire almost never culminate in a concrete satisfaction for *us;*

instead, they feed a thoroughly commodified social self whose needs become more pressing than the needs of our own bodies, as every person knows who works twelve-hour days for the sake of rewards as intangible as "reputation" and "the career."

But think, if you will give yourself the freedom to, about the different kinds of pleasure people get from their most mundane involvements with the world—watching leaves shake in the hot summer wind, listening to the sound of rain, tracing the smooth, wet curve of a child's spine with the palm of a soapy hand. And think, if you can stand it, about all the essays written ten or fifteen years ago that began with the claim to be writing "on the margin"; or of all the works today that call themselves "genealogies"; or of all the dissections of cinematic gaze that open with a summary of the mirror stage. The writers of these works are not simply sycophants or opportunists. To write in this way is to *become* Derrida, to *become* a second Foucault or a little Lacan. In the same way, Madonna's fans dress like Madonna, walk and talk like her, and read books about her life.

I see it as crucial to recognize, though, that these practices of impersonation are not new to the academy. Well before the present postmodern interlude, scholars made their reputations, as many still do now, by writing themselves into the lives of their great man. The Beckett specialist somehow became his incarnation; the Stevens scholar learned to speak in Stevens's voice. The time has come to acknowledge that academic literacy, at least as we have constructed it so far, is deeply complicit with the same culture of disembodiment that makes possible Elvis look-alikes and the stalking of the stars by their admirers, who cannot break free from obsession except by murdering their idealized alter egos. While we might prefer to dismiss as naive all the people who watch movies like *Terminator II,* we in the academy unknowingly share their fundamental orientation. No one goes to the theaters for emotional catharsis, and no one could be more absurdly deceived than we are when we close-read the bad android's metamorphoses as signifying the protean character of late capitalism. The cultural force of film derives, instead, from the chance that it offers the viewer to become someone else—to leave behind everyday existence for an imaginary realm, and this is exactly what we do when we read poems as "texts" and not as speech addressed to us, commentaries on our actual affairs.

Textuality is one way to know the world, but language does not become a "text" until we contemplate it from the standpoint of alienation. Language becomes "text," I am trying to suggest, only after it has failed to correspond to the character of our lived worlds and then, instead of making changes in our actual lives, we suppress the world itself. But when our words do their proper work by making the world more fully present to us, they disappear below the surface of consciousness, and their disappearance indicates that we have moved beyond our isolation. In an essay on the Western Apaches' sense of place, Keith Basso remembers learning from one old man that their landscape is everywhere made meaningful to them by a fabric of ancient narratives. "All these places have stories," the old man told him; and the stories, Basso learned, hold the Apaches' universe together, so tightly together that word and place can no longer be distinguished (102). For the Apaches, stories bring about a fusion of horizons far more radical than the one that Gadamer describes, linking culture to nature and perception to collective myth and history.

But what future might such stories have in our society, where our Great Mysterium is not the earth and its perennial rhythms but the frenzy of exchange? People who find themselves at home in the world are typically poor consumers, and the academy needs to sell *ideas* just as Detroit sells cars and Fifth Avenue sells clothes. Deferral and displacement, difference and the endless play of signs—this is not how things really are but how things seem in a society where domination takes the form of control over access to the world itself. It should come as no surprise that the postmodern condition resembles nothing so much as Robert Murphy's mental state in the last months of his life. "Given the magnitude of this assault on the self, it is," he wrote, "understandable that [a] major component of the subjective life of the handicapped is anger" (106). And if anger is, as some might say, the prevailing mood within the academy, it is also the ruling passion of our society as a whole. To pursue attunement, to renew emotional coherence, is not simply to challenge the existing order, but to help fashion an alternative.

For all our celebrations of resistance and revolt, no alternative is more revolutionary than our resistance to disembodiment and the pursuit of wholeness in our immediate experience. But how might such a wholeness lie within our reach, when theory and critique have unmistakably become the preeminent forms of knowledge in our time, as highly valued by Peter Drucker, the Wall Street savant, as they are by Marxists like Etienne Balibar (Drucker 64; Balibar 165)? If theory and critique free us from nothing finally, but contribute to a routinizing of expression unparalleled in our history, then perhaps the way out lies in a domain that the "linguistic turn" has caused us to overlook: I mean the domain of "the arts," understood not as the cunning lies told by an elite, nor as the property of specialists whose goal is technical virtuosity, but as traditions of attunement with the world, available to everyone everywhere but also now diligently suppressed.

"Art" as I want to define it here is what James Scott calls a weapon of the weak. Far from enticing us to overlook contradiction, practices that rise to the level of an art respond to cognitive dissonance by taking us beyond ourselves and back into the world. Initially, this movement can feel like a loss, as when a writer seems to drop the thread of her argument or when a painter's subject, so long looked upon, suddenly becomes "unseeable." What disappears, however, is not the world, but the constructions—the established "ways of seeing"—that prevent us from embracing it, as it is right now. This is why, perhaps, "great artists" have so often claimed to break free from conventions of every kind. "No theories! Only works," Cézanne wrote. "Theories corrupt" the "shimmering chaos" that "we are" (qtd. in Fischer 74). And this is why, perhaps, art as

experience has been so thoroughly suppressed—*especially* in "postmodernity"—because it unfolds in an open space that no one can own or close down.

For more reasons than I have the time to talk about here, that open space
is not the one in which we tend to do our work. Anyone who contemplates the
testing empire of the ETS and the new alliances of schools and industry; anyone who thinks about the sophisticated inertia of our professions and the spread
of electronic media that encourage mass passivity; absolutely anyone, in other
words, can see that our society is unprepared to choose Cézanne's shimmering
chaos over the steady light of instrumental certainty. But whether we like reading by that dull gray light or not, there is a violence at the heart of our society,
where the powerlessness of the many sustains the power of the few. And in the
absence of any real alternatives, this violence will continue to overturn every
kind of knowledge that we manage to devise, Platonic truth as well as deconstructive play. What our society needs most urgently is not another theoretical "advance"—toward a new discipline called grammatography, let's say, or
psycho-dialectical materialism—but a better understanding of the practices
through which everyone might enter the open space where Cézanne felt himself at home. Yet, in order to discover and protect such practices, English studies needs to undergo a change more profound than many people might like. We
will need to become ethnographers of *experience:* I do not mean armchair readers of the "social text," but scholar/teachers who find out how people actually
feel. And far from bringing English studies to a dismal close, the search for basic grammars of emotional life may give us the future that we have never had,
a future beyond the university.

Works Cited

Balibar, Etienne. "Politics and Truth: The Vacillation of Ideology, II." *Masses, Classes,
   Ideas: Studies on Politics and Philosophy Before and After Marx.* Trans. James
   Swenson. New York: Routledge, 1994. 151–74.

Basso, Keith H. "'Stalking with Stories': Names, Places, and Moral Narratives Among
   the Western Apache." *On Nature: Nature, Landscape, and Natural History.*
   Ed. Daniel Halpern. San Francisco: North Point, 1986. 95–116.

Benjamin, Walter. "Eduard Fuchs: Collector and Historian." *The Essential Frankfort
   School Reader.* Ed. Andrew Arato and Eike Gebhardt. New York: Continuum,
   1987. 225–53.

Bereiter, Carl, et al. "An Academically Oriented Pre-School for Culturally Deprived
   Children." *Pre-School Education Today.* Ed. Fred M. Hechinger. Garden City:
   Doubleday, 1966. 105–35.

Bhabha, Homi K. "Postcolonial Criticism." *Redrawing the Boundaries: The Transformation of English and American Literary Studies.* Ed. Stephen Greenblatt and
   Giles Gunn. New York: MLA, 1992. 437–65.

Bickerton, Derek. *Language and Species.* Chicago: University of Chicago Press, 1990.

Bordo, Susan. *Unbearable Weight: Feminism, Western Culture, and the Body.* Berkeley: U of California P, 1993.

Bourdieu, Pierre. *Distinction: A Social Critique of the Judgment of Taste.* Trans. Richard Nice. Cambridge: Harvard UP, 1984.

Butler, Judith. *Gender Trouble: Feminism and the Subversion of Identity.* New York: Routledge, 1990.

Campbell, Bernard. "Ecological Factors and Social Organization in Human Evolution." *Primate Ecology and Human Origins: Ecological Influences on Social Organization.* Ed. Irwin S. Bernstein and Euclid O. Smith. New York: Garland STPM, 1979. 291–312.

Culler, Jonathan. "Criticism and Institutions: The American University." *Post-Structuralism and the Question of History.* Ed. Derek Attridge et al. Cambridge: Cambridge UP, 1989. 82–98.

Derrida, Jacques. *Of Grammatology.* Trans. Gayati Chakravorty Spivak. Baltimore: Johns Hopkins, 1976.

Dewey, John. "Political Science as a Recluse." *The Middle Works, 1899–1924.* Vol. 11: 1918–1919. Ed. Jo Ann Boydston. Carbondale: Southern Illinois UP, 1982. 93–97.

Drucker, Peter F. "The Age of Social Transformation." *Atlantic Monthly* November 1994: 53–80.

Eliot, T. S. *The Complete Poems and Plays 1909–1950.* San Diego: Harcourt, 1952.

Fischer, Ernst. *The Necessity of Art: A Marxist Approach.* Trans. Anna Bostock. London: Penguin, 1978.

Gadamer, Hans-Georg. *Truth and Method.* 2d ed. Trans. Joel Weinsheimer and Donald G. Marshall. New York: Crossroad, 1990.

Giddens, Anthony. *The Transformation of Intimacy: Sexuality, Love, and Eroticism in Modern Societies.* Stanford: Stanford UP, 1992.

Goldwater, Robert, and Marco Treves. *Artists on Art: From the XIV to the XX Century.* New York: Pantheon, 1972.

Gregory, Marshall. "From Ph.D. Program to B.A. College; or, The Sometimes Hard Journey from Life in the Carrel to Life in the World." *ADE Bulletin* 107 (Spring 1994): 20–24.

Haber, Samuel. *The Quest for Authority and Honor in the American Professions, 1750–1900.* Chicago: U of Chicago P, 1991.

Horkheimer, Max. "Traditional and Critical Theory." *Critical Theory: Selected Essays.* Trans. Matthew J. O'Connell et al. New York: Continuum, 1982. 188–243.

Levi, Primo. "Beyond Judgment." *New York Review of Books* 17 December 1987: 10, 12–14.

Martin, Bernice. "Symbolic Knowledge and Market Forces at the Frontiers of Postmodernism: Qualitative Market Researchers." *Hidden Technocrats: The New Class and New Capitalism.* Ed. Hansfried Kellner and Frank W. Heuberger. New Brunswick, NJ: Transaction, 1992. 111–56.

Marx, Gary T. "Reflections on Academic Success and Failure: Making It, Forsaking It, Reshaping It." *Authors of Their Own Lives: Intellectual Autobiographies by Twenty American Sociologists.* Ed. Bennett M. Berger. Berkeley: U of California P, 1990. 260–84.

Matravers, Derek. *Art and Emotion.* Oxford: Clarendon Press, 1998.

Murphy, Robert F. *The Body Silent.* New York: Norton, 1990.

Nagatomo, Shigenori. *Attunement Through the Body.* Albany: SUNY P, 1992.

Said, Edward W. *Culture and Imperialism.* New York: Vintage, 1994.

Scholes, Robert. *Textual Power: Literary Theory and the Teaching of English.* New Haven: Yale UP, 1985.

Scott, James C. *Weapons of the Weak: Everyday Forms of Peasant Resistance.* New Haven: Yale UP, 1985.

Sheets-Johnstone, Maxine. "On the Origin of Language." *The Roots of Thinking.* Philadelphia: Temple UP, 1990. 134–66.

Siegel, Bernie S., M.D. *Love, Medicine, and Miracles: Lessons Learned about Self-Healing from a Surgeon's Experience with Exceptional Patients.* New York: Harper, 1990.

Spivak, Gayatri Chakravorty. "A Literary Representation of the Subaltern: A Woman's Text from the Third World." *In Other Worlds: Essays in Cultural Politics.* New York: Routledge, 1988. 241–68.

Sykes, Charles J. *Profscam: Professors and the Demise of Higher Education.* New York: St Martin's, 1988.

Winnecott, D. W. *The Child, the Family, and the Outside World.* Reading, MA: Addison-Wesley, 1987.

The Rhetorician As an Agent of Social Change

Ellen Cushman

In his "Afterthoughts on Rhetoric and Public Discourse," S. Michael Halloran finds that "the efforts of citizens to shape the fate of their community . . . would surely have been of interest to American neoclassical rhetoricians of the late eighteenth and early nineteenth centuries" (2). Unfortunately, he sees an "apparent lack of interest in such 'Public Discourse' among new rhetoricians of late twentieth-century English departments" (2). One way to increase our participation in public discourse is to bridge the university and community through activism. Given the role rhetoricians have historically played in the politics of their communities, I believe modern rhetoric and composition scholars can be agents of social change outside the university.

Some critical theorists believe that the primary means of affecting social change is to translate activism into liberatory classroom pedagogies. This paper seeks to address other ways in which we can affect social change, something more along the lines of civic participation. As Edward Schiappa suggests, "pedagogy that enacts cultural critique is important but it is not enough. . . . We should not allow ourselves the easy out of believing that being 'political' in the classroom is a substitute for our direct civic participation" (22). I agree. I hope here to suggest ways we can empower people in our communities, establish networks of reciprocity with them, and create solidarity with them. Using a self-reflexive rhetoric, I'll describe the limitations of my own role as a participant observer in a predominately Black (their term) neighborhood in a city in upstate New York. I hope to reveal a tentative model of civic participation in our neighborhoods, which I believe illuminates some paradoxes in postmodern approaches to composition.

Approaching the Community

One of the most pressing reasons why composition scholars may not work in the community has to do with deeply rooted sociological distances between the two. Many universities sit in isolated relation to the communities in which they're located—isolated socially and sometimes physically as well. Rensse-

College Composition and Communication, 47 (February 1996), pp. 7–28. Copyright © 1996 by the National Council of Teachers of English. Reprinted with permission.

laer, for example, where I'm a fourth year PhD candidate, is isolated socially and physically from the community.

The Hudson borders Troy on the East, rolling hills on the West. Most of downtown developed along the river valley, while RPI expanded up one of these hills. People in the city generally call those associated with RPI "higher ups." Rensselaer students often call people in Troy "Troylets," "trash," or "low lifes." RPI was originally built closer to the city, beginning at the West edge of the valley, but for reasons too complicated to go into here, RPI expanded up the hill. The relationship between Rensselaer and Troy is best symbolized by the Approach, what used to be a monument of granite stairs, pillars, and decorative lights, but is now barely recognizable as a walkway.

The city gave the Approach to Rensselaer in 1907 as a sign of the mutually rewarding relationship between the two. Once an access way to the university on the hill, literally and figuratively, the stairway was pictured on many of the notebooks of students in the Troy City school district. Walk into any diner in the city and folks can remember the Approach pictured on their notebooks when they were growing up. Even in the late 1950s, students and city officials worked together to maintain this connection as part of a "civic betterment project."

Unfortunately, the Approach fell into disrepair during the early 1970s as a result of disagreements between the city and university about who should have responsibility for maintenance. Now angry graffiti, missing stairs, and overgrowth symbolize the tattered relationship between the city and RPI. Young fraternity boys are rumored to use the Approach for initiation during rush week, and certain ski club members have skied down the Approach as a testament to their ability and courage. While Troy natives look at the Approach in fury and disgust, the city and RPI continue to negotiate over its upkeep and hopeful repair.

I spend time describing this symbol of the relationship between the university and the city because I don't think this relationship is an isolated example of the sociological distance between the university and the community. It's precisely this distance that seems to be a primary factor in prohibiting scholars from Approaching people outside the university. Everyday, we reproduce this distance so long as a select few gain entrance to universities, so long as we differentiate between experts and novices, and so long as we value certain types of knowledge we can capitalize on through specialization. This history of professionalization might be one reason academics have so easily turned away from the democratic project that education serves to ensure—civic participation by well-rounded individuals.

Malea Powell, an Eastern Miami and Shawnee Indian, suggests that the theorizing of academics necessitates a distance from the daily living of people outside academe, particularly those people we study. Although she's found "a location for healing in theory," she also knows these theories are used to "civilize unruly topics," with a similar assumption of manifest destiny that colonists use(d) to civilize unruly Native Americans. "Central to telling the 'American' story is the settlers' vision of the frontier, a frontier that is 'wilderness,' empty of all 'civilized' life." In order to colonize, the settlers denied the very existence of Turtle Island's original people. Powell sees that

> this denial, this un-seeing . . . characterizes our "American" tale. For the colonizers it was a neccessary un-seeing; material Indian "bodies" were simply not seen . . . the mutilations, rapes, and murders that made up 'the discovery' and 'manifest destiny' were also simply not seen. Un-seeing Indians gave (and still gives) Euroamericans a critical distance from materiality and responsibility, a displacement that is culturally valued and marked as "objectivity."

Scholars reproduce this colonizing ideology when we maintain a distance from people. In search of an area of interest, we look to stake our claim over a topic, or in Powell's words, "define a piece of 'unoccupied' scholarly territory . . . which will become our own scholarly homestead." If the scholarly territory happens to be occupied by other scholarly endeavors, our job demands that we show how these original scholars fail to use their territory well, thereby giving us manifest justification for removing their theories from the territory through expansion, co-option, or complete dismissal. In some fundamental ways, we shirk our civil responsibility and always already enact violence under the guise of objective distance, and the thin veil of 'creating' knowledge.

Powell (and I) "don't mean to disable scholarly work here." But I believe that in doing our scholarly work, we should take social responsibility for the people from and with whom we come to understand a topic. I'm echoing Freire, who shows that when we theorize about the oppressed, we must do "authentic thinking, thinking that is concerned about *reality,* does not take place in ivory tower isolation, but only in communication" (64). Once we leave the classroom, we're again in ivory tower isolation, unless we actively seek our students in other contexts — particularly the community context.

Activism begins with a commitment to breaking down the sociological barriers between universities and communities. And if we see ourselves as both civic participants and as preparing students for greater civic participation, then activism becomes a means to a well-defined end for Approaching the community. Recent work by Bruce Herzberg reveals one model for how rhetoricians can enter into the community. His thoughtful article on "Community Service and Critical Teaching" shows how he manages to link his writing courses with community agencies.

> The effort to reach into the composition class with a curriculum aimed at democracy and social justice is an attempt to make schools function . . . as radically democratic institutions, with the goal not only of making individual students more successful, but also of making better citizens, citizens in the strongest sense of those who take responsibility for communal welfare. (317)

I'm not asking for composition teachers to march into the homes, churches, community centers, and schools of their community. I'm not asking for its to

become social workers either. I am asking for a deeper consideration of the
civic purpose of our *positions* in the academy, of what we do with our knowledge, for whom, and by what means. I am asking for a shift in our critical focus away from our own navels, Madonna, and cereal boxes to the ways in which
we can begin to locate ourselves within the democratic process of everyday
teaching and learning in our neighborhoods. For the remainder of this paper, let
me offer some brief considerations of what such activism might ideally entail,
as well as some practical limitations of trying to live up to this ideal. For these
considerations, I draw upon my own activist research in a primarily African-
American inner city.

Shortchanged

Most current accounts of activism in cultural studies don't do justice to social
change taking place in day-to-day interactions. I think activism call lead to social change, but not when it's solely measured on the scale of collective action,
or sweeping social upheavals. Rather, we need to take into our accounts of social change the ways in which people use language and literacy to challenge
and alter the circumstances of daily life. In these particulars of daily living,
people can throw off the burdens placed upon them by someone else's onerous
behavior. In other words, social change can take place in daily interactions
when the regular flow of events is objectified, reflected upon, and altered. Daily
interactions follow regular patterns of behavior, what sociologist Anthony
Giddens terms "routinization." These interactions result from every individual
reenacting the social structures that underpin behaviors. Giddens' notion of the
"duality of structure" captures the ways in which individuals' behaviors manifest overarching social structures. When the routine flow of events is impeded
or upset, we have an example of deroutinization — of what can be the first steps
to social change on microlevels of interaction. I've found that people disrupt
the status quo of their lives with language and literacy and that the researcher,
when invited to do so, can contribute resources to this end.

For instance, Raejone, a 24-year-old mother of two, applied to a local university. As she composed her application essay, I offered some tutoring and access to Rensselaer computers. This was the first time she had applied to college.
In another example, Lucy Cadens moved to a safer, suburban apartment complex. With my (and others') letters of recommendation, she obtained decent
housing that accepts her Section 8. To facilitate the process of transferring her
social services from one county to another, she asked me to complete a letter
of certification which stated how many children she has in her new apartment.
This is the first time Lucy has lived outside of the inner city. These precedents
mark the very places where people deroutinize the status quo of wider society,
together, during activist research. Over the course of two and a half years of research, these people and I have worked together during numerous literacy
events to create possibilities, the promising, if minute, differences in opportu-

nity: together we've written resumes, job applications, college applications, and dialogic journals; when asked to do so, I've written recommendations to landlords, courts, potential employers, admissions counselors, and DSS representatives; one teen and I codirected a literacy program that allowed six children to read and write about issues important to them and that united resources from Rensselaer, Russell Sage College, the public library, and two philanthropic organizations. Since together we unite resources and grease the mechanisms of wider society institutions, all of these literacy acts carve possibilities from the routine ways these institutions, agencies, courts, and universities have historically worked in constraining ways.

I need to emphasize the difference between missionary activism, which introduces certain literacies to promote an ideology, and scholarly activism, which facilitates the literate activities that *already* take place in the community. For example, the Cadens' household had become too crowded with extended family. Lucy's daughter, Raejone, and her two children decided to seek housing from the philanthropic organization that rented to Raejone's mother. This agency had many units available and a short waiting list, but as the months passed, Raejone realized that her name never moved up the list. Her sisters also applied for housing but encountered similar foot-dragging. Raejone found housing through a private landlord and then wrote a letter to this housing agency In it she protested the inadequate treatment she received. Raejone and the directors of this housing program met to discuss the letter, and since then, Raejone's sisters have been offered housing by this agency. Raejone's letter caused the people who were simply reproducing their typical behavior to pause and consider the impact of their actions. In effect, the people in this housing program have altered the ways in which they treat Raejone and her family. Raejone, without any of my assistance, potently enacts her agency in order to challenge the routine foot-dragging she faced.

Often this type of social change would be overlooked or underestimated with the emancipatory theories we currently use. Those who choose to say resistance only counts when it takes the form of overt and collective political action might describe us as using nothing more than coping devices with this literacy. Choosing to see this interaction in isolation, they may be correct; however, Scott reminds us that thousands of such "'petty' acts of resistance have dramatic economical and political effects" (192). These daily verbal and literate interactions mark the very places where composition teachers can begin to look for the impact of our critical pedagogy and activism, both in the classroom and when we approach the community.

Red Robin Hoods

If we view social change at a microlevel of interaction, we can begin to see where activism fits into the particulars of daily living. Activism means accepting a civic duty to empower people with our positions, a type of leftist stealing from the rich to give to the poor. To empower, as I use it, means: (a) to enable someone to achieve a goal by providing resources for them; (b) to facilitate actions—particularly those associated with language and literacy; (c) to lend our power or status to forward people's achievement. Often we are in a position to provide the luxuries of literacy for people. Since we're surrounded with the tools for literacy all day long, we often take for granted the luxury of the time and space needed for our literacy events. We schedule our workdays around papers we read and write; our research is often carried out in libraries—clean, well lit, with cubicles and desks to use as we silently mine books for information; and we return to our homes or offices to trace out an idea with pen and paper or at the keyboard. Our time is devoted to reading and writing with spaces and institutional resources often provided for us. But when we approach the community, often we will be forced "to recall the material conditions of writing," to remember that "we do confront such complex material questions as how to provide equality of access to computers for word processing" (Gere, 86).

The reading and writing used for individual development in many communities is a valued, scarce, and difficult endeavor. We may say to ourselves that reading and writing is more important than some daily worries, such as cleaning, taking care of children and grandparents, and cooking, but often one of the primary ways people build a good name for themselves outside of work is to be solid parents, providers, doers. Mike Rose reminds us in *Lives on the Boundary* as he describes Lucia, a returning student and single mother, and notes "how many pieces had to fall in place each day for her to be a student. . . . Only if those pieces dropped in smooth alignment could her full attention shift to" the challenges of literacy for her own development (185). In *All Our Kin,* Carol Stack also describes similar domestic demands which must take priority over time for oneself in order for people to maintain their social networks of reciprocity. In other words, before people can devote their time to reading and writing to improve themselves, their social and family duties must be in place. Many women in the neighborhood in which I am immersed say they "wish there were more than 24 hours in a day," or they qualify their literate goals with, "if I had time, I could study that driver's manual." Yet, for a researcher, seeing the need for time is only half of the equation; the other half is doing something about those needs.

Empowering people in part enables them to achieve a goal by providing resources for them. Since it's difficult for many of these women to clear time alone while they're at home, we often schedule one or two hours to be together during the week when they know they won't be missed. We've spent time in places where we have many literate resources at our disposal including bookstores, libraries, my apartment (not far from this neighborhood), as well as the Rensselaer computer labs and Writing Center. During these times we've cleared together, we've studied driver's manuals, discussed books, gone through the college application process, as well as worked on papers, resumes and letters they wanted to write. Because we have worked together, these people who want time away from the neighborhood have achieved their literate goals.

Empowerment also happens when we facilitate people's oral and literate language use as well as lend our status for their achievement. The people in this neighborhood recognize the prestige of the language resources and social status I bring from Rensselaer and ask for assistance in a number of their language use activities.* One woman had just received an eviction notice and asked me to "help [her] get a new place." She asked if we could practice mock conversations she might have with landlords over the phone. She thought this practice would "help [her] sound respectable, you know, white." As we practiced in her dining room, she wrote what we said on the back of a Chinese take-out menu for future reference. Once she set appointments to see an apartment, she contacted me so we could view the apartments together because "having you with me will make me seem respectable, you being from RPI and all." She differentiates between the social languages we speak and she wants to practice these languages with me. She also identifies one way she can use my position for her own ends. She eventually got an apartment and thanked me for what she saw as my contribution. I've found that the luxury of literacy can easily be transferred from the university to our neighborhoods when we expand the scope of our scholarly activities to include activism. While empowerment may seem one-sided, as though the scholar has a long arm of emancipating power, the people in communities can empower us through reciprocity.

Much Obliged

The terms governing the give-and-take (reciprocity) of involvement in the community need to be openly and consciously negotiated by everyone participating in activist research. As Bourdieu terms it, reciprocity describes a gift-giving and receiving behavior which can produce a mode of domination if the gift is not returned. "A gift that is not returned can become a debt, a lasting obligation" (126). Depending on the terms of the exchange, this obligation can either be in the form of a monetary debt, which imposes "overtly economic obligations by the usurer," or, in the form of an ethical debt, which produces "moral obligations and emotional attachments created and maintained by the generous gift, in short, overt violence or symbolic violence" (126). Reciprocity in exchange networks quickly produces power relations where the likelihood of oppression depends upon the terms of the giving and receiving.

While Bourdieu depicts reciprocity networks by studying the bonds maintained in relations between kin-people and tribal chiefs, this notion of reciprocity applies to the ways in which we enter into the community. With an idea

---

*In addition to language resources, I make available many of my material resources: clothes, small amounts of money, food, and rides to the doctor, stores, and DSS offices.

of how exchanges create and maintain oppressive structures, activists can pay conscious attention to the power structures produced and mainiained during their interactions with others outside of the university. Reciprocity includes an open and conscious negotiation of the power structures reproduced during the give-and-take interactions of the people involved on both sides of the relationship. A theory of reciprocity, then, frames this activist agenda with a self-critical, conscious navigation of this intervention.

Herzberg's work exemplifies reciprocity well when interpreted in terms of the give-and-take relationship between the researcher and community. Through a "service-learning program," students at Bentley became adult literacy tutors at a shelter in Boston and wrote about their experiences in Herzberg's composition classroom. At the outset, the rules were established for what types of information could be exchanged between the tutor and learners. The students "were not allowed (by the wise rules of the shelter and good sense) to quiz their learners on their personal lives and histories" (315). Before these tutorial sessions began, the boundaries for exchange of information were set. Students tutored, wrote, and received college credit; Herzberg gave his time and energy, which eventually earned him a spot in this journal; and although this article does not make clear what the people in the shelter received and gave from this involvement, he indicates "the tutoring, as best [as they] could determine, appeared to be productive for the learners at the shelter" (316). From his work, we begin to see how bridging the university and community establishes give-and-take relationships that must be openly and carefully navigated.

It may seem that the activist research I described in the previous section is one-sided, that I may sound like a self-aggrandizing liberator of oppressed masses. But this just isn't the case, since these people empower me in many ways. Referring back to my original definition of empowerment, they've enabled me to achieve a primary goal in my life: getting my PhD. They've let me photocopy their letters, personal journals, essays, and applications. They've granted me interviews and allowed me to listen to their interactions with social workers, admissions counselors, and DSS representatives. They've told me stories and given me the history of this area through their eyes. They've fed me, included me in their family gatherings for birthdays and holidays, and have invited me to their parties and cookouts. They've read my papers and made suggestions; they listened to my theories and challenged them when I was off mark. As I write my dissertation, they add, clarify and question. In some very important ways, we collaborate in this research. In fact, the two women whose writing I refer to most frequently in this article signed a release form so that you may read about them today. To quote from the *CCC* "consent-to-reprint" forms, Raejone and Lucy understood that they "will receive no compensation" for their work and that they "assign publishing rights for the contribution to NCTE, including all copyrights." They have given me the right to represent them to you and have facilitated my work in doing so. They've also lent me their status. They've legitimized my presence in their neighborhood, in masque, and in some institutions simply by associating with me. Through reciprocity, they've enabled me to come closer to achieving my goal every day; they've facilitated my actions; and they've lent me their status.

The Access in Praxis

Often we don't have to look far to find access routes to people outside of the university. Any kind of identification we may have with people in our communities, to some extent, acts as a point of commonality where our perspectives overlap, despite our different positions. These points of convergence, I think, come closest to Freire's notion of solidarity. Solidarity manifests itself when there are common threads of identity between the student and teacher. To achieve empowerment through critical consciousness, the teacher "must be a partner of the students in his relations with them" (62). A partnership connotes people working together toward common goals. Freire finds "one must seek to live with others in solidarity. . . [and] solidarity requires true communication" (63). I believe that access to people with whom we identify is the initial building block for the solidarity and communication needed in activism.

Many access routes into the community have been established by philanthropic organizations, churches, community centers, and businesses. Before an access route is chosen, though, significant research needs to be done to see how the community developed, what types of contributions are needed, and whether or not there's precedent for the work proposed. After I spoke with representatives in many philanthropic and social service agencies, I volunteered in a bridge program between Rensselaer and a community center. Once there, I proposed a summer literacy program, but when this was over, I soon realized that I needed to reposition myself in the community. When I stopped volunteering, the women in this community found it easier to identify with me as a person and not as an organizational member.

Although I'm white, the women in this neighborhood and I identify with each other in many ways: we're no strangers to welfare offices, cockroaches, and empty refrigerators. We've held our chins out and heads up when we haven't had enough food stamps at the checkout line. We've made poor (and good) choices in men and have purple and pink scars to prove it. We know enough to take out our earrings before we fight. We know abuses and disorders and the anonymous places people turn to for them. Since many of these people came from the Carolinas, and since my great-great-grandparents were in the Trail of Tears, we know why, on a crisp January day, a cardinal in a pine tree gives us hope.

Once we locate an access route into the community, we can begin the long process of self-disclosure and listening from which we can begin to identify with each other. For Freire, communication is the main way to achieve this identification: "Through dialogue, the teacher-of-the-students and the students-of-the-teacher cease to exist and a new term emerges: teacher-student with students-teachers. The teacher is no longer the-one-who-teaches, but one who himself is taught in dialogue with the students, who in turn while being taught also teach" (67). Through communication, the exchange of questioning and asserting, we come to identify with each other and challenge the bases for our differences.

While this type of dialogue can take place in the classroom, the very power structure of the university makes it difficult to establish and maintain dialogue and solidarity. There's only so much we can get to know about our students within the sociological confines of the academic composition classroom. Yet when we approach the community, we maneuver around the sociological obstacles that hinder us in the classroom from communicating with our students in ways that show our identification with them. Said another way, activism starts with some kind of identification with people outside of the university, an identification that often can flourish in a context where both the scholar and people together assess and redraw lines of power structures between them.

No Mother Teresas Here

With the initial components of activism roughed out this way, I need to provide some important caveats. Let me show a few of the limitations of this kind of praxis with reference to shortcomings and mishaps in my own ethnographic fieldwork. My first concern in folding open activism this way is that these principles will be read as altruistic, when in my experience activism establishes an interdependency. Activism can't be altruistic because we have to be in a position to participate in our communities. The very same position as scholar which distances us from the community also invests us with resources we can make available to others. And we need these luxuries in order to be stable enough to give our time, knowledge, and resources. This means we must work very hard in the academy with the support of our community in order to garner the status and resources that we then return to the community.

I don't mean to simplify the process of gaining luxury here because I recognize that becoming an agent of social change in our neighborhoods requires time and energy. As a funded graduate student, I'm particularly fortunate to have the time and money to do this activist research. My teaching assistantship requires an average of twenty hours of work per week, and since I'm through with course work, I'm only on campus when I'm teaching, writing on the computers, or researching in the library. While I know my professors have 3/2 and 3/3 course loads, I've heard of other professors who have 5/5 course loads and hundreds of students every semester. Yet, at the risk of sounding pollyannic, we've already seen precedents for the type of scholarly civic participation I suggest. Perhaps through the reciprocity of activism, we might fold together our scholarly and civic duties.

Since the relationship established in activism centers upon reciprocity, an interdependency emerges. One of the ways in which we've maintained a mutually empowering relationship is through open and careful navigation of the reciprocity we've established. While this reciprocity may sound easy to maintain, many times requests have to be turned down. I've asked to record certain people and have been refused; I've also asked for examples of certain types of writing people didn't feel comfortable giving me, so I went without. Likewise, one person asked me to co-sign on a car loan (which I couldn't); and another person asked me to sign over any royalties I receive from a possible book to the families on the block (which I'm still considering). Everyone in this research realizes what we stand to gain from the work, and reciprocity helps prevent the work from becoming altruistic.

If we ignore the give-and-take established in activist research and instead choose to paint ourselves in the bright colors of benevolent liberators, we risk becoming what Donald Macedo so delicately terms "literacy and poverty pimps" (xv). When we adopt a fashionable theory of emancipatory pedagogy and activism without considering the structural constraints imposed by reciprocity, we capitalize on other's daily living without giving any of these benefits in return. But here's the paradox—we need to make activism part of our research and teaching, so that we can make a living in the university. How else will we be able to give in equal amount to what we take?

Accessive Force

The degree to which we gain entrance into the daily lives of people outside the university in some measure depends upon who we are. The boundaries of our access must be negotiated with the people. Often, leftist posing assumes a here-I-am-to-save-the-day air, takes for granted immediate and complete entrance into a community, presumes an undeniably forceful presence. In my own work, I've overstepped the boundaries of my access working under similar assumptions. Six months into this research on a summer afternoon, I joined a large group of teens and adults playing cards, sipping beer, and talking on a front stoop. I was dealt into a game of 21 and listened to gossip and news. Lucy Cadens had a boyfriend (Anthony) who was seated in one of the folding chairs at the end of the stoop. Lucy had been gone for a few minutes, and he and I chatted until it was my turn to deal.

Later that day, Lucy called me away from the stoop and asked, "You want to tell me about Anthony?" I thought she was referring to a complaint a parent made to the center staff about him, and told her I wasn't at liberty to talk about it. She looked confused and asked me if I was talking to him that day. I told her of what I thought was an innocent conversation about gambling in Atlantic City. "They told me he was fishing with you," she said with her hands on her hips. I was shocked; what I thought was a simple conversation was actually him flirting with me. I told Lucy that I would keep a much safer distance from him and asked if she thought I should make that a unilateral decision about interacting with men in the neighborhood. She said I should be careful about whom I talked to and about what, but that I could be polite to them. Since then, I've negotiated this boundary much more carefully and have gathered the majority of my notes from the children and women of the neighborhood. In this way, the access I presumed I had was fundamentally limited along gender lines. The lines of access must be charted, recharted, and respected in activist research. I had overstepped a boundary, albeit unintentionally, and realized my liberal presumption of unlimited access was pompous and shortsighted.

The Best Laid Approaches

Civic participation requires careful understandings of how our position will work, or not, within the given organizations of people. As mentioned earlier, I originally gained access to this neighborhood as a literacy volunteer and researcher through a bridge program between Rensselaer and the neighborhood center located in the heart of this community. As a volunteer, the social workers expected that I follow the same rules of conduct that they were institutionally bound to follow. However, I soon realized that the roles of researcher and volunteer contradict each other in important ways.

As a volunteer, a team player, I was expected to tell the social workers any details I might be privy to which concerned the private lives of the people in this neighborhood. I often visited the homes and sat on the stoops with people when the social workers were bound to stay in the center—their liability insurance did not cover them if something happened to them outside the center. As a researcher, though, I needed to walk between both worlds, the home and community center, but I was bound to the ethics of participant observation which dictate I cannot reveal information about my informants. Unfortunately, the center staff felt threatened by my peculiar position and worried that I would jeopardize their standing within the community with the information I had about the workings of their institution. As a result, they asked me to discontinue my volunteer work with them.

When we first consider bridging with communities, especially if we hope to do research at the same time, we must chart the internal workings of the institutions in order to see the ways we might, or might not, fit in. I initially believed I could simply volunteer and do research—"surely people will welcome the time and resources I offer." Here I was guilty of leftist posing disguised as philanthropy. Because I assumed this, I didn't negotiate my role within this organization well at all.

Even with these limitations, we can begin to participate in our communities despite (to spite) the sociological distances we must cross. Cultural studies models of empowerment and critical pedagogues are derelict in their civic duties by not including an expanded version of activism. Through activism, we've taken the first, tentative steps toward social change outside of the social confines of the university classroom. Finally, we not only fill a civic responsibility with activism, but also inform our teaching and theories with the perspectives of people outside the university. We begin to see just how deficient our estimations

of our students are when we immerse ourselves and contribute to their everyday literacy and hidden belief systems.

The roads into the communities aren't paved with yellow bricks and sometimes may seem unapproachable, but access can generally be gained with observation and informal interviews to see who is already in the neighborhood
and how they got there. Along the way relationships need to be navigated
openly and consciously with close attention paid to boundaries and limitations
in our access and intervention. Of course, I'm ignoring one potential means of
access into the community—our students. But then, this assumes that we have
solid enough relations with them to be able to follow them beyond the moat surrounding the ivory tower.

Works Cited

Bourdieu, Pierre. *The Logic of Practice*. Stanford: Stanford UP, 1990.

Freire, Paulo. *Pedagogy of the Oppressed*. New York: Herder, 1971.

Gere, Anne Ruggles. "The Extracurriculum of Composition." *CCC* 45 (1994): 75–92.

Halloran, S. Michael. "Afterthoughts on Rhetoric and Public Discourse." *Pre/Text: The
First Decade*. Ed. Victor Vitanza. Pittsburgh: U of Pittsburgh P, 1993. 52–68

Herzberg, Bruce. "Community Service and Critical Teaching." *CCC* 45 (1994): 307–19.

Macedo, Donald. Preface. *Politics of Liberation*. Ed. Peter McLaren and Colin Lank-
shear London: Routledge, 1994. xiii–xix.

Powell, Malea. "Custer's Very Last Stand: Rhetoric, the Academy, and the Un-Seeing
of the American Indian." Unpublished essay. 1995.

Rose, Mike. *Lives on the Boundary*. Boston: Penguin, 1989.

Schiappa, Edward. "Intellectuals and the Place of Cultural Critique." *Rhetoric, Cultural
Studies, and Literacy*. Ed. Frederick Reynolds. Hillsdale: Erlbaum, 1995. 26–32.

Scott, James C. *Domination and the Arts of Resistance*. New Haven: Yale UP, 1990.

Stack, Carol. *All Our Kin: Strategies for Survival in a Black Community*. New York:
Harper, 1997.

Writing As Performance

Susan B. Andrews

As a teenager who trained for a professional career in ballet on the East Coast, who ended up teaching English composition and journalism to primarily Eskimo college students in Alaska, I cannot pretend that my youth and adulthood mesh like the smooth floorboards of a dance studio. However, my dance experience does inform my teaching of writing in an essential way: I ardently believe teachers of writing should encourage their students to perform "before" an audience, because of the tremendous incentives for excellence that publication engenders.

As co-editor of a University of Alaska writing project that publishes student essays in newspapers throughout the state, I regularly witness students' motivation to write beyond typical classroom expectations when publication is the goal. The project, called Chukchi News and Information Service, has been operating since 1988 and draws student participants from throughout rural Alaska who attend writing classes by audioconference from Chukchi Campus, a division of the University of Alaska, based in Kotzebue, which lies 30 miles above the Arctic Circle in northwest Alaska.

Most students in this region are Inupiaq Eskimo. (Inupiaq is used as an adjective and also names the language, while Inupiat is a noun that means "the people.") However, because we teach by distance delivery, we also serve Yup'ik Eskimo, Indian, and Aleut students. Yup'ik students live primarily in southwest Alaska; Athabascan Indians in Interior Alaska; Tlingit, Haida, and Tsimshian Indians in southeast Alaska [the Panhandle]; and Aleuts along the Aleutian Chain. Other rural Alaskans whom we serve are called non-Natives. These include primarily Caucasians and Asians. Now in its sixth year of continuous operation, the Chukchi News project has published more than 200 student pieces in Alaska newspapers and magazines ranging from the largest press, the *Anchorage Daily News,* to smaller weekly papers such as the *Tundra Times* or the *Arctic Sounder,* to specialized magazines, such as *Mushing,* for sled dog enthusiasts.

Teaching English in the Two-Year College, 21 (October 1994), pp. 199–205. Copyright © 1994 by the National Council of Teachers of English. Reprinted with permission.

Lessons from the Dance World

Although I trained for a professional career in dance at the Academy of the Washington Ballet in the nation's capital, I was somewhat "learning disabled" in dance: I was slower at picking up steps than my peers and lacked the required physical attributes, such as high insteps, long legs, and great flexibility. A professional career was not to be. With the sometimes grueling training that I underwent—as did my peers, some of whom suffered from anorexia nervosa—why would I encourage anyone to aim for performance, especially in the intensely competitive field of writing? After all, few people will become famous, recognized writers just as few people will become professional dancers. True, but instead of being fixated on being "the best," part of the thinking behind the Chukchi News and Information Service project is a democratic ideal: everyone should be afforded an opportunity to be published, to "perform."

Opportunities for Amateur Performance Valuable

My belief in performance stems not so much from those difficult teen years but from a particularly valuable lesson that came late in my life as a dancer (at the "old" age of 25), when I was lucky enough to meet a talented teacher-choreographer who reawakened in me the deep feeling of satisfaction from performance. This occurred in 1985, a couple of years after I had moved to Alaska, when I was dancing with a small company in Fairbanks, called the North Star Ballet. Mark Schneider was a visiting choreographer for the company that year.

My experience in this company left me with a great appreciation for amateur performance. Unfortunately, we often attribute negative connotations to the term "amateur," but amateurs can be highly skilled and hugely successful. After all, aren't the people participating in the Olympics officially amateurs? Derived from the Latin *amare*, to love, amateur should mean doing something we love, regardless of whether we are professionally ranked.

But do not mistake me here: Mark Schneider worked us hard as if we were professionals. At the same time, he was able to magically bend the rules of ballet, shaping them to fit us, rather than trying to squeeze us into shapes and positions and body types that we could never fit.

For me, this is also the beauty of Chukchi News and Information Service. The project publishes student work in newspapers and magazines throughout Alaska, which means asking the journalism industry to bend its rules, to open its pages to non-journalistic writing and nonprofessional writers, who, nevertheless, have a tremendous vision and product to share with readers, especially the accounts of Alaska Native people, whose stories and experiences otherwise would be given short shrift by the media.

For example, consider a Chukchi News and Information Service piece by Mark Tucker, a Yup'ik Eskimo from Emmonak, Alaska, who describes how he and a friend discovered and dug up a mask in the frozen ground, which precipitated a strange illness in both of them. They sought advice from an elder about what to do with the mask:

> "That mask was probably worn by a witch doctor or shaman to treat sick people in the early days before there were hospitals nearby. Take that mask away where nobody will find it, and tell it you are more than sorry you had ever bothered it," Andrew advised us. "Also, bring a little food and water to put under the ground with the mask." Later that day, after we'd followed Andrew's instructions, I started to feel much better.

Just as a reviewer for the *Fairbanks Daily News-Miner* said of the North Star Ballet, "The dancers clearly *want* to dance for him, and Schneider has a way of finding whatever flash of beauty or grace or majesty lies hidden in his dancers" (Perkins A-10), I see my job as co-editor of the publication project as assisting students in sharing through writing whatever *flash of beauty* or *grace* or *majesty* lies in their experience, particularly as Alaska Native people. Mark Tucker's grace lies not only in his experience but also in his storytelling: not the product of a Western writer consciously trying to build suspense and tension, but an unadorned voice that speaks directly to his readers.

Challenges of Editing a Multicultural Project

I have found from dealings with editors and publishers, unfortunately, that an "unself-conscious" voice such as this risks being underappreciated, at least initially, by Western eyes that expect certain conventions in writing. As an editor, I rarely impose a prescribed form on students—except in persuasive writing and research papers—nor do I substantially edit their work myself. Obviously, heavy editing on my part exclusive of students is undesirable because it omits the process of student learning. Persuasive writing and research papers are also so thoroughly Western in concept and form that to teach students otherwise would be impractical and would do them a disservice for future college courses. But in descriptive, narrative, autobiographical, and to a lesser extent "how-to" pieces, I try to leave the form and content as open as possible to encourage students to write from their world view, which, even with the influence of omnipresent television, is best described as Inupiat, Yup'ik, Athabascan, Tlingit, Haida, Tsimshian, and Aleut—not Western.

Student work published through Chukchi News and Information Service is neither strictly an English composition essay nor a piece of journalism. Rather, it is akin to "cultural journalism," which has been defined by one of America's leaders in teaching writing, Eliot Wigginton, who founded the renowned Foxfire publication program of rural Georgia, as meaning "featuring, highlighting, and documenting aspects of the traditions, customs, and values of a culturally distinct group of people through some format—newspapers, magazines, radio, slide-tape—which can be done by anybody, by *amateurs*" [my emphasis]" (Olmstead 33).

Just as Western eyes sometimes have to adjust to the lack of conventions in these student pieces, similarly, newspaper and magazine editors do not always immediately appreciate the lack of "reporting" or "news value," conventions of journalism. In fact, one of the biggest challenges of co-editing the project is working with editors in Alaska—some of whom do not get the idea of cultural journalism initially—and others who never do at all. Fortunately, though, more than a year ago, my co-editor, John Creed, and I were able to negotiate a regular feature in the *Anchorage Daily News,* which has helped alleviate the "hit-or-miss" difficulties of continually approaching different editors to use the student pieces.

Amateur Writers, Powerful Communication

Again, the word "amateur" is key to the concept of writing as performance. The goal in motivating students through publication is not to seek out a Hemingway who turns up once a century, but in a more democratic, culturally affirming way, to find in all student writers their idiom, their expression, and publish it.

The Alaska Native (Eskimo, Indian, Aleut) participants in the project, most of whom are older than traditional college-age students, are able to draw from their rich cultural heritage and lifetime experience, and in the process, record valuable information that otherwise might not be preserved and passed on to successive generations.

For instance, Chukchi News and Information Service writer, Carol Harris, an Inupiaq Eskimo, describes how to make seal oil from ugruk (bearded seal):

> To prepare the blubber, first cut it away from the skin in blocks. Then cut the blubber into thin strips and put them in wooden barrels or five-gallon buckets. After cutting the blubber, put it in "cold storage," which for us is a hole in the ground about three feet deep, six feet long, and six feet wide. The top is built like an A-frame house, which is covered with moss and sod from the tundra. Check the blubber every day to see if it is ready to add the dried meat. When the blubber is all melted, it has become what is called "seal oil," and it is ready for the meat to be added.

By affirming knowledge of subsistence, student writers make a statement about its importance not just to the past but for the future, and in some cases, they also address the politics of subsistence. For instance, consider the writing of Eva Menadelook whose experience growing up on Alaska's Little Diomede Island during the Cold War prevented her from knowing her relatives on Big Diomede, the neighboring island in the Bering Strait held by the Soviets:

> The Ice Curtain, as it was called by many was an appropriate name for the border. The curtain erased our ability to know our relatives and cut in half

the lands and seas that were once bountiful for all. It left the Alaskan and
Siberian Natives with their hands outstretched but not quite touching.

For her, this "bureaucratic decision from afar," as she calls the hostility between the former Cold War enemies, disrupted the subsistence way of life
between the islanders as well as their sense of family.

Opportunities for Educating Public

This kind of writing needs to be done and shared with others, and not just
with Native people. For instance, by publishing Native writing in the state's
largest daily, the *Anchorage Daily News,* the Chukchi News project also
reaches non-Native, urban Alaskans who lack understanding about Native and
rural people.

Unfortunately, in Alaska, the indigenous people still are battling second-
class citizenship. According to a report on the continuing problem of racism
against Alaska Natives by the *Anchorage Daily News,* Natives are treated as if
they are invisible. This is particularly true in Alaska's largest Native "village,"
Anchorage: "The message comes across in small ways, day by day. A store
clerk waits on several white people before you. A business seems to have few
Native employees. A landlord takes your name and never gets back to you"
(O'Harra G12).

The antidote to racism, of course, is complex, but in this same *Daily News*
article, "The Hatred Among Us," Anchorage history teacher and Native activist
June Degnan points to education and role models as part of the solution. This
is the approach of Chukchi News and Information Service: its participants are
both educating their readers and serving as role models. For instance, when
Hannah Paniyavluk Loon explains village English, a local English used in rural
Alaska, she takes pride in the language, and rightfully makes no apology for
its being a nonstandard English: "There's no such thing as 'correct' village
English. I structure my sentences any way I desire. Rules don't limit village
English as long as the listener understands." Loon cherishes village English's
flexibility as well as its special meaning and function for rural Alaskans. A piece
such as this can play a role in bridging cultural and racial divides by changing
attitudes, for instance, about local Englishes.

Arriving at Performance-Level Writing

Preparing a piece for publication is not unlike preparing for performance on
stage. Naturally, the best place to start is with a lot of practice. Johannah S.
Franke, a physical education teacher who was retrained as a writing teacher at
Lehman College in New York, made this connection between dance and writing after her mentor cited writing expert Peter Elbow who says: "Writing is like

a muscle. It needs to be exercised to get stronger." Franke discovered in the English classroom that:

> Writing wasn't just a matter of mastering a set of principles or a series of grammatical rules—it wasn't a body of knowledge teacher passed on verbally to student, as we had thought. Rather, writing, like dance and sport, was an activity that could be improved through practice. So, we wrote a lot—in our journals, in class and at home. And we began to feel a little muscle. (275)

Indeed, once Chukchi News and Information Service participants have practiced toning and flexing their prose, they typically settle on one or two pieces a semester to polish for publication. Then begins a series of "rehearsals" in which the student writers refine, rework, and fine-tune their piece(s) through the process of rewriting, often multiple times. While most students are not used to this process and may at first resist, they come to understand and appreciate the importance of polishing for publication, particularly because newspapers demand clarity *and* accuracy.

According to Peter Elbow, even if a piece of writing is not going to be shared with anyone else, just thinking about audience can be instrumental in the writing process:

> The truth is that even if you are writing something that won't ever go to an audience, you often can't get it the way *you* want it till you spend some of your writing or revising time thinking of this piece in terms of a particular audience and situation. (197)

After students have carefully worked through their pieces, they often take part in a "dress rehearsal" in which only a limited number of people familiar to the writer read the work: this might mean reading aloud to a spouse, a friend, a parent—and/or sharing drafts with the instructor and other students in peer work or workshops. Typically, students are spread across hundreds of miles in a distance-delivery class in Alaska, but they can, nevertheless, hear each other and fully participate in an audioconference workshop. Although audioconferencing lacks the valuable element of body language for the writer to gauge the audience response (also, sometimes the transmission over telephone lines can be poor), audioconferencing does offer a particular advantage to the writer: he or she is reaching many parts of the state and typically more than one cultural group simultaneously, which better approximates the ultimate readership of a piece than a workshop in a single classroom would.

These workshops and informal readings for family, friends, and peers prepare the writer and the piece of work for a broader audience of people; in the case of Chukchi News and Information Service, this means readers of Alaska's newspapers and magazines. Once "performance" has occurred and a piece is published, students typically receive substantial positive feedback in their own communities and sometimes from other parts of the state as well. Of course, students who polish a piece for publication must work well beyond classroom expectations, which means they have simultaneously achieved academic excellence. Finally, students often get paid for their submissions, which is an added reward.

Performance and Process Both

The end product of publication is critical because of the stunning incentive for excellence it breeds in students, yet the learning process of arriving at publishable work is equally important. Professor and student alike must be committed to working together on a series of edits, rewrites and fine-tuning to prepare for publication. Even though publication is the goal, a faculty member can—and should—emphasize both the product-approach and the process-approach to writing.

Ideally, all students should have opportunities to test their writing skills beyond the classroom, if not in a project that publishes in existing media as Chukchi News and Information Service does, then perhaps by starting with a desktop-published, in-house collection of student writing or a Foxfire-style project. Or campus newspapers may be interested in running pieces that provide a diversity of student voices.

Publishing in existing media is worth pursuing in other settings. For instance, this kind of project would work well in a community with a large minority population where small presses flourish that are targeted for the minority audience. An example of this would be a localized, weekly paper, say, for the Jewish community. The same opportunities can sometimes be found in rural areas where there is a concentrated minority population, such as on or near Native American reservations, where newspapers are published. A relationship also could be forged with a nonmainstream, weekly newspaper in an urban setting that would welcome divergent voices. Even in a suburban setting, the publishers of tabloid "shoppers" often welcome submissions around which they wrap their advertising. Other populations come to mind: students writing from prison, elderly students, and new immigrants. Most important, the idea is to share the voices of those who otherwise would not be heard, while building the self-esteem of the writer.

No matter the publication, students who participate in this kind of project experience the thrill of performance when they see their byline next to a published piece of writing. And I know from experience that even after the thrill is gone, the self-esteem lasts. While I no longer perform on stage, the power of dancing in Mark Schneider's "Northern Lights" ballet transformed me. In that one performance, all the pain and regrets of those teenage years were swept away, as if I truly was the Aurora Borealis zigzagging through the sky on a clear, dark winter night.

Works Cited

Elbow, Peter. *Writing with Power.* New York: Oxford UP, 1981.

Franke, Johannah S. "Coaching, Dancing, and Writing: Parallel Skills." *Teaching English in the Two-Year College* 4 (1989): 274–79.

Harris, Carol. "Making Seal Oil." *Arctic Sounder* 3 April 1992: 4.

Loon, Hannah, "There's No 'Correct' Village English." *Tundra Times* 17 Dec. 1990: 13.

Menadelook, Eva. "Ice Curtain Divided Families." *Anchorage Daily News* 6 Sept. 1993: B4.

O'Harra, Doug. "The Hatred Among Us." *Anchorage Daily News* Feb. 1994: G6–13.

Olmstead, Kathryn J. "Expanding Cultural Awareness." *English Journal* 3 (1988): 32–35.

Perkins, Leroy. "North Star Ends Season on High Note," *Fairbanks Daily News-Miner* 12 May 1985: A-10.

Turker, Mark. "Shaman's Mask Teaches Lesson That's Not Just a Halloween Tale." *Anchorage Daily News* 21 March 1994: B5.

Kitchen Tables and Rented Rooms

The Extracurriculum of Composition

Anne Ruggles Gere

> Two prisoners in contingent cells communicate by blows struck
> on the wall. The wall separates them, but it also permits them to
> communicate.
>
> —Simone Weil

In a rented room on Leavenworth Street in the Tenderloin District of San Francisco a group of women gathers on Friday afternoons from two to five to provide one another advice and feedback on their writing. The Tenderloin District, identified by many as a home for drug dealers, welfare recipients, criminals, and mental health patients, also provides a home for several writing groups including the Tenderloin Women's Writing Workshop. Carol Heller, who has studied this group, notes that although these women have little formal education, they take their writing seriously; they offer one another encouragement as well as criticism and suggest revisions. As Carolyn, a member of the group, put it, "We can disagree with each other's views, but the point of this workshop is to do the work" (Heller, *Multiple Functions* 225).[1]

In Lansing, Iowa, a small farming community, a dozen writers gather around Richard and Dorothy Sandry's kitchen table. They meet on Monday evenings during the lull between fall harvest and spring planting and spend two hours reading and responding to one another's writing. In their prose they look at the experience of farming, old equipment, the process of milking cows, and country schools. Frequently writers talk about their plans before they begin writing, gathering suggestions and ideas for shaping their material. These writing workshops are part of what Robert Wolf, the workshop facilitator, calls the Rural Renovation Proposal, which aims to revitalize both the economy and democracy of small towns by building community and consensus among individuals who can then address local problems.

Participants in groups like the Tenderloin Women's Writing Workshop and the Lansing, Iowa Writers' Workshop represent a tiny portion of the enormous

College Composition and Communication, 45 (February 1994), pp. 75–92. Copyright © 1994 by the National Council of Teachers of English. Reprinted with permission.

number of individuals who meet in living rooms, nursing homes, community centers, churches, shelters for the homeless, around kitchen tables, and in rented rooms to write down their worlds. These writers bear testimony to the fact that writing development occurs outside formal education. As Simone Weil reminds us, walls can be a means of communication as well as a barrier, and I propose that we listen to the signals that come through the walls of our classrooms from the world outside.

Hobbled by poverty, histories of alcoholism and drug addiction, along with the indignities of aging, the women in the Tenderloin Women's Writing Workshop take strength from finding that their experience is worth expressing. As one member of the Women's Writing Workshop says, "You write down your world and then you read it to other people and they affirm you for it" (Heller, *Writers* 6). Anita Ardell, a recovering cancer patient, expresses a similar view, "I had never before written. They've encouraged me incredibly. . . . You are given the freedom to try. You feel brave here. You feel brave at the women writers group" (Heller, *Multiple Functions* 174). Participants in the Lansing, Iowa Writers' Workshop also find that writing enhances their self-esteem. Bob Leppert, a farmer with little formal education, says, "I never felt like I had anything that anyone was interested in hearing" (Wagner). Eighty-three-year-old Clara Leppert, the oldest member of the Lansing Workshop, echoes this feeling, "We didn't think we could write . . . " (Wagner, *Writers*). Despite their inexperience, workshop participants gain confidence and begin to think of themselves as writers.

In addition to increasing positive feelings, workshops outside classroom walls discipline participants to hone their craft as writers. Mary TallMountain, a member of the Tenderloin Women's Writing Workshop and a published author, explains, "They're my readers. I write down everything they say and at some point in time, when it's quiet and spiritually proper, when my mind and whole system are attuned to the writing, I go through it" (Heller, *Multiple Functions* 83). Maria Rand, another member of the workshop affirms this: "Some of the women are hesitant because nobody ever asked them their opinions about anything. But unless you read your work and get reactions from different groups of people, you're not a writer. You're just dilettanting around. You gotta get rejected and get applause. You gotta get both sides. I'll always be in writing groups. That's where I get my energy from" (Heller, *Multiple Functions* 91–92). The Lansing, Iowa, group also helps members develop their writing skills. A local reporter explains, "They offer positive criticism of one another's work. They read books and essays by established writers and pick the work apart, talking about the elements that make it effective" (Wagner).

Opportunities for performance provide a major incentive for writers to develop their skills. The Tenderloin Reflection and Education Center, which sponsors the Women's Writing Workshop, holds regular public readings where workshoppers present their work to a live audience. Despite the anxieties they feel at reading their writing aloud to strangers, individual members and the group as a whole enjoy the opportunity to display their work. As Heller notes, these readings strengthen the relationship between the storyteller and those who hear the story, along with the larger community as a whole (Heller, *Multiple Functions* 130). The Center also helps maintain a local newsletter, *Tender Leaves,* to which workshop participants contribute regularly, and the Tenderloin's Exit Theater has produced plays written by Workshop participants. When he began working with the Lansing group, Robert Wolf explained that "public readings with discussions afterwards" would be the heart of the project (*Voices* 2). Publication also features prominently in this group's work. Several members of the workshop contributed to *Voices from the Land,* a book that has attracted national attention. Bill Welsh, one of these contributors, observes, "I never dreamed of this. I don't feel like any kind of a big shot. I still wear my overalls" (Wagner, *Writers*).

Reaching out into the community with prose performances develops in participants the perception that writing can effect changes in their lives. The stated purpose of the Lansing, Iowa Writers' Workshop—to build community in order to solve local problems—is enacted by individual members (Wolf, *Newsletter*). Greg Welsh, a member of the Workshop, employed writing to deal with the time when his family's cattle herd was accidentally poisoned by a contaminated bale of hay. Greg explains, "Writing about it was one way for me to understand how I felt. It was a way for me to reconcile some differences I had with members of my family" (Wagner). In addition to changing the quality of personal relationships, workshop participants often use writing to alter the material conditions of their lives. A piece by one of the Tenderloin women writers led to a fund-raising event for a publication called *Homeless Link* along with increased activism on behalf of homeless people, and a Black History study group developed because of another participant's play, "Ain't I Right Too?" (Heller, *Multiple Functions* 216). The public readings of the Lansing group have led individuals to consider organic alternatives to chemical farming (Wagner).

Positive feelings about oneself and one's writing, motivation to revise and improve composition skills, opportunities for publication of various sorts, the belief that writing can make a difference in individual and community life— these accomplishments of workshops outside classroom walls mirror the goals most of us composition teachers espouse for our students. Workshops outside classroom walls frequently, however, succeed with those individuals deemed unsuccessful by their composition instructors. Few of the participants in the Tenderloin Women's Writing Workshop or the Lansing, Iowa Writers' Workshop had much formal education, and many had negative experiences with schooling. They did not think of themselves as writers because teachers had taught them they could not write. Yet these individuals wrote effectively in workshops, published their writing, and gained personal and community recognition for their work. Although it remains largely invisible and inaudible to us, writing development occurs regularly and successfully outside classroom walls.

One explanation for our relative unfamiliarity with groups such as those in Lansing and the Tenderloin lies in the way we tell our history. Like representatives of most emerging fields, we in composition studies have sought to establish our right to a place in the academy by recounting our past, and this historiography has focused inside classroom walls. One version of composition's history has concentrated on American instructional practices of the nineteenth and twentieth centuries. Albert Kitzhaber's study of rhetoric in nineteenth-century American colleges helped establish this tradition. Drawing upon nineteenth-century textbooks, Kitzhaber describes the theory and practice of composition in higher education during the latter part of the nineteenth century. Historians such as Donald Stewart, Robert Connors, and James Berlin, even though they adopt differing stances toward their materials, emulate Kitzhaber's model in looking to composition texts, course descriptions, statements of instructions, and other institutional artifacts as sources for information about composition theory and practice. A related historical narrative constructs for composition a genealogy that extends back to Classical Rhetoric. Scholars such as James Murphy, Edward P. J. Corbett, and Winifred Bryan Homer have aided this construction by delineating the composition-rhetoric connections. Robert Connors, Lisa Ede and Andrea Lunsford extol the benefits of this union, asserting that until recently "rhetorical scholars in speech communication emphasized theoretical and historical studies, while those in composition focused on pedagogy," but the wedding of rhetoric and composition has provided the former with an "outlet for application" and relieved the latter of its "historical and theoretical vacuum" (12–13). In addition, they claim, this merger has helped "to make composition and its necessary theoretical background in rhetoric acceptable to departments of English" (13).

While we might debate how acceptable composition has become in English departments, the terms in which composition's history has been represented arouse little dissent: In concentrating upon establishing our position within the academy, we have neglected to recount the history of composition in other contexts; we have neglected composition's extracurriculum. I borrow this term "extracurriculum" from Frederick Rudolph, who uses it to describe the literary clubs, the fraternity system, and the organized athletics instigated by undergraduates during the nineteenth century. Rudolph argues that this extracurriculum served to make undergraduates "a remarkably important element in the power structure of the American college" (136). Arthur Applebee also uses the term "extracurricular," but for him it describes one of three traditions—the ethical, the classical, and the extracurriculum—from which English studies emerged. Applebee defines the extracurriculum as the nonacademic tradition that contributed to the development of English studies. Like Rudolph, he employs the term extracurriculum to describe eighteenth- and nineteenth-century college literary clubs and recounts how these groups discussed vernacular literature not judged worthy of academic study. As Applebee explains, college literary clubs also sponsored libraries, speakers, and magazines, providing a context where students could "polish their skills in English composition" (12). Applebee's extracurriculum does not include fraternities or athletic groups but it confirms Rudolph's point that the extracurriculum lent undergraduates power in American colleges because the curriculum was adapted to their interests. Gerald Graff emulates Applebee's description of extracurricular literary clubs, noting their contribution to the development of English studies.

Significantly, Rudolph, Applebee, and Graff all describe the extracurriculum as a white male enterprise. Literary societies at women's colleges and women's literary groups on co-ed campuses receive no more attention than do those of African Americans. In addition, each of these narratives positions the extracurriculum as a way station on the route toward a fully professionalized academic department, thereby implying that the extracurriculum withered away after helping to institutionalize English studies. There is no suggestion that the extracurriculum continues to exist or perform cultural work. This erasure of the extra-professional takes on particular irony in Graff's work as his discourse advances the very professionalism he decries. As Jonathan Freedman puts it, "The effacement or replacement of the non-academic perspective by a thoroughly academicized one that professionalism accomplished is recapitulated in the narrative form in which the story of professionalism is told."

In contrast, my version of the extracurriculum includes the present as well as the past; it extends beyond the academy to encompass the multiple contexts in which persons seek to improve their own writing; it includes more diversity in gender, race, and class among writers; and it avoids, as much as possible, a reenactment of professionalization in its narrative. In looking at the relationship between composition studies and the "outside/other" represented by the extracurriculum, my project shares much with Susan Miller's *Textual Carnivals,* a text which also discusses the extracurriculum. This excellent book has informed my thinking, and I share Miller's interest in considering the relationship between nonacademic writing and composition instruction, although Miller gives more attention to the political forces surrounding composition's institutional location, and I am more interested in the cultural work undertaken by various groups of writers, our projects converge.

My methodology for looking at composition's extracurriculum owes much to recent accounts of literacy practices outside formal education. Investigations of community literacy practices by Shirley Brice Heath, of workplace literacy by Glynda Hull, of multiple discourse communities by Patricia Bizzell, and of "unofficial literacy" by Ruth Hubbard all provide angles of vision for looking at composition's extracurriculum. They suggest the need to uncouple composition and schooling, to consider the situatedness of composition practices, to focus on the experiences of writers not always visible to us inside the walls of the academy. Drawing on this tradition, my account focuses explicitly on self-sponsored pedagogically oriented writing activities outside the academy. In defining the extracurriculum this way, I deliberately exclude from my story the writing instruction carried out in workplaces, extension courses, and workshops for which participants pay large fees. The extracurriculum I examine is constructed by desire, by the aspirations and imaginations of its participants. It posits writing as an action undertaken by motivated individuals who frequently see it as having social and economic consequences, including transformations in personal relationships and farming practices.

Just as accounts of literacy practices outside the walls of the academy uncouple literacy and schooling, so my account of the extracurriculum of composition separates pedagogy from the traditional pedagogue. Composition's extracurriculum acknowledges a wide range of teachers, including texts published for aspiring writers. From the Colonial Period to the present, publications designed for persons who seek to improve their writing have contributed to composition's extracurriculum. One of the most popular, George Fisher's *The American Instructor: Or, Young Man's Best Companion* was first published in Philadelphia in 1748, and issued in 17 editions between 1748 and 1833. Aimed at the emerging entrepreneurs of the period, Fisher's book emphasized the importance of composition for business and asserted: "To write a good fair, free and commendable hand, is equally necessary in most if not all the affairs of life and occurrences of business" (A2). Fisher goes on to offer sentences to copy, models of letters for various occasions as well as instructions for making a quill pen, holding the pen in the hand, positioning the light, and making red and black ink. He also includes directions for keeping ink from freezing or molding: "In hard frosty Weather, Ink will be apt to freeze; which if once it doth, it will be good for nothing, for it takes away its Blackness and Beauty. To prevent which (if you have not the Convenience of keeping it warm, or from the Cold) put a few Drops of Brandy, or other Spirits, into it, and it will not freeze. And to hinder its Moulding, put a little Salt therein" (43). This form of composition's extracurriculum continued after the Revolutionary War with publications such as *The Complete Letter Writer* (1793), *The Farmer and Mechanic's Pocket Assistant* (1818), and *The Art of Epistolary Composition* (1826).[2]

Not only did publications like these offer an alternative to the academy's instruction in composition, they frequently criticized the way composition was taught in schools. *A Help to Young Writers*, a self-help guide published in 1836, found fault with the "vapid subjects" assigned by teachers and with the tendency of schools to teach composition as though it bore no relationship to good conversation. This self-help guide went on to assert that "composition is nothing more than conversation put on paper" and demonstrated this by advising writers in question and answer form (Heath 34).

As magazines developed during the nineteenth century, composition's extracurriculum flourished in their pages as well. As Nicole Tonkovich Hoffman has shown, Sarah Hale, editor of *Godey's Ladies Magazine* from 1828–1878, offered considerable advice to writers. Like the authors of self-help books, Hale includes material on the technology of writing. Instructions for cutting a pen point and models of handwriting appear in the pages of *Godey's*. Hale also gives attention to the processes of writing. An 1838 column, for example, recommends what Hale calls "mental composition" for developing more active reading. According to Hale, mental composition "can be pursued at any time and place without the requisite paraphernalia of written composition. . . . it greatly conduces to the development of the judgment, to make frequent pauses, and trace out the inference, and the particular bearing and tendency of detached portions of it; and upon its completion to consider the general scope, its moral tone, the correctness of the sentiments advanced and the character of the style" (191). Hale goes on to recommend writing in response to reading, not note taking but "the keeping of a common-place book, to sketch down one's views, opinions, and sentiments, upon every subject or topic, which may have interested the mind in the perusal of a work" (191).

Godey's was not the only magazine to include advice for individuals interested in developing their composition skills, but it was the most influential women's magazine until the last two decades of the nineteenth century when it was supplanted by the more consumer-oriented *The Ladies Home Journal*. Although less didactic than *Godey's, The Ladies Home Journal* continued composition's extracurriculum. Editor Edward Bok's column in an 1890 issue of *The Ladies Home Journal,* for example, included admonitions to aspiring writers such as, "Whenever possible use the typewriter. If you have not a machine yourself, send your manuscript to some typewriting establishment and let it be copied. The expense is trifling, but the value to a manuscript can hardly be overestimated. . . . Avoid corrections, erasures and interlineations. Don't do on paper what you ought to do mentally. Again—and on this point I cannot be too emphatic—do not roll your manuscript. If there is one thing more than any other which irritates a busy, practical editor, it is a rolled manuscript" (12). An 1894 column by J. MacDonald Oxley includes directives for a "Mutual Research Club" whose "essential feature is the preparation of papers on given subjects and the rule is that each member should have a paper ready for every meeting." Oxley continues, "The modus operandi is as follows: A subject having been selected, and a night of meeting decided upon, the members proceed to prepare their papers. These, at least ten days before the meeting, are sent in to the secretary who binds them together, adding several blank pages at the back. They are then circulated among the members, who pass them on from one to the other, having first entered any note or comment that may suggest itself on the blank pages provided for the purpose. Then at the night of the meeting each member reads his or her paper, and the reading concluded, a general discussion takes place" (16).

Although we can never know precisely how these publications of composition's extracurriculum were used, their number, multiple editions, and wide circulation document that they *were* used. We can speculate that at least some of them played a role in the many self-help groups that also constituted composition's extracurriculum. The egalitarian view of knowledge that character-ized European settlers who arrived on this continent led them to organize for self-improvement. Cotton Mather started a self-help group in Boston during the colonial period and in 1728, Ben Franklin joined with several friends to form a mutual improvement group that required each member to "once in three months produce and read an essay of his own writing on any subject he pleased" (Goodman 98). As the new republic took shape, many young men formed self-improvement groups. In Boston in 1833, for example, more than 1,500 young men belonged to groups that gave composition a central place in their activi-ties. Individuals wrote reports on local issues and these reports were read and discussed at meetings. The Lyceum, founded in 1826, had 3,000 clubs in 15 states by 1836, and fostered self-improvement through writing, as did the Chautauqua Literary and Scientific Circle (CLSC), founded in 1878. This 1904 letter from a CLSC member in Syracuse, New York, demonstrates the extra-curriculum of composition in action:

> The members are expected to write two papers upon subjects assigned to them by the president who selects carefully such as pertain strictly upon the year's study. This part of the program is thoroughly enjoyed as a special effort is put forth by each member to put only such thoughts upon paper which may prove helpful. An able critic from whose valuable assistance much benefit has been derived is usually in attendance unless professional duties demand her ab-sence. (CLSC, 1904 Record Book)

Many self-help groups included a critic among the officers. Usually elected on the basis of skill in identifying errors, this critic assumed special responsibility for noting faults of syntax and diction in papers read before the group. The critic's commentary, combined with the general club discussion, provided mem-bers significant guidance for improving their prose. The Bay View Circles, an offshoot of Chautauqua, also followed an annual course of study which included writing papers on topics under discussion. In 1897, the *Bay View Magazine,* which published the curriculum for the Circles, included this re-minder: "Work has a two-fold purpose: The first is to share with the circle the results of research; the other is the benefit the member receives in knowledge and in discipline of writing." It also offered this advice: "In preparing papers, never be content to give dry and detailed facts, but invest the subject with your own individuality" (7).

Spurned by many of these groups, middle class African Americans formed self-help associations of their own early in the nineteenth century. Typical of these, the New York Garrison Society, founded in 1834, concentrated its dis-cussions on education and liberty and devoted its meetings to "singing, praying and the reading of original compositions" (Porter 568). Other African Ameri-can expressions of composition's extracurriculum included the Philadelphia Association for Moral and Mental Improvement of the People of Color, The

Young Men's Literary and Moral Reform Society of Pittsburgh and Vicinity, the New York African Clarkson Society, the Washington Convention Society, the Young Men's Lyceum and Debating Society of Detroit, and the Boston Philomathean Society. Many of these groups included both men and women, but African American women led the way in organizing single-sex forms of composition's extracurriculum by establishing ladies literary societies in Philadelphia, Washington, D.C., New York, Boston, Buffalo, and Rochester before 1836. William Lloyd Garrison, editor of *The Liberator,* addressed the Female and Literary Society of Philadelphia in 1832. When members of this society entered the meeting room, they placed their anonymous weekly compositions in a box from which they were later retrieved and criticized. Garrison was so impressed with the writing produced by The Female and Literary Society that he subsequently published several selections in *The Liberator,* thus instituting a tradition of African American clubwomen publishing their work.

Faced with the double challenge posed by their race and gender, African American clubwomen embraced writing's capacity to effect social and economic change, to enact their motto, "lifting as we climb." The Women's Era Club, founded in Boston by Josephine St. Pierre Ruffin in the latter part of the nineteenth century, issued a newspaper *The Woman's Era* in which clubwomen published their writing, and African American women appeared frequently in the pages of *The Liberator* as well as *The Guardian, The Conservator* and *Voice of the Negro.* Prior to the Civil War, African Americans living in the south created another kind of extracurriculum in the form of secret schools. These schools—composed of one person who could read and write and a group of individuals who wanted to learn—would meet during the night or on Sundays when slaves had a bit of free time. The mandate for graduates of these secret schools was to teach others. Kept secret because the punishment for trying to learn to read and write was severe beating or even death, these schools enabled a number of graduates to write their own passes to freedom. As Thomas Holt puts it, "Just as blacks maintained an invisible church, separate from the one that whites provided for them, they also maintained secret schools. These schools could be found in every major southern city and in countless rural communities and plantations. Their teachers were often barely literate themselves, but they passed on what little they knew to others in what one may call a chain letter of instruction" (94).

White women also contributed to composition's extracurriculum. Between 1839 and 1844, Margaret Fuller offered well-educated women subscription memberships to conversations designed to provide women an opportunity to reproduce their learning as men did, and although talk was the dominant mode, Fuller required participants to write. She explained: "At the next meeting I read these [writings] aloud and canvassed their adequacy without mentioning the names of the writers" (Hoffman 299). Clearly Fuller saw writing as a means of fostering thinking and she encouraged women to write as part of their self-education. For example, she advised one woman this way:

I should think writing would be very good for you. A journal of your thoughts and analyses of your thoughts would teach you how to generalize and give firmness to your conclusions. Do not write down merely your impressions that things are beautiful or the reverse, but what they are and why they are. (Hoffman 302)

White women's clubs wielded considerable cultural force during the period between 1880 and 1920, and most clubs required members to write papers. The Saturday Morning Club of Boston, for example, stipulated in its bylaws: "Papers shall be read to the president (or to someone designated by her) at least a week before the discussion date" (Rudolph, SMC Yearbook). Since newer members wrote a higher percentage of the papers, this system of supervision guaranteed that less experienced writers received more direct instruction in this form of the extracurriculum. Elizabeth Moore et al.'s *English Composition for Women* (1914) demonstrates the ubiquitous nature of club papers during this period by including a chapter on the club paper. In addition to sample papers and suggestions for topics, the chapter includes this description: "A club paper may be considered a popular exposition of some subject of general utility or interest" (67).

The extracurriculum of composition reached across class lines. One account of a working-class women's club appears in Lucy Larcom's *A New England Girlhood*. Larcom, who worked in the textile mills of Lowell, Massachusetts, describes "The Improvement Circle" in which she and her coworkers met "for writing and discussion" (174). Papers read in the Improvement Circle were often published in "The Lowell Offering," a journal edited by a young woman who worked in the mills. Other forms of composition's extracurriculum appeared in the clubs organized in Settlements—such as Jane Addams' Hull House in Chicago, the Philadelphia Guild of Working Women, founded in 1893, and the Women's Educational and Industrial Union, founded in 1877. In these and other such associations, working-class women wrote their worlds and helped one another become better writers.

This brief account documents some of the publications and groups that sustained the extracurriculum of composition in the past. Current publications such as William Zinsser's *Writing Well: An Informal Guide to Writing* and magazines such as *The Writer's Market* have taken the place of *The Young Man's Companion* and columns in *Godey's Ladies Magazine*, but today's writers continue to separate pedagogy from the classroom pedagogue and seek advice from texts in the extracurriculum. The Garrison Society's "singing, praying, and reading of original compositions" and Margaret Fuller's conversational advice to women writers may be silenced, but groups such as the Tenderloin Women Writer's Workshop and the Lansing, Iowa Writers' Workshop have taken up their task of bringing together individuals of varying classes, genders, and races who meet to read and respond to one another's writing. These ongoing and vital manifestations of the extracurriculum challenge us to take a wider view of composition. In suggesting a more inclusive perspective, I am not advocating that composition studies work to appropriate the extracurriculum or tear down classroom walls. Rather, I propose that we avoid an uncritical narrative of professionalization and acknowledge the extracurriculum as a legitimate and autonomous cultural formation that undertakes its own projects. Such an inclusive perspective can lead us to tap and listen to messages through the walls, to consider how we can learn from and contribute to composition's extracurriculum in our classes.

That word *class* suggests possibilities, since it designates at once a political/economic social group and the site where we in composition studies enact much of our working lives. Normal usage separates social class from academic class, but a look at the origins of the word suggests a close relationship between the two. The Latin word *Classis* referred to the most prosperous Roman citizens, the ones who paid the highest taxes. In the second century Aulus Gellius used the name of these wealthy citizens to designate the best writers. As Richard Terdiman says, "This subterranean valorization of *economic power masquerading as quality* has stuck to 'class' ever since" (226). If we look at the relationships between economic power and attributions of quality in our writing classes, we cannot avoid noting that those with least economic power, often people of color, are most likely to be designated as "basic writers." Significantly, writing centers, which lie outside classes yet remain intimately related to them, offer rich opportunities for communicating with worlds outside the academy. Students often bring extracurricular texts such as self-sponsored poems, resumes, and personal letters to these liminal sites. By stepping outside our classes in both economic and academic terms, we can contribute to and learn from the extracurriculum as we reconsider relationships between economic power and attributions of quality in the writing of our student bodies.

The term *student body* suggests potential for creating another bond through the walls separating the classroom and the extracurriculum. Schooling implies a disciplining of the student's body. Nineteenth-century images of classrooms with the instructor standing on a raised dais over students seated in desks bolted to the floor, of teachers caning students' bodies, and of students standing to recite have given way to the more familiar images of instructors seated near students, of moveable desks arranged in a semicircle, and of students' fingers poised over a keyboard. But schooling in general and composition in particular still inscribes itself on students' bodies. The relaxed physical environment of the extracurriculum suggests that we rethink the relationship between physical and mental discipline. Why, for example, has the move toward whole language pedagogies among our colleagues in elementary schools been accompanied by the introduction of cushions, beanbag chairs, and carpets in classrooms? How do we see the correlation between whole language—a pedagogy that unites reading and writing while affirming students' inherent language abilities—and a blurring of domestic and academic scenes? This blurring suggests new ways of looking at the relation of public and private life, even of eliding distinctions between the two. It also recalls the material conditions of writing. While few of us are concerned with providing our students recipes for making red ink or instructing them in ways to prevent it from molding or freezing, we do confront such complex material questions as how to provide equality of access to computers for word processing. Reconsidering the relations between domestic and classroom economies may help us develop creative responses to the material constraints of writing. Thinking along these lines we would do well to recall Kenneth Burke's image of intellectual history as a parlor where participants enter and leave the ongoing conversation. This domestic/academic image resonates with feminist explorations of the trajectories of public and private.

In urging that we look again at the relationship between domestic and academic scenes, I am emphatically not suggesting that we move away from professionalism in our field. We know too well the history of the Harvard Reports issued at the turn of the century. These reports, which had an enormously negative impact on composition studies, demonstrate what can happen when questions about composition are answered by nonprofessionals: The most superficial aspects of writing receive the greatest attention, and the more complicated and important questions remain unasked and unanswered. We who teach composition, and particularly we who claim membership in CCCC, have, in recent years, given considerable energy to professionalism. We have asserted that writing instructors have or require specialized training and that they deserve the respectability born of educated knowledge. I applaud these efforts, particularly where they have served to improve the working conditions of writing teachers. But I'd like to suggest that we scrutinize the culture of professionalism. For instance, professionalism incorporates both material and ideological functions. Its economic function creates a link between education and the marketplace by insisting, for example, that composition teachers ought to be paid adequately because they possess special training. Embracing this economic function implicates us in an ideology that justifies inequality of status and closure of access. Composition's extracurriculum can remind us of the need for increased access in writing instruction. In response we can strengthen our vigilance against reductive forms of assessment and against instructional practices and curricular plans that make writing a barrier to be overcome rather than an activity to be engaged in. We can also learn to value the amateur. The culture of professionalism, with its emphasis on specialization, abhors amateurism, but composition's extracurriculum shows the importance of learning from amateurs. After all, as the Latin root *amatus* reminds us, members of the Tenderloin Women's Writing Workshop or the Lansing, Iowa Writers' Workshop write for *love*.

An unswerving concentration on professionalism can also blind us to the power relations in our classrooms. One of the clearest messages of the extracurriculum concerns *power*. As Frederick Rudolph noted, the extracurriculum of the nineteenth century vested students with power in curriculum decisions.

We see that power acknowledged (and usurped) today as student film societies become departments of and courses in film studies. In a related way composition studies can draw upon and contribute to circulations of power in its extracurriculum. Our incorporation of the workshop practices that originated in student literary societies exemplifies one way. Another is suggested by a sketch Mary TallMountain read at the Tenderloin Women's Writing Workshop. This sketch portrays a fellow Indian who loses his identity and ultimately his life in San Francisco:

> I watched that man for six months in the line at St. Anthony's shelter. I watched him and watched him and watched him. I could see beyond the dirt and all the things holding him back. He was a brave man to me. I felt he had come to the end of his way. The next thing he knew he was riding through the prairies on his horse. And the filthy street changed into the long grass in a strangely familiar valley and Bilijohn was riding. Riding. He didn't hear the high keening screech of brakes, didn't see the lithe swerve of the shining town car. He heard only a distant call: Bily! Bily John! and his own answering holler. Yeah, I'm coming as fast as I can! He didn't feel the massy jolt as the sharp hood scooped him skyward, his eyes still measuring the weeping clouds. The half-empty, gray-green bottle arced into the gutter and tumbled down the torrent of flotsam, the Thunderbird belching out of it. Indian Bilijohn galloped on through the long amber grass, heels pummeling the bright flanks. (Heller, "Writers" 77–78)

Mary TallMountain demonstrates the power of representing one's own community. In insisting on Bilijohn's dignity and humanity against mainstream accounts of poverty and alcoholism among Native Americans, she exemplifies the point made by a good deal of fashionable critical discourse: the importance of considering who will represent whom in what terms and in what language. Like medical doctors who learn from nutritionists, shamans, and artists without compromising their professional status, we can benefit from examining how the extracurriculum confers authority for representation and how we might extend that authority in our classes. Our students would benefit if we learned to see them as individuals who seek to write, not be written about, who seek to publish, not be published about, who seek to theorize, not be theorized about. Ultimately, however, we in composition studies would benefit from this shift because, as Susan Miller reminds us, "placing those who teach composition in the role of hired mother/maid has a great deal to do with the presexual, preeconomic, prepolitical subjectivity imposed on composition *students*" (192). By helping to change the subjectivities of our students, we open the possibility of enhancing our own (professional) positions.

The fact that sketches like Mary TallMountain's are read regularly at the Tenderloin Women's Writing Workshop speaks to the issue of *performance* in the extracurriculum. Here, as Maria Rand says, "You gotta get rejected and get applause." Clubs that mandated oral readings of papers, the office of the critic who commented on syntax and diction in self-help groups, the presumption of the editor of *The Ladies Home Journal* that writers would be sending their manuscripts, rolled or not, to busy editors—all of these items from the history of composition's extracurriculum show the direct relationship between writing and performance. Like the British working-class balladeer of the mid-nineteenth century who exchanged original compositions for a pint of ale, writers in the extracurriculum demonstrate how writing effects changes, both tangible and intangible. Thinking of writing as performance reminds us that it occupies an uncertain space between the concrete and the symbolic. This might prompt us to reconsider performance in our own teaching and research. As Porter Perrin shows, college composition before 1750 in this country centered on the declamation, a pedagogical practice which required students to read aloud to an audience compositions they had previously written. Pedagogies of performance like these reinforce writing's liminal status between materiality and idea and demonstrate it as "a centered space from which we do not exit in the same form" (Bentson 435).

The transformative quality of writing's performance speaks to the cultural work it accomplishes. Within classroom walls, composition frequently serves a gatekeeping function by providing an initiation rite that determines whether newcomers can master the practices and perspectives of academic discourse. Those who do not succeed in composition classes rarely last long in higher education. For a significant number of those who survive this initiation, alienation results. These are students who succeed in composition by distancing themselves from persons and experiences important in their everyday lives. Composition thus accomplishes the cultural work of producing autonomous individuals willing to adopt the language and perspectives of others. Composition's extracurriculum frequently serves the opposite function by strengthening ties with the community. In his study of the development of schooled literacy among the British working class of the nineteenth century, David Vincent observes that, "Composition was eventually admitted to the official curriculum in 1871, but as a means of exploiting the Penny Post, not of imitating penny dreadfuls" (218). Penny dreadfuls, episodic narratives that rely strongly on the songs and melodramatic tales common among working-class people, were held in low regard by school instructors who saw composition as a means of copying the sentences of others. Yet, as Vincent shows, working-class children educated in these schools were as likely to use their skills to write penny dreadfuls as letters for the penny post. Similarly, when our own students enter the extracurriculum, they frequently write their own versions of penny dreadfuls. That is, the form and content of what they write reflects their connections with their own communities. For women of the nineteenth century the genre of club paper represented one such connection, and the extracurricular selections that students bring to our writing centers manifest another. When persons in groups such as the Tenderloin Women's Writing Workshop and the Lansing, Iowa Writers' Workshop write about people they know, about homeless, about farming, composition's extracurriculum accomplishes the cultural work of affirming and strengthening their connections with their own communities.

These communities outside our classroom walls have, if books on the best-seller list in recent years provide any indication, demonstrated considerable dissatisfaction with much of what transpires in higher education. While one reasonable response is to counter with books telling the story from our side of the classroom wall, we run the risk of talking past those on the other side, of constructing walls as divisions rather than means of communicating. A more productive alternative involves considering our own roles as agents within the culture that encompasses the communities on both sides of the classroom wall.

This consideration implies rethinking the narratives we construct about composition studies. Instead of a historiography based exclusively on textbooks used in schools and colleges, on the careers and works of prominent teachers and scholars, on the curricular decisions made by universities and on texts produced by students, we can consider the various sites in which the extracurriculum has been enacted, the local circumstances that supported its development, the material artifacts employed by its practitioners, and the cultural work it accomplished. This expanded historical account will attend to the New York Garrison Club along with Porter Perrin's discussion of the teaching of rhetoric in the American college before 1750. It will recognize that a group of unschooled young men who met on Friday evenings to share and respond to one another's writing contributes to the story of composition as surely as does an examination of textbooks written by Fred Newton Scott. It will look to *Godey's Magazine* as well as Hugh Blair's *Lectures on Rhetoric and Belle Lettres* for information on how writers of another age learned their craft.

While history offers a source of inspiration for the future, its vision cannot be realized without cultural work in the present. As we consider our own roles of social agency we can insist more firmly on the democracy of writing and the need to enact pedagogies that permit connections and communication with the communities outside classroom walls. This does not mean appropriating the extracurriculum but merely assigning it a more prominent status in our discourses. Whether or not we rise to this challenge, composition's extracurriculum will persist and our students can join it as soon as they step outside our classroom walls and enter what Tillie Olson calls "all the life that happens outside of us, beyond us." We may discipline their bodies with school desks and hand positions for keyboarding, but they write outside and beyond us in an extracurriculum of their own making. They may gather in rented rooms in the Tenderloin, around kitchen tables in Lansing, Iowa, or in a myriad of other places to write their worlds. The question remains whether we will use classroom walls as instruments of separation or communication.

Acknowledgments

An earlier version of this article was presented at the 1992 Penn State Rhetoric Conference, and many conference participants helped me think toward revisions. In particular, Stephen Mailloux, Deborah Minter, Jack Selzer and Nancy Shapiro offered very useful comments. Members of my writing group—Arnetha Ball, Deborah Keller-Cohen, Rosina Lippi-Green, Pamela Moss, and Annemarie Palincsar—urged me through multiple revisions, and Karen Burke-Lefevre provided a very timely and generous reading when I needed it most. I thank them all.

Notes

1. I am grateful to Carol Heller for sharing with me her extensive work with and ideas about the Tenderloin Women's Writing Workshop.

2. I wish to thank Deborah Keller-Cohen for introducing me to these early American texts.

Works

Applebee, Arthur. *Tradition and Reform in the Teaching of English.* Urbana: NCTE, 1974.

Bentson, Kimberley W. "Being There: Performance as Mise-en-Scène, Abscene, Obscene and Other Scene." *PMLA* 107 (1992): 434–449.

Bok, Edward. "Editor's Column." *The Ladies Home Journal* 7 (1890): 12.

Chautauqua Literary and Scientific Circle Record Book, CLSC Clubhouse, Chautauqua, New York, 1904 (unpaged).

"Column." *Bay View Magazine* 5.2 (1897): 6.

Connors, Robert, Lisa Ede and Andrea Lunsford. *Essays on Classical Rhetoric and Modern Discourse.* Carbondale: Southern Illinois UP, 1984.

Fisher, George. *The American Instructor: Or, Young Man's Best Companion.* Philadelphia: Franklin and Hall, 1748.

Freedman, Jonathan. "Beyond the Usual Suspects: Theorizing the Middlebrow." Unpublished paper, U of Michigan, 1993.

Goodman, Nathan, Ed. *A Benjamin Franklin Reader.* New York: Crowell, 1945.

Graff, Gerald. *Professing Literature: An Institutional History.* Chicago: U of Chicago P, 1987.

Hale, Sarah Josepha. "Editor's Column." *Godey's Ladies Magazine* 16 (1838): 191.

Heath, Shirley Brice. "Toward an Ethnohistory of Writing in American Education." *Writing: The Nature, Development and Teaching of Written Communication.* Ed. Marcia Farr Whiteman. Hillsdale, NJ: Lawrence Erlbaum, 1981.

Heller, Carol Elizabeth. "Writers of the Tenderloin." Unpublished essay. U of California, Berkeley, 1987.

——. "The Multiple Functions of the Tenderloin Women's Writing Workshop: Community in the Making." Diss. U of California, Berkeley, 1992.

——. *Until We Are All Strong Together: Women Writers in the Tenderloin.* New York: Teachers College Press, 1997.

Hoffman, Nicole Tonkovich. "Scribbling, Writing, Author(iz)ing: Nineteenth Century Women Writers." Diss. U of Utah, 1990.

Holt, Thomas. "'Knowledge is Power': The Black Struggle for Literacy." *The Right to Literacy.* Eds. Andrea A. Lunsford, Helene Moglen, and James Slevin. New York: MLA, 1990. 91–102.

Hubbard, Ruth. "Notes from the Underground: Unofficial Literacy in One Sixth Grade." *Anthropology and Education Quarterly* 20 (1989): 291–307.

Kitzhaber, Albert Raymond. "Rhetoric in American Colleges, 1850–1900." Diss. U of Washington, 1953.

Larcom, Lucy. *A New England Girlhood.* Boston: Houghton, 1889.

Miller, Susan. *Textual Carnivals: The Politics of Composition.* Carbondale: Southern Illinois UP, 1991.

Moore, Elizabeth, Dora Gilbert Tompkins, and Mildred MacLean. *English Composition for College Women.* New York: Macmillan, 1914.

Oxley, J. MacDonald. "Column." *The Ladies Home Journal* 9 (1894): 16.

Perrin, Porter Gale. "The Teaching of Rhetoric in the American Colleges Before 1750." Diss. U of Chicago, 1936.

Porter, Dorothy B. "The Organized Educational Activities of Negro Literary Societies, 1828–1846." *The Journal of Negro Education* 5 (1936): 555–576.

Rudolph, Frederick. *American College and University: A History.* New York: Vintage, 1962.

——. Saturday Morning Club Yearbook, 1898, Schlesinger Library, Cambridge, MA.

Terdiman, Richard. "Is There Class in This Class?" *The New Historicism.* Ed. H. Aram Veeser. New York: Routledge, 1989.

Vincent, David. *Literary and Popular Culture: England 1750–1914.* Cambridge: Cambridge UP, 1989.

Wagner, Jay P. "Alamakee Farmers Cultivate Writing Habits." *Des Moines Register* 12 March 1991.

——. "Writers in Overalls." *The Washington Post* 2 January 1993.

Wolf, Robert. *Free River Press Newsletter* 1 (January 1993): 1.

——, ed. *Voices from the Land.* Lansing, Iowa: Free River Press, 1992.

The Writing Process Goes to San Quentin

Jane Juska

San Quentin Prison looms over San Francisco Bay. It offers one of the world's most beautiful views and houses 6,000 men, among them the world's most violent offenders, including those on California's Death Row. A little west of Death Row is my classroom building. Downstairs, in Room 2, for three hours every Wednesday night, I meet 15 students who are serving life sentences and who have elected to take my course, English 101: Reading and Writing Fiction.

Prewriting: "A so-called prewriting activity may simply be another activity done for its own sake—a discussion, improvisation. . . ."
—James Moffett in *Active Voice*

Rasheed and Max are yelling at each other across what Max has named our "Circle of Kings Plus One." "You can't have empathy with my situation," shouts Max for the third time. He pushes his glasses back up to the bridge of his nose where they tilt, smudged and crazily askew. "I can!" yells back Rasheed, "That's what I been telling you!" Rasheed stretches his heavily muscled upper body out from his chair, so does Max, and the fingers they point at each other look like God's and Adam's on Michelangelo's ceiling.

Where is my whistle. The prison authorities directed me to wear a whistle around my neck at all times. Either that or carry the beeper they offered to lend me. "But be careful," they warned. "This is extremely sensitive . . . "—the guard held the beeper aloft—" if it goes off, we go on lockdown with guns out." So I don't carry a beeper, and the whistle I bought to abide by the rules is somewhere not around my neck. This is the first time in the eight weeks I have met with my class that I have been nervous, though not for my own safety. I introduced the word "empathy" because I wanted my students to establish characters in their writing with whom the reader would have it. Look where it led.

The argument stems from the fact that Max is doing life without a date. Rasheed is serving 15 to life, which means a possibility of parole after 15 years.

The Quarterly of the National Writing Project, 19 (Fall 1997), 1–5. Reprinted with permission.

"If a person's got no date," explains Max, "nobody can understand." "I can," insists Rasheed, and thus it goes.

The other students, some with dates, most without, listen respectfully. Dwinell winks at me in silent reassurance. I forget about my whistle.

L.C. says in his elegant baritone, "Listen, you all, I'm going to tell you a story." We turn to him. "Since, let me remind you," he smiles, "that's what we're here for."

We smile back. Max and Rasheed, too, though not at each other. L.C. soothes us, as he has before, with the darkness of his lilt: "When I was a little boy, I saw a certain film time and time again. Scared me half to death, don't know why. It was called 'The Onion Field Killer.' In case you don't know, it's about this guy who goes berserk and kills a cop; they called him the onion field killer because that's where it happened. Or so I have been led to believe." Am I the only one in here, I wonder, who knows that Max is in for murder? Rasheed knows, I'll bet. "When I grew up, one of the places I got myself into was Folsom Prison, y'all know where that is. I was a young man then." L.C. has relaxed in his chair, his long legs stretched out before him, hands locked behind his head. He looks above our heads, staring at a time and space beyond the walls of our classroom. He is enjoying himself. He says, "One of the first nights I was there, come time to see a film. And guess what that film was. Yes, indeed, it was 'The Onion Field.' And I was sitting there watching and remembering when suddenly the guy next to me, an older guy he was, says, 'That's me.' I looked around and he's pointing at the screen. It was the Onion Field Killer himself."

What a story! We are entranced, we are impressed. Now comes the lesson. L.C. unfolds his hands, returns to a more formal position in his chair, and looks around the circle at us. "What I want to say is I wasn't terrified of this fella. We both were serving life sentences. And I could go along with him. I believe that's what you call 'empathy.'"

We are quiet for a moment. Then Max says, "Yeah, I still say . . ." Hectar, who rarely speaks in class, raises his hand and says, "Can we go on now?"

I remember where my whistle is: in my briefcase which sits in the corner of the classroom, outside our circle where it belongs.

Stan stays after class which means he will miss showers. He tells me that an inmate, in here 22 years, asked him, "Tell me what it feels like to pet a dog." Stan tried to describe his own dog's coat, the dog he hasn't seen for seven years. "What does a dog's bark sound like?" the man asked. Stan barked. Still another inmate wanted Stan to tell him how BART works. He's seen it on TV but has been in longer than BART's been alive. Stan did all this. Is this empathy, he wants to know.

Two men on Death Row want to sign up for more than one course. Most inmates will take only one class since they work in the prison forty hours a week. Those on the Row, exempt from prison work, will sign up for more. One says, "I want a degree and I don't have all that much time." Because of the un-usual circumstances, I give them a little test:

Writing Prompt: Write about someone who had a strong influence in your life.

One response:

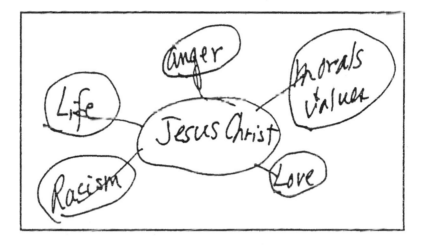

And another:

I guess I would have to say it's my mom who influenced me the most. At the
age of three, she taught me to get the candy out of the gumball machine. At five,
I could open any hotel door with a credit card. I guess if it wasn't for my mom,
I wouldn't be where I am today.

Both passed the test.

Most of my students have been in prison longer than the writing process
has been in town, so early on in the course I give the presentation I have given
so many times in so many institutions: "An Introduction to the Writing Process." I make a big noise about revision, about how Less Is More, Slow Is
Fast. They listen politely; they even take notes, and at the end Thomas says,
"I know this story I want to write has to have people talking; otherwise, it isn't
a story. But there's something about those marks (he holds up his hands and
curls the first two fingers of each hand) that I never learned. I'm not writing any
story until I know what to do about those marks." He crosses his arms over his
chest and narrows his eyes into what passes for a belligerent stare. Correctness comes first for these men. It is what they failed to learn in school; not following the rules has got them into trouble. "Gimme some rules!" Thomas demands. "Coach me!"

Writing: *"Members of a writing workshop may come together only for one*
session . . . or they may stay together for weeks or months and enjoy the benefits
of increasing trust and familiarity."
                                                                    —Moffett, p. 24.

With or without rules, they are fluent, though they don't know it. Once I have
convinced them that writing is not about spelling and punctuation—that we
can worry about that down the line—then their favorite part of the class, they
will tell me in their end-of-semester course evaluation, is when I say "Let's
write." Then we are all quiet for ten or fifteen minutes. And afterwards, just
about everybody reads. The prompts they like best are ones I, and eventually
they, make up on the spot; they go like this: "Give me a color." "Red." "Give
me a body part." "Teeth." "Give me some weather." "Thunder." "Let's write."
Sometimes, we write from what John Gardner tells us: "Write a dialogue in
which each of the two characters has a secret. Do not reveal the secret but make
the reader intuit it." Intuit becomes a favorite word. But this John Gardner stuff
is really hard, we agree, so we take it "home," and work on it. Is that revision,
I wonder.

Response: *"After a writer has done some version of her composition or*
begun to put together some material she has collected, it's often helpful to get
advance audience reactions while changes can still be made."
                                                                    —Moffett, p. 19

Donald, a former Oakland cop, sits way over there, unwilling to join us in anything let alone a response group. No amount of encouragement from me would
budge him. Eventually, after a few of the other students motion him out of his
corner, he joins our circle and writes about his experiences with the Black Pan-
thers. ("Donald, this is supposed to be a story, not a police report," I tell him to
no avail. The final draft, complete with dialogue, interior monologue, and figu-
rative language, still sounds like a police report: "It was alleged that night had
fallen. . . ."). Although I demonstrate and talk about the value of writing groups,
and though the students get into them once in a while, neither Donald nor any
of the others are convinced that their writing might benefit from peer response,
if that's what this is. No, the response that matters is the teacher's. Conferenc-
ing is big.
      We sit behind my desk. Each student in his turn pulls his chair close to
mine, and I become aware of the powerful smell of men in prison. It is dark and
musty and enormously sad. Though we sit close together, neither our knees nor
our shoulders, nor even our fingers touch. Yet this is one of the most intimate
experiences of my life.
      Max has written the following and brought it to conference:

> Snakelike brown muddy water dribbling down, the magical melting chocolate
> river, you see the saint get ducked, comes up anew in funk. Sweet brown sugar
> residue still in the corner of the mind like the Python leaving the scene on full.

The bridge was taken long ago, hypnotized, intoxicated, now victimized without bail.

I am impressed and say so. "This is a prose poem." "Yeah?" he says. "Is that good?" "Yes," I say, "but I wonder what it's about. Do you think, when you revise, you could. . . ." Max's face falls and he looks at me through his glasses smudged and crooked on his nose. "It's my mind, man! It's my mind on heroin!" He wipes his sleeve across his nose: "And it could happen again! Don't you get it?" I do, so I shut up.

Stan wants to show me a story he's working on in which the main character is getting ready to leave for the golf course. He describes his sleeping wife with whom he has made long-night's love. "She lies there not moving, pale, slender, her breasts twin globes," etc., etc. I ask, "Stan, is she alive?" "Oh, yes," he assures me. "And then just after that the cops dropped out of nowhere and slapped the cuffs on me. The next thing I know I'm standing in front of the judge for sentencing." "Wow," I say, and shut up again.

Revision: *"All writing has to be an edited and revised version of the inner speech someone produces at a particular moment under the influence of random or controlled circumstances."*

—Moffett, p. 27

Victor begs me, "Please, Professor, fix my verbs." Do I say, "Go back to your group"? No. Besides, the groups seem to have dissolved right while I was fixing Homer's verbs. One night, Tim tells me, "I been reading my writing to my cellmate. He likes it and all, but thinks it's kind of long. What do you think?" I think he's got a smart cellmate and I tell Tim so. L.C. adds, "I find that since I have been discussing my writing, I have more to talk about with other folks. My conversation is much more interesting."

Publication: *". . . a cardinal rule is, 'Put writing to some realistic use after it is done, and make clear in advance of writing what purpose and audience are.'"*

—Moffett, p. 23

I am insistent on two requirements; in the syllabus I hand out the first night of class, I have written: 1) At the end of this course, you will submit to me and to your classmates a portfolio of your work, complete with drafts and cover letters. 2) You will submit at least one of your pieces to a newspaper, magazine, or journal for publication. When a few students murmur that they have no typewriters, no stamps, no envelopes (no confidence, I would add), I do not relent. "We're doing this," I say, nodding grimly. "You tell 'em, Professor," says Kareem.

It's a nightmare. Prisoners are not allowed to buy stamps. The prison must see and pass on everything that is sent out from the prison. Those are the rules. Add to the rules the fact that they are paid 14 cents an hour for their work and so I pay considerable money for the materials necessary to uphold my dictum. Then there is the matter of where to send their stuff. I buy *Writers' Market*. Victor gets increasingly anxious over completing the requirements, "Here I am doing time, and I haven't got any." It's OK, they're going to do it. And they do, every last one of them. The last night of class looks like this:

We are enjoying ourselves. Gino and Jack write furiously; so does Tui. Bob and Tom and Jonas and Donald exchange portfolios, bend into them, read quickly and write their remarks on Post-its. Occasionally they laugh, tease each other. "I couldn't get over you, man," Jonas teases Tom. "There you are in your cell banging away on your new typewriter, and there's no paper in it!" What has happened is that Tom has cleaned out his prison account (his life savings) and sent away for an electronic typewriter. He explains to me that the typewriter is necessary so "I won't lose my hard-earned writing skills." I nod and smile and return to my own writing. Every once in a while, someone motions me over. Jack wants to be sure he puts the address in the right spot on the envelope. "Where," he says, "show me exactly where." I draw a square on the envelope. "OK, thanks." The sun has begun to go down behind the wall-sized, multipaned window. In the winter the radiator against this wall bangs and hisses throughout class. This spring the sun has beaten its way onto our heads and into our eyes so that sometimes, until evening comes on, we find ourselves huddled together in the corner of the room the sun has yet to scorch. Now it is cool and quiet. Near the end of class, as people make ready to leave, I say almost to myself, "I always feel better after this class." Gino's smile breaks across his face. "Me, too," he says. "By the end, I always feel good." He hands me his portfolio. "You know, I took this class because I thought it would be fun. And it was, but the work! You worked us hard! Whew!" and he wipes his hand across his brow. As they file out of class, we shake hands, all my prisoners and I, and they say nice things. "What I could say about you," says Tim, "boy, you'd feel like a queen." (Later, at the end-of-the-year ceremony he does and I do.) Smiles all around.

We will miss each other. We will miss the quiet concentration on reading and writing and talking that takes them (and in a sense me) far away from the night that descends on us in the yard as we leave the classroom. We will miss the way we like each other. Max asks, "Do you think we've grown as a class? You know, like a unit?" Yes, I do. "We get along good, don't we," says Gino. Yes, we do.

Post-Writing: *"The benefits will transfer to future writing."*
                                                                    —Moffett, p. 24

Teaching in prison gets turned all around. Not just the writing process, but every expectation. I expected that surely, unlike high school, absences and tardies would not exist; my students would all be in class; where else could they go? Turns out, they can go lots of places, like the hole, which is where I am told Hectar is, "Don't expect him back anytime soon." And the teacher's ideas of what teaching is about get shaken up until Lord knows they could drop right out of you. To wit: I come armed with my Pollyanna smile and 30 years of practicing homilies in the classroom. *The truth shall make you free. Knowledge is power. Writing is power. Writing can give you knowledge. And power. And freedom.* I said them over and over to myself and to my high school kids. Freedom for my convicts would be freedom from San Quentin, so during my first few weeks of teaching there, I revise my thinking to read: *Knowledge is powerful. It can stir one up; it can make a whirlwind inside the head, a windmill in the gut.* What is my responsibility to my students for opening a can of worms that smells to high heaven? I don't want it. I write about it in my journal.

They are talking about their truth. Will they write it? What purpose is served by talk of the truth of despair, anger, pain? Wasn't it better for them to stick to politeness? Maybe it's good we meet only ten times. Let's Pretend served us well for most of the quarter.

So for this class they have written about any damn thing they want to, and not a one of them has chosen to write about what got him sentenced to life in prison. Jason will tell us frequently, "I participated in the taking of another human life," but he won't write about it. And I do not insist. I get humbler all the time.

And the writing process, where did it go? Well, in fact, it never went anywhere at all. It was right there all the time, getting jerked around by living human beings just as it got screwed with by the high school kids. Sometimes, it looked as though it would get blasted right out of existence. But it didn't. It shifted here and there, ducked some powerful artillery, fluttered in the winds of discourse but held its ground. In the end, talking and writing and talking some more, then rewriting, got this from David:

> My first engine was an International Harvester DT 4656, an inline six-cylinder diesel engine for a grain mill. She was like my first girlfriend. Once you've been down deep into an engine all the way down to the pistons and have held them in your hands, and have held and cleaned every single part and assembled every piece with care hoping it will be a success and last forever it's like an intimate relationship. If the engine runs well and doesn't blow up well then that relationship was a success, and you don't want to give the truck back to the owner, he won't know how to take care of her. Seeing the trucks rolling down the highway that I have had involvement with is like seeing old girlfriends. You remember the long, intimate nights together, like women you really love but don't own and can't hold on to, you wish the trucks well and send them on their way.

> And that's the truth.

Part Six

Spiritual Sites of Composing

Our intellect has achieved the most tremendous things, but
in the meantime our spiritual dwelling has fallen into disrepair
—Carl G. Jung, *The Archetypes*
of The Collective Unconscious

The conclusion of this book pays tribute to those invisible forces within our discipline, indeed, within the world at large, that seek out the best part of ourselves, that mend and heal, focus on essence rather than image, and bring to full circle and make whole. All this and more is captured in a single word, *spiritual,* which before the 1990s was disdained by the profession. How many times, with thinly veiled sarcasm, has the question been asked, "Well, just what is it you mean by the word . . . *spiritual?*" This concluding section is dedicated to those pioneers among us who have worked faithfully, despite criticism and ridicule, lost tenure and lost jobs, not only to make the word acceptable in the mainstream but to make its reality available to students as well as the profession at large.

The title of this section, "Spiritual Sites of Composing," is taken from a panel presentation at the Conference on College Composition and Communication in Cincinnati in 1992. The presentation was then printed in the *CCC* journal and appears here as the lead essay. The panel, chaired by Ann Berthoff, included Beth Daniell, JoAnn Campbell, and Jan Swearingen, with James Moffett offering a concluding response. In many ways the presentation was a watershed event, for it formally introduced ideas into the profession that before had largely been underground.

In the introduction, Ann Berthoff raises an interesting question. Why is it that American educators have ignored the religious aspects of the pedagogy of the oppressed? As well as a traditional church and a liberal church, Freire has posited a "prophetic church," which Berthoff tells us is not a creed or sect but a speculative instrument, with the energy to create other images. This suggests that a spiritual dimension runs through literacy learning, perhaps through all learning. It also suggests that although there are apparent differences between Freire's peasants and our own students, there is a crucial common link, a spiritual poverty in both communities.

Beth Daniell continues this theme, demonstrating that the spiritual is an important though neglected aspect of rhetoric and composition. She goes on to describe her work in discerning the spiritual foundations of literacy, especially as they are manifested in the writing of six women in Al-Anon. She identifies three stages in their writing: (1) "The healing came." (2) "I had to let go of being perfect, and then it became perfect." (3) "We can't carry our message if we don't have our own language" (299). One wonders whether these three stages may represent something universal in the writing process.

In future years JoAnn Campbell's "Writing to Heal: Using Meditation in the Writing Process" will likely be regarded as one of the twentieth-century's most important statements about the teaching of writing. The author calls our attention to the role of healing in the writing process, an insight capable of transforming not only the way we teach but the way we see ourselves and others. She goes on to describe the practice of meditation as a path toward integrating healing and writing. Perhaps one of the challenges for writing teachers is to come to see that healing is a process, too, that its energy is enormous, and we have just begun to see how profound it is.

In "Women's Ways of Writing, or Images, Self-Images, and Graven Images" Jan Swearingen describes an intensive, weeklong workshop that she and two colleagues teach: "Women's Spaces: Exploring Our Creative and Spiritual Selves." Participants often come to the workshop with unconscious, self-imposed limitations, pressures from family and culture, and the tension between "being good" and "telling the truth." Designed to release the creative energy of the participants, the workshop features journal exercises, photography, and active meditation as well as opportunities for sharing stories and creative products.

James Moffett's "Response" should be read slowly, thoughtfully. Before his untimely death in 1996, Jim made several prophetic statements about the broader purposes of education. Those who were lucky enough to have known him remember him as a brilliant thinker whose insights were always clear and full of common sense, and yet simultaneously, a spiritual giant whose depth was profound, at times even baffling. To his credit, he continued to share his vision, even during his illness.

Modern illiteracy grows from too much language, not from a lack of language, argues Lynn Nelson in "Bringing Language Back to Life: Responding to the New Illiteracy." Because we are inundated with words—by radio, school, TV, movies—we do not allow opportunities for silence and reflection. Nelson describes a classroom that has its roots in spiritual growth, journal writing, meditation and reflection, listening, sharing, always starting with the heart. "In my classroom, small is beautiful" (325), he writes. Every word counts; every thing has a reason for being; every person is important.

Although Don Murray doesn't use the word *spiritual* in "One Writer's Curriculum," he does suggest its shadowy presence in the creative process. The first step of the process is restlessness, unease, anger; the final step is reading the finished product aloud to an audience. But the audience for the poem also includes those who contributed to its creation, both living and dead, who continue to live in the dreams and the solitude of the author.

Any attempts to comprehend those elements that are spiritual inevitably come to the topic of transcendence. In "Surprised by Bird, Bard, and Bach: Language, Silence, and Transcendence," Charles Suhor shows how transcendence touches all the arts, from the perspective of both consumer and creator. Without some element of transcendence, writing remains a sterile, joyless activity. Teachers of writing may note the way transcendence interacts with competence, both of which are worthy goals of the composition curriculum.

Maxine Hairston's description of the paradigm shift in composition ("Winds of Change") was published in 1982, and now some two decades later Susan A. Schiller has shown how that paradigm has expanded to include spiritual sites of composing. In "Writing: A Natural Site for Spirituality" the author describes a dream, a vision of the future, but it is a dream rooted in shifts of consciousness that are very real and are occurring at the present time.

"In today's age of educational reform," Schiller writes, "we are just now beginning to dream toward a spirit-based education" (345). Indeed it is as though we are standing on the threshold of the possible. Those who are able to bring together all the recent developments in the discipline and then find at its very center a living spiritual energy are the teachers we need for the twenty-first century.

Spiritual Sites of Composing

Introduction

Ann E. Berthoff

The 1992 *CCCC* panel on spiritual sites of composing, from which this Interchange derives, was dreamed up and subsequently composed by Beth Daniell. Beth has told me that a question I raised in an earlier *CCCC* session provided her point of departure. I had wanted to know why the panelists, who had stressed the political aspects of the pedagogy of the oppressed, had neglected to take into account Freire's religious convictions, commitments which had made him one of the chief influences on Liberation Theology. The panelists' response showed that they hadn't a clue of what I was talking about, but Beth Daniell heard the question as a reminder of a context essential for an understanding of critical consciousness. Articulating the spiritual and political aspects of all that we do in teaching reading and writing was Beth's aim for the panel and continues to be the purpose in offering the written versions here.

Let me stress the strategy of *articulation* because confusion continues in this regard. Articulation, not bifurcation: those who make a dichotomy of Freire's pedagogy of the oppressed and his pedagogy of knowing have understood neither. It is not literacy *per se* which liberates, but the fostering of critical consciousness, for which literacy, won in social contexts, serves as principal model. A pedagogy of knowing puts the individual at the center, yet that individual is not a solitary waif, but a social being—necessarily! It should not come as a surprise to discover that language is, as Sapir put it, a social product, but that does not mean that the language animal has no soul. The chief benefit of attending to spirit is that we can thereby more efficiently slay the killer dichotomy of the individual and society.

I would like now to offer an assisted invitation to form the concept of "spiritual sites." Paulo Freire has observed that there are three churches: There is the traditional church, in the hands of those he has called "men of the Middle Ages," who would have all attempts to direct the church to problems of modern life abandoned. There is the liberal church, which offers goodwill and audiovisual equipment, but that is not enough. And then there is the prophetic

College Composition and Communication, 45 (May 1994), pp. 237–63. Copyright © 1994 by the National Council of Teachers of English. Reprinted with permission.

church, which guides us in imagining how we could transform cultural practices, how we could teach, what we could all become, doing so without utopian
vagueness or partisan passion (*Politics* 137). The prophetic church is not a
creed or a sect or a particular congregation but an image—with power to create other images; indeed, the prophetic church creates spiritual sites, and they
are far from the altar. The prophetic church is an idea to think with, a speculative instrument for reclaiming representation which the radical skepticism of
the present day identifies with "copy" and sends into exile. If we lose the concept of representation, there is no way to apprehend what Schleiermacher
called his "highest intuition," that "each man represents humanity in his own
way" (41). The idea of the prophetic church can awaken us to the root meaning
of *religion* as binding force. And it offers a powerful antidote to the new posi-
tivism, which is called "antifoundationalism," a variant of context-free ideology. The point is not to discard foundations, which is logically impossible to
do anyway, but to examine them with a critical consciousness. *Spirit* is a very
powerful speculative instrument for this enterprise.

Let the dialogue proceed.

Composing (As) Power

Beth Daniell

At the 1988 meeting of the Conference on College Composition and Communication, Ann Berthoff fundamentally altered my view of reality, and I hope
to convince you that the issue she brought to my attention is one that deserves serious exploration by researchers in rhetoric and composition. Beginning the discussion following a panel that had used the work of Paulo Freire
to critique college writing programs, Berthoff reminded the two or three hundred people in the audience that Freire's pedagogy of the oppressed results as
much from his Catholicism as from his Marxism. Yes, that's it, I thought. Economic and political analyses had never seemed adequately to account for the
success of Freire's method; a fuller, more convincing explanation includes
the fact that Freire taps into that striving in his students, in his teachers, and
in his readers for something beyond ourselves. Seeking a connection with
God, the universe, the life force, humankind, one's own higher "self"; attempting to give life coherence and purpose beyond professional, economic, or personal goals—which is precisely the definition of spirituality. While Freire uses
Christian terms and imagery to discuss this search for wholeness, in this series
of papers we do not mean to imply that this quest is necessarily associated with
any formal religion. But still, as I remember, the room at *CCCC* filled with
embarrassed silence. For all our erudition, we did not possess a language
that would permit us to discuss in an academic setting the spiritual aspects of
Freire's work.

Later that same year I read James Moffett's *Storm in the Mountains,* an
extended analysis of a schoolbook censorship case. Moffett argues that one

reason that public education sometimes alienates rather than enlightens is that it fails to take seriously the spiritual and religious values of students and parents. He is right. As scholars and teachers in America, we have been carefully trained not only to separate religion from civic life but also to dismiss the spiritual. Similarly, in *The Culture of Disbelief,* Stephen L. Carter, professor of constitutional law at Yale, argues that American law and government actually trivialize religious belief, treating it as if it were a hobby rather than that which gives meaning and purpose to the lives of many people.

What makes the dismissal of the spiritual and the religious so troubling in academic discussions of literacy is that, according to historical studies like those by Jack Goody, the Resnicks, and Harvey Graff, spiritual and religious motives have traditionally impelled human beings to seek literacy and, in America, to enact statutes that require it. Even though adult literacy workers all over the United States testify to their students' religious motives for learning to read, only a few ethnographic studies, most notably Shirley Brice Heath's "Protean Shapes" and *Ways with Words,* have seemed to take seriously any contemporary interaction of religion or spirituality with reading and writing. Signs indicate that this may be changing, however. More recently, Andrea Fishman has studied reading and writing among the Amish, Beverly Moss has analyzed language and literacy in three black churches in Chicago, and Keith Walters has discussed the literate foundation of a Quaker meeting. In addition, books like Christina Baldwin's *Life's Companion: Journal Writing As a Spiritual Quest* are currently selling well in nonacademic markets. Yet despite Heath's work, recent ethnographic projects, and popular interest in writing for spiritual growth, it is nonetheless fair to say that contemporary intersections of literacy and spirituality have gone largely unrecognized in our discipline.

Neglecting the truly personal, the emotional, or the spiritual is not just a problem in rhetoric and composition. According to feminists in many disciplines, academic inquiry often hinders or precludes discussion of our closest, and most significant, issues. One consequence of our failure to examine such issues is the gaps it leaves in our knowledge. But this is not the only result. Academic language often actually alienates human beings from their own emotions and experiences. German theologian Dorothee Soelle, for example, argues that "scientific" theology not only devalues religious experience, which is after all the source of theology, but also disallows emotional response to these experiences. She says, "In learning the language of domination, these students learn to give up their subjectivity, their emotionality, their range of experience, their partisanship" (85).

In composition studies, as James Berlin has shown, there have always been scholars and teachers attempting to disrupt the language of domination. In the 1960s, expressive rhetorics called for freewriting and authentic voice; in the 1980s, social rhetorics employed various deconstructive moves. But we need to go further: We need a language that will allow us to talk not only about the cognitive, intellectual, social, political, and economic aspects of writing but also about its emotional and spiritual aspects.

After what I call my Berthoff-Moffett epiphany, I decided to investigate those aspects of writing, and over the past few years, I have interviewed six women about how they use literacy in their spiritual lives. These women range in age from their midthirties to midfifties. Their education is from GED to master's student. All six of these women know each other. All are members of Al-Anon.

Patterned after Alcholics Anonymous and formally organized in the early 1950s, Al-Anon is, in its own words, "a fellowship of relatives and friends of alcoholics who share their experience, strength, and hope in order to solve their common problems. . . . The Al-Anon program is based on the Twelve Steps (adapted from Alcoholics Anonymous) which we try, little by little, one day at a time, to apply to our own lives" (Al-Anon 41). Members of Al-Anon believe that the spiritual awakening that is supposed to result from applying the Steps to their own lives will allow for solutions to the problems of living with an alcoholic.

The literate bias of Al-Anon is readily apparent. Members are exhorted to "read the literature." Meetings begin with various members reading aloud the Suggested Welcome, the Twelve Steps, the Twelve Traditions, and the day's page in a book entitled *One Day at a Time in Al-Anon*. Discussion often consists of sharing interpretations of text in this book or in some other Al-Anon publication. The Fourth Step—"Made a searching and fearless moral inventory of ourselves"—is almost universally taken to mean a *written* inventory; the Eighth Step is usually understood as making a *written* "list of all persons we had harmed." Those who know the history of AA, the model for Al-Anon, will not find this emphasis on reading and writing surprising. AA's founders were highly literate and well educated, a New York stockbroker and an Akron physician. Middle-class assumptions about the value of literacy seem to have been part of "the program," as it is called, since its earliest beginnings.

Because reading and writing are significant activities in Al-Anon, because Al-Anon claims that its program is inherently spiritual, and because my six informants had been involved in Al-Anon from three to ten years, I expected them to be able to talk about their spirituality and their reading and writing in the same breath. They did not let me down. I have 19 hours of audiotape.

Initial analysis reveals that spirituality and literacy intertwine in rich and complex ways in these women's lives. Indeed, for these women, there is no such thing as decontextualized literacy. In re-forming themselves by means of this Twelve-Step program, they use both written and spoken language—reading and writing, speaking and listening. As they experience what they call "recovery," they begin to tell stories of their lives to each other and to newcomers. All my informants take seriously the Al-Anon admonition to "share our experience, strength, and hope," and they all articulate a deeply held belief in the power of language to heal and to bring about and deepen spiritual experience. They would agree with an AA member writing about the role of storytelling in both the healing and spirituality of the program: "In AA we dry moist souls on the *logos,* the Word" (Elpenor 48). In listening to the stories of my informants, I am reminded of the first paragraph of *Diving Deep and Surfacing,* where theologian Carol Christ writes:

> Women's stories have not been told. And without stories there is no articulation of experience. . . . Without stories [a woman] cannot understand herself. Without stories she is alienated from those deeper experiences of self and world that have been called spiritual or religious. She is closed in silence. . . . If women's stories are not told, the depths of women's souls will not be known. (1)

My informants read Al-Anon literature, of course, but they also read or have read books about alcoholism and about families of alcoholics. They read meditation books, some of which are directed specifically at "recovering" persons, some of which are religious in origin or focus. They read novels—Toni Morrison, Alice Walker, and Robert B. Parker are great favorites—and there is much discussion of their books. At the time of the interviews, two of the women had returned to the university and so were reading "tons" of academic articles and books. In addition to various kinds of reading, my informants write many different kinds of things. With the qualification in mind that if pushed too hard, genre lines blur and distinctions break down, I have categorized their writings as: Fourth Steps, journals, "God Can" notes, "Dear God" letters, letters (to be mailed or not), poems, short stories, essays for publication, and school papers. Their written discourses vary in length from one or two words to many thousand.

Because of space, I'm going to focus in this paper on the writing of only two of my informants, whom I call here Jennifer and Tommie, though those are not their real names.[1] Between them, Jennifer and Tommie write or have written all the genres I have identified, though, as you will see, they don't necessarily share my terminology. When I interviewed Jennifer in 1990 she was 36 years old, had been divorced for two years, had no children, and was midway through a master's in counseling. Tommie was 41 years old, married to her second husband, the mother of three children, a married daughter and two teenaged boys. Tommie dropped out of high school in eleventh grade to get married; in 1984 she earned her GED.

I want readers to hear Jennie's and Tommie's voices, but at the same time I want to make the data accessible. So at the risk of oversimplifying the rich complexity of these women's perceptions, I have organized this paper around what seems to me to be three stages in the quest for personal growth. Each stage is perhaps best summarized by a sentence from Tommie: First, "The healing came." Second, "I had to let go of it being perfect, and then it became perfect." And third, "We can't carry our message if we don't have our own language."

"The healing came" for both Jennifer and Tommie with the Fourth Step, "the fearless moral inventory." Central to the spiritual lives of both, this step seems to mark the beginning of the end of the personal confusion that had brought each of them to Al-Anon. This is what Tommie says about the Fourth Step: "I was in such pain. But I couldn't write the *Blueprint*." (*Blueprint for Progress* is a workbook published by Al-Anon designed to help a person look at his or her behaviors and values.) She explains her trouble:

> I kept writing the same answers to every question. Then when I focused on the gory details, I got hung up on the completeness of it all. So I had to throw all that away. My first Fourth Step didn't have gory details. I decided: Keep this simple. It didn't have to be everything, it only had to be what I knew. I wrote about a page and a half, an enormous prayer: God, here are the things I don't like about myself. In that Fourth Step was stuff I was afraid to say to any-one. I kept it for a year, finally burned it. The healing came.

Jennie didn't care for the *Blueprint,* either, but unlike Tommie, who invented her own form, Jennie persevered. This is how Jennie tells it: "The first thing I wrote after getting into the program was connected with my Fourth Step. I used the *Blueprint.* I felt like I was doing an assignment for English class. I could not see any connection between what I was doing and what it was supposed to result in. But it was helpful to my sponsor." (A sponsor is a combination confidant and spiritual guide.) Jennie continues, "I just gave her the booklet to read. We talked about my answers as she read." Even though Jennie sees value in that first Fourth Step, she no longer uses this method, having found another, more helpful way to write the three or four Fourth Steps she has completed in her seven years in the program. She explains, "I do a Fourth Step whenever I get stuck. When something permeates my life, I need to get it on paper."

In the next stage it becomes important to let go of expectations of how things ought to be; in Tommie's words, "I had to let go of it being perfect, and then it became perfect." In this stage, each woman uses various literate forms to come to her own solutions. In this stage, the main genre appears to be the journal. Both Jennie and Tommie are journal writers, though neither writes every day or follows a strict form. Again, as with the Fourth Step, Jennie and Tommie's experiences with journals are different.

Tommie traces the evolution of her journal: "I started writing, keeping a journal in October of 83. I came into the program in March of 84. I started writing because people couldn't listen to me any more. I wrote as release and analysis. I started writing in a notebook where I also had recipes and wrote kids' notes. Then I started writing Dear God letters and prose." The Dear God letters began, she says, after she read *The Color Purple.* For the pieces Tommie calls prose, readers of *CCC* would use the term poetry. Read aloud, they sound like poetry; on the page, they look like poetry. But, according to Tommie, "Prose doesn't rhyme. It has meter, but it doesn't rhyme. Poetry rhymes."

For Tommie, the journal is very much a means of claiming ownership of her life: "I write the journal for me," she says. "It's not an assignment." Tommie believes that sharing her journal is a way of sharing her spiritual growth. She explains:

I tell other people in the program that part of my recovery is keeping a journal. I write for me, but when I show it to you, it helps you. I show my journal to people I'm talking to. Even with some Dear God letters not being finished. See, I had to let go of it being perfect, and then it became perfect. If I'd 'a' done it the way I thought you had to do it, I'd 'a' never done it.

Jennifer does not use the term *journal* for writings that seem to function for her in same way that the journal does for Tommie. In fact, Jen says with certainty "I don't keep a journal or diaries, but I have. Once when my sponsor went out of town. Once when my husband was in treatment. It was a way of recording what went on." Nonetheless Jennie talks about the writing she does "in my steno pad." Here she writes letters she does not intend to mail, records dreams, defines words, and freewrites about issues in her life in order to attain clarity or find connections.

Just as Tommie uses the Dear God letters in her journal as a way to attain emotional detachment from the problems in her life, so Jennie uses her God Can notes. In her kitchen, Jen keeps a can—Folger's coffee, I think—that has pasted on it a label declaring "I Can't. God Can." Jennie explains how this works: "I can't just visualize putting somebody or some problem in God's hands. That doesn't work for me. I condense it into a few words, on an inch- or a 2-inch piece of paper, ½ inch wide. When I put it in the God Can, I can let go."

In this middle stage, both Jen and Tommie devise various literate strategies for coming to terms with their experiences, dealing with their emotions, reassessing other people's rules and cultural expectations—in short, for letting go of their own private struggles. Using various written forms —prose, Dear God letters, journals, God Can notes—these women are, as Robert Brooke might say, negotiating their own identities. And thus they reach the third stage: "We can't carry our message if we don't have our own language."

Despite all her writing, Jennie did not in 1990 think of herself as a writer. She told me, "I've not gotten back into writing. I've had writer's block for years. I used to write poetry. I'm hoping I'll get that back. I remember writing as a teenager. I liked writing then." When I interviewed Jennie, most of what she was writing was for her classes. Returning to graduate school after a hiatus of ten years probably accounts at least partially for the initial difficulty Jennie reported in writing her school papers. Halfway through her master's program her writing was becoming easier and better, because she now was able to claim authorship of school assignments in a way she had not done previously. Here's how Jen explains it:

There's a different part of me that produces now. It's coming out now like I have to write. Like this morning, I had to do this reaction paper on Reality Therapy. The assignment was to read the book and then tell what you like and don't like. But this other part of me says, "Wait a minute, this is what you believe." You have to understand that what I believe is *not* normally what I'd put in a class paper. There's something in me different that's putting together what

I want to say. Writing it, ideas come from some place else, and it's not what I
intended to write at first. What I ended up with was more integrated and at a
higher level intellectually. I need to relax and let that come out.

So for Jennie, then, even her academic writing has a spiritual aspect—in her
words, "Something that comes from somewhere within me. Like last night, just
all of a sudden came the words 'I believe' and I wrote on a deposit slip so that
I could use this idea in my paper this morning. It feels like it's—in me—but
from somewhere other than my thinking."

In discovering this something that comes from somewhere other than her
thinking, Jennie is learning to trust the power of her own words, a power that is
both generative and freeing. Tommie also believes in the connection between
language and spirituality, in the power of language to heal and to liberate. In
fact, for Tommie, healing and liberation from the past come in and through language: "In [Steps] Six and Seven, you get your own language. See, we can't
carry our message," Tommie says, "if we don't have our own language."[2] To
illustrate, Tommie tells of a woman she met once in a meeting in another city
who described herself before Al-Anon as "a parrot" endlessly repeating what
everyone else told her to say. Celebrating this other woman's transformation,
Tommie explains, "She has come to her own language," a phrase strikingly
similar to bell hooks' much quoted "coming to voice."

In *Talking Back* hooks defines "coming to voice" as "moving from silence
into speech," which she identifies as a "revolutionary gesture . . . especially
relevant for women who are speaking and writing for the first time . . . a rite of
passage where one moves from being object to being subject" (12). What hooks
is talking about, and what my informants both talk about and illustrate, is making meaning out of human experience, using both spoken and written language
to name and claim their lives—in short, empowerment. Perhaps it is possible
to theorize then that at the intersection of literacy and spirituality we find both
meaning and power. William Coles, weaving together images of a program of
recovery, teaching writing, and—wonderfully—playing the horses, said more
than a decade ago:

> I value [writing] as a form of language using, language using understood as
> the primary means by which all of us run order though chaos, thereby giving
> ourselves the identities we have. . . . [W]riting [is] an avenue to a special kind
> of power, the only power I know that is uncorrupting and that for my money
> it therefore makes any sense to have: the power to choose with awareness, to
> change and adapt consciously, and in this sense to be able to have a share in
> determining one's own destiny. (253)

At our conferences and in our journals when we have discussed writing
and power, we have meant intellectual, economic, social, or political power.
Perhaps it is time for us to include the spiritual. Perhaps it is time for us to see

all the multifaceted ways actual human beings use literacy to compose power in their daily lives.

Writing to Heal: Using Meditation in the Writing Process

JoAnn Campbell

Unifying the many definitions and practices of meditation is the notion of training the mind, which suggests that the technique of meditation could usefully supplement courses designed to train people to think and write critically, analytically, or academically. In *Riding the Ox Home: A History of Meditation from Shamanism to Science,* Willard Johnson argues that "meditation has no intrinsic goal or meaning; it is rather a technique, a way of developing consciousness" (3). Coming from a Hindu tradition, Ekneth Easwaran similarly defines meditation as "a systematic technique for taking hold of and concentrating to the utmost degree our latent mental power" (9). Most frequently meditation is discussed within a spiritual context, yet for beginning college students, who often report difficulty keeping their minds on what they read, practice in meditation could be as useful as other study techniques frequently taught, such as focused freewriting, mapping, and dialogic reading logs.

Yet work linking writing and meditation remains on the fringes of our discipline. In this essay I want to review the scholarship on the connections between meditation and writing, analyze objections to the use of meditation in a writing classroom, and suggest that writing teachers consider using meditation with apprehensive or blocked writers, a population I have studied and seen it serve. Most of my experience with meditation and writing has occurred outside the academy; I've led workshops at a bookstore, in a therapist's office, and most frequently through Unity, a center for spiritual growth. Teaching at a spiritual site helped me shift my focus from helping writers produce good prose to helping them enjoy the process of meditating and writing regardless of the outcome. I have also guest taught in elementary and high school classes and typically offer an optional day of meditating and writing in my university writing courses. Despite enthusiastic student response, the marginality of meditative practice within the academy has discouraged me, as an untenured faculty member, from regularly offering meditation to writing classes. Peter Elbow relates a similar reluctance to bring new practices into his university classes: "The question in teaching is always where to find an occasion to try something out, because it always feels you can't try it out in your regular teaching. We need arenas to do these things" ("Interview" 19).

Although the workshops I've led were not associated with a university, many participants were undergraduate and graduate students hoping to rediscover some joy in writing or seeking help with writing blocks. Their stories, as well as hundreds of other literacy histories I've read, reveal the wounds too frequently inflicted by English teachers. I've used the word "heal" in the title of this essay (despite being warned that I could be sued for claiming something I cannot deliver) because, if given a choice between wounding or healing, I want to move toward the latter. "Healing" is rarely heard in academic discussions of writing and teaching, perhaps because it has become the province of those credentialized to heal: physicians, psychologists, perhaps ministers—but surely not writing teachers. Don't we already have enough to do? In a context of traditional western medicine the word *healing* may connote a passivity of the healed and a power of the healer that I do not intend. Rather I invoke the etymological sense of healing as being from the holy, the spiritual, an interplay of forces with which I am a participant rather than creator.

James Pennebaker, a psychologist who has studied the physiological effects of writing, reports on experiments where "those subjects who had written about their thoughts and feelings about traumatic experiences evidenced significant improvement in immune function compared with controls" (162). These beneficial physical and psychological effects of writing have been used outside the academy, for example, in the Twelve-Step programs that Beth Daniell examines. Writing exercises are frequently included in self-help books, such as *Courage to Heal* by Ellen Bass and Laura Davis, which instructs survivors of sexual abuse to narrate their experiences. In other popular texts, meditation is added to writing exercises to enrich the writer's experience. Christina Baldwin's *Life's Companion: Journal Writing as a Spiritual Quest* includes a guided meditation at the end of each section to expand and complicate the reader's awareness of issues she has explored through journaling. In her popular book, *Writing from the Inner Self,* Elaine Farris Hughes, a college writing teacher, has collected a number of guided visualization exercises designed to help writers tap into topics they might not otherwise explore. And Gabriele Rico's *Pain and Possibility* includes reports from workshop participants testifying to the power of meditation and writing combined.

Very successful outside the academy but cited infrequently in composition studies is Ira Progoff, whose books and journal workshops are based on a systematic study of depth psychology and incorporate "process meditation" with writing prompts. Progoff defines meditation broadly as "all the forms and methods by which we reach toward meaning in our lives and by which we seek the depth beyond the doctrines of religion and philosophy" (226). While any journal prompt might be said to reach toward meaning, Progoff includes meditation to "access the power of the unconscious."

In the early history of composition, meditation was sometimes included as a part of writing instruction. D. Gordon Rohman's 1965 article "Pre-Writing: The Stage of Discovery in the Writing Process" suggested imitation, analogies, and meditation as techniques to help students "imitate the creative principle itself which produces finished works" (107). Meditation allowed students to experience their subjects "concretely" and "personally" because it was "a heuristic model, something which served to unlock discovery" (110). Rohman maintained that once students had experienced their subject "the urge to 'get it down' usually increases to the point that the will directs the actual writing of words to begin" (110).

But it has been the work of James Moffett that has so far brought the use of meditation in a writing classroom closest to legitimacy. Coming from a prominent composition theorist, Moffett's 1982 article "Writing, Inner Speech, and Meditation" provides an overview of meditation practices (including his own) from many cultures and locates the common trait in "some notion of transcending intellectual knowledge" (235). He proposes inner speech as the "bridge" between meditation and writing and writes that meditation helps one gain "some control of inner speech ranging from merely watching it to focusing it to suspending it altogether" (236). This allows a writer to engage in "authentic authoring" by helping the writer perceive "the deeper self that abides at least somewhat independently of the outside," a trait he believes necessary for effective writing (236). The article concludes with an exhortation to teachers who meditate to "come out of the closet" as well as a proposal to include meditation training in regular staff development programs (246).

College English published three responses to Moffett's article: a wholehearted acceptance of the article with minor adjustments, a sarcastic dismissal of Moffett and his sources, and a detailed response from James Crosswhite, in which he objects to the idea that we can transcend our circumstances to perceive a "higher" knowledge, arguing that all abilities are rooted in language and history. He calls Moffett's proposal "illiberal," because "being critical of language in a historic and political and cultural way" is the root of a liberal education (402). Crosswhite's objection sounds like one that might come from many social constructionists, anti-foundationalists, and postmodernists today, namely, that there is nowhere to transcend *to* and no absolute to found our notions *on,* so we must be aware that when we privilege a discourse or idea that we are also privileging and serving a particular group of people. Moffett anticipated objections that his approach was too personal by acknowledging the social and historical forces in language, observing that "one's revised inner speech may reflect convention so much as hardly to bear a personal mark" ("Writing" 233). But rather than fight for the supremacy of his theory he seems to want schools to include any technique that helps a student understand: "Human beings rely on several authorities for their knowledge. The only problem comes from excluding some. If it is a mode of knowing, it belongs" ("Comment" 404).

Perhaps the continued exclusion of meditation as a classroom practice is based in part on a distrust of the idea of a "deep" self so often sought by the meditating spiritual seeker. Swami Muktananda, for example writes, "We do not attain the Self through spiritual practices, because the Self is already attained. The Self is always with us. Just as the sun cannot be separated from its light, the Self cannot be separated from us" (12). The capitalized "Self" seems to indicate a singular essence at the core of each individual, similar to that valorized by many advocates of expressive writing. For example, Ira Progoff uses as a basic metaphor for the individual a water well which in turn is "connected to an underground stream . . . that is the source of all wells" (33). For Progoff, unity is possible amidst individual differences, for once "we have gone deeply enough we find that we have gone through our personal life beyond our personal life" (34). Or in Moffett's words "spirituality depends on widening the identity" of the person and institution ("Censorship" 117).

In postmodern theory, this idea of transpersonal unity is not possible or desirable, and instead difference is foregrounded. Lester Faigley defines the postmodern subject "as a play of differences that cannot be reduced to a whole" (232), and he cites the damage done to marginalized people when a single, unified voice is demanded in a writing classroom. Faigley's word *reduced* reflects past religious or liberal treatments of difference where unity is evoked without acknowledging difference—you can be one with us if you leave your race, class, gender, or sexual orientation at the door. Drawing on the work of political theorist Iris Young, Faigley writes that, "In order to practice a politics of differences, there must be discourses and spaces where differences are preserved and appreciated" (232).

Because religious groups have historically suppressed differences, with tragic consequences, in the name of a single path to God, any technique used by religion seems suspect to some. This conflation of religion and spirituality leads both postmodernists and fundamentalists to distrust meditation as a practice of peace. Postmodernists essentialize difference and religious fundamentalists fear it. But in the spirituality that stems from mediation, the perception of oneness does not erase difference but creates an arena where that difference is not only named and celebrated but ultimately loved. Faigley's aim is to bring ethics back into rhetoric, not in order to study absolute right and wrong but to accept "the responsibility for judgment," "reflect on the limits of understanding," and "to respect . . . diversity and unassimilated otherness" (239). Meditation can facilitate all three ends, whether a person seeks a unified self in the process or uses meditation as a technique to create one of a number of selves.

Even those who acknowledge the value of meditation may have reservations about writing teachers employing it in a classroom, objecting that we aren't trained as therapists and should not pretend to be. While I understand the concern for students in these objections, it is important (and potentially radical) to acknowledge that students are not only intellectual but also physical, emotional, and spiritual beings—and that these elements are as present in a classroom as the politics and power we now address. Further, I would contend that a teacher is actually less intrusive during meditation than during most other pedagogical acts, as she can only offer suggestions for physical relaxation without monitoring its results.

For blocked or anxious writers, meditation offers a practical technique to move through that pain. Moffett writes that "the key to meditation is a relaxed body and an alert awareness" ("Writing" 244), and that combination can help apprehensive writers discover the physical location of their fear of writing and begin releasing it. For instance, several women I have worked with in getting past writing block have had histories of headaches, even migraines, before or during a project. As they meditated in and on places of perceived safety, the headaches disappeared, and they could express their ideas in writing. As Rohman has argued, meditation can also facilitate invention, which can ease anxiety of composing. Meditating before writing helps writing run through a whole series of images or phrases before committing any of them to writing. When I led an exercise at a high school, the students seemed most impressed with how easy it was to write once they had visualized a subject. Many of the fifth and sixth graders I worked with doubled the amount of writing they usually produced in one sitting and were astonished at the power of their imaginations the meditation had tapped. One boy wrote "That was incredible! I have never experienced anything like that in my life! It was so realistic! I could hear birds twerping, feel the mist through my body, see the cabin, and then slowly come back to the room."

Meditation and writing often work well in conferences with individual blocked or apprehensive writers. For instance, over the course of four meetings, Marianne, a graduate student I worked with, began to get past her writing block only after she saw her dissertation director in a meditation and continued writing the dialogue with him she started there. Our conversations and further meditations helped her change her working habits so that she was able to write daily, to use a different voice in her writing, to include personal information for an academic audience, and to finish her project in time to submit it for publication. The article was accepted.

It's perhaps a particularly capitalist perspective to think of meditation as a means to an end. In Buddhism the *practice* of meditation is all, and meditators are cautioned against becoming attached to outcomes or insights. Yet in a discipline which talks of process but where teachers often must still evaluate products, and in universities where students want class activities to feed directly into the papers they write, it's difficult to avoid arguing for the practical benefits of offering meditation—at the very least, to students with writing block. Just as Elbow argues for the inclusion of personal writing in the curriculum because, as he puts it, "Life is long and college is short" ("Reflections" 136), I urge meditating writing teachers to combine meditation with writing to provide an anodyne for the wounds of schooling and to offer a model for healthy living.

Women's Ways of Writing,
or, Images, Self-Images, and Graven Images

C. Jan Swearingen

In his most recent—and he claims last—study of childhood, *The Spiritual Life of Children,* Harvard psychologist Robert Coles brings his work on children full circle by recounting one of its starting points. Working in the Deep South during the early 1950s with grade school children who were among the first to integrate the public schools, he experienced a conversion of sorts. He came face to face with the power of religious conviction as something far more than psychiatric neurosis as he listened to an eight-year-old patient, Laurie:

> I was all alone, and those people were screaming, and suddenly I saw God smiling, and I smiled. . . . A woman was standing there [near the school door], and she shouted at me, "Hey, you little nigger, what you smiling at?" I looked right at her face, and I said, "At God." Then she looked up at the sky, and she looked at me, and she didn't call me any more names. (19–20)

Steeped in Freudian psychology, Coles had been trained to regard religion at its worst, as hate-filled, mean-spirited, ignorantly superstitious—as a social lie based on the need people have for self-deception. Yet, he asks, what would Freud have made of Laurie, from Greenville, North Carolina, "or, for that matter, of the heckler who was stopped in her tracks by a child who knew exactly how and when to invoke God? Might [it] have moved the great Viennese doctor, if not to the doors of faith, to a more nuanced sense of what some of us, of whatever age, can manage to do with our convictions?" (20).

Our most firmly held beliefs, some of them hard won, are not often what we are asked to put into writing in academia. Like the embarrassment and self-effacing stigmata that too often accompany discussions of the therapeutic purposes and effects of pedagogy, spiritual and belief-centered elements in creativity, writing, and scholarship are shunned. Even among the most radical of canon bashers still reign the canons of skepticism, criticism, and analysis that have long governed the goals and conventions of academic discourse, writing, and thinking.

Yet all around us, in myriad cultures inside and outside of academia, we observe, to paraphrase Coles, the mind's search for meaning, conviction, and purpose through storytelling, through a faith in and received in legends, handed down in homes and in places of worship, in songs and poems and prayers. This process should not be construed necessarily or arbitrarily as a lie or as a form of self-delusion (20–21). Coles: "The issue, as always, is that of context and intention. Novelists spin stories aimed at the penetration by writer and reader alike of many layers of truth, whereas liars spin stories *meant* to deceive, mislead, trouble, and harm. Freud constructed his own story, a story of the human mind, its battles, its protagonists and antagonists, its victories and defeats" (21). From Laurie and from other children like her, Coles learned another story. He quotes another patient, a fourteen-year-old Catholic girl named Connie: "The whole big world out there, it's God's worry, and it's mine, I guess, because I belong to him." Coles remarks: "Maker and searcher, the divine and external 'object' of religious faith [work] with the investigator in each of us who puts in so brief an earthly appearance" (21).

How do religious faith and spirituality—so poorly imagined, imaged, or understood in much psychology, academia, and secular culture—function in our creative lives as makers and searchers? How can we begin to characterize and draw on—rather than flatly avoiding, as Coles describes himself as doing in his early years—the spiritual lives of those we profess to teach, and the spiritual contexts and purposes of composing alongside other forms of creative work? How can we draw on the power of spiritual conviction and invoke it in the tasks of making meaning, in creating images of self and images of the world for ourselves and our communities—images of the world as it is, and as we hope it may come to be?

This question has been a constant in the teaching that I and two others have undertaken during the past five summers in a weeklong workshop on spirituality and creativity, "Women's Space: Exploring our Creative and Spiritual Selves."[3] It was initially conceived as a workshop that would support and nourish a variety of forms of creative work—including writing, painting, photography, and fabric arts—by attending to the lives of creative women, past and present, whose energies have been tested in the crucible of the tensions created by cultural views of women, and by those corollary tensions that many women feel divide their loyalties to family and professional work. In a study of working-class women's gradual acculturation into academia, Mary Belenky and her colleagues characterize one aspect of this tension as the conflict between "telling the truth" and "being good." Not only as students, but as creative artists and writers, women often want to "tell the truth"; however, cultural roles assigned and rewarded make them feel torn in special ways by what society and their own values tell them is "being good"—with all of its familial, moral, social, and emotional ramifications.

We have learned from five summers in a circle of twenty-five—a different twenty-five each summer. We have come to some understanding of aspects of the creative process that take distinctive forms in women's lives, and this has led us to want to define those contexts in ways that can be nourishing. To help participants build or recover a strong self image, we have developed a number of images of both self and creativity that we use in teaching self-image, self-worth, motivation, and conviction. These serve as antidotes to the deep fear and self-doubt that women, like other marginalized groups, must overcome in order to write the first sentence, paint the first stroke. We have crafted exercises for journal writing that exorcise the inner critic, those voices that say, "You can't," "Who do you think you are?" "You'll never finish," "Puttin' on airs, are you?" Some of the exercises have in turn become starting points for stories, for talking about storytelling and story making and about literature, past and present. Literature, we emphasize, sustains its ties with the narratives and externalized "objects of faith" that—along with stories—religion has always provided as images of self, of what it is to be human, of what it is to live and make a life that has meaning and purpose.

We have also learned of the enormous pressure, often unspoken, that women feel from family and from the culture. Work, especially creative work, is in the experience of many women treated as indulgent, as a rival for attentions

and emotions, as abandonment of emotional and other duties to relationships
or to family. If mother is cleaning the toilet, fine; if she's painting, she might as
well be a painted woman. Our circle has been a place to abandon such pressures,
to put them aside for a week, and to ignore the hecklers—male—who even at
our conference center look in the window and sometimes whisper, "You're
talking about us, aren't you?" One year we indulged in a choral rejoinder
and sang to the hecklers and scorners at the window Carly Simon's refrain and
title: "You're So Vain, You Probably Think This Song Is About You." And
we've fended off the hecklers—male and female—who whisper the old saw,
intended to intimidate, "Lesbians."

We have compiled short journal exercises that serve as warm-ups and
starters for creative work, whether in writing or in other media. In these exercises writers dialogue with, run to ground, and finally defer inner critics and
hecklers: "Talk to me later, when I'm revising, or in the book reviews." In one
journal exercise each writer furnishes a "house of the spirit"—a special room
in a special place that is holy, full of mementos and meanings that help her to
create and to take her creations seriously. We write dialogues with adversaries
and with treasured friends as a way of getting the inner voices of discussion going. In journal entries never to be read by anyone but the writer, unless she
chooses; otherwise, we confront the envy and resentment we feel toward one
another's accomplishments, or families, or looks, or all of the above. Some of
the voices that emerge in journal writing become, not self-images, but alter
egos: personas, or for novelists, separate characters. Stages of separation in images of self allow us to understand that we are seeing parts of ourselves in those
we envy, as well as in those we love.

The enterprise of self-imaging exercises may seem highly psychologized—
self-help, self-esteem, selfish—but the exercises entail active mediation and
interpretation of received and desired images, with the emphasis on active
meaning making that Ann Berthoff likes to give to Peirce's triadicity: "Mediation is logically dependent on the idea held by the interpreter. The necessary
condition of interpretation is the logical role of the interpretant, the idea which
mediates between the symbol and what it represents" (3). Our participants re-
direct their interpretations of images of self. Traits they envy or admire in others are seen instead as part of a repertoire—a social and spiritual world of characters that is far larger than those of us around the circle.[4] We reanimate
concepts of images, self-images, and graven images as a constantly evolving
aesthetic and cultural pantheon that we draw on in our thinking and writing, our
meaning finding and meaning making, our ways of understanding, and our
ways of being.

Roughly half of the participants in our workshop each summer have no religious beliefs and no interest in acquiring any. Nonetheless, most say that they
have come because they feel a spiritual poverty in their lives. Among these participants, as well as those who have an active religious life, we have observed
many compatabilities. They share understandings of the importance of art,

their experiences of the creative process, the many ways of weaving relationships among images and stories and self-image, and the centrality of community to the spiritual and creative viability of individuals. For students in classrooms, the institution of the school can provide a community. For those who work alone, at home, at odd moments, freelance, the sense of community is harder to come by. Participants in our workshop have found it helpful simply to know more about each others' experiences and to learn about the history and experiences of other women in similar situations who worked, wrote, or painted while they also raised children, worked outside the home, or lived alone. Our circle is an immediate community, but it is short-lived. Like a compressed semester, our circle brings together a group of strangers who for all practical purposes will not meet again— with all the valuable containment and poignant partings that such communities entail.

As well as crafting new understandings of image and self-image for themselves, our creative participants have assigned us images. One year a workshop participant, working on a Ph.D. in Jungian feminist counseling, dubbed us a trinity: I was to my great discomfort anointed the talking head "Father"—I'd rather say academician and scholar—of the trinity; our photographer became the "Son" or "Image"; and our journal writing expert cum visionary was, of course, the "Holy Spirit." Our photographer has created a popular innovation in traditional journal writing and creative work exercises. She teaches participants to use photographic self-portraiture as a vehicle for finding and enhancing images of self and of creativity that will prompt creative motivation and provide a repertoire of images. The photographic self-images need not be of one's face or even of one's body. Instead, much like T. S. Eliot's notion of poetic images as objective correlatives for emotion or Keats' metaphor of the chameleon on the mirror, the images may be of rocks and trees and streams, or of children playing in apple trees, or of a bare bottom beneath a tuxedo jacket. Imagistic as well as verbal materials have given creativity and spirituality many resources and renewed their life in many times and cultures. We have learned from correspondence with participants that the materials we present on women writers and artists of earlier eras provide an additional stimulus, a resource of older images and stories that are enormously helpful after the workshop ends. Along with reconfigured and enhanced self-images drawn from journaling and photography exercises, images of women from the past provide additional images of self and life stories as paradigms that, as one participant put it, "enable me to walk on water."

Space permits only a few examples of the historical materials I have presented over five summers as the stand-up talking head, the academic lecturer in our trinity. I review various social settings and individuals from past eras in order to emphasize two points. First, women are more prominently represented among the writers, thinkers, and artists of past eras than most of us knew until very recently. And, second, contrary to widely held beliefs, women's communities, particularly in the Middle Ages, were not exclusively mendicant orders whose primary tasks were to tend to the poor, the elderly, the fields, the flocks, and the baking of bread. Histories of women who were actively intellectual and artistic, often in religious communities during the Middle Ages, need to be retrieved, in part because they provide images of productive and accepted intellect among women.[5]

It was not until the 1240s within Thomist Dominican doctrines that women were officially forbidden by the church to teach and to be ordained; educated women in the Middle Ages and earlier often acquired and practiced their learning in convents or double houses, some of which had double abbots—one male and one female. Similar correction of long held images of women in earlier periods is being conducted in studies of the public and private discourse of women in Greek and Latin classical culture and in Jewish tradition in the Hellenic, medieval, and modern periods. Nonetheless, longstanding practice as well as social attitudes kept all but a very few women, and particularly women educated in theology and philosophy, out of the public arena and out of publication. The few exceptions to this rule—and now we are discovering more numerous exceptions—are revealing for the common pattern they manifest. The letters of Heloise and Abelard, for instance, reveal Heloise to be a thoughtful, well-read, and insightful theologian who could argue pointedly with the doctrines—derived from Aristotle and Augustine primarily—concerning women's intelligence and nature (see Pagels). Her letters employ, in addition to subtle logical arguments, historical examples of women teachers, philosophers, and religious figures drawn from secular as well as sacred histories stretching back through the classical period and into the New Testament and Hebrew scriptures. A similar combination of these two modes—subtle argumentation clearly honed by formal training in logic and detailed historical examples—is also employed by Sor Juana Inez de la Cruz, a seventeenth-century colonial Mexican nun, largely self-educated through access to the 6,000-volume library of her maternal grandfather. Like many women authors, Heloise and Sor Juana chose as their public vehicles genres acceptable for women: letters and literary works. Because she had become widely acclaimed in Spain as well as in the New World for her voluminous productivity as a literary author, Sor Juana's letter, *La Respuesta,* stands out because it is a response to—and refutation of—her bishop's request that she stop writing entirely. Like Heloise's self-defense that is simultaneously a defense of women writers and of women's intellect, Sor Juana's *Respuesta* is a composite of erudite logic, autobiography, and historical example.

What distinguishes these and other works by women is that they draw on a body of knowledge that we—save for few highly specialized scholars—have in effect lost. E. D. Hirsch's list provides little mention of women like Hypatia, Aspasia, Sappho, the Queen of Sheba, Deborah, Abigail, Esther, Anna the mother of Samuel, Polla Argentaria, Zenobia, Leontium, Gertrudis, even Isabella of Spain. We find Hymen, but not Hypatia; Isabella (with Ferdinand), the Queen of Sheba, and Esther, but not Miriam and Deborah, who were political leaders. Sor Juana applauds Isabella, the patron of Columbus, for her astronomical research and cites her as a scholarly patron and ancestress (*Respuesta* 64–66). But Heloise, Sor Juana, Christine de Pisan (writing *The Book of the City of Ladies* under Isabella's patronage) and Gilles Menage (writing his *History of Women Philosophers* in the French court of the seventeenth century) had access to these figures and to details of their lives and work. Material that was common knowledge to the educated in earlier eras has thus been lost and needs to be reclaimed.

Two related issues emerge from this history. First, was it largely within communities of women that educated women could flourish and write, conduct scholarship and exchange their work with others, and evade the compulsion to defend their ability as well as their right to write and engage in intellectual activity? Though Heloise's, Sor Juana's, and Menage's work preserve for us a list of women and a group of defenses of women's intelligence that had become common topics by the fifteenth century, they were not known primarily for this element in their work in their own time. (Sor Juana's letter was published posthumously.) Instead, Heloise and Sor Juana spent their lives in communities of women where the *practice* rather than the defense of women's intellect to an outside world was a primary activity. I believe this pattern persists—and exerts continuing influence—in the intellectual conduct, education, and practice of women in our culture today.

Modern histories of women's communities during the Middle Ages have not until recently emphasized the presence or practice of intellectual women in their midst. Many are social histories that emphasize conventional roles for women. Late medieval beguinages—religious communities that were like convents for laywomen—provided women haven in an economic and social world in which they had few economic homes apart from marriage. Despite the conventional paradigms of most histories of beguines, it is tempting to speculate, at the risk of wish-fulfillment, that amidst these communities of women there were homes for intellectual women as well—and that perhaps until very recently this role was a well-kept secret. The existence of intellectually active and productive women during the Middle Ages and Renaissance is becoming increasingly well documented (see King; Wilson). At great pains and under duress, the women of the Renaissance, Middle Ages, and earlier eras produced work known in their own time that has been lost. Is this not true, still, of the work, images, and self-images of many women within this century? To give only one example, the African American anthropologist and novelist Zora Neale Hurston, author of *Their Eyes Were Watching God*, died in a poorhouse and was buried in an unmarked pauper's grave in Florida in the 1930s. Her work languished unknown for decades until Alice Walker found her grave, marked it, and saw to the republication of her work.

Our workshop participants have found it sustaining to know that such women existed, and that their lives and work are now being recovered. Just as Robert Coles underwent a conversion in his understanding of religion when he listened to how and why Laurie said "I am smiling at God," participants in our workshop, and students in our classes, benefit from observing other individuals, both past and present, constructing and defending images of their creative and spiritual selves. I hope that the ongoing recovery of the history of women in the Renaissance and in the medieval beguinages, and in other eras as well, will increasingly emphasize their creative and intellectual work because that gives many modern women permission and courage that they have been without. "It makes me feel like I can walk on water." Like Laurie's account to Robert Coles, women's stories of self and creativity draw together the stories and patterns and meanings that connect the spiritual and the intellectual, the knower and the known, the quest for meaning and the will to make it.

Response

James Moffett

Instead of trying to critique these papers, I would like to respond to them in kind by adding to their authors' knowledge and personal experiences some of my own, partly by way of corroboration. I'm especially happy to take part in this interchange because writing to heal and to grow is close to my heart and because it is alien to universities, which have much to learn from these spiritual sites of composing.

Probably nothing is harder for the academy to come to terms with than therapy and spirituality, which Alcoholics Anonymous has brought into a conjunction that seems right to many members of our society. Look at the rapidly increasing number of Twelve-Step programs among other wounded and wounding people who have banded together like Beth Daniell's informants for a "recovery" program that no educational institution provides.

A huge amount of both amateur and professional writing represents efforts to do the "fearless moral inventory" of Step Four, to take stock of our experience and find out who we are and where we stand. Students need badly to use writing to do their own moral inventory. You don't have to be alcoholic or in some other crisis. Just being young and growing—or even just taking part in this world—gives you enough reason to want to assess what you are up to and what you are.

For their part, teachers have reasons for choosing the profession they're in, and going about it the way they do, that concern their own efforts to heal, grow, and find themselves. When I was a young adult, I wrote some stories that indirectly dealt with my experience as a child of an alcoholic. From this I learned a great deal that I later used in teaching literature and writing. I think we all become better teachers when we bring out and draw on our personal efforts to do what we know our students are now trying to do also—heal the feelings so the spirit can develop.

Meditation has been a major means of self-development for as long as anyone knows. I'm always interested in how someone else teaches meditation with writing, because it's difficult to know how to go about it. The connections JoAnn Campbell has indicated between writing and relaxing, concentrating, and visualizing are ones I hope other teachers will consider seriously in the light of today's emphasis on holistic functioning, if for no other reason.

I've been meditating since 1971 and have incorporated meditation several times into a writing course that I've given from time to time at the Breadloaf School of English, Middlebury College, where the master's candidates are nearly all teachers and inclined to try in their own classes what we do. Here's a big methodological question for me: How *closely* should students interweave their meditating and their writing? I have them experiment with this by sometimes writing immediately after meditating or even stopping to take notes during meditation. Or they just keep both going on separate schedules. We discuss the differences in the short- and long-term effects. Another question concerns how much to meditate together and how much alone. Sometimes I start with group in-class meditation, partly to initiate novices, partly to provide common experience, and partly to let them compare these sessions with those in solitude.

Many students have reported that fragments of unfinished thought or writing came together during or because of meditation so that they were able and pleased to be able to complete them. Most testified also that meditation freed them from ephemera and petty concerns to get deep into themselves for more interesting and important writing material.

During a couple of ten-day workshops with teachers from the Northern Virginia Writing Project at George Mason University, I experimented more intensively with a variety of nonverbal activities such as focusing, meditating, yogic stretching, fasting, breathing, and chanting as they are alternated abruptly with talking, thinking, reading, and writing. Undergoing this gamut tends to rearrange the inner furniture and to reconnect thoughts and feelings in new ways within each person and across people. The main issues in writing, after all, concern the composing of the inner life.

Surely it's of value to writing teachers to know where and with whom people of the past found some community to nourish their writing. At nearly the same time that I was learning about beguinages from reading Jan Swearingen's paper, another colleague, Karen Carlton at Humboldt State in California, gave me a trilogy on the subject written by the abbot of the Cistercian monastery near where she occasionally goes on retreat. She in fact helped him, an elderly Flemish scholar, to finish this work, which has to be the most definitive done in America on beguinages—*Beatrice of Nazareth and the Thirteenth-Century Mulieres Religiosae of the Low Countries* by Roger de Ganck. *Mulieres religiosae* was a set term in the Middle Ages for laywomen leading a spiritual life. While a great number of men were off killing and being killed in the crusades, many women were going to God in a more appropriate way. De Ganck corroborates Jan's conjecture that beguinages provided not merely a haven when husbands were scarce but an intellectual home where minds and spirits could thrive.

Even in the seventeenth century one could join the spiritual activities at Port Royal, where an abbey sheltering a women's religious community became so popular that laymen of letters, like Pascal, came there to meditate, study, do manual labor, write, and run an unconventional school. But by then, and later, worldly aristocrats were creating communities of the mind and spirit in the salons of their own mansions, where writers like Pierre Corneille, Madame de Sévigné, Madame de LaFayette, de La Rochefoucauld, and Madame de Staël found the peers and mentors, atmosphere and audience, that make for spiritual sites of composing.

These three papers give some idea of what has replaced beguinages and salons. I appreciate them especially for dealing with the relations between writing and therapy, writing and spirituality, and hence between therapy and spirituality. What strikes me most is that to do this they had to go off campus for all their examples. Not only are women still making shift to find or create spiritual sites of composing, in special groups or courses, but men too cannot find them in their own male-created institutions. Why can't people write to heal or to develop spiritually *on* campus?

You can say that the business of colleges is something else, that those people who want spiritual sites of composing can continue to take workshops or form private groups. Public institutions are concerned with public matters. So college composition courses should continue to prepare students to write term papers and do well on essay exams, that is, to fit into the institution's evaluation system in the other courses. Or, at a bit higher elevation, to do the kinds of writing that keep business and government and research moving (in whatever direction). Therapy and spiritual growth should be on your own time and don't require a university.

But my pitch is not so much that the university should provide spiritual sites of composing for the sake of therapy and spirituality, which have done without universities since before the latter were founded, as that the university needs spiritual sites of composing for its *own* sake. For my point here, consider what therapy, spirituality, and the university's missions are essentially about. I'll designate them all three by one term, *getting better*—getting better in the sense of *healing,* getting better in the sense of *becoming a finer person,* and getting better in the sense of *becoming more competent* at some activity.

Now the university acts, and the writing program right along with it, as if getting better at doing something is really all it's concerned with. But writing programs, and the universities along with them, will never get any better themselves so long as they don't take together all three senses of this goal. People don't learn to write well just to accommodate an institution and then the one after that, even if they try to and think they should. We get good at doing something as a part of getting well and realizing our deepest being. I know, the university feels it shouldn't play doctor or priest, dirty its hands with therapy and its mind with religion. But if it has real live students on its hands, its hands are already dirty. And the time has come for intellectuals to quit confusing spirituality with superstition and sectarianism. Unhealed wounds and undeveloped souls will thwart the smartest curriculum.

Notes

1. This study was reviewed by the Clemson University Committee for the Protection of Human Subjects. All my informants are aware of the purpose of my work, and their anonymity has been assured. Both women featured in this essay have read an earlier version and have either confirmed or corrected my report.

2. Step Six reads, "We're entirely ready to have God remove all these defects of character." Step Seven says, "Humbly asked Him to remove our shortcomings." Tommie also refers in this speech to Step Twelve: "Having had a spiritual awakening as a result of these Steps, we tried to carry this message to others, and to practice these principles in all our affairs."

3. My co-teachers, in both senses, for I have learned much from them, are Lesley Poling-Kempes and Terry Evans. Lesley Poling-Kempes is a freelance author, grant writer, and novelist who has worked with public television and collaborated with other New Mexico artists in environmental projects. Terry Evans has for many years been an active documentary, art, and environmentalist photographer based in Salinas, Kansas. Before being deeded to the Presbyterian Church's National Board of Christian Education as an adult and clergy study center, Ghost Ranch, the conference center where we teach, had been a dude ranch much frequented by the New Mexico art intelligentsia of the 1920s and 30s, including Georgia O'Keeffe, who began to reside there in the summers. Lesley Poling-Kempes' history of the early pre-Presbyterian years of Ghost Ranch features many of the expatriate New York art and literary world women who happily settled in the West for a number of reasons. Her work on these women and her expertise as a journal writing leader have been valuable and acclaimed elements in our workshop.

4. I am indebted to Terry Evans and Lesley Poling-Kempes for constructing this conversion of envy into an identification of admired traits.

5. Dronke; Grafton and Jardine, especially their chapter "Women Humanists: Education for What?" (29–57); and King are excellent examples of scholars working to reclaim women's lives and voices that have been left out of most histories.

Works Cited

Abelard, Peter. *The Letters of Abeland and Heloise.* Trans. and intro. by Betty Radice. Harmondsworth: Penguin, 1974.

Al-Anon Family Groups. *Al-Anon and Alateen Groups at Work: The Basic Manual of Principles and Practices.* New York: Al-Anon Family Group Headquarters, 1976.

Baldwin, Christina. *Life's Companion: Journal Writing As a Spiritual Quest.* New York: Bantam, 1991.

Bass, Ellen and Laura Davis. *Courage to Heal.* New York: Perennial, 1988.

Belenky, Mary Field, Blythe McVicker Clinchy, Nancy Rule Goldberger, and Jill Mattuck Tarule. *Women's Ways of Knowing: The Development of Self, Voice, and Mind.* New York: Basic, 1986.

Brooke, Robert E. *Writing and Sense of Self: Identity Negotiation in Writing Workshops.* Urbana: NCTE, 1991.

Carter, Stephen L. *The Culture of Disbelief: How American Law and Politics Trivialize Religious Devotion.* New York: Basic, 1993.

Christ, Carol. *Diving Deep and Surfacing: Women Writers on a Spiritual Quest.* Boston: Beacon, 1980.

Coles, Robert. *The Spiritual Life of Children.* Cambridge: Harvard UP, 1990.

Coles, William E., Jr. "Literacy for the Eighties: An Alternative to Losing." *Literacy for Life: The Demand for Reading and Writing.* Eds. Richard W. Bailey and Robin Melanie Fosheim. New York: MLA, 1983. 248–262.

Crosswhite, James. "Comment and Response." *College English* 45 (1983): 400–403.

de la Cruz, Sor Juana [Juana Asbaje]. *A Woman of Genius/La Respuesta.* Trans. and ed. Margaret Sayers Peden. Salisbury, CT: Lime Rock, 1982.

de Ganck, Roger. *Beatrice of Nazareth and the Thirteenth-Century Mulieres Religiosae of the Low Countries.* Kalamazoo: Cistercian Publications, 1991.

de Pisan, Christine. *The Book of the City of Ladies.* Trans. Earl J. Richards. New York: Persea, 1982.

Dronke, Peter. *Women Writers of the Middle Ages.* New York: Cambridge UP, 1984.

Easwaran, Ekneth. *Meditation, an Eight-Point Program.* Petaluma, CA: Nilgiri, 1978.

Elbow, Peter. "Reflections on Academic Discourse: How It Relates to Freshmen and Colleagues." *College English* 53 (1991): 135–55.

———. "An Interview with Peter Elbow: Going in Two Directions at Once." John Boe and Eric Schroeder. *Writing on the Edge* 4 (Fall 1992): 9–30.

Elpenor. "A Drunkard's Progress: AA and the Sobering Strength of Myth." *Harper's* October 1986: 42–48.

Faigley, Lester. *Fragments of Rationality: Postmodernity and the Subject of Composition.* Pittsburgh: U of Pittsburgh P, 1992.

Fishman, Andrea. *Amish Literacy: What and How It Means.* Portsmouth, NH: Heinemann, 1988.

Freire, Paulo. *Pedagogy of the Oppressed.* New York: Seabury, 1970.

———. *The Politics of Education: Culture, Power, and Liberation.* Trans. Donaldo Macedo. South Hadley, MA: Bergin, 1985.

Goody, Jack. "Introduction." *Literacy in Traditional Societies.* Cambridge UP, 1968. 1–26.

Goody, Jack and Ian Watt. "The Consequences of Literacy." *Comparative Studies in Society and History* 5 (1963): 304–45.

Graff, Harvey. *Legacies of Literacy: Continuities and Contradictions in Western Culture and Society.* Bloomington: Indiana UP, 1987.

Grafton, Anthony and Lisa Jardine. *From Humanism to the Humanities*. Cambridge: Harvard UP, 1986.

Heath, Shirley Brice. "Protean Shapes: Ever-Shifting Oral and Literate Traditions." *Spoken and Written Language: Exploring Orality and Literacy*. Ed. Deborah Tannen. Norwood, NJ: Ablex, 1982. 91–117.

———. *Ways with Words: Language, Life, and Work in Communities and Classrooms*. Cambridge UP, 1983.

Hirsch, E. D., Jr. *Cultural Literacy: What Every American Needs to Know*. Boston: Houghton, 1987.

hooks, bell. *Talking Back: Thinking Feminist, Thinking Black*. Boston: South End, 1989.

Hughes, Elaine Farris. *Writing from the Inner Self*. New York: Harper Collins, 1991.

Johnson, Willard. *Riding the Ox Home: A History of Meditation from Shamanism to Science*. London: Rider, 1962.

King, Margaret L. *Women of the Renaissance*. Chicago: U of Chicago P, 1991.

Menage, Gilles. *The History of Women Philosophers (Historia Mulierum Philosopharum, 1690)*. Trans. Beatrice H. Zedler. Lanham, MD: University P of America, 1984.

Moffett, James. "Comment and Response." *College English* 45 (1983): 404–406.

———. "Censorship and Spiritual Education." *The Right to Literacy*. Eds. Andrea Lunsford, Helene Moglen, and James Slevin. New York: MLA, 1990. 113–119.

———. *Storm in the Mountains: A Case Study of Censorship, Conflict, and Consciousness*. Carbondale: Southern Illinois UP, 1988.

———. "Writing, Inner Speech, and Meditation." *College English* 44 (1982): 231–246.

Moss, Beverly J. *The Black Sermon as a Literacy Event*. Diss. U of Illinois at Chicago, 1988.

Muktananda, Swami. *I Am That*. Revised. South Fallsburg, NY: SYDA, 1983.

Pagels, Elaine. *Adam, Eve, and the Serpent*. New York: Vintage, 1989.

Paz, Octavio. *Sor Juana, Or, The Traps of Faith*. Trans. Margaret Sayers Peden. Cambridge: Harvard UP, 1988.

Pennebaker, James W. "Self-Expressive Writing: Implications for Health, Education and Welfare." *Nothing Begins with N: New Investigations of Freewriting*. Eds. Pat Belanoff, Peter Elbow, and Sheryl L. Fontaine. Carbondale: Southern Illinois UP, 1991. 157–170.

Progoff, Ira. *At a Journal Workshop*. Revised ed. Los Angeles: Tarcher, 1992.

Resnick, Daniel P. and Lauren B. Resnick. "The Nature of Literacy: An Historical Exploration." *Harvard Educational Review* 47 (1977): 370–385.

Rico, Gabriele. *Pain and Possibility*. Los Angeles: Tarcher, 1992.

Rohman, D. Gordon. "Pre-Writing: The Stage of Discovery in the Writing Process." *College Composition and Communication* 16 (1965): 106–112.

Schleiermacher, Friedrich E. *Schleiermacher's Soliloquies.* Trans. H. L. Friess. 1926. Westport, CN: Hyperion, 1984.

Soelle, Dorothee. "Mysticism—Liberation—Feminism." *The Strength of the Weak: Toward a Christian Feminist Identity.* Philadelphia: Westminster, 1984. 79–105.

Walker, Alice. *In Search of Our Mothers' Gardens: Womanist Prose.* New York: Harcourt, 1983.

Walters, Keith. "Not-So-Hidden Literacy in an Unprogrammed Quaker Meeting." MLA Responsibilities for Literacy Conference, Pittsburgh, September 15, 1990.

Wilson, K. M., ed. *Women Writers of the Renaissance and Reformation.* Athens: U of Georgia P, 1987.

Bringing Language Back to Life

Responding to the New Illiteracy

G. Lynn Nelson

The basic word I-You can only be spoken with one's whole being.
The basic word I-It can never be spoken with one's whole being.
— Martin Buber, *I and Thou*

As I write this, we have just been told that the SAT verbal scores have declined for the fourth straight year. It is no great surprise, just one more reminder of what we already know. After years of our testing and protesting and lamenting and returning-to-the-basics, Johnny and Jane still can't read or write very well. Nothing we do in American education seems to slow for very long the inexorable drift toward larger numbers of language disabled in our society. And while the finger of blame is most often pointed at English teachers, any careful observer knows that Jane and Johnny are not our offspring—they are the children of an entire culture in the process of change.

But even though we English teachers are not the cause of the growing inarticulateness of America's youth, we could be a much greater part of the solution than we generally are. We could help our students much more than we do to take back their words, to bring their language back to life. But first we must understand the major cause of modern inarticulateness.

This cause is hard for us to see, because it has only fully emerged, like some new disease, in recent years—and because we, the doctors, have the disease, too. While illiteracy and poor language skills are an age-old problem, in the past their cause has most often been a lack of exposure to language—a lack of schools and books and education. This is why modern illiteracy so perplexes us. We have all these schools, all these English classes, all these new computers—and still the inarticulateness and inability grow. *Because most modern illiteracy arises not from a paucity of language but from overexposure to language—from too much language, too many I-It words.*

Our students' lives are polluted with words—loud, cheap, manipulating, heartless words. They awaken to disc jockeys shouting time, temperature, and

English Journal, 80 (February 1991), pp. 16–20. Copyright © 1991 by the National Council of Teachers of English. Reprinted with permission.

traffic conditions at them on their clock radios. On the schoolbus, ubiquitous headset radios blare mostly mindless lyrics as the students roll past the garish language of billboards and marquees. At school, the intercom drones instructions, and in classes of thirty to fifty fellow students, the teacher lectures. At the end of the day, they go home—perhaps to do homework from impersonal textbooks, certainly to be exposed again to the typical language of movies and TV programs and commercials. Eventually, they fall asleep, as they awoke, to endless words emanating from the clock radio. . . .

Sketchy, yes, and obviously not exclusively true, but it demonstrates the point—most modern literacy problems do not arise from a lack of exposure to language. On the contrary, our culture gluts the lives of our youth with an endless stream of words. It deadens them to language. Most of the words of their days constitute an impersonal, sterile, meaningless stream of I-It language *addressed to no real person.* Few of the spoken or written words they experience are addressed to them as unique and meaningful people. Almost none of the language is the living "I-Thou" language of which Martin Buber speaks—language that is caring and careful and meaningful. "O mysteriousness without mystery, O piling up of information! It, it, it!" (1970, *I and Thou,* New York: Scribner's, 56).

And so their sensitivity for language dies, and a part of them dies with it. As English teachers, we can never make our students care about a semicolon if they do not care about language. And they will not care about language if the language they are surrounded with does not care about them.

I think no one has seen this modern illness more clearly nor described it more sensitively than N. Scott Momaday in his *House Made of Dawn* (1966, New York: NAL).

> In the white man's world, language . . . and the way in which the white man thinks of it—has undergone a change. The white man takes such things as words and literatures for granted, as indeed he must, for nothing in his world is so commonplace. On every side of him there are words by the millions, an unending succession of pamphlets and papers, letters and books, bills and bulletins, commentaries and conversations. He has diluted and multiplied the word, and words have begun to close in upon him. He is sated and insensitive; his regard for language—for the Word itself—as an instrument of creation has diminished nearly to the point of no return. It may be that he will perish by the word. (89)

This is the dilemma of the youth in our schools—the dilemma of us all in the age of mass media and technology. In a language-polluted and language-deadened environment, our students learn subconsciously and defensively to let language roll off of them. The commercial and materialistic aspects of our culture—which have destroyed the magic of language and reduced it to commodity—have thus forced our students to desensitize themselves as a matter of survival. Like a fox in a trap chewing off its paw, they kill a part of themselves in order to survive. Except on a very superficial level, our students learn not to see words, not to hear words. They become blind and deaf to language.

This may well be the fundamental literacy problem of our time, basic to all other language problems. My own teaching experience suggests that it is, suggests that when I deal with this problem, all the other language problems begin to diminish. So how do we deal with it? What can we do in our classrooms to change this? Here are some things I am doing in my own teaching that make a difference.

Teaching Silence

Silence is an important part of my lesson plans. Not "Sit down and shut up!" silence, but dynamic silence—outer stillness so that we can enter the inner stillness and learn from it. Just as the space between the notes is necessary for the music, so silence around our words is necessary if our words are to be meaningful.

Early on, I introduce my students to their cerebral cortex, so they are aware that there are many ways to learn—and that one way is to "be still and know." They begin to understand that we humans know more than we know we know, so it is legitimate pedagogy to learn from ourselves. They begin to see that ours is a predominantly left-brained, noisy, outgoing culture and to have an inkling of what such a culture is doing to their psyches and their spirits. They know that we are going to have to work deliberately and diligently if we hope to be whole and if we wish our words to have a heart.

So we almost always start class with five to ten minutes of soft music and "quiet writing" in our journals. We also do "silent breathing" at various times—short periods of sitting still ("silence of body, silence of speech, silence of mind") and simply watching the miracle of our breath coming and going. I set the timer for five minutes, and we sit with spines straight and feet flat on the floor and simply "breathe." We are quieting the chatter of the left brain so that we can begin to hear beyond it.

At first this may be a little awkward for my students and some may feel self-conscious, but gradually they become accustomed to it and begin to feel its value. And I begin to see its value in their writing and their being. Always after such sessions, we return to our work more settled and focused and alert. Our words are more care-full and we see and hear them more clearly.

Keeping a Personal Journal

The personal journal has become basic to all work with language in my classroom. I have witnessed more of my students (from junior-high through college graduate students) begin to touch the power of themselves and their own language through the journal than through any other single activity. Recently, I taught a five-week intensive writing course for high-school Hispanic girls, part of a program to keep them in school and encourage them to go on to college. All of our writing tasks started with my asking them to explore something in their journals; then we moved it out into public writing, revised it, helped each other with it; and then we published it for the class. After the course was over, I received a letter from Cathy, one of the young women in the class. The following is an excerpt from her letter.

> I miss you. You . . . showed me a whole new, endless world of writing, inside something very important, me. Writing feelings down and turning them into something to share has allowed me to see inside myself. You have reminded me of something I seem to have forgotten. That I am important.
>
> Because of you [read "my writing"], I have just left a relationship that was both mentally and physically abusive. After three and a half years, leaving was the hardest thing to do, but I did it. . . . I know I deserve better than what I had, because nobody deserves that. . . . I'll get through it. . . .

The change is evident. Words have come to life and turned into a power beyond her English class for this student. This happens only when the words come from within us, when we care about what we write. This happens only when we start with personal writing, the journal, and work outward from there.

Starting with the Heart

My Native American students have taught me about the Feather Circle, in which the eagle feather is passed and each person speaks from the heart. Because they come from the heart, the words spoken in the Feather Circle are almost always simple, strong, and powerful—the way all good writing and speaking should be. So I incorporate this into my classes. All our speaking and writing must come from our hearts, must be "emotionally honest," as Ken Macrorie says.

So we work at taking back our feelings, along with our words. We are, after all, feeling creatures—though we have been taught, at deadly price to our words and our being, to deny our emotions and pretend that we are rational, logical, analytical creatures. The poet e. e. cummings said it best: "since feeling is first / who pays any attention / to the syntax of things / will never wholly kiss you" (1959, *100 Selected Poems,* New York: Grove, 35). So in my classes, we try to speak and write as whole people, saying "I" and owning our feelings, even as we work our words into formal syntax and logic.

All our writing tasks start with the heart, start with exploring our feelings about something in our journals, whether it is about our personal lives or about how Hamlet treats Ophelia. Then some of our words find their way out and into the forms of public writing. Cathy's feelings of fear, first written in her journal and later expressed in the letter to me quoted earlier, worked their way in class into a carefully structured poem called "Fear." It was a strong and meaningful piece of public writing. She worked hard to get it technically correct—because she cared about it. My experience has shown me that the heart (feeling, content, creativity) can generate a skeleton (form, structure, mechanics) but a skeleton can seldom generate a heart.

Publishing

All real and meaningful communication is always some version of that wonderful "Show-and-Tell" of kindergarten — using my words to share something I care about with others I care about. Too often, we ask students to write in a vacuum — or worse, to write for an English teacher with a red pen waiting to find all their errors. I-Thou language always has a living audience. I-Thou words are always addressed to real people for real purposes.

When we work on a piece of public writing in my classes, we always have an audience for our writing. Usually, the audience is the rest of the class. We make copies for everyone. We read our writing in class. They write notes back to us. This is not artificial language; it is real communication.

If we are not writing for the class, we are writing letters to other people, letters to the editor, articles for the school paper, poems to be put up on the wall, pieces for our class publication, and the like. A real audience causes our words to come alive. I-Thou language becomes vibrant with the blood of life. This cannot be taught; it can only be infused.

Writing Small

In my classroom, small is beautiful. We write lots of small pieces — poems, paragraphs, and vignettes. Writing small restores my students' sensitivity to language more than a fifteen-page term paper. I like to get my students excited about something, eagerly writing about it — and then tell them that the public writing can be no more than seventy-five words, or one hundred fifty words, or whatever. So they must be very care-full. They must make every word count. This reverses the usual pattern of trying to fill a large container with language, throwing in dead words, empty words, I-It words, just to get the form filled.

Always, I have them give their piece a title ("Must it have a title, Mr. Nelson?" "Of course," I say. "It is your baby. Your child must have a name." And they smile, knowingly). And I challenge them to place the piece carefully on the page, working with form and symmetry, working with the empty space, the silence around their words.

Listening

Because our society's words have become mostly I-It words, we have forgotten how to listen to one another. As Paul Simon's "Sounds of Silence" foresaw, we have become "people hearing without listening." But when we speak and write

I-You words from our heart to others, we begin to listen to each other. So that becomes a concomitant rule in my classes—not only must we try to speak and write from out hearts but also we must listen carefully to others' words.

When we "publish" our writing, we have reading circle. All are encouraged to read their piece aloud to us. When one person is reading, the rest of us listen carefully. Sometimes the words are so real the reader cries. Always, it is a powerful, dynamic experience.

As we all do this, we begin to understand internally that this miracle of language is dependent upon an I and a Thou. All words are empty and meaningless if they are not spoken to someone and if someone is not listening. As Sheldon Kopp explains in *If You Meet the Buddha on the Road, Kill Him,* when we set out on the narrative journey, when we begin to tell our stories, "There must be another there to listen" (1973, New York: Bantam). When we find that someone is really listening to our words—not judging them or grading them but listening to them—then we begin to care about what we say and how we say it. Then both we and our words begin to change.

Writing Thank-You Notes

Early on in my classes, we begin writing thank-you notes. After each "publishing" of a piece of writing, the assignment for the next class meeting goes something like this.

> Read care-fully the publishings you received today. As you read them, mark things that "work" for you—things you like; things that sound good; things that feel good, right, true, powerful; things that touch you or help you.
>
> And then, write personal notes to these people thanking them for these "gifts" given to you in their writings. Be specific. Try to tell them specifically what you liked about their publishings—what worked for you, what helped you. It may be as small as just the way they expressed something or a word that they used. Or they may have shared something that touched you or helped you in your own life. Telling them specifically and carefully will help both you and the other writers. It will make you both more aware of the power in real writing and more aware of what works in your own writing—and of the gifts we can give each other.

At the next class meeting, we take time to give these notes to each other, and we continue this throughout the semester. These I-Thou notes are powerful, affirming us as writers and as people. They do more to improve public writing ability than hours of my red-pen marking of "errors." Such messages acknowledge that we have been heard and that our words have actually touched someone in positive ways. My students begin to think of themselves as writers, and they go back to our next writing with renewed energy and heightened self-concept.

These, then, are some of the ways that I and my students are working to bring our language back to life. Such attitudes and activities as these help us move back toward the source of the stream which has been so badly polluted— the intermingled stream of life and language.

It is, ultimately, a question of survival. For how do you separate sensitivity to and reverence for language from sensitivity to and reverence for one another and the earth? They are inseparable. We are always playing for bigger stakes than we know

For too long in education, we have treated reading and writing as mechanical processes, as I-It transactions, and have been increasingly dismayed at our students' diminishing abilities. It is time now to help restore those abilities through restoring our sensitivity to language, through restoring mystery and reverence. For all language is dead unless it involves an I and a Thou.

> On account of that which cannot be spoken about, I can say in my language, as all can say in theirs: You. For the sake of this there are I and You, there is dialogue, there is language, and spirit whose primal deed language is, and there is, in eternity, the word. (Buber 143)

One Writer's Curriculum

Donald M. Murray

Last spring the writing machine started to creak, clunk and then broke down. I didn't look to see what had gone wrong, but what, in the past, had gone well.

Since I attend a one-room, one-person schoolhouse every morning where I am both teacher and student, I had responsibility for the curriculum.

I have stayed in the same grade for years so I cannot—like some—blame last year's teacher, or the principal, or the superintendent, or the school board, or socioeconomic conditions, or the genetic design of the parents of my student. Well, I can complain about that—mostly in poetry.

I have learned not to blame and not to look at what has gone wrong, but to look at what has gone right in the past. I looked back to when the writing had gone well and constructed a curriculum that would recreate the conditions that produced effective writing.

I studied the successful drafts—the ones that had gone easily—in memory to see what conditions had made each go well. "Going well" is an interesting term. I wasn't interested in looking at my best writing—I try to stay away from such evaluations. I wanted to remember those pieces of writing that had been written with ease to rediscover what elements made the writing easy. And despite the cliché to the contrary, I find easy writing usually makes easy reading.

I want to share what I found and to suggest some implications for other composition classrooms. To demonstrate this curriculum at work I am going to share one of my most recent poems with you and show how it was produced by this writer's course of study.

The Swords Survive

In the museum at Thessaloniki
the guide's voice fades, echoes
from another room. I stand

before a glass case: metal beaten
into armor that did not protect,
tiny swords once warm with blood.

Small men commanded from village,
forced to wear breastplate, plumed
helmet, spent their last night

English Journal, 80 (April 1991), pp. 16–20. Copyright © 1991 by the National Council of Teachers of English. Reprinted with permission.

328

sleepless on cold stones before
rising with the red sun to attack
other village men who had stranger

gods, served an alien king. I do not
know their cause but remember our
blood cries, how young our legs

felt as we ran toward the enemy.
In this glass case are their remains.
swords bent with use, one dented

shield. This old soldier stands
at attention, in angry tribute
to men like him who were eager

to leave home, willing to believe
in a cause, until the sword missed
bone, drove to another's soft heart.

He feels the ease of giving death
in his own hand, hears his own warrior
cry, witnesses their sudden death.

Now let's examine my curriculum.

I found ten elements that made writing go well for me. The first three elements—*solitude, experience,* and *faith*—precede the page and make it possible for me to believe that writing will give meaning to my world.

Solitude

My world is crowded with community. Minnie Mae upstairs, Tom Newkirk across the street, Don Graves and Chip Scanlan on the phone, hundreds of others at the Bagelry, at the supermarket, at NCTE, in letters, magazines, books, on TV, radio, CD. My mother, like most American mothers, became worried if I spent much time alone: at home, at church and tavern, at school, at work, we are commanded to be outgoing.

But writing is ingoing. The efforts at collaborative writing are an interesting variation on a theme. But the theme is solitude. Writers must be comfortable with aloneness: free of guilt at delight in our own company. We must find our own way to achieve quiet so that we can hear the whisper of the emerging text. We must, without shame, withdraw, shut the door, and confront ourselves. While writing, we talk and listen to ourselves. That is where it all begins, alone.

This then is what we must give our students: insulation from the external world, time to be with themselves, instruction in reflection. We need classes of daydreamers with all the desks turned, so they can stare out the window instead of at the board.

I like to begin a class—or a day—with a few moments—five, ten, fifteen—with quiet, pen uncapped, daybook open, waiting without expectation. Our discussion afterwards will include such words as patience, receptivity and, most blessed of all, surprise.

The poem began when I was on a tour in Greece. We were herded from historical ruin to excavation to museum, but I was the reluctant student who hung back, wandered off, stood by myself. I had detached myself from the guide's glorification of war, and I finally went outside to sit, with my daybook, on the steps of the museum. Happy to be alone with my reflections.

Experience

The most important experience I bring to my writing desk is not experience with language, punctuation, form, although all of those are necessary. I have a history of surprise. I know that language will lead me to meaning. I will write what I do not expect to write.

I know that as I write I will receive the blessings of failure and accident: the failure will be instructive, the accident insightful. I will write what I do not intend in voices we have not yet heard because failure and accident will point the way.

Fortunately it is easy to have students experience discovery in writing. Invite them to write with you—I prefer to do this on 3 × 5 cards—about a person, place, or event important to them. Have them write fast and then share what they wrote that surprised them. They will begin to develop a history of surprise, a record of writing what they had no intention of writing.

They will have failed to say what they meant to say. Congratulate them. Show how the failure is instructive, how the text is pointing the way toward meaning.

We teach safety, forcing our students to be conservative, to avoid the possibility of error in thought or expression. Of course, our final drafts must be edited, but first we have to discover what we have to say and construct an experiential history of discovery through writing.

I did not know if I would write about this museum but my experience told me that language would lead me to meaning.

Faith

Each day I must recover the writer's essential arrogance: my story is significant. But I watch my own words appearing on the page and hear myself say, "So, Murray, you had an unhappy childhood? What else is new?" "So you learned 45 years ago that you could kill? You weren't the first or the last soldier in the world." "So you teach yourself to write? So what?"

I don't find it easy—believe it or not—to be arrogant. I find it difficult to maintain faith in my stories, to believe that my experience is significant. And yet the more personal the stories I write, the more readers recognize their own stories. We articulate the experience of others when we speak of our world in our own voices.

Our students need our listening. They do not know—as I did not know—that what I had to say was of value to others. We must instill and support the always-fragile faith in our students that their stories are significant. We do it by sharing our stories and the stories of their classmates and by listening to what each student says and what is not yet quite said.

The museum was filled with people who each had his own reaction, appropriate to his needs. I would not compete with them if I wrote of my visit, but I might articulate the feelings of a few veterans—German, Japanese, Italian, British, Canadian—who were staring at these ancient weapons and thinking of their own wars. I would, most of all, attend to myself, arrogantly faithful that my story is the story of others.

Now, to be ready to write, I have to mobilize the following parts of my curriculum: *need, tension, pattern,* and *voice.*

Need

I am driven to write by an internal need or obsession. I do not so much write for love, praise, attention, money—although I accept all of the above—as I write because I must. As Simone de Beauvoir said, "a day in which I don't write leaves a taste of ashes."

And I have found our students must write once they have discovered how writing makes the life they have lived, the life they are living, more meaningful. They need to write as I do: to celebrate, to explore, to persuade.

We must go within ourselves to discover and accept our obsessions, those things that *irrationally* interest us, the mysteries that haunt us and are, also, the mysteries of everyone.

Our students need to be instructed that they have their own mysteries to explore and they are in place early. As Willa Cather said, "Most of the basic material a writer works with is acquired before the age of fifteen." That is true of me, and it was true of my students.

And if we help our students discover and explore their obsession in writing, they will receive the great gift of concentration, of being lost in the work.

One of my obsessions is war. I was in combat as a paratrooper in World War II, and I still need to try to understand that experience. I am writing a novel, this poem and others, as well as an occasional essay, out of the mystery of combat I experienced nearly fifty years ago.

And the troops in Saudi Arabia in my old outfit magnify my obsession.

Tension

As I look back on the writing that has gone well it has been ignited by a tension that is usually caught in a phrase, a fragment of language that captures the energy that will unlock a draft.

I must keep reminding my lone student to rehearse, to fiddle around, to play with language and ideas, to delay writing until I have captured the central tension that lies within my subject.

I remember staring at the weapons in that museum and muttering to myself, "the swords survive." I did not need to add that the soldiers did not. The tension was there: we celebrate the soldiers, but it is only their weapons that survive.

I did not know what this really meant, but I knew that I had spoken a phrase that I would worry into meaning, probably by writing.

Pattern

The positive experience of writing this talk and the concurrent difficulty I was having with a novel caused me to reinstruct myself in the importance of pattern. I had the title and I drafted the lead, but I did not plunge in to write. I stopped and fooled around for weeks—at home and in Greece—with the elements in my curriculum.

I wrote the crossheads as a form of outline so that I had the design of the entire talk. Then I messed around with design and fitted notes and fragments of writing into it. And finally I filled in the design, and during the last draft, changed it again.

I forget the power of design in all its forms—genre, structure, order—and see them after the fact, as they appear in a written draft of others. They seem powerful and rigid when they are in place, but pattern is flexible; it is molded by meaning. Through pattern I begin to see the subject.

I have to remind my student to shape pattern, to use genre as a lens, use order as a way of seeing how a subject may be seen. These are tools of exploration. The novelist, Ernest Gaines, reminds us:

> A novel is like getting on a train to Louisiana. All you know at the moment is that you're getting on the train, and you're going to Louisiana. But you don't know who you're going to sit behind, or in front of, or beside: you don't know what the weather is going to be when you pass through certain areas of the country: you don't know what's going to happen south; you don't know all these things, but you know you're going to Louisiana. (Dan Tooker and Roger Hofheins, 1976. *Fiction! Interviews with Northern California Novelists,* New York: Harcourt, 92)

I need a destination and a plan to make surprise possible. My destination was another walk through the museum in memory, recording my reactions to discover what they were. I did not know who I would meet, but I got on that train to Louisiana.

Voice

I heard a voice before I wrote. The voice may a whisper or less; others do not need to hear the music in what may sound like an ordinary line, but I must hear that fragment of melody before I write.

This is my voice, yes, but more than that it is the voice of the text, my voice as it may be tuned to my subject and my reader.

I need to read aloud and write aloud. Voice, after meaning, is the most important element in effective writing. An individual human voice is what we seek in a text, that voice is what keeps us reading and makes us believe what is written. And I must help my student hear the shadow of the voice in the early drafts and remind my student to keep writing out loud so the heard quality of writing will rise from the page.

On October 15 I left my tour inside the museum and angry, but not understanding my anger, sat on the front steps of the museum in Thessaloniki and wrote a number of fragments in my daybook. The first of those lines was prose. "The soldiers are dead but their weapons survive; swords swung against forgotten enemies, medals cast to unknown gods."

Yet in that line an angry voice and the echo of the bitter voice I remember from my own months of combat.

I had found the *need* — my undefined anger at this museum and others I was visiting—the *tension*—the survival of the artifacts but not the soldiers—the *pattern*—a poem that would connect this living veteran with those dead ones—and the voice I was able to write.

Now to write the first draft, I had to call on the final sequence in my curriculum: *ease, productivity,* and *readers.*

Ease

I want to teach my lone student a craft of ease—without guilt. My student still feels guilt when he writes easily, and that is truly stupid.

When I began to teach. I was told my worst students would write too easily. I would have to teach them how hard writing was. I went into the classroom and found that my students *struggled* to produce poor writing. The students who wrote more easily were the best students, but they felt guilty, tried to make writing hard—and too often succeeded.

My curriculum takes its theological base from that great theologian of writing, William Stafford.

I believe that the so-called "writing block" is a product of some kind of disproportion between your standard and your performance. . . . One should lower his standards until there is no felt threshold to go over in writing. It's *easy* to write. You just shouldn't have standards that inhibit you from writing. (1978, *Writing the Australian Crawl,* Ann Arbor: U of Michigan P, 118)

I lower my standards. I write easily. And I write fast. Velocity is central to my curriculum. Fast writing allows me to keep ahead of the critic that lives within me, and velocity causes the accidents of insight and language that instruct.

I wrote the poem as fast as I could to hear what I had to say. I rewrote it a bit and may rewrite it some more, but it came easily, flowing out of my fingers without a struggle. And to hell with John Calvin, I'll accept this example of easy writing.

Productivity

My student's craft must be exercised. On the wall of my one-room schoolhouse is the motto *nulla dies sine linea,* never a day without a line. I never know when the writing will go well, I never know when the writing will go. The writer must be promiscuous, wasting language, wasting ideas to find the few that work.

It is not a saving business. One of my texts comes from Annie Dillard.

One of the few things I know about writing is this: spend it all, shoot it, play it, lose it, all, right away, every time. Do not hoard what seems good for a later place in the book, or for another book: give it, give it all, give it now. The impulse to save something good for a better place later is the signal to spend it now. Something more will arise for later, something better. These things fill from behind, from beneath, like well water. (1989, *The Writing Life,* New York: Harper, 78–79)

My single student writes frequently, writes fast, never saves an idea, a line, a word for a better day. When one project doesn't go, he turns to another, writing a newspaper column, a poem, yet another textbook, an academic article, a food or home feature, a novel.

The writing breeds the writing. One morning I was writing something else when something—perhaps a news report, perhaps a memory not yet captured, perhaps the whisper of another voice—made me stop and write the poem. Since it is my habit and my need, I wrote it. In this schoolroom the student writes. That is first priority.

Readers

My curriculum begins in solitude and ends in community.

On October 31, sixteen days after I sat on the step of the museum at Thessaloniki and scribbled in my daybook, I attempted this poem. It had been conceived in solitude, but now, as I drafted it, I was aware of all my companion readers crowding into my one-room schoolhouse.

There was Jack Kelley, a poet and veteran of Vietnam, who knows more of combat and its lasting effects than I do and with whom I can communicate without words. If he had not been standing in the corner of my mind in Thessaloniki, I might not have written this poem.

My companion readers keep changing with each text, but while writing this poem I remember Mekeel McBride standing behind the computer monitor. Don Graves was sitting in the rocker, Lisa Miller standing beside Jack, my wife who stayed in the museum while I sat on the steps outside was now looking over my shoulder.

The classroom was full: Earl Brown from high school who left with me for my war and did not return, Bonnie Sunstein, the first dead German soldier I saw—so bloodied, so young—, Tom Romano, myself rising from a ditch in Belgium, Roma Huk, Chip Scanlan, and many more.

At the beginning of each day's lesson I am alone but as I write my classroom is packed with the living and the dead, those I know will laugh at this line, grow sad at that one, nod at the significant detail, appreciate how this line turns, how that word surprises.

Surprised by Bird, Bard, and Bach

Language, Silence, and Transcendence

Charles Suhor

Most of us can claim peak aesthetic experiences not only from contact with our favorite literary works but also from connections with other arts. Novelist Iris Murdoch (Murdoch and Krishnamurti 1984) claims painting as an art that yields intense aesthetic experiences. Imamu Baraka, best known as a playwright and poet, has cited jazz and blues as rich sources of aesthetic pleasure (Jones 1963). I've met many English teachers who, like me, derive as much satisfaction from listening to and playing music as from reading and writing.

Long before I ever had a genuine, transporting experience with a work of literature, I learned through jazz what art could do for me and to me. Born in New Orleans, I was raised in a neighborhood where jukeboxes played the music of Baby Dodds, Ray Bauduc, Irving Fazola, and other great early jazz artists. But the idea that the arts are interconnected didn't really hit home until one day when I was a sophomore in college, sitting in the library and reading Shakespeare's Sonnet 116 ("Let me not to the marriage of true minds") for the first time. I got to the couplet—"If this be error and upon me proved / I never writ nor no man ever loved"—and something in me shouted. I shouted "Yeah!" exactly as I had done for years when I heard a jazz musician play a great phrase.

If other students were disturbed by my spontaneous yawp, I didn't notice, because at that moment I sensed that Charlie Parker and Louis Armstrong were somehow in the same mind-blowing, spirit-soaring game that Shakespeare was in. Shortly afterward, I came across Gerard Manley Hopkins and grunted volubly as I subvocalized the densely compacted prosody of his sonnets. I learned about and experienced inscape, and I knew that it related not only to gazing at dappled things but also to climbing through the architecture of a Bach fugue or following a jazz musician's dazzling improvisational lines.

At about the same time, I was surprised when I read a curious statement by Jean Cocteau. "Literature is impossible. One must get out of it," he wrote in a letter to philosopher Jacques Maritain (Maritain and Cocteau 1948, 54). I loved literature, of course, and couldn't understand a great writer of our age saying that we should get out of it. Reading on, I found that Cocteau was talking about

English Journal, 80 (February 1991), pp. 21–26. Copyright © 1991 by the National Council of Teachers of English. Reprinted with permission.

getting out of literature and into silence—the silence of transcendence towards which literature and all the other arts ultimately point us. Having connected my aesthetic experiences in music and literature, I had some sense of what he meant.

Decades of aesthetic experiences (and life experiences) later, I can now relate strongly to Cocteau's viewpoint. And in recent years I've met more and more English teachers who, while certainly not "getting out" of literature, are seeking transcendence more directly. They are looking elsewhere for the sense of the timeless and eternal communicated indirectly through literature and the other arts.

Cocteau and Maritain thought of transcendent experiences as glimpses of God, but the question of transcendence is by no means limited to discussions of theology. As a theist, I'm comfortable with a recent common-sense definition of transcendence from Salman Rushdie, who wrote candidly as an atheist. I'll adopt his definition for purposes of this article:

> What I mean by transcendence is that flight of the human spirit outside the confines of its material, physical existence which all of us, secular or religious, experience on at least a few occasions. (1990, 103)

Sidetracked by the Humanities

It would be ludicrous to suggest that we can dispense transcendence like worksheets in the classroom, but good teaching in every subject should deal with the joy of discovery. As teachers of English, we have the special advantage—as do teachers of music and art—of working with rich artistic material. But each subject, whether catalogued in the arts, sciences, or humanities, has its own mysteries and underlying poetry.

Maritain understood this when he defined poetry as insight (1952). He saw poetry—insight—as the center of innumerable intuitive experiences that involve making connections. You're having a poetic understanding, he said, when you're "seeing into" human relationships, as writers do; or relationships among numbers and geometric forms, as mathematicians do; or highly emotive combinations of sounds, as composers do; or patterns in the stock market, as financiers do.

In the high-school curriculum, we usually think of humanities courses and other interdisciplinary programs as the best place to cultivate expansive, overarching insights. What better way to help students make exciting connections among the arts and academic disciplines such as literature, history, psychology, and philosophy? But the very things we have treasured most about the humanities—their ability to put us in touch with enduring values and evoke a sense of the transcendent—have too often been denied by the teaching of humanities as information *about* great artists' works and great thinkers' reflections. Student response to artistic and literary texts takes second place to coverage of ground in a forced march through representative works or snippets from such works. Fascinating newer connections among disciplines (physics and Eastern philosophy, music and computer technology, literature and television) seldom seem to enter the syllabus.

Of course, many humanities and interdisciplinary programs are well-conceived and brilliantly taught. But the presumed universal significance of the humanities is contradicted by the tendency to gear courses towards brighter students. If the wonders of the arts and humanities are indeed for all humankind, why have so many programs consisted of ability-grouped, oversized surveys of literary, historical, and artistic traditions—usually Western traditions?

The evocation of wonder, the nurturing of "Yeah!" experiences, is an all-too-meager part of the tradition of humanities education. The neo-progressive movement of the late 1960s and early 1970s was an attempt to involve students of all ability levels directly in creative processes that link literature and language with the graphic and performing arts. During those years I saw some marvelous student writings, drawings, collages, mobiles, films, sculptures, musical performances, and multimedia creations that related literature to other disciplines in inventive ways.

But the radical temper of the times, along with insufficient theoretical guides, subjected this hands-on humanities instruction to easy criticism. Professional journals carried articles with titles like "Hook Up, Plug In, Connect: Relevancy Is All" (Grenier 1969) and "The English Teacher as Interior Decorator" (Artman 1972), giving the impression that the new approaches were frivolous, Tinkertoy efforts (and, of course, in many cases they were). The back-to-basics movement followed in the midseventies, and a trend towards rigorous cultural heritage programs dominated until the recent revival of interest in response theory.

Following Response into Silence

With response-centered instruction, we again have the interests and the psychology of the learner at the center of literary study. Response theory calls for an emphasis on the aesthetic that inherently leads to larger questions: What is the nature of this fine sense of transcendence that arises from our interaction with texts, and how can we explore it more fully? Ultimately, the proper study of literature leads us, as Cocteau suggests, "out of literature" and indeed out of the arts, into a more general and more thrilling quest for spiritually wonderful things.

It is important to pause here and recognize that aesthetic experiences are by no means the most important or the most common points of human contact with the transcendent. Some of the deepest sources of spiritual awareness have always been in family relationships, various forms of prayer, communion with nature, human sexuality, and other experiences that require good will and effort but neither special talent nor formal education. They don't happen every day to most of us, but as Rushdie says, they are accessible to us all.

These commonplace realms of human development converge in nourishing ways with educational pathways to the transcendent. A joyful response to Robert Cormier's (1982) short story, "Guess What? I Almost Kissed My Father Goodnight," resonates in the minds of our students, and that merges with intense classroom talk about this excellent work, and that ties in with tender and ambivalent feelings in the students' family lives and our own, and that recalls poignant feelings from musical themes or paintings we've seen, and . . . we aren't quite sure what else, because transcendent experiences converge as they rise to meet each other in our conscious and unconscious minds. In *Sleepers Joining Hands,* Robert Bly (1985) puts it this way:

> I see in my own poems and the poems of so many other poets alive now fundamental attempts to right our own spiritual balance, by encouraging those parts in us that are linked with music, with solitude, water, and trees, the parts that grow when we are far from the centers of ambition. (50)

And here we're brought back to the question of silence. At this point, I'll propose outright that it's reasonable to consider silence as a part of English programs and other subjects that deal with aesthetic experiences.

After all, the core of aesthetic response is movement towards the transcendent, the ineffable, the wordlessly splendid. To say this is not to undermine our traditional goals. In talking about literature and the arts we nurture students' cognitive growth, language development, and literary understanding in important ways. But we're all aware that the paraphrase is not the poem, the description is not the painting, the review is not the concert. Arts educators have long railed against the linguistic and analytical bias in schools. As Wordsworth once put it, in overanalyzing we murder to dissect.

But before I get too lofty, let me list a few ways in which silence is *already* part of our tradition. Mainly we value silence in English classes when there's a need to concentrate. Teachers at all levels allow time for silent reading. Some schools continue to use structured Sustained Silent Reading periods or DEAR (Drop Everything And Read) times in which students, faculty, and staff put other things aside in order to read in silence. During test-taking, too, everybody wants silence.

Silence is at a premium during in-class writing time. In fact, many teachers build silence into process writing instruction at several points. Some allow silent reflection during invention time, when students can consider their choices of a topic. Before brainstorming, students might be asked to gather silently their thoughts and make notes on their initial impressions. In the drafting stage, students might quietly review their notes from brainstorming or class discussion and begin their first drafts. "To write is to enter into silence," Jean Sulivan said (1988, 8). And Annie Dillard, "The page, that eternal blankness, . . . that page will teach you to write" (1989, 58–59).

Purposeful silence also occurs, albeit for short intervals, during good class discussion. Teachers build "wait time" into discussion after they pose complex questions, allowing students to reflect before responding. Frequently, the class observes useful silence when seeking textual evidence for a comment made about a literary work. In peer editing, silence precedes discussion as students examine each other's work. To teachers and students who talk frequently and well, none of these are awkward silences. They are useful gaps in which reflection takes place.

The point here is that a fertile language environment, in the classroom or in daily life, is one in which a dynamic interaction exists between talk and silence. We correctly deplore the systematic suppression of language, the shut-up-and-do-your-seatwork sort of silence. But appropriately spaced silences are organic to sensitive listening, speaking, and reading, all of which are essential to good English teaching.

The Answer Is the Question

If you've followed me to this point, you're probably ready for some sort of punch line, an answer of sorts to paradoxical questions about silence in our classrooms. I don't have a theological ace up my sleeve, nor do I have a plan for integrating nonlanguage into the language arts. But the wonderful story about Gertrude Stein's last words is helpful here. She asked her friend, Alice B. Toklas, "What is the answer?" Alice didn't know, so Gertrude backed things up a bit: "In that case, what is the question?" (Toklas 1963, 173).

With regard to the place of silence in the English classroom, what we have is a really good question. Some people have ready answers, like silence = silent prayer; silence = nonsectarian mediation; and (perennially) silence = punishment. I mistrust those answers, but we needn't discard the question. We can listen to people who have something to say about silence, listen to ourselves as we respond to them, recollect all of this in tranquility, and move our thoughts on the subject a few paces further. We don't have an answer simply by virtue of asking the question, but we do have a start.

And we're starting from a familiar position. After all, our traditional classroom goals include cultivating and understanding the experiences that elevate us in literature and life. We could do much worse than focus on the relationships among silence and literature, the arts, and other experiences that point us towards transcendence.

Some concrete ideas have been advanced for extending the classroom uses of silence. The most fully articulated proposal is in James Moffett's 1981 essay, "Writing, Inner Speech, and Meditation." Working from his expansive theories of language and language learning, Moffett forthrightly advocates nonsectarian meditation as part of the English program. He discusses techniques such as visualization, witnessing one's consciousness, observation of breathing, incantation and mantras, and suspending inner speech, even while acknowledging the potential hazards of such practices—denominational intrusion, manipulation of students, and trivializing of meditation.

Several specific techniques have been described by teachers or found in instructional materials. "Listen to the Silence," for example, is a freewriting exercise in which students silently attend to the sounds in their environment, sounds that are usually a mere din of background noise. They write about what they hear, commenting on the nature of the noise and on how they feel as they focus attention on sounds in solitude. Simple variations on this activity might include asking students to attend to their breathing, body sensations, or stream of consciousness.

An exercise in *Tactics for Thinking,* published by the Association for Supervision and Curriculum Development (ASCD), involves students' focusing attention strongly on a spot on the wall or other stimulus and asking them to notice what it's like to turn intensive attention onto something (Marzano and Arredondo 1986). A teacher reported a similar technique in which students are asked to concentrate on a black dot while listening to Mozart, a relaxation activity that is carried out for progressively longer time periods.

I hasten to note that even these modest attempts to extend the instructional uses of silence have been controversial. A colleague of the teacher who does the Mozart exercise saw it as a form of thought control. The ASCD activity, intended as a metacognitive exercise, was attacked by a conservative coalition in Indiana and equated with hypnosis, mind control, and New Age religion (Jenkinson 1988). In fact, Christian fundamentalists have been busily advocating prayer in the public schools on one hand and attacking those who advocate meditation-like techniques on the other. In *Dark Secrets of the New Age,* Texe Marrs (1988) links Maria Montessori, Fascism, and New Age meditation as conspirators bent on forming a one-world Satanic religion.

A nonideological rationale for cultivating techniques of silence is clearly stated by Moffett: "People who can suspend discourse think and speak better when they turn it back on" (171). The statement strikes me as reasonable and is true to my observations and experiences. Moffett's idea is also supported by a recent Stanford meta-analysis of research which found that meditation and other relaxation techniques are useful in easing stress and reducing anxiety (Eppley et al. 1989).

But what about the theology of it all? When we consider ways to nurture peacegiving silence in our classrooms, are we opening the door for right-wing fundamentalists or those spooky New Age types? Some form of meditation is the most obvious way of exploring the aesthetics of silence within a language environment. But isn't that, *prima facie,* cryptoreligion?

Maybe so, but probably not. I believe that public education is, despite its detractors, a tough enough institution to deal with such problems. English teachers can expand the repertoire of classroom activities and teaching techniques that make use of silence, just as they have expanded the repertoire of discussion techniques. In saying this, I take it as axiomatic that public-school teachers must be committed to pluralism. Just as we have striven to remain philosophically neutral in studying literary works that have theological implications, we can orchestrate silence without proselytizing for a belief system.

Erich Fromm (1956), often an aggressive atheist, made an insightful and surprisingly conciliatory observation in *The Art of Loving* (72). One way of interpreting our experiences of transcendence is nontheistic. That, Fromm says, happens to be his way. Another is theistic. That's my way, although my theistic beliefs about transcendence are very different from those of Maritain or Marrs. My views are also different from Fromm's and Joseph Campbell's (1972) and Bly's, and from those of many of my theistic and nontheistic colleagues.

But as Fromm notes, those who hold differing views about spiritual reality need not be enemies in a culture that values love and reason. We have all seen destructive arguments over philosophy and religion, but we've also experienced productive ways of sharing our sense of spirituality. We can take pleasure in discussing these things, weaving our way in and out of literature, other disciplines, and personal experiences as we talk.

As teachers and as coworkers, we're all working with the same raw and refined material—the joyful experience of literature. There is no reason why we can't find ways in which the joy of silence fits into our classrooms and our world in common.

Works Cited

Artman, John. 1972. "The English Teacher as Interior Decorator." *English Journal* 61.2: 289–91, 295.

Bly, Robert. *Sleepers Joining Hands.* 1985. New York: Harper.

Campbell, Joseph. 1972. "The Confrontation of East and West in Religion." *Myths to Live By.* New York: Bantam. 83–106.

Cormier, Robert. 1982. "Guess What? I Almost Kissed My Father Goodnight." *8 + 1— Stories by Robert Cormier.* New York: Bantam. 115–34.

Dillard, Annie. 1989. *The Writing Life.* New York: Harper.

Eppley, Kenneth et al. 1989. "Differential Effects on Relaxation Techniques on Trait Anxiety: A Meta-Analysis." *Journal of Clinical Psychology* 45.6: 957–74.

Fromm, Erich. 1956. *The Art of Loving.* New York: Harper.

Grenier, Charles F. 1969. "Hook-up, Plug In, Connect: Relevancy Is All." *English Journal* 58.1: 23–29.

Jenkinson, Edward. 1988. "New Age: Target of the Censor." *Newsletter of Intellectual Freedom* 37.6; 189–220, 222.

Jones, LeRoi (Imamu Baraka). 1963. *Blues People.* New York: Morrow.

Maritain, Jacques. 1952. *Creative Intuition in Art and Poetry.* Princeton: Princeton UP.

Maritain, Jacques, and Jean Cocteau. 1948. *Art and Faith: Letters Between Jacques Maritain and Jean Cocteau.* New York: Philosophical Library.

Marrs, Texe. 1988. *Dark Secrets of the New Age: Satan's Plan for a One World Religion.* Westchester, IL: Crossways.

Marzano, Robert, and Daisy Arredondo. 1986. *Tactics for Thinking—Teacher's Manual.* Alexandria, VA: ASCD.

Moffett, James. 1981. "Writing, Inner Speech, and Meditation." *Coming on Center.* Ed. James Moffett. Upper Montclair, NJ: Boynton.

Murdoch, Iris, and J. Krishnamurti. 1984. "J. Krishnamurti und Iris Murdoch." Videotape. Oji, CA: Krishnamurti Foundation.

Rushdie, Salman. 1990. "Is Nothing Sacred?" *Granta* 31 (Spring): 97–111.

Sulivan, Jean. 1988. *Morning Light.* Trans. J Cunneen and P. Gormally. New York: Paulist.

Toklas, Alice B. 1963. *What Is Remembered.* New York: Holt.

Writing

A Natural Site for Spirituality

Susan A. Schiller

The Dream

I was a new student. Sitting in the classroom I could sense a difference. All the students could enter or depart the room at any moment—whenever the urge struck. It was obvious that specific class enrollment was outdated. A tacit understanding and respect for others' learning and teaching filled the air, and most students stayed for an hour to participate in the experience.

I was in an English class, still as Dr. Schiller, but as a student. Dr. Jasper, a woman my age, was talking about poetry in film. She had just introduced a new book on film, yet this was a poetry class, and students came to write poetry. We all kept notebooks for our poems and randomly, sympathetically shared our work with one another. Everyone expressed interest in each other's work. As the hour ended, a new teacher came into the room; some of the students stayed, some left. I left, walking down the hall in search of a German class that I had signed up to take.

I could see I was walking on the second floor and, down below, the hallway opened onto a mezzanine. The space was circular, bright, spacious, and full of excitement. People were milling around. Some sat eating snacks. Some sat in front of TV monitors. Some sat in lounge areas talking. Some were headed for other classrooms. At one point, I stood with four other people outside a large lecture hall where people were discussing paleontology. One or two of the others took seats in the room, but I did not, since I needed to be somewhere else. In the classroom next door, a teacher was showing slides about brain research and the way sound is manifested in our brains. This interested me, but I was trying to find the German class. I went down the stairs and, as I started to walk across the mezzanine, I was drawn to a table near a lounge area where a large screen was showing a film. I suddenly changed my focus away from the German class; now I was pulled in a different direction, and I clearly had permission to follow my intuition.

The Spiritual Side of Writing: Releasing the Learner's Whole Potential. Edited by Regina Paxton Foehr and Susan A. Schiller. Portsmouth, NH: Boynton/Cook Heinemann, 1997. Copyright © 1997 by Boynton/Cook Publishers, Inc. Reprinted with permission.

I stood at the table with a young man who had been watching the film in the lounge area. A young woman came up and asked him, "Did you have fun in the film?" He said, "Yes." I looked at them oddly because I was stunned. I suddenly understood that these students could maintain passive and active positions in the learning process. They could jump into the film as an actor, actress, producer, or director at the same time as they sat in the audience watching the film and their own involvement in it. The film required their participation, but they also had to observe themselves in the learning. They had to see, not just with their eyes, but with their bodies. They had to feel the spirit in the learning so that the learning could reciprocate and feed their spirit.

Finally, I saw that this was an experiential school in which spirit guided learning. Lecture time was minimized. Its usefulness was noted, but a reliance on it was considered outdated. Its purpose was understood and utilized, but experience was given the premium value. I looked around and felt everyone's thirst for knowing and discerned their collaborative habits. In this school, particularly apparent on the mezzanine, students and teachers blended into one learning body. In the teaching, teachers learned, too. Students knew this, helped it along, and could stand and assume the teacher role whenever it became necessary for learning. As a result, distinctions between student and teacher were practically nonexistent. Tests were thought to be harmful, curriculum requirements were abandoned, and the four-year degree belonged to schools from the past. Instead, people relied on their natural interests to shape and eventually develop a core of instruction that would lead to career choices. People could drop out but could also return to school at any time, pick up where they had left off, or start afresh. This type of educational system was accepted by the culture, was valued for its reliance on intuition, and was regarded as superior to all systems that had gone before it. Learning reigned. With authority ascribed to learning rather than to people or systems, spirit caused a thirst for sharing and growing together, and it was good that way.

Is this just an idealistic dream? Perhaps. But as educators, we must dream; for if we do not, realities do not shift. That student in the back row who cannot envision success would still sleep if not for our efforts to reach out, to show the power in vision. That idea that needs exposure would be unheard if not for our attempts to get it published. That paradigm of thought would stagnate if not for our questions and ways of reseeing. Dreams realized, manifested into action, shape our culture. Our actions can begin quite simply, but our dreams are powerful with imagination, powerful in challenge. In today's age of educational reform, we are just now beginning to dream toward a spirit-based education, which I define as an education that honors affect, intuition, inner knowing, and connections to God, to the Earth, and to human beings. If we let it, if we are open to its power, spirit-based education can guide us and can foster change. Where does it start? It starts in our hopes, in our idealism, in our courage to live as spiritual beings. It starts today, in our classrooms. The easiest, most natural place to begin is in the composition classroom.

In the Academy

Writing is a natural site for spirituality. Every time we pick up a pen to express language, sometimes language that stretches our reach, we push inward to discover new realms of experience. The journey inward automatically imposes a quest for connections between the known and the unknown, between the cognitive and the intuitive, between the self and the other. We know that through writing we construct our worldview, that we encourage ourselves to accept new ideas and life habits. Many writers have already made this connection and rely on spirit to guide their work. Those of us who teach composition can follow these writers' lead as we define and develop spirit-based writing assignments/ environments for ourselves and for our students.

Fortunately, today, a growing number of people want to inculcate a spirit-based approach. Still in the inchoate stages, their efforts to introduce change through carefully planned pedagogy and composition theory are contributing to the way we talk about composition studies. But to create spirit-based teaching, as educational reformer Parker Palmer advises, "we must cultivate personal experience of that which we need to profess" (1993, 113). We must invite and develop a spirit-based life. It begins with centering on what it means to be spiritual.

First, we need to accept and value the fact that spirituality can be defined in myriad ways because it is mysterious. The infinite potential offered to us by such mystery is an advantage, for it allows affirmation of far more than we will ever fully know. It offers the opportunity for lifelong learning and discovery, which in turn opens us up to accepting knowledge as a spiraling evolution of information and insight. The implications for pedagogy and composition theory are infinite. Just by looking at a few definitions we can see this point.

William James says the "idea of universal evolution lends itself to a doctrine of general meliorism and progress which fits the religious needs of the healthy-minded so well that it seems almost as if it might have been created for their use" (1961, 88). I think it safe to assume that people want to be healthy-minded and that teachers are in the profession of guiding other people to healthy-mindedness. It seems clear also that health must embody spirit. Spirituality, for James, is a personal connection with what he calls "God" and all that flows out of the divine (1961, 95). The flow is circular and comes in degrees so that we might distinguish the evolutionary process of knowing spirit. He doesn't care by what term people name God, whether they use "Kindly Light, Providence, the Over-Soul, Omnipotence, or whatever . . ." (1961, 95). This openness creates a space for the nonreligious also to be spiritual, and it can open our view of writing as a spiritual event.

People can also choose to be spiritual without placing themselves within an organized religion; they can find spirituality almost anywhere, including classrooms. Statistics indicate a growing population who, while still spiritual, do not attend church or consider themselves affiliated with any organized religion.[1] According to a *Newsweek* poll in November 1994, "fifty-eight percent feel the need to experience spiritual growth, thirty-three have had a religious or mystical experience, twenty percent of Americans have had a revelation from God in the last year, and thirteen percent have seen or sensed the presence of an angel" (54). People are seeking spirituality.

As global interests challenge nationalistic tendencies, people are also accepting diversity with regard to faith commitments. Such diversity is a healthy signal that a shift in reality is happening. We can see it in education, too. Every time we ask a student to expand and stretch his or her abilities, we are asking for a spiritual act, even if we do not name it as such. Every time we ask students to develop language and rhetorical skills, we are asking that they reshape their world, that they recast their reality. This may be considered a tiny shift, but shift after shift accrues until people are changed, until dreams are realized. Multiple definitions, as acts of language, empower us because they dissolve boundaries and inspire our imaginations to envision even more.

Joseph Campbell, who spent a lifetime studying comparative religion, believed we accept either a personal or an impersonal entity when we define *spirit.* For instance, naming the source of spirit "God" indicates a personalized vision of spirit. In contrast, spirit seen as an infinite energy with varying degrees embodied in the physical and metaphysical world indicates an impersonal source. He says we can choose to experience the ultimate mystery—spirit—without form or with form. We can name it *God,* thereby reducing it to a concept and giving it form, or we can resist concepts in order to welcome *experience* rather than *idea.* Campbell, who chooses the impersonal, says, "God is the vehicle of the energy [Brahman, the energy that is the whole universe] not its source" (1988). For Campbell, one's definition of spirit and way of practicing faith becomes an individual decision. Today people are leaving traditional forms found in organized religion and instead are seeking the mystery of spirit in the forms of their professional lives. Hence, we see a proliferation of spirit occurring across medicine, psychology, popular culture, and finally education. It seems clear that people need to *experience* spirit—*even if they do not name it God.* This does not mean that people should do whatever they want and then call it spirit; it means that they are released from dogma associated with traditional forms in order to discover additional ways of knowing spirit. It means they can find the natural mystery of spirit in their own efforts to improve the human condition.

Others offer their definitions that are all different but that are all connected. Beth Daniell, educator and compositionist, defines *spirituality* as "seeking a connection with God, the universe, the life-force, humankind, one's own higher 'self'; attempting to give life coherence and purpose beyond professional,

---

1. David Briggs. 1994. "Boomers' Spiritual Quest and Church Integrity Not Necessarily Compatible." *Morning Sun,* 13 May. Briggs, an AP religion writer, offers statistics about the growing trend among baby boomers who are looking for spirituality outside organized religion.

economic, or personal goals" (1994, 239). James Moffett, educational reformer, says, "spirit can be thought of as the subtlest frequency, the one that propagates the spectrum of increasingly slower vibrations. To be spiritual is to identify with spirit across these vibrations" (1994, 22). Inayat Khan, a Sufi teacher, offers four ways to understand the word *spirit:*

> One meaning is essence. The second meaning of spirit is what is understood by those who call the soul spirit when it has left the body on earth and has passed to the other side. The third meaning is that of the soul and mind working together. It is used in this sense when one says that a man seems to be in low spirits. And the fourth meaning of spirit is the soul of all souls, the source and goal of all things and all beings, from which all comes and to which all returns. (1982, 38)

Jean Houston, who practices sacred psychology, places spirit in consciousness and psyche. For her, there is a great "no-thing-ness," a vacuum, that is the foundation of all being (1987, 21). This can be likened to the vibrational world of Moffett, the essence Khan refers to, and the universal in Daniell's view. These multiple definitions reach for understanding the oneness demanded by the spiritual. They can help us understand the infinite possibilities for teaching writing as a spiritual act. Spirituality in writing can be self-defined by the student so that it specifically fits his or her own readiness for experience and learning. Teachers have to lead, however, by building flexibility and tolerance into our assignments. We also have to share our spiritual life with our students and be willing to explore the oneness that can be found in learning from them as we teach them.

Spirituality in Pedagogy

After we reach a personal understanding of spirituality, we need to let writers who have allowed spirituality to guide them act as our teachers. By following their example, we can help students develop into more competent writers and into more spiritual people. Successful writers seem to be spiritually motivated in ways that we rarely hear about in composition classes. Their communication of the ways spirit weaves itself into writing can teach us to see the writing process as a spiritual event of the highest order. If they can feel its mystery, can be challenged by the paradox of discovery, and then be enriched by the potential of learning that takes place when they reach inside their creativity and imagination, so too can we. So too can our students.

When writers write about what it means to be a writer, they often refer to the challenges they face in solitude. They say solitude is the writer alone, facing the page, one-on-one, face-to-face, with the angst of the blank page. Some view the challenge with a sense of discovery as their stories' characters emerge and live through decisions and actions. Others view writing as a journey into self or into community—a joyful journey, but not one that is risk free. Alice

Walker and Isabel Allende agree that as writers they place themselves into the role of storyteller and witness. They use *witness* in the Christian sense; to witness is to proclaim the lessons they have learned. They witness to others that which their life-lessons have revealed—lessons of mind, body, and spirit. Allende thinks of her characters as "spirits." She says:

> There is a prophetic or clairvoyant quality in writing. It comes from the fact that you are alone for so many hours concentrating on something that you start living the story . . . all my books come from a very deep emotion that has been with me for a very long time. And those emotions are usually painful—abandonment, pain, anger, death, violence. But there are also joyful emotions that go with the writing. . . . So there's a mixture of both things—the love and the pain. (Writer's Life, 1993, 84)

The solitude is necessary, not always easy, not always without pain, but necessary and rewarding because it brings Allende closer to her own spirit life.

Allende's spirit-based approach is similar to Walker's experience. Walker states:

> *The Temple of My Familiar* was amazing for me because I felt that I had really connected with the ancient knowledge that we all have, and that it was really a matter not of trying to learn something, but of remembering. And that propelled me right through that book. And honestly, I just knew some of the things in it. I didn't learn them. I found I knew them. And this was a great delight. (Writer's Life 1993, 85)

Walker relied on cellular knowledge, on that which was stored in her body, which came from personal ancestry and ancient memory. She drew out of her what was deepest inside and she did it through connections to her spirit.

Frederick Buechner, minister and author of twenty-three books, echoes Allende in his essay "Faith and Fiction," in which he connects faith and writing and understands the inseparable bond they share. He says:

> In both faith and fiction [writers] *fashion* out of the raw stuff of [their] experience. If [they] want to remain open to luck and grace, [they] shape that stuff, less to impose a shape on it than to discover what the shape is. And in both, [writers] *feign*. Feigning is imagining—making visible images for invisible things. (1988, 115)

It is obvious that imagining takes faith just as faith takes imagining. Writers have to have faith that they will imaginatively reflect in symbols—that is, in the written word—the essence of an experience. Their symbology must intensify the essence so that it can be completely transmuted from writer to page to reader. The reception of the essence must result in a lived-through experience for the reader if the writer is effective.

David Bradley, novelist and educator, "realized that no matter how good [he] became at manipulating symbols [he] could never hope to move anyone without allowing [himself] to be moved—that [he] would only arrive at slight truths if [he] wasn't willing to reveal truths about [himself]" (1988, 79). Again an inner journey precipitates writing. Writing becomes a solo journey that requires faith, intuition, compassion, and a willingness to open up to solitude and inner knowing. Even more, it requires a commitment to revealing self and to laying bare all the emotions and thoughts that create self.

Allen Ginsberg offers a superb understanding of this process when he states:

> It's the meditative practice of "letting go of thoughts"—neither pushing them away nor inviting them in, but as you sit meditating, watching the procession of thought forms pass by, rising, flowering and dissolving, and disowning them, so to speak: you're not responsible any more than you're responsible for the weather, because you can't tell in advance what you're going to think next. . . . So it requires cultivation of tolerance towards one's own thoughts and impulses and ideas—the tolerance necessary for the perception of one's own mind, the kindness to the self necessary for acceptance of that process of consciousness and for acceptance of the mind's raw contents. (1988, 150)

Composition isn't taught this way very often. But when it is, people soon understand the joys and rewards of listening to intuition. An ability to watch words appear in a surprising flow arises from a comfortable faith in one's own courage and spirit. The most common composition methods that attempt to draw on this surprising flow—freewriting, brainstorming, clustering, and mapping—value spontaneity, but a vision of the final product can still dominate neophytes by blocking them from the spontaneous knowing that can be played out.

In this sense, professional writers "play" and turn inward to touch their spirit base, but students have not been taught to see the play. If we, as teachers, are to create spiritual sites for writing like those that professional writers describe, we must take faith in the play we see in writing and create pedagogy that motivates not just a paradigm shift but *a whole-system transition.*

A Whole-System Transition

What is a whole-system transition and how is it different from a paradigm shift? According to Thomas Kuhn, a paradigm shift occurs when intellectual systems break down. Old ways of thinking and solving problems do not work; new ways and major changes occur. One conceptual model is replaced with a new one (Hairston 1984, 14). In composition studies, the most talked about paradigm shift has been the shift from teaching writing as product to teaching it as process. Recently, compositionists have based composition pedagogy on theories borrowed from literary criticism and, even more recently, compositionists have argued for a shift from exclusively cognitive models to one that combines cognition with noncognitive approaches like intuition, spirituality, silence, among others (see Brand and Graves 1994). Paradigm shifts, while useful in promoting change, are actually minor when compared to the whole-system transition Jean Houston describes. A whole-system transition is a global shift, whereas a paradigm shift is usually contained in a specific discipline.

In *The Search for the Beloved*, Jean Houston discusses five factors (1987, 13) that are critical to bringing about such a monumental shift.

1. Planetization posits that we all have a responsibility to maintain a healthy planet.

2. The rise of the feminine champions female sensibility, recognizing the feminine as an essential and crucial component in the human mind pool. Interconnectedness of psyche and nature will help to bring about new values for process and cultural differences.

3. The emergence of a new science and new scientists, accompanied by a miniaturization of technology, means that information, rather than industry, will shape our world.

4. The new understanding of the potential for extending both human capacities and the ecology of consciousness will release dormant human abilities.

5. The emergence of a global spiritual sensibility will reveal that consciousness and psyche occupy the vacuum of existence and will suggest that consciousness might be "the fundamental stuff of reality" (1987, 21).

There is now evidence that all five steps are actively changing education. In composition studies, recently published environmental rhetorics are one piece of evidence that planetization is occurring. The emergence of feminine literary criticism indicates that feminine sensibility is manifesting itself. Word processing, e-mail, World Wide Web, and fax machines have changed the way we process information and, in composition studies, have changed the ways some of us teach. Additionally, current research into learning styles is reshaping our notions of human abilities, and the proliferation of spiritual book titles currently appearing across disciplines encourages us to believe that a global spiritual sensibility is emerging.

While composition pedagogy can find roots in all five of these factors, I want to emphasize the fifth. If consciousness is the fundamental stuff of reality, then through writing we can turn inward, understand our individual process of learning, and create interconnections with each other. Spirit-based pedagogy can thus significantly contribute to profound levels of consciousness and offer opportunities to connect Houston's five factors within holistic education.

Houston's whole-system transition is simply another lap on the evolutionary spiral, but it is a significant lap because this shift, a shift in reality itself, can transcend fundamental and often limiting differences between diverse groups. If we accept the notion that the infinite power of God circulates in *all* people and through *all,* then we also have to value our differences and tensions that cause *us* to create polarities that divide. By accepting God or Spirit in that which we oppose, we can release ourselves from negative relationships that destroy us or confine us. We are, after all, all part of the same whole. Spirit-based pedagogy, whether it is in science, composition, literature, psychology, math, geography, or music and art, offers a holistic attachment to the oneness of which we are a part. It can connect each of us to one another in ways that foster compassion, acceptance, and growth. Through a spiritual connection, we can recognize and honor ourselves in each other as we stand face-to-face, for each of us *is in the other.* That is oneness. Discovery of this connection can naturally occur when we write and share our writing with one another.

It is imperative to understand that a spirit-based life means finding and maintaining connections with oneness. In the academy, such an idea too frequently gets connected to religion, but it can as easily be disconnected from religion since civil law calls for a separation of *church* and state, not of *spirit* and state. If reaching into the oneness, into the no-thing-ness, can bring about acceptance, tolerance, and a willingness to confront conflict and problem solving with a positive attitude, which I believe it can, the academy needs to take a closer look. The academy needs to question, test, speculate, validate, and sift through what is useful in developing intelligent, fearless citizens, especially as we greet the emerging whole-system transition.

Spirit-based pedagogy can assist in bringing about the whole-system transition because it connects body, mind, and spirit. It is experiential and focused in action, and it allows students and teachers to "follow their bliss." Campbell tells us that our bliss is something inside each of us that lets us know we are in the center, on the beam. In his words, "If we get off the beam we lose our life." In a pedagogy that aims at global change, we will stay on the beam if we develop such qualities as love, compassion, patience, generosity, courage, and wisdom. We will learn writing by writing; by doing; and by experimenting with style, word choice, images, symbols, voice, and all the other rhetorical devices available. Competence will develop naturally if we allow "the flow of life to set the rhythm, like the tides, instead of fighting each new wave of experience, [and] harmony [will be] found through subtle adjustments" (Sams 1993, 199). Since writing competence does not appear overnight or as a result of one experience, we will patiently coax its growth, and we will practice writing, knowing that change is inevitable. As educators, we will have the courage to follow our bliss, to dream, to share our visions, and to transform our world into one that is balanced and harmonious. We will model this lifestyle for our students so that they, too, will learn that writing is essentially a spiritual act.

Works Cited

Bradley, David. 1988. "Bringing Down the Fire." In *Spiritual Quests: The Art and Craft of Religious Writing,* ed. William Zinsser, 55–82. Boston: Houghton Mifflin Company.

Buechner, Frederick. 1988. "Faith and Fiction." In *Spiritual Quests: The Art and Craft of Religious Writing,* ed. William Zinsser, 193–230. Boston: Houghton Mifflin Company.

Campbell, Joseph. 1988. *Masks of Eternity.* Videocassette, ed. Bill Moyers Prod. WNET New York, 60 min.

Daniell, Beth. 1994. "Spiritual Sites of Composing: Composing As Power." *College Composition and Communication* (45): 238–46.

Ginsberg, Allen. 1988. "Meditation and Poetics." In *Spiritual Quests: The Art and Craft of Religious Writing,* ed. William Zinsser, 143–66. Boston: Houghton Mifflin Company.

Houston, Jean. 1987. *The Search for the Beloved.* New York: Putnam Publishing Group.

James, William. 1961. *The Varieties of Religious Experience.* New York: Macmillan Publishing Company.

Khan, Hazrat Inayat. 1982. *A Mediation Theme for Each Day,* ed. Pir Vilayat Khan. New Lebannon, NY: Omega Publication.

Moffett, James, 1994. *The Universal Schoolhouse: Spiritual Awakening Through Education.* San Francisco: Jossey-Bass.

Palmer, Parker J. 1993. *To Know As We Are Known: Education As a Spiritual Journey.* San Francisco: Harper Collins Publishers.

Sams, Jamie. 1933. *The 13 Original Clan Mothers.* San Francisco: HarperSan Francisco.

(continued from p. iv)

"Happiness and the Blank Page: Csikszentmihalyi's Flow in the Writing Classroom," by Gina Briefs-Elgin was originally published in *Journal of the Assembly for Expanded Perspectives on Learning*, 3 (Winter 1997–1998). Reprinted by permission of the Publisher.

"Entering Wonder" reprinted by permission of Sherry Swain. In *The Spiritual Side of Writing*, edited by Regina Paxton Foehr and Susan Schiller (Boynton/Cook Publishers, Portsmouth, NH, 1997).

"Wait, and the Writing Will Come: Meditation and the Composing Process" reprinted by permission of Donald R. Gallehr. In *Presence of Mind*, edited by Alice Glarden Brand and Richard L. Graves (Boynton/Cook Publishers, Portsmouth, NH, 1994).

"What I Learned from Verle Barnes," by Richard Graves was originally published in *Teaching English in the Two-Year College*, 15 (February 1988). Copyright © 1988 by the National Council of Teachers of English. Reprinted with permission.

"Focusing Twice Removed," by Leslie Rex was originally published in Freshman English News, 14 [now *Composition Studies*] (Spring 1985). Reprinted by permission of the Publisher.

"Like Happy Dreams—Integrating Visual Arts, Writing, and Reading," by Ann Alejandro was originally published in *Language Arts*, 71 (January 1994). Copyright © 1994 by the National Council of Teachers of English. Reprinted with permission.

"Are Today's Students Better Writers?," by Mary M. Licklider was originally published in *English Journal*, 81 (February 1992). Copyright © 1992 by the National Council of Teachers of English. Reprinted with permission.

"Teaching Writing to Dyslexic Students: A Guide for the Composition Instructor," by John R. Corrigan was originally published in *Teaching English in the Two-Year College*, 24 (October 1997). Copyright © 1997 by the National Council of Teachers of English. Reprinted with permission.

"Family Stories and the Fictional Dream," by Tom Romano was originally published in *English Journal*, 82 (September 1993). Copyright © 1993 by the National Council of Teachers of English. Reprinted with permission.

"Educating the Imagination," by Es'kia Mphahlele was originally published in *College English*, 55 (February 1993). Copyright © 1993 by the National Council of Teachers of English. Reprinted with permission.

"The Language of Coats," by Nancy Sommers was originally published in *College English*, 60 (April 1998). Copyright © 1998 by the National Council of Teachers of English. Reprinted with permission.

"Car Wrecks, Baseball Caps, and Man-to-Man Defense: The Personal Narratives of Adolescent Males," by Lad Tobin was originally published in *College English*, 58 (February 1996). Copyright © 1996 by the National Council of Teachers of English. Reprinted with permission.

"Grammar, Grammars, and the Teaching of Grammar," by Patrick Hartwell was originally published in *College English*, 47 (February 1985). Copyright © 1985 by the National Council of Teachers of English. Reprinted with permission.

"After Theory: From Textuality to Attunement with the World," by Kurt Spellmeyer was originally published in *College English*, 58 (December 1996). Copyright © 1996 by the National Council of Teachers of English. Reprinted with permission.

"The Rhetorician As an Agent of Social Change," by Ellen Cushman was originally published in *College Composition and Communication*, 47 (February 1996). Copyright © 1996 by the National Council of Teachers of English. Reprinted with permission.

"Writing As Performance," by Susan B. Andrews was originally published in *Teaching English in the Two-Year College*, 21 (October 1994). Copyright © 1994 by the National Council of Teachers of English. Reprinted with permission.

"Kitchen Tables and Rented Rooms: The Extracurriculum of Composition," by Anne Ruggles Gere was originally published in *College Composition and Communication*, 45 (February 1994). Copyright © 1994 by the National Council of Teachers of English. Reprinted with permission.

"The Writing Process Goes to San Quentin," by Jane Juska was originally published in *The Quarterly of the National Writing Project*, 19 (Fall 1997), pp 1–5. Copyright © 1997 by Jane Juska. Reprinted by permission.

"Spiritual Sites of Composing," by Ann E. Berthoff et al. was originally published in *College Composition and Communication*, 45 (May 1994). Copyright © 1994 by the National Council of Teachers of English. Reprinted with permission.

"Bringing Language Back to Life: Responding to the New Illiteracy," by G. Lynn Nelson was originally published in *English Journal*, 80 (February 1991). Copyright © 1991 by the National Council of Teachers of English. Reprinted with permission.

"One Writer's Curriculum," by Donald M. Murray was originally published in *English Journal*, 80 (April 1991). Copyright © 1991 by the National Council of Teachers of English. Reprinted with permission.

"Surprised by Bird, Bard, and Bach: Language, Silence, and Transcendence," by Charles Suhor was originally published in *English Journal*, 80 (February 1991). Copyright © 1991 by the National Council of the Teachers of English. Reprinted with permission.

"Writing: A Natural Site for Spirituality" reprinted by permission of Susan A. Schiller. In *The Spiritual Side of Writing*, edited by Regina Paxton Foehr and Susan Schiller (Boynton/Cook Publishers, Portsmouth, NH, 1997).